Woody Allen: Interviews
Revised and Updated

Conversations with Filmmakers Series
Gerald Peary, General Editor

Woody Allen
INTERVIEWS
Revised and Updated

Edited by Robert E. Kapsis

University Press of Mississippi / Jackson

www.upress.state.ms.us

The University Press of Mississippi is a member
of the Association of American University Presses.

Copyright © 2016 by University Press of Mississippi
All rights reserved
Manufactured in the United States of America

First printing 2016
∞

Library of Congress Cataloging-in-Publication Data

Names: Allen, Woody, 1935– author. | Kapsis, Robert E., editor.
Title: Woody Allen : interviews / edited by Robert E. Kapsis.
Description: Revised and updated [edition]. | Jackson : University Press of
  Mississippi, 2016. | Series: Conversations with filmmakers series |
  Includes index.
Identifiers: LCCN 2015043309 (print) | LCCN 2015046193 (ebook) | ISBN
  9781628466935 (hardback) | ISBN 9781496804457 (paperback) | ISBN
  9781496804402 (epub single) | ISBN 9781496804419 (epub institutional) |
  ISBN 9781496804426 (pdf single) | ISBN 9781496804433 (pdf institutional)
Subjects: LCSH: Allen, Woody—Interviews. | Motion picture producers and
  directors—United States—Interviews. | BISAC: PERFORMING ARTS /
  Individual Director (see also BIOGRAPHY & AUTOBIOGRAPHY / Entertainment &
  Performing Arts). | PERFORMING ARTS / Film & Video / Direction &
  Production. | BIOGRAPHY & AUTOBIOGRAPHY / Entertainment & Performing Arts.
Classification: LCC PN1998.3.A45 A3 2016 (print) | LCC PN1998.3.A45 (ebook) |
  DDC 791.43/092—dc23
LC record available at http://lccn.loc.gov/2015043309

British Library Cataloging-in-Publication Data available

Contents

Introduction ix

Chronology xxiv

Filmography xxxi

Woody Allen Interview 3
    Robert Mundy and Stephen Mamber / 1972

Woody Allen Says Comedy Is No Laughing Matter 21
    Kathleen Carroll / 1974

A Conversation with the Real Woody Allen 24
    Ken Kelley / 1976

Woody Allen on Woody Allen 43
    Gary Arnold / 1977

Scenes from a Mind: Woody Allen Is Nobody's Fool 47
    Ira Halberstadt / 1978

An Interview with Woody 55
    Frank Rich / 1979

Creators on Creating: Woody Allen 60
    Robert F. Moss / 1980

Allen Goes Back to the Woody of Yesteryears 67
    Charles Champlin / 1981

Woody Allen, Inside and Out 71
    Gary Arnold / 1982

Interview with Woody Allen 79
    Robert Benayoun / 1984

Woody on the Town 83
    Joe Klein / 1986

Woody Allen 90
    Alexander Walker / 1986

Husbands and Wives 101
    Stig Björkman / 1993

If You Knew Woody Like I Knew Woody 109
    Douglas McGrath / 1994

Interview with Woody Allen: "My Heroes Don't Come from Life, but from Their Mythology" 120
    Michel Ciment and Yann Tobin / 1995

The Imperfectionist 131
    John Lahr / 1996

Woody Allen: "All My Films Have a Connection with Magic" 152
    Michel Ciment and Franck Garbarz / 1998

Reconstructing Woody 161
    Peter Biskind / 2005

Still a Working Stiff 176
    Scott Foundas / 2005

Interview with Woody Allen 183
    Scott Tobias / 2008

Interview with Woody Allen 190
    Douglas McGrath / 2008

In Conversation: Woody Allen 204
    Adam Moss / 2008

Woody Allen on Life, Films, and *Whatever Works* 211
    Terry Gross / 2009

Woody Allen: The *Film Comment* Interview (Expanded Version) 224
    Kent Jones / 2011

Woody Allen Interview 231
    Scott Foundas / 2011

Woody Allen on *Blue Jasmine* 235
    Catherine Shoard / 2013

Index 241

Introduction

The present volume is the second edition of *Woody Allen: Interviews*; the first edition came out in 2006. In the years since, Allen has continued making movies, more than forty in all in a forty-five-year career as a filmmaker. My introduction, originally written for the first edition, also has been expanded and revised.

Unlike other filmmakers, Allen has enjoyed almost complete autonomy as a director, making exactly the films he wants to make. He also has starred in many of his films, especially during the first three and a half decades of his career, and has created a widely recognized on-screen persona—that of the highly neurotic *schlemiel*.

"On-screen, Allen is a loser," wrote John Lahr in 1996, "who makes much of his inadequacy; offscreen, he has created over the years the most wide-ranging oeuvre in American entertainment." While he started out making films strictly for the laughs—*Take the Money and Run* (1969), *Bananas* (1971), *Everything You Always Wanted to Know about Sex* (*but Were Afraid to Ask)* (1972), and *Sleeper* (1973)—his work quickly shifted to more complicated concerns, as in *Love and Death* (1975), *Annie Hall* (1977), and *Interiors* (1978). A few of his more bittersweet and somber comedies like *Annie Hall* (1977), *Manhattan* (1979), and *Hannah and Her Sisters* (1986) achieved greater commercial success and critical acclaim than his earlier, zanier efforts. Indeed, *Annie Hall* won four Academy Awards, including Best Picture and Director. But others of Allen's darker films, like *Zelig* (1983), *The Purple Rose of Cairo* (1985), *Another Woman* (1988), *Husbands and Wives* (1992), and *Deconstructing Harry* (1997), were limited in their profitability, though well received by the critics.

Since the early 1990s, Allen's critical reputation in the United States has deteriorated. A frequent charge is that he is repeating himself, that he has lost his magical touch. It has forced him to do what he seems to loathe: engage in self-promotion. For most of his career, he had shied away from public appearances and interviews, and there were periods where he seemed to disappear from the spotlight altogether. When he did make himself available for interviews, typically he would agree to only a few of them, favoring more widely circulating, prestigious publications like the *New York Times* and *Rolling Stone* over both the popular press and specialized film magazines like *Film Comment* and *Film Quarterly*.

And therein lies the challenge of assembling a book of Allen interviews drawn from all phases of his directorial career—an apparent shortage of good interviews to choose from, especially during certain key phases of his career. Consider, for example, the period between 1988 and 1992, an especially prolific one for Allen in which he directed seven films—*Another Woman*, *Crimes and Misdemeanors*, "Oedipus Wrecks" (one of three stories in the anthology film *New York Stories*), *Alice*, *Shadows and Fog*, and *Husbands and Wives*. For this period, we were unable to find a single interview published in the United States in which Allen discusses any of these films. If, as Janet Maslin has noted, Hitchcock "is one of the most over-interviewed people imaginable" (*Boston After Dark*, June 12–20, 1972), then Allen is surely one of the most under-interviewed among people of similar stature or renown. His unwillingness to be interviewed is only part of the problem. The other is when he allows an interview to take place. A number of journalists who were able to speak with Allen have come away frustrated from the experience. Graham McCann, writing for the British magazine *Films and Filming*, put it this way:

> Meeting Woody Allen is not the most promising method of acquiring a better understanding of his work. He greets one with a limp, almost apologetic handshake, and responds to questions in a thoughtful, hushed tone of voice. During interviews he will shift uneasily in his chair, and either stare at his shoes or gaze steadily into his interrogator's eyes. He is a gentle, kindly person who seems rather embarrassed at the interest one shows in him. One feels that if Allen has learned anything from thirty years in analysis, it is the need to leave certain aspects of his psyche undisturbed (*Films and Filming*, August 1989).

In recent decades, Allen has enjoyed a better relationship with European than American critics, and his films also do better in Europe, especially in France. In 2003 Richard Schickel reported that Allen "mentioned [to him] that several of his recent releases have done more business in Paris alone than in the entire United States" (*Woody Allen: A Life in Film*, 2003). But following the release of *Match Point* in 2005, Allen has seen his work viewed more favorably at home than during the previous fifteen years, and two of his films, *Midnight in Paris* and *Blue Jasmine*, were major hits. Still, the acclaim and enthusiasm for his oeuvre has never approached what it was during the 1970s and 1980s. Then, the most influential American critics, most notably Vincent Canby of the *New York Times* and Charles Champlin of the *Los Angeles Times*, advanced the opinion that Allen was among the all-time great author-directors and rarely could do wrong.

Since the mid-1980s and until only most recently, Allen has made himself more accessible for interviews by journalists from abroad, especially Europeans.

In order to fill some of the gaps in covering Allen's career for the first edition, six interviews were selected from non-American sources: three from France, one from Scandinavia, one from Australia, and one from Canada. While many interviews from the original edition have been retained in the present volume, nine new entries extend the coverage of Allen's directorial career through 2016. In addition, there is a new in-depth interview (Mundy and Mamber, *Cinema*, 1972) from the period covered in the first edition.

The first four interviews in this new volume, from *Cinema*, the *New York Daily News*, *Rolling Stone*, and the *Washington Post*, are from the early to mid-1970s. We learn from this set of interviews that Allen had at that point been working exclusively in comedy for over twenty years, as a gag writer, a stand-up comic, a short story writer and playwright, and then as the writer-director-star of four extraordinarily zany films: *Take the Money and Run*, *Bananas*, *Everything You Always Wanted to Know about Sex* (*but Were Afraid to Ask)*, and *Sleeper*. According to these interviewers, Allen had already joined "the ranks of Hollywood's greatest comic artists, the Marx Brothers, Buster Keaton, Harold Lloyd, and even Charlie Chaplin" (Carroll 1974). Perhaps Stephen Mamber who, along with Robert Mundy, interviewed Allen for the *Cinema* piece referenced above, came the closest among these contributors to nailing Allen's uniqueness: "Woody Allen is not the best new American comedy director, or the best comedy writer, or the best comedy actor, he's simply the finest combination of all three." These early pieces are eye-openers, revealing a Woody Allen who is serious and earnest—a straight man when it comes to discussing his career in comedy, often forcing the interviewer to take on the role of the comic.

In "Woody Allen Says Comedy Is No Laughing Matter," Kathleen Carroll frames her *New York Daily News* interview as an amusing profile of a comic genius who is so uncomfortable with his celebrity status that he showed up for the interview in disguise. "He was wearing a battered Army surplus jacket," writes Carroll, "and the receptionist couldn't help but stare. She is a movie company receptionist and is expected to know a star when she sees one, but this one she couldn't figure. She picked up the phone and called one of the executives. 'There's a bum out here who says he wants to see you,' she said. The bum? Woody Allen." The profile closes with Allen putting on his Army jacket and "the rest of his 'disguise,' a soiled rain hat, which he pulls down so it all but covers his ears," while the interviewer leaves him behind in the lobby, wondering whether he will be safe. Sandwiched between these opening and closing descriptions are revelations about Allen's seriousness ("I'm amusing with close friends . . . but I'm generally quiet and serious. I'm the opposite of a cut-up. I do know comedians that are on all the time. They wake up in the morning and they're ready to go on stage"); a discussion about the "ephemeral" nature of comedy ("so relational and so dependent on how the audience feels"); how the making of his latest film, *Sleeper*, was pure torture ("I found myself working over and over on one particular scene, the kind of scene where I'm seen dangling from a ladder and, maybe out of incredible planning, I might get a minute of film"); his plans to turn out one comedy film a year and to perform again on Broadway; and his love of New York—a recurring theme in these interviews ("I'm a big New York lover despite all its problems. The city has so much going for it. I enjoy the country only if I'm with nice people. Here you don't have to be with nice people to enjoy it. You can be with the muggers").

Ken Kelley's "A Conversation with the Real Woody Allen (or Someone Just Like Him)" in *Rolling Stone* (1976) also has its witty moments, but once again, most of the wit and humor is supplied by the interviewer. In his farcical introduction, Kelley gushes that "after weeks of delicate negotiations," he was able to pull off an interview with "the real Woody Allen," but then ends up interviewing "Allan Stewart Konigsberg . . . the 'éminence grise' (which translates loosely from the French as 'grizzled antler') behind Woody Allen" instead. "After six hours, I knew I had made the right choice, though when Konigsberg claimed to be the reincarnation of Kierkegaard, Nietzsche, and Freud, I turned the tape recorder off. During the entire session he smiled three times—an event tantamount to the arrival of Halley's Comet, I later learned—and cracked not a single joke."

To Kelley, with a self-effacing honesty and openness, Allen admitted to the following:

He is not obsessed with being Jewish. "I use my background when it's expedient for me in my work. But it's not really an obsession of mine."

He gets no pleasure from making films. "None of [my movies] have been any fun at all. They've all been terrific anxiety and hard work. . . . I would consider all the movies that I've done failures. . . . I always finish and say, "Ugh—I only got 60 percent of that idea that worked and what a shame."

Luck has a lot to do with the total control he enjoys as a filmmaker. "I do movies because I have the opportunity, and I'm living in a world where everybody wants to do movies. And I'm in, through no fault of my own, through a series of bizarre quirks, a position where I write, direct, and star in my own films. I have total control over them, final cut. No one approves the script. I have everything going for me. And it all happened so accidentally—had you told me fifteen years ago that I was going to be the lead in a movie I would have thought you were crazy."

He has many heroes and they are all unconventional. "Sugar Ray Robinson, Willie Mays, Louis Armstrong, Groucho, Ingmar Bergman . . . the Marx Brothers. . . . My heroes are all pure . . . not diluted [by] politics."

He is attracted to foreign directors who make serious films. "Really the only ones I have any interest in at all are Bergman, Antonioni, Renoir, Buñuel—basically serious stuff. I don't have an enormous interest in comedies."

He wants to take risks as a filmmaker. "I'd like to keep growing in my work. I'd like to do more serious comical films and do different types of films, maybe write and direct a drama. And take chances—I would like to fail a little for the public. . . . What I want to do is go on to areas that I'm insecure about and not so good at. This next movie I'm going to do [which turns out to be *Annie Hall*] is very different than anything I've ever done and not nearly a sure thing."

Considering that *Annie Hall* was a bold departure for Allen, it is understandable that he did more promotion for it than for his earlier comedies. One of the more elegant interview-profiles from this period, by Gary Arnold, appeared in the *Washington Post* shortly before *Annie Hall* opened. In it, Allen reveals the challenges of the new film, for example in his comments on how comedy must adapt to the contemporary world: "Chaplin and Keaton operated in a very physical world where people worked and struggled to cope with tangible obstacles and frustrations. I think the conflicts are interior now. They're psychological conflicts, and it's difficult to find a vocabulary to express those inner states, to make them visual." Later in the interview, Allen praises cinematographer Gordon Willis for helping him develop such a vocabulary. "Shots like Diane's mind leaving her body are not opticals," says Allen. "Gordy knows how to get special effects like that in the camera." Finally, Allen announces that his next project will be "a straight dramatic film," without a part for himself, acknowledging that if the film fails he may have to return to comedy. But if the film is successful, continues Allen, "I think I'd find it far more satisfying [than doing comedy]."

That "straight dramatic film" was *Interiors*, and the next interview, "Scenes from a Mind" (from *Take One*), is a real find. The interviewer, Ira Halberstadt, worked on *Interiors*—he was a DGA trainee at the time—and Allen opens up uncharacteristically and is unusually communicative. He devotes considerable time to fleshing out what he articulates as his personal concerns: bravery, integrity, the meaning of life, and the conflict between pursuing art and cultivating rich human relationships. According to Allen, the character Renata (Diane Keaton) in *Interiors* embodies all of these. Renata is a successful writer who comes to realize that having artistic talent is meaningless—a dead end. "Art is like the intellectual's Catholicism," says Allen. "It's the promise of an afterlife, but of course it's fake—you're only doing it because *you* want to do it." Searching for meaning in her life, Renata will discover that "the only thing anyone has any chance with is human relationships."

Elsewhere in this interview, Allen critically assesses his earlier films, including *Annie Hall*, which the Academy Awards had recently honored as the best film of 1977 (honoring Allen also as best director), and *Love and Death*, which of all his films up to this point in his career he calls his personal favorite—the one film that "expressed [him] the most." Of *Love and Death* he says, "I was very concerned with the filmmaking aspect, and with wanting to do darker things, not deal with a lot of conventional stuff." *Annie Hall*, by contrast, was too conventional for Allen's taste—"a very middle-class picture," says Allen, that appealed to people because it reinforced "middle-class values."

In this probing interview, Allen also elaborates on his practices as a filmmaker, such as the difference between filming comedy and drama: "When you're making crazy comedy . . . make the movie with cuts," while with a more serious picture, "you can make dolly shots, because relentless speed is not what you're after." He also explains that he always budgets for reshoots, because every picture he has ever done has required that he "shoot more material." He adds, "You can't be married to what you set out to do, because film takes on a different quality when . . . you shoot it . . . put a frame around it, [and] edit it."

Frank Rich, writing in *Time*, offers a brief but scintillating profile of Allen and the city he loves on the eve of the release of his latest film, *Manhattan* (1979). Rich points out that the montage of "romantic cityscapes" that opens the film was "largely shot from the director's own terrace," but the film is no fluff piece. Its characters, says Allen, "create problems for themselves" and seek distractions such as "playing sophisticated games" to avoid confronting their own mortality. Other characters, such as the one Allen plays, struggle "to live a decent life amidst all the junk of contemporary culture."

The release of *Stardust Memories* in 1980 marks an important turning point in Allen's career. Allen defended this film when it came out, declaring that he considered it his most fully realized film to date, and (as recently as 1994) he still regards it as among his three or four more successful works (see McGrath 1994). But audiences and critics alike hated the film. The interviews by Robert F. Moss (*Saturday Review*, 1980) and Charles Champlin (*Philadelphia Inquirer*, 1981) shed light on this anomaly. Well before the release of *Stardust Memories*, Allen worried that audiences would misunderstand the film. He told Moss, "I think people will regard *Stardust Memories* as very autobiographical because it's about a filmmaker/comedian who's reached a point in his life where he just doesn't find anything amusing anymore and so he's overcome with depression. This is not me, but it will be perceived as me." Champlin interviewed Allen several months after the release of *Stardust Memories*. The interview brings out that *Stardust Memories* deals fundamentally with "spiritual emptiness" and the ambivalent relationship between the public and the artist, and it makes it clear that American audiences perceived that Allen had severed his contract with them. It was becoming increasingly apparent that Allen's deepest affinities were with the Europeans. As Allen wryly put it, "I do better now in Milan than in Moline."

After the *Stardust Memories* debacle in 1980, Allen interviews become even more infrequent. This is particularly frustrating because Allen was then entering his most creative and prolific period as a filmmaker. For the next decade or so, he would create an almost unbroken string of works of film art on the highest level, each, as Charles Champlin has aptly put it, "a startling departure from the last": *A Midsummer Night's Sex Comedy* (1982), *Zelig* (1983), *Broadway Danny Rose* (1984), *The Purple Rose of Cairo* (1985), *Hannah and Her Sisters* (1986), *Radio Days* (1987), *September* (1987), *Another Woman* (1988), "Oedipus Wrecks" (*New York Stories*) (1989), and *Crimes and Misdemeanors* (1989). "His career," writes Champlin, "offers a unique opportunity to follow a filmmaker's steep-rising curve of assurance and mastery, from early offerings that are little more than photographed jokes . . . to films whose continually surprising diversity in form and intention, whose personal revelations and emotional force, and total, supple command of the resources of the medium place Woody Allen in the top rank of author-directors anywhere." (Essay by Charles Champlin in *Woody Allen at Work: The Photographs of Brian Hamill*, edited by Derrick Tseng. New York: Harry N. Abrams, 1995.)

The interviews discussed next from the 1980s, including pieces appearing in the *Washington Post*, the *New York Times*, *Positif*, and *Cinema Papers*, start from Champlin's premise that Allen was in the top rank of author-directors and was currently at the top of his form. The publication of the *Washington Post* interview with Gary Arnold coincided with the national release of his new film, *A Midsummer Night's Sex Comedy* (1982), which was the first of thirteen films that he would cast with Mia Farrow. The interview dramatically illustrates how Allen's creative juices were flowing at the time. Allen had been working on a black and white "surrealistic comedy" (*Zelig*, as it turned out) when he came up with the idea of "doing a serious film as a companion piece." What started as a serious project, "in the style of *Interiors* almost," became *A Midsummer Night's Sex Comedy*, a bedroom farce with a Chekhovian "subtext." Allen didn't complete *Zelig* before nearly finishing work on *A Midsummer Night's Sex Comedy*, because, in an inspired moment, he decided to "structure . . . and film them together."

The *New York Times* profile by Michiko Kakutani (from the original edition but not included here) is primarily about *Zelig*, which had just come out and had received near unanimous praise from the critics. The hero of this film, Leonard Zelig (played by Allen), is a human chameleon who is so anxious to be liked that he assumes the personality and physical characteristics of the people around him. Kakutani draws parallels between Zelig's eventual cure and Allen's own "discovery . . . of a distinctive cinematic voice," and Allen, in the course of their exchange, obliges, supplying Kakutani with the necessary quotes. "Ironically enough," writes Kakutani, "Mr. Allen started in show business relying—not unlike Zelig—on a gift for mimicry . . . providing such stars as Bob Hope, Sid Caesar, and Pat Boone with lines. Later, during his early days as a stand-up monologist, he recalls that 'there was a tendency at first to lean on other comedians I liked, like Mort

Sahl. When you have such a response to other people's work, it can creep into your bone marrow,' he said, 'but as you relax and become more accomplished, it encourages your own growth and development'" (*New York Times*, July 18, 1983).

The interview in the French film journal *Positif* by Robert Benayoun (1984) also finds Allen at the height of his creative powers. Benayoun comments on his great productivity, but also on the enormous range of his work. *Broadway Danny Rose* had recently opened, and Allen was already shooting his next film, *The Purple Rose of Cairo*. In contrast to *Zelig*, which Allen described as involving "two years of strenuous shooting and unceasing technical experimentation," *Broadway Danny Rose* was a much more "spontaneous film." "I like to grab hold of an idea on the fly," says Allen "and work it out without delay, like when I was leaving a restaurant with Mia and she mentioned something she'd like to do. We'd noticed at the neighboring table one of those wig-wearing Latin women, talking a blue streak, loud and insulting, with dark glasses planted on her face, and Mia told me that it would be funny for her to play a role like this, at the opposite pole from the skinny ingénues she's all too often made to play. I took her at her word, writing the role . . . and shooting the film right away. Of course, I asked her to put on a few pounds and finally, I rounded her out with a little padding!"

At the time of the interview, Allen was shooting *The Purple Rose of Cairo*, and his synopsis of that film as he then conceived it is a revelation. He explains that the heroes of the film are "out-of-work actors who go to the movies to kill time and go several times in a row to see an imaginary movie called *The Purple Rose of Cairo*"—while in the version that was released, the out-of-work actors have been replaced by a single character, played by Mia Farrow, who escapes into the imaginary film, but is ultimately forced to choose reality over fantasy. As Allen tells Alexander Walker in a later interview (*Cinema Papers*, 1986), "Of course, you can't choose fantasy, because there lies madness." Walker's interview is one of several in which we learn that Allen's completed films typically deviate quite dramatically from his original conception, requiring him to set aside considerable funds for extensive reshooting. In the case of the drastically altered *The Purple Rose of Cairo*, Allen ended up with a film that he considers among his three or four most fully realized works. Another film on which many creative changes were made during the reshooting phase was *Hannah and Her Sisters*. But in the final analysis, Allen told Walker, he remains disappointed with all his films because "they're so far removed from all the great masterpieces I felt I was conceiving."

Joe Klein's sharply etched piece in *GQ* (1986) on Allen's love affair with New York City (co-star of so many of his movies) is a refreshing change of pace from the other, more broadly conceived interviews from the 1980s. "I know I've romanticized the city," Allen tells Klein, "I constantly run into Europeans whose only sense of New York comes from *Manhattan* and *Annie Hall*. . . . If that's what they're expecting to find, I guess they're disappointed." This interview provides invaluable insights, both autobiographical and sociological, into the importance of New York settings not only in the films referred to in the interview—*Annie Hall*, *Manhattan*, *Broadway Danny Rose*, *The Purple Rose of Cairo*, and *Hannah and Her Sisters*—but also in several of Allen's future films, especially *Radio Days*, *Bullets over Broadway*, and *Everyone Says I Love You*.

Between 1987 and 1992, Allen created some of his most daring and original works—*September*, *Another Woman*, *Crimes and Misdemeanors*, *Alice*, *Shadows and Fog*, and *Husbands and Wives*—but with few exceptions, he avoided being interviewed about them; the two major indexes of film literature (*Film Literature Index* and the *International Index to Film Periodicals*) record virtually no English-language interviews from 1987 until the fall of 1992. Then, however, interviews of a different sort, about Allen's heretofore closely guarded private life, began to appear: a scandal had erupted over Mia Farrow's discovery that Allen had fallen in love with her adult adopted daughter, Soon-Yi Previn. Farrow broke with Allen, accusing him also of abusing their seven-year-old adopted daughter Dylan, an allegation that was never proved, and Allen sued Farrow for custody of their biological son Satchel and their adopted children Moses and Dylan. In 1993 he lost the custody suit, but was granted limited visiting rights with his children.

The scandal hit the news media shortly before the US release of *Husbands and Wives*, which Allen wrote, directed, and starred in (ironically, he and Mia Farrow portrayed a couple in a failing marriage), and as he was developing *Manhattan Murder Mystery* (1993), which he also wrote (with Marshall Brickman), directed, and starred in. The following year, he wrote (with Douglas McGrath) and directed the acclaimed *Bullets over Broadway* (seven Oscar nominations and one statuette). The volume includes two interviews from this period: the chapter in which Allen discusses *Husbands and Wives* from Stig Björkman's excellent full-length interview book, *Woody Allen on Woody Allen* (published in Swedish in 1993 and in English in 1994), and Douglas McGrath's remarkable profile of Allen, which appeared in 1994 in *New York* magazine.

Allen's conversation with Björkman about *Husbands and Wives* took place after the scandal broke, and yet Allen is uncharacteristically pleased, even joyful, when discussing his experiences working on this film, especially its technically daring aspects, such as the use of a handheld camera and jump cuts to give the film a rough and raw look that paralleled the disrupted lives of the characters. Except for when it touches on the film's subject matter—failed relationships—there is no hint during the interview that Allen's personal life is in disarray.

McGrath's profile was one of the most unusual and insightful pieces in the original collection, and I am grateful to him for granting me permission to include it in the new edition. McGrath is a close friend of Allen's, and at the time of this interview he had recently collaborated with him on the screenplay for *Bullets over Broadway*. Allen comes across as unusually relaxed as he talks about his movies and how he has been coping with the scandal, and he shares with McGrath a few wonderful anecdotes, including a remarkable one about the background of some of the actors who played gangsters in *Bullets over Broadway*. When Allen realized that one of the actors was a gangster and that they had attended the same Brooklyn high school, he asked him about some of their classmates: "I said, 'How's Greg Mottola?' and he said, 'You mean Greg the Nutcracker?' And I'd say, 'What about Vincent Spinelli?' and he'd say, 'You mean Vinnie the Snake?' He did this for everyone I asked about." From McGrath's profile, we also get an extraordinary sense of what it must be like working on an Allen film. Actors kid Allen about his tendency to only rarely cut to a close-up within a scene. After working on *Hannah and Her Sisters*, says Allen, "Michael Caine told Gena Rowlands, 'Don't save your best stuff for the close-ups. He's not going to shoot any.'" Lastly, in this intimate portrayal of Allen, we also learn quite a bit about the scandal and how it affected him. "The only value of a film," Allen told McGrath, "is the diversion of doing it. . . . I'm so involved figuring out the second act, I don't have to think about life's terrible anxieties."

Each of the next four interviews and profiles described here focuses primarily on one of Allen's later films—*Bullets over Broadway* (1994), *Everyone Says I Love You* (1996), *Deconstructing Harry* (1997), and *Sweet and Lowdown* (1999). These are among Allen's finest works, and the interviews are unusually informative about them. We learn how Allen's command of the film medium has deepened over the years, but we also learn how little his thematic concerns, work habits, personal philosophy, tastes, life style, and self-evaluation had changed in the thirty years covered up to this point in the volume.

Michel Ciment's and Yann Tobin's coverage of *Bullets over Broadway* (from *Positif*, 1995) nicely complements McGrath's. While there is extensive attention here to the filmmaking process, there is also some substantial probing into the meaning of the film. Allen told the interviewers that in *Bullets over Broadway*, he was preoccupied with "the problem of the artist: how people imitate the outside appearance of an artist without really being able to imitate what happens inside." A related concern of his was whether one could be an artist and, "at the same time an abominable human being." In the case of *Bullets over Broadway*, a hit man for the Mafia turns out to be the real artist. Note that Allen raised similar concerns in conversations about *Interiors* from the late 1970s.

Both the John Lahr piece (from the *New Yorker*, 1996) and the Michel Ciment and Franck Garbarz piece (from *Positif*, 1998) are a reminder that the human need for magic and illusion has also been a major theme in many of Allen's films, especially *The Purple Rose of Cairo*, *Alice*, *Zelig*, *A Midsummer Night's Sex Comedy* and

Everyone Says I Love You, which ends with two characters literally dancing in the air. "Allen's art," writes Lahr, "mediates between the need for illusion and the need to reach some accommodation with the real." Or as Allen told Lahr, "The only hope any of us have is magic. . . . If there turns out to be no magic—and this is simply it, it's simply physics—it's very sad." (One of Allen's earliest memories of New York, captured in the Klein interview from 1986, is when he was six years old and his father took him to Times Square and to a famous magic shop on 52nd and Broadway.)

With Ciment and Garbarz, Allen also discusses the main theme of *Deconstructing Harry*—the thin line separating the artist's work from his personal life—and admits to being haunted by this theme. "[Harry] is a character I feel within myself," says Allen. "I could never portray an astrophysicist or an engineer. I wouldn't know how to behave. Whereas I feel capable of portraying a writer or an actor, or anyone who expresses himself by the word and by recourse to fiction. . . . Because the dividing line between . . . my own life and art is so indistinct, [it has become] an obsessional theme with me." (Compare his earlier discussion of *Stardust Memories* with Charles Champlin, 1981.)

The dominant theme of Fred Kaplan's 1999 interview in the *Boston Globe* (part of the original collection but not included in the revised edition) is Allen's love of music, especially New Orleans jazz. From the earliest interviews, we learned that Allen played the clarinet, practiced daily, and performed every Monday night at a club on Manhattan's East Side, as a member of a band specializing in New Orleans jazz. In 1977, when *Annie Hall* was nominated for five Oscars, Allen chose to stay home, as the story goes, so he would not miss his Monday night gig. In several other interviews, Allen indicated that he would like someday to make a film about the history of jazz. *Sweet and Lowdown* turned out to be that film, and Kaplan uses the occasion of its release to explore with Allen the strong musical element that runs through all his work. "The putting in of music," says Allen with uncharacteristic enthusiasm, "[is] the highest form of pleasure I get in making a film. . . . I get to go through my record collection and select anything, from Beethoven to Monk to Errol Garner. It's so much better than hiring someone to write a score."

Woody Allen was approaching his seventieth year at the time the original volume was completed (2004) and showing no signs of slowing down, still averaging one new film per year. He also continued to be a reluctant interview subject, and his most recent films, starting with *Small Time Crooks* in 2000 and continuing with *The Curse of the Jade Scorpion*, *Hollywood Ending*, *Anything Else*, and *Melinda and Melinda* all received some of the worst reviews of his career and yielded little in the way of interview material that added significantly to the insights that can be garnered from earlier sources included here. Therefore, I had decided to end the original collection on an unconventional note, with a 2001 feature in which

Allen discusses *Shane*, one of his favorite American films, with *New York Times* film journalist Rick Lyman (August 3, 2001; not included in the present edition). This was one in a series of discussions with prominent members of the film industry about movies that have a special significance to them. As he comments on *Shane*, Allen also expounds on his views of American filmmaking, contextualizing his own philosophy of filmmaking as expressed in the eighteen preceding interviews.

Before analyzing the film, Allen introduces a number of disclaimers. "If I were, for example, to list my ten or even fifteen favorite movies . . . aside from *Citizen Kane*," says Allen, "all of the films would be foreign." The examples he gives are films by Bergman (*Wild Strawberries*, *The Seventh Seal*), Renoir (*Grand Illusion*), Buñuel (*Los Olvidados*), Kurosawa (*Rashomon*, *Throne of Blood*), De Sica (*The Bicycle Thief*), and Truffaut (*The 400 Blows*). Nearly thirty years earlier in the *Rolling Stone* interview included in our collection, Allen had also listed only foreign directors among his favorites, including three of the directors whose films he mentions here: Bergman, Renoir, and Buñuel.

Reading from a prepared statement, Allen presents his rationale for selecting an American film—he "wanted to make sure that the people who read this, at least a portion of them, [had] seen the movie." And why, one might wonder, did he choose *Shane*, a Western, instead of one of his favorite post-silent comic movies like *The Shop around the Corner* or *Born Yesterday*? "I hesitated . . . about viewing a comedy," says Allen, "because on a list I might make of, let's say, the ten or fifteen great American films, there'd be almost no comedies. Certainly not from the talking era" (and he includes his own films in that assessment). Nearly thirty years had passed since the early interviews, and Allen still didn't regard comedy as something to be taken as seriously as other types of films. On the other hand, when Allen discusses why he likes *Shane*, we realize he has picked a film that he wouldn't have listed among his favorites thirty years ago. After numerous viewings, Allen had come to realize that, unlike *High Noon* and other finely crafted Westerns, *Shane* is more like "poetry." If poetry is what he is after, it is no wonder that Allen has been so hard on himself over the years—too self-critical, as the interviews in both the original and expanded volumes amply document, to notice how often his own films have succeeded as art, including several he has made in the decade since the first volume came out.

Four exceptional films in particular—*Match Point* (2005), *Vicky Cristina Barcelona* (2008), *Midnight in Paris* (2011), and *Blue Jasmine* (2013)—receive the most attention in the remaining interviews selected for this expanded edition. Collectively, these four films received numerous awards, including eight Oscar nominations and three statues. A less successful film, *Whatever Works* (2009), also gets coverage, mainly for its novelty and sentimental value at this stage of Allen's career—his only post-2004 film set and shot entirely in Manhattan.

Except for *Whatever Works* and *Blue Jasmine*, all the films Allen has directed between 2004 and 2014 have been shot in European settings—four in London, one in Barcelona, one in Rome, and two in France. Allen's European exodus all started with *Match Point*, the first of three successive films set in London. In a *Vanity Fair* profile by Peter Biskind, appearing shortly before *Match Point* opened in the United States, we learn of the financial reasons "this quintessential New York filmmaker has been shooting in London." As Allen explains it, "In recent years, the studios' attitude has changed. . . . It's 'Look, we're not just the bank. . . . We'd like to have input.' I don't feel that they're qualified to give the input. They wouldn't know a good script from a problem one or how to cast a picture, not the first thing about it. That's not the way I want to make films." In England, by contrast, we learn that the investors basically leave Allen alone with only a few requirements and these he can tolerate —a largely British cast and crew and British locations.

The *L.A. Weekly* profile by Scott Foundas, also appearing at around the same time, contains passages of Allen elaborating on the serious nature of *Match Point*: "I wanted to do something on the subject of luck being a force that people are afraid to acknowledge in their lives. . . . People like to boast and say, 'I make my own luck.' But the truth of the matter is we're all at the mercy of luck much more than we realize." Foundas also provides Allen with space to once again counter a misconception many people have of him: "The picture people have of me is the character that I play on the screen and I'm not that . . . I'm a middle-class person playing the part of a neurotic intellectual. People mistake that for who I am, but actually, I'm the guy who sits next to you at the ballgame or the movie house. I'm the guy who will be home tonight with a beer watching the Knicks on television. I'm not going to have my nose in my Kierkegaard."

The next three interviews are from late summer to early fall 2008. Allen's latest film, *Vicky Cristina Barcelona* had recently opened to mostly rave reviews and Allen, still very much the workaholic, had already shot and was now editing his next film, *Whatever Works*, a comedy set in Manhattan and starring Larry David—marking Allen's return to New York after having made four consecutive films in Europe.

Allen's conversation with Scott Tobias (from *A.V. Club*, August 13, 2008) focuses almost entirely on the making of *Vicky Cristina Barcelona* and is unusually revealing about Allen's work habits as both the writer and director of close to forty feature films.

The next piece, by Douglas McGrath, is the second interview he has graciously granted me permission to include here and is reminiscent of the previous one in that it reveals a Woody Allen more relaxed and less guarded than usual. In the following exchange, Allen poignantly admits to McGrath his frustration with how he turned out as a person—in the sense of failing to fulfill his promise. For Allen, this is an unusual outpouring of emotion that adds real depth and insight into his frequent claim in the earlier interviews that unbeknownst to most of his critics and fans, he is not at all like the character he plays in his films:

>**DM:** This is an old-fashioned idea, but . . . would you say that you've fulfilled your promise?
>
>**WA:** I don't think that I've fulfilled my promise, no. I think that the sabotaging of my promise began in childhood because, you know, I was not led in the right direction by my parents really.
>
>**DM:** Why? What direction did they lead you in?
>
>**WA:** I mean, I never read a book until I was eighteen years old. I never read a single book. I was a smart kid and I was not understood by my parents.
>
>**DM:** Were they encouraging you to be something other than what you were?
>
>**WA:** They were like all Jewish parents. They hoped that I would be studious enough to become a doctor or a lawyer or some professional thing. They were creatures of the Depression—they would have been thrilled if I had become a pharmacist or something reliable. But I don't think that I've ever fulfilled my promise. I think that I was born lucky with a very good sense of humor and a reasonably good native intelligence. But I should have studied and been bookish. I should have gone to college and become a philosophy major. I should have studied literature. I should have aimed much higher than I aimed. I mean, I was interested in show business and magic tricks and tap-dancing and joke-telling—these were, you know, the trivial, escapist activities of my childhood. I should have been interested in writing novels and serious plays and poetry and things like that. Had I been better directed as a child, those are things that I think would have stood me better in life. I could have utilized whatever natural gifts I had in a more profound and deeper way. Now, I don't know this to be true—it's just something that I think.

The third interview from 2008 appeared in *New York* magazine and provides Allen once again with an opportunity to reminisce about his life-long love for New York. And what stands out is how little his view of New York has changed over the years. Below is a sampler:

>**NY:** If you could live forever in the New York of one of the past four decades, which decade would it be?
>
>**WA:** I can't go back earlier than that, right? Okay, 'cause I just want to add, parenthetically, the period leading up to World War II, that was really the time to be here. But, I guess, the seventies. There were a lot of good movies in the seventies, and politically we weren't completely in the toilet.

The remaining interviews and profiles in this volume include a contentious yet penetrating one with Public Radio's *Fresh Air* host Terry Gross, appearing around the time *Whatever Works* (2009) opened, and three pieces covering two of Allen's latest triumphs—*Midnight in Paris* (2011) and *Blue Jasmine* (2013).

As with all books in the *Conversations with Filmmakers* series, the interviews are reproduced as they originally appeared and have not been edited in any significant way. Indeed, the repetitions that will be found here are compelling evidence of the recurring concerns and obsessions that have haunted Woody Allen throughout his career. (Typographical errors and a few significant errors of fact have been corrected.)

I would like to express my gratitude to all those who granted us their permission to make this material available. In addition, I would like to thank those who assisted me on the first edition, notably, Rebecca Finkel, my unusually versatile and gifted research assistant, for her invaluable contributions, especially early in the project, which proved critical to its successful launching and eventual completion; Dr. Harry I. Shuman, for allowing me to borrow freely from his nearly complete DVD collection of Woody Allen films; Walter Biggins and Anne Stascavage, my editors at the University Press of Mississippi, for their guidance and encouragement; and Susan Kapsis, who was always available for editorial counsel. I am also grateful to the Professional Staff Congress-City University of New York (PSC-CUNY) for providing financial support. Finally, particular thanks must go to Kathie Coblentz, who served as my coeditor and also capably translated three interviews from French. She has also provided valuable assistance on the revised edition.

For the present edition, I would like to add thanks to Leila Salisbury and Valerie Jones of the University Press of Mississippi for their guidance and support, and a special word of thanks to the series editor, Gerald Peary, for his many helpful suggestions. I am particularly appreciative to Andy Beveridge of Queens College for assisting me in securing much-needed financial support, especially for covering permissions fees that, in some cases, became prohibitively expensive. This was the sole reason why three articles from the original collection had to be dropped. Finally, I dedicate this volume to the memory of Peter Brunette, now deceased, who as general editor of the Conversations with Filmmakers series offered me this project in 2003, my second in the series (the first was on Clint Eastwood).

REK

Chronology

Unless otherwise noted, films are listed according to release year, though the production year may differ. Details of Academy Awards and nominations may be found in the Filmography. Other major awards (but not nominations) are listed here.

1935	Allan Stewart Konigsberg is born to lower middle-class Jewish parents, Martin Konigsberg (1900–2001) and Nettie Cherry Konigsberg (1908–2002), in the Bronx, December 1.
1935–53	The Konigsbergs move numerous times to several Brooklyn addresses, frequently sharing apartments with extended family members. From an early age he often goes to the movies; he especially enjoys Bob Hope, the Marx Brothers, and W. C. Fields.
1941	Martin Konigsberg takes his son to Manhattan for the first time and Allan falls in love with the city, the location for many of his future films.
1943	The Konigsbergs' second child, Letty, is born; as an adult, Letty Aronson will work as executive producer or producer on many of Allen's later films.
1949	Enters Midwood High School. Hates school and prefers to play hooky and go to the movies with his friend Mickey Rose, with whom he will co-write two films. Develops an interest in magic and auditions for two television shows, unsuccessfully.
1950	Obsessed with New Orleans style jazz; takes up the clarinet, which he still plays regularly in Manhattan nightclubs.
1951	Performs in public for the first time, doing magic tricks at a Catskills resort.
1952	Allan Stewart Konigsberg changes his name to Woody Allen. First published in Nick Kenny's column for the *Mirror*. Soon his jokes are used by *New York Post* columnist Earl Wilson. Hired for twenty dollars a week as a joke writer for publicist David Alber.
1953–54	Graduates from Midwood; enrolls in New York University to please his parents. His courses include one in film production. Skips classes

	to go to the movies. Fails first semester; takes another film course at City College of New York but drops out. Studies playwriting privately with Lajos Egri. Returns to NYU for summer courses, but drops out again. Becomes a Bergman aficionado after seeing *Summer with Monika* (1953).
1954	Overwhelmed after hearing Mort Sahl perform stand-up comedy. Shows his material to his mother's distant relative Abe Burrows. Burrows loves his jokes, but suggests he write for the theater rather than television or film, so Allen starts to read Tennessee Williams, Arthur Miller, Ibsen, Chekhov, and others.
1955	Hired by NBC writer's development program. Goes to Hollywood to write for *The Colgate Comedy Hour* (later *The Colgate Variety Hour*). Begins writing comedy sketches.
1956	March 15: Marries seventeen-year-old Harlene Rosen, from his Brooklyn neighborhood. *The Colgate Variety Hour* folds in May and the couple returns to New York.
1958	Hired for a Sid Caesar special, which airs on NBC (November 8). It wins Allen (with Larry Gelbart) a Sylvania Award and an Emmy nomination. Continues to write for various television shows.
1959	Begins Freudian psychoanalysis, which he will continue until the 1990s.
1960	Writes for *The Garry Moore Show* for $1,700 a week, but wants to get out of television. Begins writing his own plays and projects. A one-night audition at the Blue Angel is successful, but he is not ready for wide exposure. Works on his act at the Upstairs at the Duplex in Greenwich Village in front of very small audiences.
1960–69	Becomes a popular stand-up comedian in New York and other cities and on television variety programs.
1961	Separates from Harlene; begins living with Louise Lasser, an aspiring singer from a privileged background.
1962	Divorces Harlene.
1964	Film producer Charles K. Feldman attends a performance, which leads to an offer to script and act in *What's New Pussycat?* (Clive Donner, 1965); Allen travels to Rome and Paris to film it. Following its success, he is hired to re-dub and transform the Japanese thriller *Kokusai himitsu keisatsu: Kagi no kagi* into *What's Up, Tiger Lily?* (1966).
1966	Marries Louise Lasser, February 2. They divorce three years later, but she continues to work with him, appearing in five of his films, 1969–80. *What's New Pussycat?* is nominated by the Writers Guild of America for Best Written American Comedy, the first of eighteen

films scripted by Allen to be nominated for a WGA award (four won). His first *New Yorker* piece is published. Continues to write comic pieces for the *New Yorker* and the *Kenyon Review* for next two decades. Travels to London to appear in *Casino Royale* (Guest and others, 1967) for Feldman. November 17: Allen's *Don't Drink the Water* opens on Broadway. It runs for a year and a half. Filmed twice, once starring Jackie Gleason (Howard Morris, 1969), once for TV, directed by and starring Allen (1994).

1969   February 13: Allen's *Play It Again, Sam* debuts on Broadway, starring Woody and Diane Keaton; it runs for 453 performances. Keaton will work with Allen in Herbert Ross's film version (1971) and eight of Allen's own films, 1971–92. Keaton and Allen begin a relationship; she lives with him for about a year. Writes (with Mickey Rose), directs, and stars in *Take the Money and Run*.

1971   Writes (with Mickey Rose), directs, and stars in *Bananas*. Publishes *Getting Even*, a collection of essays and stories. Writes, directs, and stars in a PBS program including the mock documentary *Men of Crisis: The Harvey Wallinger Story*, a satire of the Nixon administration. Scheduled for telecast in 1972, the show is considered too politically controversial and is shelved.

1972   Writes, directs, and stars in *Everything You Always Wanted to Know about Sex* (*but Were Afraid to Ask)*.

1973   Writes (with Marshall Brickman), directs, and stars in *Sleeper*.

1975   Writes, directs, and stars in *Love and Death*, one of the few films he shoots outside New York, in France and Yugoslavia. Publishes *Without Feathers*, his second prose collection; includes two plays, *God* and *Death*.

1976   *Inside Woody Allen*, a newspaper cartoon drawn by Stuart Hample, with jokes by Allen, premieres. It will run for eight years and be seen in 180 newspapers in sixty countries. Stars in *The Front* (Martin Ritt), the first film he appears in that he did not write.

1977   Writes (with Marshall Brickman), directs, and stars in *Annie Hall*. Wins four Academy Awards; a Golden Globe; the Directors Guild of America Award for Outstanding Directorial Achievement in Motion Pictures; the WGA Award for Best Comedy Written Directly for the Screen; and five British Academy of Film and Television Arts Awards, including Direction, Screenplay, and Best Film.

1978   Writes and directs his first dramatic film, *Interiors*, which disappoints audiences expecting another comedy.

1979   Writes (with Marshall Brickman), directs, and stars in *Manhattan*. Shown at the Cannes Film Festival. Wins BAFTA Awards for

	Screenplay and Best Film, and the French César Award for Best Foreign Film.
1980	Writes, directs, and stars in *Stardust Memories*. Disliked by critics and audiences at the time, it will be more appreciated in later years, especially by foreign critics. Publishes *Side Effects*, third collection of writings. Begins relationship with actress Mia Farrow, whom he will cast in thirteen films.
1981	April 27: Allen's *The Floating Light Bulb* opens at New York's Lincoln Center to mostly negative reviews. It closes after sixty-five performances.
1982	Writes, directs, and stars in *A Midsummer Night's Sex Comedy*.
1983	Writes, directs, and stars in *Zelig*. Wins Pasinetti Award at the Venice Film Festival.
1984	Writes, directs, and stars in *Broadway Danny Rose*. Shown at the Cannes Festival. Wins WGA Award for Best Screenplay Written Directly for the Screen and BAFTA Award for Original Screenplay.
1985	Writes and directs *The Purple Rose of Cairo*. Shown at the Cannes Festival, where it wins the FIPRESCI Prize (Fédération Internationale de la Presse Cinématographique; International Federation of Film Critics). Wins a Golden Globe for Best Motion Picture Screenplay, two BAFTA awards, and the César Award for Best Foreign Film.
1986	Writes, directs, and appears in *Hannah and Her Sisters*. Shown at the Cannes Festival. Wins three Academy Awards; the Golden Globe for Best Motion Picture—Comedy or Musical; a WGA award; and BAFTA awards for Direction and Original Screenplay.
1987	Wins the WGA's Laurel Award for Screen Writing Achievement, a lifetime award. Writes, directs, and narrates *Radio Days*. Shown at the Cannes Festival. Wins two BAFTA awards. Writes and directs *September*, a drama. December 19: Mia Farrow gives birth to Allen's son, Satchel.
1988	Writes and directs *Another Woman*, a drama.
1989	Writes, directs, and appears in *Crimes and Misdemeanors*. Wins WGA award. Writes, directs, and stars in "Oedipus Wrecks" in the anthology film *New York Stories*. Shown at the Cannes Festival.
1990	Writes and directs *Alice*.
1991	Stars in Paul Mazursky's *Scenes from A Mall*. December 17: Allen and Farrow become joint adoptive parents of two of Farrow's adopted children, Moses and Dylan.
1992	Writes, directs, and stars in *Shadows and Fog*. Writes, directs, and stars in *Husbands and Wives*. Wins BAFTA Award for Original Screenplay. Scandal erupts when Mia Farrow discovers Allen's relationship

	with her adult adopted daughter, Soon-Yi Previn. Farrow breaks with Allen and accuses him of abusing their seven-year-old adopted daughter Dylan, an allegation that is never proved. Allen sues Farrow for custody of Satchel, Moses, and Dylan.
1993	Writes (with Marshall Brickman), directs, and stars in *Manhattan Murder Mystery*. Loses custody suit, but is granted limited visiting rights with his children.
1994	Writes (with Douglas McGrath) and directs *Bullets over Broadway*, which premieres at the Venice Festival. Wins an Academy Award (Actress in a Supporting Role: Diane Wiest).
1995	Writes, directs, and appears in *Mighty Aphrodite*. Wins an Academy Award and a Golden Globe (both for Actress in a Supporting Role: Mira Sorvino). Allen is awarded a Career Golden Lion at the Venice Festival. Appears in John Erman's TV remake of *The Sunshine Boys*.
1996	Writes, directs, and appears in the musical *Everyone Says I Love You*.
1997	Writes, directs, and appears in *Deconstructing Harry*. *Wild Man Blues*, Barbara Kopple's documentary of Allen's tour of Europe with his New Orleans jazz band, is released. December 23: Marries Soon-Yi Previn. They will adopt two children, Bechet and Manzie.
1998	Writes and directs *Celebrity*. Voice of Z in the animated film *Antz*.
1999	Writes, directs, and appears in *Sweet and Lowdown*.
2000	Writes, directs, and stars in *Small Time Crooks*.
2001	Writes, directs, and stars in *The Curse of the Jade Scorpion*. January 8: Allen's father, Martin Konigsberg, dies, aged one hundred. Files lawsuit against long-time friend Jean Doumanian, who since 1993 has financed his films through her Sweetland Films production company, after Hollywood backed out over the Mia Farrow scandal. Doumanian countersues.
2002	Writes, directs, and stars in *Hollywood Ending*. Opens the Cannes Festival; Allen appears in Cannes for the first time. January 27: Allen's mother, Nettie Konigsberg, dies. Allen and Doumanian reach a settlement during the trial of their lawsuits, but their friendship is ended.
2003	Writes, directs, and stars in *Anything Else*. Premieres at the Venice Festival. Directs two of his one-act plays off Broadway under title *Writer's Block*; his first work as a director for the stage.
2004	Writes and directs *Melinda and Melinda*. Premieres at the San Sebastián International Film Festival, where Allen receives a Lifetime Achievement Award, and is shown at several European festivals;

released in the US in 2005. Writes and directs an off-Broadway play, *A Second Hand Memory*.

2005 Writes and directs *Match Point*, the first of three successive films he will shoot in London with a largely British cast. Shown at the Cannes Festival. His best reviewed film in over a decade. Nominated for several awards, including the Golden Globe for Best Motion Picture—Drama and the Academy Award for Best Writing, Original Screenplay.

2006 Writes, directs, and appears in *Scoop*.

2007 Writes and directs *Cassandra's Dream*. Premieres at the Venice Film Festival and has its first North American screening at the Toronto International Film Festival.

2008 Writes and directs *Vicky Cristina Barcelona*, which is shot in Spain with a largely Spanish cast. Shown at the Cannes Festival. Wins two Golden Globes (Best Motion Picture—Comedy or Musical; Best Actress in a Supporting Role: Penélope Cruz) and an Academy Award (Best Actress in a Supporting Role: Penélope Cruz). Directs his first opera production, Puccini's *Gianni Schicchi*, at LA Opera, Los Angeles.

2009 Writes and directs *Whatever Works*—the first film he has shot in New York since *Melinda and Melinda* in 2003.

2010 Writes and directs *You Will Meet a Tall Dark Stranger*. Shown at the Cannes Festival.

2011 Writes and directs *Midnight in Paris*. Opens the Cannes Festival. Receives excellent reviews and becomes his top-grossing film to date. Wins several awards, including the Academy Award for Best Original Screenplay, the Golden Globe for Best Screenplay, a WGA Award, and an AFI Movie of the Year Award. "Woody Allen: A Documentary" airs on PBS's *American Masters* TV series.

2012 Writes, directs, and appears in *To Rome with Love*. Makes cameo appearance in *Paris-Manhattan*, a film by Sophie Lellouche about a Woody Allen–obsessed Parisienne.

2013 Writes and directs *Blue Jasmine*. Kate Blanchett receives numerous awards for her performance in the film, including the Academy Award for Best Actress and the Golden Globe for Best Actress in a Motion Picture, Drama.

2014 Allen receives the Golden Globe Life Achievement Award. A Broadway musical version of his 1994 film *Bullets over Broadway* opens. Allen co-stars in *Fading Gigolo*, a film written and directed by John Turturro. Writes and directs *Magic in the Moonlight*.

2015 Writes and directs *Irrational Man*. Shown at the Cannes Festival. Writes and directs his first TV series, a half-hour series exclusive to

Amazon Prime Instant Video to be released in 2016. Writes and directs his next film, a still-untitled period piece shot in New York and Los Angeles, for the first time in Allen's career in digital.

Filmography

As Director

WHAT'S UP, TIGER LILY? (1966)
American International Pictures
Executive Producer: Henry G. Saperstein
Associate Producer: **Woody Allen**
Director: **Woody Allen**
Screenplay: **Woody Allen**, Julie Bennett, Frank Buxton, Louise Lasser, Mickey Rose, Bryan Wilson
Dubbed/Edited from: *Kokusai himitsu keisatsu: Kagi no kagi* (1964; Director: Senkichi Taniguchi; Cinematography: Kazuo Yamada (Tohoscope/Eastmancolor))
Editing: Richard Krown
Music: Jack Lewis, The Lovin' Spoonful
Cast: Tatsuya Mihashi (Phil Moscowitz), Akiko Wakabayashi (Suki Yaki), Mie Hama (Teri Yaki), Tadao Nakamaru (Shepherd Wong), Susumu Kurobe (Wing Fat), **Woody Allen** (Himself/Dub Voice/Projectionist), Frank Buxton (Dub Voice), Louise Lasser (Dub Voice)
80 minutes

TAKE THE MONEY AND RUN (1969)
Heywood-Hillary Productions/ Cinerama Releasing Corp.
Executive Producers: Sidney Glazier, Edgar J. Scherick (uncredited)
Associate Producer: Jack Grossberg
Producers: Charles H. Joffe, Jack Rollins (uncredited)
Director: **Woody Allen**
Screenplay: **Woody Allen**, Mickey Rose
Cinematography: Lester Shorr (black and white, Technicolor)
Editing: Paul Jordan, Ron Kalish
Art Direction: Fred Harpman
Music: Marvin Hamlisch
Cast: **Woody Allen** (Virgil Starkwell), Janet Margolin (Louise), Marcel Hillaire (Fritz), Jacquelyn Hyde (Miss Blair), Lonny Chapman (Jake), Jan Merlin (Al),

James Anderson (Chain Gang Warden), Jackson Beck (Narrator), Henry Leff (Father Starkwell), Ethel Sokolow (Mother Starkwell), Louise Lasser (Kay Lewis), Dan Frazer (Psychiatrist), Mike O'Dowd (Michael Sullivan)
85 minutes

BANANAS (1971)
United Artists
Executive Producers: Charles H. Joffe, Jack Rollins
Associate Producer: Ralph Rosenblum
Producers: Axel Anderson, Antonio Encarnacion, Jack Grossberg, Manolon Villamil
Director: **Woody Allen**
Screenplay: **Woody Allen**, Mickey Rose
Cinematography: Andrew M. Costikyan (DeLuxe)
Editing: Ron Kalish, Ralph Rosenblum
Production Design: Ed Wittstein
Music: Marvin Hamlisch
Cast: **Woody Allen** (Fielding Mellish), Louise Lasser (Nancy), Carlos Montalban (General Emilio M. Vargas), Natividad Abascal (Yolanda), Jacobo Morales (Esposito), Miguel Angel Suarez (Luis), David Ortiz (Sanchez), Jack Axelrod (Arroyo), Charlotte Rae (Mrs. Mellish), Stanley Ackerman (Mr. Mellish)
82 minutes

MEN OF CRISIS: THE HARVEY WALLINGER STORY (TV) (1971)
WNET Channel 13 New York (withdrawn before scheduled 1972 telecast)
Executive Producer: Charles H. Joffe
Associate Producer: Mary Ann Donahue
Producer: Jack Kuney
Director: **Woody Allen**
Screenplay: **Woody Allen**
Editing: Eric Albertson
Art Direction: Gene Rudolf
Cast: **Woody Allen** (Harvey Wallinger), David Ackroyd, Conrad Bain, Louise Lasser, Diane Keaton
25 minutes

EVERYTHING YOU ALWAYS WANTED TO KNOW ABOUT SEX* (*BUT WERE AFRAID TO ASK) (1972)
United Artists
Executive Producer: Jack Brodsky

Associate Producer: Jack Grossberg
Producers: Charles H. Joffe, Jack Rollins
Director: **Woody Allen**
Screenplay: **Woody Allen**
Book: David Reuben
Cinematography: David M. Walsh (black and white, DeLuxe)
Editing: Eric Albertson
Production Design: Dale Hennesy
Music: Mundell Lowe
Cast: Woody Allen (The Fool/Fabrizio/Victor Shakapopulis/Sperm #1), John Carradine (Dr. Bernardo), Lou Jacobi (Sam), Louise Lasser (Gina), Anthony Quayle (The King), Tony Randall (The Operator), Lynn Redgrave (The Queen), Burt Reynolds (Sperm Switchboard Chief), Gene Wilder (Dr. Doug Ross)
87 minutes

SLEEPER (1973)
United Artists
Executive Producers: Charles H. Joffe, Jack Rollins
Associate Producers: Marshall Brickman, Ralph Rosenblum
Producer: Jack Grossberg
Director: **Woody Allen**
Screenplay: **Woody Allen**, Marshall Brickman
Cinematography: David M. Walsh (DeLuxe)
Editing: O. Nicholas Brown, Ron Kalish, Ralph Rosenblum
Production Design: Dale Hennesy
Music: **Woody Allen**
Cast: **Woody Allen** (Miles Monroe), Diane Keaton (Luna Schlosser), John Beck (Erno Windt), Mary Gregory (Dr. Melik), Don Keefer (Dr. Tryon), John McLiam (Dr. Aragon), Bartlett Robinson (Dr. Orva)
89 minutes

LOVE AND DEATH (1975)
United Artists
Executive Producer: Martin Poll
Associate Producer: Fred T. Gallo
Producer: Charles H. Joffe
Director: **Woody Allen**
Screenplay: **Woody Allen**, Mildred Cram (uncredited), Donald Ogden Stewart (uncredited)
Cinematography: Ghislain Cloquet (DeLuxe)

Editing: Ron Kalish, Ralph Rosenblum, George Hively (uncredited)
Production Design: Willy Holt
Non-Original Music: Sergei Prokofiev
Cast: **Woody Allen** (Boris Grushenko), Diane Keaton (Sonja), Feodor Atkine (Mikhail Grushenko), Henri Czarniak (Ivan), Olga Georges-Picot (Countess Alexandrovna), Jessica Harper (Natasha), Alfred Lutter III (Young Boris Grushenko), James Tolkan (Napoleon Bonaparte)
85 minutes

ANNIE HALL (1977)
United Artists
Executive Producer: Robert Greenhut
Associate Producer: Fred T. Gallo
Producers: Charles H. Joffe, Jack Rollins
Director: **Woody Allen**
Screenplay: **Woody Allen**, Marshall Brickman
Cinematography: Gordon Willis (DeLuxe)
Editing: Wendy Greene Bricmont, Ralph Rosenblum
Art Direction: Mel Bourne
Cast: **Woody Allen** (Alvy Singer), Diane Keaton (Annie Hall), Tony Roberts (Rob), Carol Kane (Allison), Paul Simon (Tony Lacey), Shelley Duvall (Pam), Janet Margolin (Robin), Colleen Dewhurst (Mom Hall), Christopher Walken (Duane Hall), Donald Symington (Dad Hall), Helen Ludham (Grammy Hall), Mordecai Lawner (Alvy's Dad), Joan Neuman (Alvy's Mom)
93 minutes
Academy Awards: Best Picture, Charles H. Joffe; Directing, **Woody Allen**; Writing, Screenplay Written Directly for Screen, **Woody Allen**, Marshall Brickman; Actress in a Leading Role, Diane Keaton
Academy Award Nominations: Actor in a Leading Role, **Woody Allen**

INTERIORS (1978)
United Artists
Executive Producer: Robert Greenhut
Producers: Charles H. Joffe, Jack Rollins (uncredited)
Director: **Woody Allen**
Screenplay: **Woody Allen**
Cinematography: Gordon Willis (DeLuxe)
Editing: Ralph Rosenblum
Production Design: Mel Bourne
Cast: Kristin Griffith (Flyn), Mary Beth Hurt (Joey), Richard Jordan (Frederick),

Diane Keaton (Renata), E. G. Marshall (Arthur), Geraldine Page (Eve), Maureen Stapleton (Pearl), Sam Waterston (Mike)

93 minutes

Academy Award Nominations: Directing, **Woody Allen**; Writing, Screenplay Written Directly for Screen, **Woody Allen**; Actress in a Leading Role, Geraldine Page; Actress in a Supporting Role, Maureen Stapleton; Art Direction—Set Decoration, Mel Bourne, Daniel Robert

MANHATTAN (1979)
United Artists
Executive Producer: Robert Greenhut, Jack Rollins (uncredited)
Producer: Charles H. Joffe
Director: **Woody Allen**
Screenplay: **Woody Allen**, Marshall Brickman
Cinematography: Gordon Willis (black and white/Panavision)
Editing: Susan E. Morse
Production Design: Mel Bourne
Non-Original Music: George Gershwin
Cast: **Woody Allen** (Isaac Davis), Diane Keaton (Mary Wilkie), Michael Murphy (Yale), Mariel Hemingway (Tracy), Meryl Streep (Jill), Anne Byrne (Emily), Karen Ludwig (Connie), Michael O'Donoghue (Dennis)

96 minutes

Academy Award Nominations: Writing, Screenplay Written Directly for Screen, **Woody Allen**, Marshall Brickman; Actress in a Supporting Role, Mariel Hemingway

STARDUST MEMORIES (1980)
United Artists
Executive Producers: Charles H. Joffe, Jack Rollins
Producer: Robert Greenhut
Director: **Woody Allen**
Screenplay: **Woody Allen**
Cinematography: Gordon Willis (black and white)
Editing: Susan E. Morse
Production Design: Mel Bourne
Music: Dick Hyman
Cast: **Woody Allen** (Sandy Bates), Charlotte Rampling (Dorrie), Jessica Harper (Daisy), Marie-Christine Barrault (Isobel), Tony Roberts (Tony)

91 minutes

A MIDSUMMER NIGHT'S SEX COMEDY (1982)
Orion Pictures
Executive Producer: Charles H. Joffe
Associate Producer: Michael Peyser
Producer: Robert Greenhut
Director: **Woody Allen**
Screenplay: **Woody Allen**
Cinematography: Gordon Willis (Technicolor)
Editing: Susan E. Morse
Production Design: Mel Bourne
Cast: **Woody Allen** (Andrew), Mia Farrow (Ariel), Jose Ferrer (Leopold), Julie Hagerty (Dulcy), Tony Roberts (Maxwell), Mary Steenburgen (Adrian)
88 minutes

ZELIG (1983)
Orion Pictures
Executive Producers: Charles H. Joffe, Jack Rollins
Associate Producer: Michael Peyser
Producer: Robert Greenhut
Director: **Woody Allen**
Screenplay: **Woody Allen**
Cinematography: Gordon Willis (black and white)
Editing: Susan E. Morse
Production Design: Mel Bourne
Music: Dick Hyman
Cast: **Woody Allen** (Leonard Zelig), Mia Farrow (Dr. Eudora Fletcher), John Buckwalter (Dr. Sindell), Patrick Horgan (The Narrator (voice)), Marvin Chatinover (Glandular Diagnosis Doctor), Stanley Swerdlow (Mexican Food Doctor), Paul Nevens (Dr. Birsky)
79 minutes
Academy Award Nominations: Cinematography, Gordon Willis; Costume Design, Santo Loquasto

BROADWAY DANNY ROSE (1984)
Orion Pictures
Executive Producer: Charles H. Joffe
Associate Producer: Michael Peyser
Producer: Robert Greenhut
Director: **Woody Allen**
Screenplay: **Woody Allen**

Cinematography: Gordon Willis (black and white)
Editing: Susan E. Morse
Production Design: Mel Bourne
Songs: Nick Apollo Forte
Cast: **Woody Allen** (Danny Rose), Mia Farrow (Tina Vitale), Nick Apollo Forte (Lou Canova), Paul Greco (Vito Rispoli), Frank Renzulli (Joe Rispoli), Edwin Bordo (Johnny Rispoli), Gina DeAngeles (Johnny's Mother)
84 minutes
Academy Award Nominations: Directing, **Woody Allen**; Writing, Screenplay Written Directly for Screen, **Woody Allen**

THE PURPLE ROSE OF CAIRO (1985)
Orion Pictures
Executive Producers: Charles H. Joffe, Jack Rollins (uncredited)
Associate Producers: Michael Peyser, Gail Sicilia
Producer: Robert Greenhut
Director: **Woody Allen**
Screenplay: **Woody Allen**
Cinematography: Gordon Willis (black and white, DeLuxe)
Editing: Susan E. Morse
Production Design: Stuart Wurtzel
Music: Dick Hyman
Cast: Mia Farrow (Cecilia), Jeff Daniels (Tom Baxter, Gil Shepherd), Danny Aiello (Monk), Irving Metzman (Theater Manager), Stephanie Farrow (Cecilia's Sister)
84 minutes
Academy Award Nominations: Writing, Screenplay Written Directly for Screen, **Woody Allen**

HANNAH AND HER SISTERS (1986)
Orion Pictures
Executive Producers: Charles H. Joffe, Jack Rollins
Associate Producer: Gail Sicilia
Producer: Robert Greenhut
Director: **Woody Allen**
Screenplay: **Woody Allen**
Cinematography: Carlo Di Palma (Technicolor)
Editing: Susan E. Morse
Production Design: Stuart Wurtzel
Cast: Barbara Hershey (Lee), Carrie Fisher (April), Michael Caine (Elliot), Mia

Farrow (Hannah), Dianne Wiest (Holly), Maureen O'Sullivan (Norma), Lloyd Nolan (Evan), Max von Sydow (Frederick), **Woody Allen** (Mickey Sachs), Daniel Stern (Dusty)

103 minutes

Academy Awards: Actor in Supporting Role, Michael Caine; Actress in Supporting Role, Dianne Wiest; Writing, Screenplay Written Directly for Screen, **Woody Allen**

Academy Award Nominations: Best Picture, Robert Greenhut; Directing, **Woody Allen**; Film Editing, Susan E. Morse; Art Direction—Set Decoration, Stuart Wurtzel, Carol Joffe

RADIO DAYS (1987)
Orion Pictures
Executive Producers: Charles H. Joffe, Jack Rollins
Associate Producers: Gail Sicilia, Ezra Swerdlow
Producer: Robert Greenhut
Director: **Woody Allen**
Screenplay: **Woody Allen**
Cinematography: Carlo Di Palma (DeLuxe)
Editing: Susan E. Morse
Production Design: Santo Loquasto
Music: Dick Hyman
Cast: Julie Kavner (Mother), Michael Tucker (Father), Josh Mostel (Abe), Renee Lippin (Aunt Ceil), Dianne Wiest (Bea), Mia Farrow (Sally White), Diane Keaton (New Year's Singer), Seth Green (Joe)

85 minutes

Academy Award Nominations: Art Direction—Set Decoration, Santo Loquasto, Carol Joffe, Leslie Bloom, George DeTitta Jr.; Writing, Screenplay Written Directly for Screen, **Woody Allen**

SEPTEMBER (1987)
Orion Pictures
Executive Producers: Charles H. Joffe, Jack Rollins
Associate Producer: Gail Sicilia
Producer: Robert Greenhut
Director: **Woody Allen**
Screenplay: **Woody Allen**
Cinematography: Carlo Di Palma (DeLuxe)
Editing: Susan E. Morse
Production Design: Santo Loquasto

Cast: Denholm Elliot (Howard), Dianne Wiest (Stephanie), Mia Farrow (Lane), Elaine Stritch (Diane), Sam Waterson (Peter), Jack Warden (Lloyd)

82 minutes

ANOTHER WOMAN (1988)
Orion Pictures
Executive Producers: Charles H. Joffe, Jack Rollins
Associate Producers: Thomas A. Reilly, Helen Robin
Producer: Robert Greenhut
Director: **Woody Allen**
Screenplay: **Woody Allen**
Cinematography: Sven Nykvist (DeLuxe)
Editing: Susan E. Morse
Production Design: Santo Loquasto
Cast: Gena Rowlands (Marion Post), Mia Farrow (Hope), Ian Holm (Ken), Blythe Danner (Lydia), Gene Hackman (Larry Lewis), Betty Buckley (Kathy), Martha Plimpton (Laura)

84 minutes

NEW YORK STORIES (1989) (segment "Oedipus Wrecks")
Touchstone Pictures
Executive Producers: Charles H. Joffe, Jack Rollins
Producer: Robert Greenhut
Director: **Woody Allen**
Screenplay: **Woody Allen**
Cinematography: Sven Nykvist (Technicolor)
Editing: Susan E. Morse
Production Design: Santo Loquasto
Cast: **Woody Allen** (Sheldon), Marvin Chatinover (Psychiatrist), Mae Questel (Mother), Mia Farrow (Lisa)

39 minutes

CRIMES AND MISDEMEANORS (1989)
Orion Pictures
Executive Producers: Charles H. Joffe, Jack Rollins
Associate Producers: Thomas A. Reilly, Helen Robin
Producer: Robert Greenhut
Director: **Woody Allen**
Screenplay: **Woody Allen**
Cinematography: Sven Nykvist (DeLuxe)

Editing: Susan E. Morse
Production Design: Santo Loquasto
Cast: Martin Landau (Judah Rosenthal), Claire Bloom (Miriam Rosenthal), Anjelica Huston (Dolores Paley), **Woody Allen** (Cliff Stern), Alan Alda (Lester), Sam Waterston (Ben), Mia Farrow (Halley Reed)
107 minutes
Academy Award Nominations: Actor in Supporting Role, Martin Landau; Directing, **Woody Allen**; Writing, Screenplay Written Directly for Screen, **Woody Allen**

ALICE (1990)
Orion Pictures
Executive Producers: Charles H. Joffe, Jack Rollins
Associate Producers: Jane Read Martin, Thomas A. Reilly
Producer: Robert Greenhut
Co-Producers: Joseph Hartwick, Helen Robin
Director: **Woody Allen**
Screenplay: **Woody Allen**
Cinematography: Carlo Di Palma (color)
Editing: Susan E. Morse
Cast: Joe Mantegna (Joe), Mia Farrow (Alice), William Hurt (Doug), Keye Luke (Dr. Yang), Judy Davis (Vicki), Alec Baldwin (Ed)
102 minutes
Academy Award Nominations: Writing, Screenplay Written Directly for Screen, **Woody Allen**

SHADOWS AND FOG (1992)
Orion Pictures
Executive Producers: Charles H. Joffe, Jack Rollins
Associate Producer: Thomas A. Reilly
Producer: Robert Greenhut
Co-Producers: Joseph Hartwick, Helen Robin
Director: **Woody Allen**
Screenplay: **Woody Allen**
Cinematography: Carlo Di Palma (black and white)
Editing: Susan E. Morse
Production Design: Santo Loquasto
Cast: Michael Kirby (Killer), **Woody Allen** (Max Kleinman), Mia Farrow (Irmy), John Malkovich (Clown), Madonna (Marie), Donald Pleasence (Doctor), Lily

Tomlin (Prostitute), Jodie Foster (Prostitute), Kathy Bates (Prostitute), John Cusack (Jack), Kate Nelligan (Eve)
85 minutes

HUSBANDS AND WIVES (1992)
TriStar Pictures
Executive Producers: Charles H. Joffe, Jack Rollins
Associate Producer: Thomas A. Reilly
Producer: Robert Greenhut
Co-Producers: Joseph Hartwick, Helen Robin
Director: **Woody Allen**
Screenplay: **Woody Allen**
Cinematography: Carlo Di Palma (color)
Editing: Susan E. Morse
Production Design: Santo Loquasto
Cast: **Woody Allen** (Gabe Roth), Mia Farrow (Judy Roth), Sydney Pollack (Jack), Judy Davis (Sally), Jeffrey Kurland (Interviewer/Narrator), Juliette Lewis (Rain)
108 minutes
Academy Award Nominations: Actress in Supporting Role, Judy Davis; Writing, Screenplay Written Directly for Screen, **Woody Allen**

MANHATTAN MURDER MYSTERY (1993)
TriStar Pictures
Executive Producers: Charles H. Joffe, Jack Rollins
Associate Producer: Thomas A. Reilly
Producer: Robert Greenhut
Co-Producer: Joseph Hartwick, Helen Robin
Director: **Woody Allen**
Screenplay: **Woody Allen** and Marshall Brickman
Cinematography: Carlo Di Palma (Technicolor)
Editing: Susan E. Morse
Production Design: Santo Loquasto
Cast: **Woody Allen** (Larry Lipton), Diane Keaton (Carol Lipton), Jerry Adler (Paul House), Lynn Cohen (Lillian House), Ron Rifkin (Sy), Joy Behar (Marilyn), Alan Alda (Ted), Anjelica Huston (Marcia Fox)
104 minutes

BULLETS OVER BROADWAY (1994)
Sweetland Films/Miramax

Executive Producers: J. E. Beaucaire, Jean Doumanian
Co-Executive Producers: Letty Aronson, Charles H. Joffe, Jack Rollins
Associate Producer: Thomas A. Reilly
Producer: Robert Greenhut
Co-Producer: Helen Robin
Director: **Woody Allen**
Screenplay: **Woody Allen**, Douglas McGrath
Cinematography: Carlo Di Palma (Technicolor)
Editing: Susan E. Morse
Production Design: Santo Loquasto
Cast: John Cusack (David Shayne), Jack Warden (Julian Marx), Chazz Palminteri (Cheech), Dianne Wiest (Helen Sinclair), Jennifer Tilly (Olive Neal)
98 minutes
Academy Award: Actress in Supporting Role, Dianne Wiest
Academy Award Nominations: Actor in Supporting Role, Chazz Palminteri; Actress in Supporting Role, Jennifer Tilly; Art Direction—Set Decoration, Santo Loquasto, Susan Bode; Costume Design, Jeffrey Kurland; Directing, **Woody Allen**; Writing, Screenplay Written Directly for Screen, **Woody Allen**, Douglas McGrath

DON'T DRINK THE WATER (TV) (1994)
Executive Producers: J. E. Beaucaire, Jean Doumanian
Co-Executive Producer: Letty Aronson
Producer: Robert Greenhut
Director: **Woody Allen**
Teleplay: **Woody Allen**, based on his play
Cinematography: Carlo Di Palma (color)
Editing: Susan E. Morse
Production Design: Santo Loquasto
Cast: Ed Herlihy (Narrator), Josef Sommer (Ambassador Magee), Robert Stanton (Mr. Burns), Edward Herrmann (Mr. Kilroy), Rosemary Murphy (Miss Pritchard), Michael J. Fox (Axel Magee), **Woody Allen** (Walter Hollander), Julie Kavner (Marion Hollander), Mayim Bialik (Susan Hollander)
100 minutes

MIGHTY APHRODITE (1995)
Sweetland Films/Miramax
Executive Producers: J. E. Beaucaire, Jean Doumanian
Co-Executive Producers: Letty Aronson, Charles H. Joffe, Jack Rollins
Associate Producer: Thomas A. Reilly

Producer: Robert Greenhut
Co-Producer: Helen Robin
Director: **Woody Allen**
Screenplay: **Woody Allen**
Cinematography: Carlo Di Palma (Technicolor)
Editing: Susan E. Morse
Production Design: Santo Loquasto
Music: Dick Hyman (uncredited)
Cast: **Woody Allen** (Lenny Weinrib), Mira Sorvino (Linda Ash/Judy Cum), Helena Bonham Carter (Amanda Weinrib), Olympia Dukakis (Jocasta)
98 minutes
Academy Award: Actress in Supporting Role, Mira Sorvino
Academy Award Nomination: Writing, Screenplay Written Directly for Screen, **Woody Allen**

EVERYONE SAYS I LOVE YOU (1996)
Sweetland Films/Miramax
Executive Producers: J. E. Beaucaire, Jean Doumanian
Co-Executive Producers: Letty Aronson, Charles H. Joffe, Jack Rollins
Producer: Robert Greenhut
Co-Producer: Helen Robin
Director: **Woody Allen**
Screenplay: **Woody Allen**
Cinematography: Carlo Di Palma (color)
Editing: Susan E. Morse
Production Design: Santo Loquasto
Music: Dick Hyman
Cast: Edward Norton (Holden), Drew Barrymore (Skylar), Natasha Lyonne (D. J.), Alan Alda (Bob), Gaby Hoffman (Lane), Natalie Portman (Laura), Lukas Haas (Scott), Goldie Hawn (Steffi), Julia Roberts (Von), **Woody Allen** (Joe Berlin), Tim Roth (Charles Ferry)
101 minutes

DECONSTRUCTING HARRY (1997)
Sweetland Films/Fine Line Features
Executive Producer: J. E. Beaucaire
Co-Executive Producers: Letty Aronson, Charles H. Joffe, Jack Rollins
Producer: Jean Doumanian
Co-Producer: Richard Brick
Director: **Woody Allen**

Screenplay: **Woody Allen**
Cinematography: Carlo Di Palma (Technicolor)
Editing: Susan E. Morse
Production Design: Santo Loquasto
Cast: Caroline Aaron (Doris), **Woody Allen** (Harry Block), Kirstie Alley (Joan), Bob Balaban (Richard), Richard Benjamin (Ken), Billy Crystal (Larry), Judy Davis (Lucy), Hazelle Goodman (Cookie Williams), Mariel Hemingway (Beth Kramer), Amy Irving (Jane), Julie Kavner (Grace), Eric Lloyd (Hilly), Julia Louis-Dreyfus (Leslie), Demi Moore (Helen), Elisabeth Shue (Fay), Robin Williams (Mel)
96 minutes
Academy Award Nomination: Writing, Screenplay Written Directly for Screen, **Woody Allen**

CELEBRITY (1998)
Sweetland Films/Miramax
Executive Producer: J. E. Beaucaire
Co-Executive Producers: Letty Aronson, Charles H. Joffe, Jack Rollins
Producer: Jean Doumanian
Co-Producer: Richard Brick
Director: **Woody Allen**
Screenplay: **Woody Allen**
Cinematography: Sven Nykvist (black and white)
Editing: Susan E. Morse
Production Design: Santo Loquasto
Cast: Kenneth Branagh (Lee Simon), Judy Davis (Robin Simon), Leonardo DiCaprio (Brandon Darrow), Melanie Griffith (Nicole Oliver), Famke Janssen (Bonnie), Winona Ryder (Nola)
113 minutes

SWEET AND LOWDOWN (1999)
Sweetland Films/Sony Pictures Classics
Executive Producer: J. E. Beaucaire
Co-Executive Producers: Letty Aronson, Charles H. Joffe, Jack Rollins
Producer: Jean Doumanian
Co-Producer: Richard Brick
Director: **Woody Allen**
Screenplay: **Woody Allen**
Cinematography: Zhao Fei (color)
Editing: Alisa Lepselter

Production Design: Santo Loquasto
Cast: **Woody Allen** (Himself), Sean Penn (Emmet Ray), Samantha Morton (Hattie), Uma Thurman (Blanche), Anthony LaPaglia (Al Torrio), Brian Markinson (Bill Shields), Gretchen Mol (Ellie)
95 minutes
Academy Award Nominations: Actor in a Leading Role, Sean Penn; Actress in a Leading Role, Samantha Morton

SMALL TIME CROOKS (2000)
Sweetland Films/DreamWorks
Executive Producer: J. E. Beaucaire
Co-Executive Producers: Letty Aronson, Charles H. Joffe, Jack Rollins
Producer: Jean Doumanian
Co-Producer: Helen Robin
Director: **Woody Allen**
Screenplay: **Woody Allen**
Cinematography: Zhao Fei (Technicolor)
Editing: Alisa Lepselter
Production Design: Santo Loquasto
Cast: **Woody Allen** (Ray Winkler), Tracey Ullman (Frances "Frenchy" Winkler), Hugh Grant (David Perret), Elaine May (May Sloan), Michael Rapaport (Denny Doyle), Tony Darrow (Tommy Beal), Jon Lovitz (Benny Borkowski), Elaine Stritch (Chi Chi Potter)
94 minutes

THE CURSE OF THE JADE SCORPION (2001)
DreamWorks
Executive Producer: Stephen Tenenbaum
Co-Executive Producers: Charles H. Joffe, Jack Rollins, Datty Ruth
Producer: Letty Aronson
Co-Producer: Helen Robin
Director: **Woody Allen**
Screenplay: **Woody Allen**
Cinematography: Zhao Fei (Technicolor)
Editing: Alisa Lepselter
Production Design: Santo Loquasto
Cast: **Woody Allen** (C. W. Briggs), Elizabeth Berkeley (Jill), Brian Markinson (Al), Helen Hunt (Betty Ann Fitzgerald), Wallace Shawn (George Bond), Dan Aykroyd (Chris Magruder), David Ogden Stiers (Voltan Polgar), Charlize Theron (Laura Kensington)
103 minutes

SOUNDS FROM A TOWN I LOVE (TV) (2001)
Director: **Woody Allen**
Screenplay: **Woody Allen**
Cast: Marshall Brickman, Griffin Dunne, Hazelle Goodman, Bebe Neuwirth (Last Woman on Cell Phone), Tony Roberts (Man on Bench)
5 minutes

HOLLYWOOD ENDING (2002)
DreamWorks
Executive Producer: Stephen Tenenbaum
Co-Executive Producers: Charles H. Joffe, Jack Rollins
Producer: Letty Aronson
Co-Producer: Helen Robin
Director: **Woody Allen**
Screenplay: **Woody Allen**
Cinematography: Wedigo von Schultzendorff (Technicolor)
Editing: Alisa Lepselter
Production Design: Santo Loquasto
Cast: **Woody Allen** (Val Waxman), Téa Leoni (Ellie), George Hamilton (Ed), Debra Messing (Lori Fox), Mark Rydell (Al Hack)
114 minutes

ANYTHING ELSE (2003)
DreamWorks
Executive Producers: Stephen Tenenbaum, Benny Medina
Co-Executive Producers: Charles H. Joffe, Jack Rollins
Producer: Letty Aronson
Co-Producer: Helen Robin
Director: **Woody Allen**
Screenplay: **Woody Allen**
Cinematography: Darius Khondji (color/Panavision)
Editing: Alisa Lepselter
Production Design: Santo Loquasto
Cast: **Woody Allen** (David Dobel), Jason Biggs (Jerry Falk), Danny DeVito (Harvey), Christina Ricci (Amanda), Jimmy Fallon (Bob), William Hill (Psychiatrist), Stockard Channing (Paula)
108 minutes

MELINDA AND MELINDA (2004; US, 2005)
Fox Searchlight

Executive Producers: Stephen Tenenbaum, Charles H. Joffe, Jack Rollins
Producer: Letty Aronson
Co-Producer: Helen Robin
Director: **Woody Allen**
Screenplay: **Woody Allen**
Cinematography: Vilmos Zsigmond (color)
Editing: Alisa Lepselter
Production Design: Santo Loquasto
Cast: Will Ferrell (Hobie), Radha Mitchell (Melinda), Chloë Sevigny (Laurel), Chiwetel Ejiofor (Ellis), Jonny Lee Miller (Lee), Wallace Shawn (Sy), Larry Pine (Max), Amanda Peet (Susan), Steve Carell (Walt), Daniel Sunjata (Billy)
100 minutes

MATCH POINT (2005)
BBC Films, Thema Productions, Jada, Kudu/DreamWorks
Executive Producer: Stephen Tenenbaum
Co-Executive Producers: Charles H. Joffe, Jack Rollins
Producers: Letty Aronson, Lucy Darwin, Gareth Wiley
Co-Producers: Nicky Kentish Barnes, Helen Robin
Director: **Woody Allen**
Screenplay: **Woody Allen**
Cinematography: Remi Adefarasin (color)
Production Design: Jim Clay
Editing: Alisa Lepselter
Cast: Jonathan Rhys Meyers (Chris Wilton), Matthew Goode (Tom Hewett), Brian Cox (Alec Hewett), Penelope Wilton (Eleanor Hewett), Emily Mortimer (Chloe Hewett Wilton), Scarlett Johansson (Nola Rice)
124 minutes
Academy Award Nomination: Writing, Screenplay Written Directly for Screen: **Woody Allen**

SCOOP (2006)
BBC Films, Ingenious Film Partners, Phoenix Wiley, Jelly Roll Productions/ Focus Features
Executive Producers: Stephen Tenenbaum; Duncan Reid, Peter Touche (Ingenious Film Partners); David M. Thompson (BBC Films)
Co-Executive Producers: Charles H. Joffe, Jack Rollins
Producers: Letty Aronson, Gareth Wiley
Co-Producers: Nicky Kentish Barnes, Helen Robin
Director: **Woody Allen**

Screenplay: **Woody Allen**
Cinematography: Remi Adefarasin (color)
Production Design: Maria Djurkovic
Editing: Alisa Lepselter
Cast: Scarlett Johansson (Sondra Pransky), Hugh Jackman (Peter Lyman), Ian McShane (Joe Strombel), **Woody Allen** (Sid Waterman)
96 minutes

CASSANDRA'S DREAM (2007)
Iberville Productions, Virtual Studios, Wild Bunch/Weinstein Company
Executive Producers: Brahim Chioua, Vincent Maraval, Daniel Wührmann
Co-Executive Producers: Charles H. Joffe, Jack Rollins
Producers: Letty Aronson, Stephen Tenenbaum, Gareth Wiley
Co-Producers: Nicky Kentish Barnes, Helen Robin
Director: **Woody Allen**
Screenplay: **Woody Allen**
Cinematography: Vilmos Zsigmond (color)
Production Design: Maria Djurkovic
Editing: Alisa Lepselter
Music: Philip Glass
Cast: Ewan McGregor (Ian), Colin Farrell (Terry), Hayley Atwell (Angela), Sally Hawkins (Kate), Tom Wilkinson (Howard), Ashley Madekwe (Lucy)
108 minutes

VICKY CRISTINA BARCELONA (2008)
The Weinstein Company, Mediapro, Gravier Productions, Antena 3 Films, Antena 3 Televisión, Televisió de Catalunya (TV3)/The Weinstein Company, MGM
Executive Producer: Jaume Roures
Co-Executive Producers: Charles H. Joffe, Javier Méndez, Jack Rollins
Producers: Letty Aronson, Stephen Tenenbaum, Gareth Wiley
Co-Producer: Helen Robin
Director: **Woody Allen**
Screenplay: **Woody Allen**
Cinematography: Javier Aguirresarobe (color)
Production Design: Alain Bainée
Editing: Alisa Lepselter
Cast: Rebecca Hall (Vicky), Scarlett Johansson (Cristina), Chris Messina (Doug), Patricia Clarkson (Judy), Kevin Dunn (Mark), Javier Bardem (Juan Antonio), Penélope Cruz (Maria Elena)

96 minutes
Academy Award: Actress in a Supporting Role, Penélope Cruz

WHATEVER WORKS (2009)
Sony Pictures Classics, Wild Bunch, Gravier Productions, Perdido Productions/Sony Pictures Classics
Executive Producers: Brahim Chioua, Vincent Maraval
Co-Executive Producers: Charles H. Joffe, Jack Rollins
Producers: Letty Aronson, Stephen Tenenbaum
Co-Producer: Helen Robin
Director: **Woody Allen**
Screenplay: **Woody Allen**
Cinematography: Harris Savides (color)
Production Design: Santo Loquasto
Editing: Alisa Lepselter
Cast: Larry David (Boris), Evan Rachel Wood (Melody), John Gallagher Jr. (Perry), Patricia Clarkson (Marietta), Henry Cavill (Randy), Ed Begley Jr. (John)
92 minutes

YOU WILL MEET A TALL DARK STRANGER (2010)
Mediapro, Versátil Cinema, Gravier Productions, Antenna 3 Films, Antenna 3 Televisión, Dippermouth/Sony Pictures Classics
Executive Producer: Javier Méndez
Co-Executive Producer: Jack Rollins
Producers: Letty Aronson, Jaume Roures, Stephen Tenenbaum
Co-Producers: Nicky Kentish Barnes, Helen Robin
Director: **Woody Allen**
Screenplay: **Woody Allen**
Cinematography: Vilmos Zsigmond (color)
Production Design: Jim Clay
Editing: Alisa Lepselter
Cast: Gemma Jones (Helena), Pauline Collins (Cristal), Anthony Hopkins (Alfie), Naomi Watts (Sally), Josh Brolin (Roy), Freida Pinto (Dia), Antonio Banderas (Greg)
98 Minutes

MIDNIGHT IN PARIS (2011)
Gravier Productions, Mediapro, Pontchartrain Productions, Televisió de Catalunya (TV3), Versátil Cinema/Sony Pictures Classics

Executive Producer: Javier Mendez
Co-Executive Producer: Jack Rollins
Producers: Letty Aronson, Jaume Roures, Stephen Tenenbaum
Co-Producers: Raphaël Benoliel, Helen Robin
Director: **Woody Allen**
Screenplay: **Woody Allen**
Cinematography: Darius Khondji (color)
Production Design: Anne Seibel
Editing: Alisa Lepselter
Cast: Owen Wilson (Gil), Rachel McAdams (Inez), Michael Sheen (Paul), Carla Bruni (Museum Guide), Kathy Bates (Gertrude Stein), Marion Cotillard (Adriana)
94 minutes
Academy Award: Writing, Screenplay Written Directly for Screen: **Woody Allen** Academy Award Nominations: Best Picture: Letty Aronson, Stephen Tenenbaum, Directing: **Woody Allen**, Art Direction: Ann Seibel and Hélène Dubreuil

TO ROME WITH LOVE (2012)
Medusa Film, Gravier Productions, Perdido Productions/Sony Pictures Classics
Co-Executive Producer: Jack Rollins
Producers: Faruk Alatan, Letty Aronson, Giampaolo Letta, Stephen Tenenbaum
Co-Producers: David Nichols, Helen Robin
Director: **Woody Allen**
Screenplay: **Woody Allen**
Cinematography: Darius Khondji (color)
Production Design: Anne Seibel
Editing: Alisa Lepselter
Cast: Judy Davis (Phyllis), Roberto Benigni (Leopoldo), Alec Baldwin (John), **Woody Allen** (Jerry), Jesse Eisenberg (Jack), Greta Gerwig (Sally), Penélope Cruz (Anna), Ellen Page (Monica)
112 minutes

BLUE JASMINE (2013)
Gravier Productions, Perdido Productions/Sony Pictures Classics
Executive Producers: Leroy Schecter, Adam B. Stern
Co-Executive Producer: Jack Rollins
Producers: Letty Aronson, Stephen Tenenbaum, Edward Walson
Co-Producer: Helen Robin
Director: **Woody Allen**

Screenplay: **Woody Allen**
Cinematography: Javier Aguirresarobe (color)
Production Design: Santo Loquasto
Editing: Alisa Lepselter
Cast: Cate Blanchett (Jasmine), Alec Baldwin (Hal), Sally Hawkins (Ginger), Bobby Cannavale (Chili), Andrew Dice Clay (Augie), Louis C. K. (Al), Peter Sarsgaard (Dwight)
98 minutes
Academy Award: Actress in a Leading Role, Cate Blanchett
Academy Award Nominations: Actress in a Supporting Role, Sally Hawkins, Writing, Screenplay Written Directly for the Screen, **Woody Allen**

MAGIC IN THE MOONLIGHT (2014)
Gravier Productions, Dippermouth Productions, Perdido Productions, Ske-Dat-De-Dat Productions/Sony Pictures Classics
Executive Producer: Ronald L. Chez
Co-Executive Producer: Jack Rollins
Producers: Letty Aronson, Stephen Tenenbaum, Edward Walson
Co-Producers: Raphaël Benoliel, Helen Robin
Director: **Woody Allen**
Screenplay: **Woody Allen**
Cinematography: Darius Khondji (color)
Production Design: Anne Seibel
Editing: Alisa Lepselter
Cast: Emma Stone (Sophie), Colin Firth (Stanley), Marcia Gay Harden (Mrs. Baker), Hamish Linklater (Brice), Eileen Atkins (Aunt Vanessa)
97 minutes

IRRATIONAL MAN (2015)
Gravier Productions/Sony Pictures Classics
Executive Producers: Ronald L. Chez, Adam B. Stern, Allan Teh
Co-Executive Producer: Jack Rollins
Producers: Letty Aronson, Stephen Tenenbaum, Edward Walson
Co-Producer: Helen Robin
Director: **Woody Allen**
Screenplay: **Woody Allen**
Cinematography: Darius Khondji (color)
Production Design: Santo Loquasto
Editing: Alisa Lepselter

Cast: Joaquin Phoenix (Abe), Emma Stone (Jill), Jamie Blackley (Roy), Parker Posey (Rita), Betsy Aidem (Jill's Mother), Ethan Phillips (Jill's Father)
95 minutes

UNTITLED PROJECT (2016)
Executive Producers: Ron Chez, Adam B. Stern, Allan Teh
Producers: Letty Aronson, Stephen Tenenbaum, Edward Walson
Director: **Woody Allen**
Screenplay: **Woody Allen**
Cinematography: Vittorio Storaro (color, digital)
Production Design: Santo Loquasto
Cast: Kristen Stewart (Theresa), Jesse Eisenberg (James), Blake Lively (Kat), Steve Carell (Aaron)

As Writer, Directed by Others

WHAT'S NEW PUSSYCAT? (1965)
United Artists
Executive Producer: John C. Shepridge
Producers: Charles K. Feldman, Richard Sylbert
Director: Clive Donner
Screenplay: **Woody Allen**
Cinematography: Jean Badal
Editing: Fergus McDonell
Production Design: Jacques Saulnier
Music: Burt Bacharach
Cast: Peter Sellers (Dr. Fritz Fassbender), Peter O'Toole (Michael James), Romy Schneider (Carole Werner), Capucine (Renee Lefebvre), Paula Prentiss (Liz Bien), **Woody Allen** (Victor Shakapopulis), Ursula Andress (Rita)
108 minutes
Academy Award Nomination: Music, Original Song, Burt Bacharach, Hal David

CASINO ROYALE (1967)
Columbia Pictures
Associate Producer: John Dark
Producers: Jerry Bresler, Charles K. Feldman
Directors: Val Guest, Ken Hughes, John Huston, Joseph McGrath, Robert Parrish
Screenplay: Wolf Mankowitz, John Law, Michael Sayers, **Woody Allen**, et al. (uncredited)

Novel: Ian Fleming
Cinematography: Jack Hildyard
Editing: Bill Lenny
Production Design: Michael Stringer
Music: Burt Bacharach
Cast: Peter Sellers (Evelyn Tremble), Ursula Andress (Vesper Lynd), David Niven (Sir James Bond), Orson Welles (Le Chiffre), **Woody Allen** (Dr. Noah/Jimmy Bond), Deborah Kerr (Agent Mimi/Lady Fiona McTarry), William Holden (Ransome)
131 minutes
Academy Award Nomination: Music, Original Song, Burt Bacharach, Hal David

DON'T DRINK THE WATER (1969)
20th Century Fox Film Corporation/AVCO Embassy Pictures
Executive Producer: Joseph E. Levine
Associate Producers: Jack Grossberg, Henry Polonsky
Producers: Charles H. Joffe, Jack Rollins
Director: Howard Morris
Screenplay: R. S. Allen, **Woody Allen** (also play), Harvey Bullock
Cinematography: Harvey Genkins
Editing: Ralph Rosenblum
Art Direction: Robert Gundlach
Music: Patrick Williams
Cast: Jackie Gleason (Walter Hollander), Estelle Parsons (Marion Hollander), Ted Bessell (Axel Magee), Joan Delaney (Susan Hollander), Michael Constantine (Krojack), Howard St. John (Ambassador Magee)
100 minutes

PLAY IT AGAIN, SAM (1972)
Paramount
Executive Producer: Charles H. Joffe
Associate Producer: Frank Capra Jr.
Producer: Arthur P. Jacobs
Director: Herbert Ross
Screenplay: **Woody Allen** (also play)
Cinematography: Owen Roizman
Editing: Marion Rothman
Production Design: Ed Wittstein
Music: Billy Goldenberg, Max Steiner

Cast: **Woody Allen** (Allan), Diane Keaton (Linda), Tony Roberts (Dick), Jerry Lacey (Bogart), Susan Anspach (Nancy)
85 minutes

SOMEBODY OR THE RISE AND FALL OF PHILOSOPHY (1989)
Director: Axel Hildebrand
Screenplay: Axel Hildebrand, based on story "Mr. Big" by **Woody Allen**
Cast: Patrick Jech ("Kaiser" Lupowitz), Unika Schaefer (Heather Buttkiss), Thomas Garlipp (Rabbi/Pope), Jörg Beller (Chicago-Phil), Axel Hildebrand (Sergeant Reed)
25 minutes

As Actor Only

THE FRONT (1976)
Columbia Pictures
Executive Producer: Charles H. Joffe
Associate Producer: Robert Greenhut
Producer: Martin Ritt
Director: Martin Ritt
Screenplay: Walter Bernstein
Cinematography: Michael Chapman
Editing: Sidney Levin
Art Direction: Charles Bailey
Music: Dave Grusin
Cast: **Woody Allen** (Howard Prince), Zero Mostel (Hecky Brown), Herschel Bernadi (Phil Sussman), Michael Murphy (Alfred Miller), Andrea Marcovicci (Florence Barrett)
95 minutes

KING LEAR (1987)
Cannon Films
Producers: Yoram Globus, Menahem Golan
Director: Jean-Luc Godard
Screenplay: Richard Debuisne, Jean-Luc Godard, Norman Mailer (all uncredited), William Shakespeare (play)
Cinematography: Sophie Maintigneux (uncredited)
Editing: Jean-Luc Godard
Cast: **Woody Allen** (Mr. Alien), Leos Carax (Edgar), Julie Delpy (Virginia),

Jean-Luc Godard (Professor Pluggy), Norman Mailer (The Great Writer), Burgess Meredith (Don Learo) (all uncredited)
90 minutes

SCENES FROM A MALL (1991)
Buena Vista
Associate Producer: Stuart H. Pappé
Producer: Paul Mazursky
Co-Producers: Pato Guzman, Patrick McCormick
Director: Paul Mazursky
Screenplay: Paul Mazursky, Roger L. Simon
Cinematography: Fred Murphy
Editing: Stuart H. Pappé
Production Design: Pato Guzman
Music: Marc Shaiman
Cast: Bette Midler (Deborah Fifer), **Woody Allen** (Nick Fifer), Bill Irwin (Mime), Daren Firestone (Sam), Rebecca Nickels (Jennifer), Paul Mazursky (Doctor Hans Clava)
89 minutes

THE SUNSHINE BOYS (TV) (1995)
Hallmark Entertainment
Executive Producer: Robert Halmi Sr.
Producer: John Erman
Co-Producer: Gerrit van der Meer
Director: John Erman
Teleplay: Neil Simon, based on his play
Cinematography: Tony Imi
Editing: Jack Wheeler
Production Design: Ben Edwards
Music: Irwin Fisch
Cast: **Woody Allen** (Al Lewis), Peter Falk (Willie Clark), Sarah Jessica Parker (Nancy Clark), Michael McKean, Liev Schreiber, Edie Falco
120 minutes

ANTZ (1998)
DreamWorks
Executive Producers: Penney Finkelman Cox, Sandra Rabins, Carl Rosendahl
Producers: Brad Lewis, Aron Warner, Patty Wooton
Editing: Stan Webb
Directors: Eric Darnell, Tim Johnson

Screenplay: Todd Alcott, Chris Weitz, Paul Weitz
Story: Chris Miller
Music: Harry Gregson-Williams, John Powell
Cast: **Woody Allen** (voice of Z), Dan Aykroyd (voice of Chip), Anne Bancroft (voice of Queen), Jane Curtin (voice of Muffy), Danny Glover (voice of Barbatus), Gene Hackman (voice of General Mandible), Jennifer Lopez (voice of Azteca)
Animated, 87 minutes

THE IMPOSTORS (1998)
Fox Searchlight/Twentieth Century Fox
Executive Producer: Jonathan Filley
Producers: Elizabeth W. Alexander, Stanley Tucci
Director: Stanley Tucci
Screenplay: Stanley Tucci
Cinematography: Ken Kelsch
Editing: Suzy Elmiger
Production Design: Andrew Jackness
Music: Gary DeMichele
Cast: Oliver Platt (Maurice), Stanley Tucci (Arthur), Alfred Molina (Jeremy Burtom), Lili Taylor (Lily), Tony Shalhoub (First Mate), **Woody Allen** (Audition Director) (uncredited)
101 minutes

COMPANY MAN (2000)
Paramount
Co-Executive Producers: Susan Cartsonis, John Ein, Carmen Finestra, Robert Greenhut, Nigel Sinclair, Matt Williams
Producers: Guy East, Rick Leed, John Penotti, James W. Skotchdopole
Directors: Peter Askin, Douglas McGrath
Screenplay: Peter Askin, Douglas McGrath
Cinematography: Russell Boyd
Editing: Camilla Toniolo
Production Design: Jane Musky
Music: David Nessim Lawrence
Cast: Paul Guilfoyle (Officer Hickle), Jeffrey Jones (Sen. Biggs), Reathel Bean (Sen. Farwood), Harriet Koppel (Stenographer), Douglas McGrath (Alan Quimp), Sigourney Weaver (Daisy Quimp), **Woody Allen** (Lowther) (uncredited)
86 minutes (U.S. cut)

PICKING UP THE PIECES (2000)
Not distributed theatrically in the U.S., premiered on Cinemax
Executive Producers: Alfonso Arau, Donald Kushner, Peter Locke, Mimi Polk
Producer: Paul Sandberg
Director: Alfonso Arau
Screenplay: Bill Wilson
Cinematography: Vittorio Storaro
Editing: Michael R. Miller
Production Design: Denise Pizzini
Music: Ruy Folguera
Cast: **Woody Allen** (Tex Cowley), Sharon Stone (Candy Cowley), Alfonso Arau (Dr. Amado), Maria Grazia Cucinotta (Desi), Cheech Marin (Mayor Machado), David Schwimmer (Leo Jerome), Kiefer Sutherland (Bobo)
95 minutes

PARIS-MANHATTAN (2012)
Vendôme Production, France 2 Cinéma, SND Films, Canal+, Ciné+, France Télévisions, A Plus Image 3, Palatine Étoile 9/Strand Releasing
Producer: Philippe Rousselet
Associate Producer: Étienne Comar
Director: Sophie Lellouche
Screenplay: Sophie Lellouche
Cinematography: Laurent Machuel
Editing: Monica Coleman
Production Design: Philip L'Évêque
Music: Jean-Michel Bernard
Cast: Alice Taglioni (Alice), Patrick Bruel (Victor), Marine Delterme (Hélène), Michel Aumont (The Father), Louis-Do de Lencquesaing (Pierre), Marie-Christine Adam (The Mother), **Woody Allen** (himself, uncredited)
77 minutes

FADING GIGOLO (2013)
Antidote Films/ Millennium Entertainment
Executive Producers: Scott Ferguson, Anton Lessine, Sasha Shapiro, Bart Walker
Producers: Bill Block, Paul Hanson, Jeffrey Kusama-Hinte
Co-Producer: James Debbs
Director: John Turturro
Screenplay: John Turturro
Cinematography: Marco Pontecorvo
Editing: Simona Paggi

Production Design: Lester Cohen
Cast: John Turturro (Fioravante), **Woody Allen** (Murray), Vanessa Paradis (Avigal), Liev Schreiber (Dovi), Sharon Stone (Dr. Parker), Sofía Vergara (Selima)
90 minutes

Woody Allen: Interviews
Revised and Updated

Woody Allen Interview

Robert Mundy and Stephen Mamber / 1972

From *Cinema*, Winter 1972/73, 14–21. Reprinted by permission.

Q: Perhaps we could begin by asking you about your own interest in movies. In *Bananas* especially there are a lot of references to other films. I wondered how long you've been liking films as well as making them.
A: I would not say I have an inordinate liking of movies. I'm just an average person who likes movies. But I'm not a fanatic, I'm not a collector, I haven't seen an inordinate amount of them, I don't spend seven days a week going to them.

Q: There are a lot of references to the Marx Brothers in *Bananas*.
A: I've seen a lot of Marx Brothers movies, because I like them. I haven't seen as many comedies as you would think. I've only seen one Buster Keaton film, only about three Chaplin films outside of the one- and two-reelers. Not that many. I've seen most of the Marx Brothers' pictures. They are particular favorites of mine. I thought *Duck Soup* was a tremendous picture.

Q: Would you say that it inspired the courtroom scene in *Bananas*?
A: No. The reason for that was that we thought the ending of *Take the Money and Run* wasn't strong enough. When I was writing *Bananas* I was trying to think of what would be a strong ending. It was either a chase or a courtroom scene. Either would have worked very well. We couldn't afford a chase, so it was a courtroom scene.

Q: *Take the Money and Run* parodies the 1940s semi-documentary style.
A: Sure, and I think that style is even prevalent now. For some reason that documentary style has always appealed to me. This little film that I made for NET, which they are not showing, was also documentary.

Q: Could you talk about that a little?
A: Sure, if you like. It's a pseudo-documentary, political, but very broad. Like *Take*

the Money and Run, a very broad kind of comedy. It was only twenty-eight minutes long. I used myself, and a lot of people I had worked with before. A few new people. It was based on Henry Kissinger, but very loosely. As loosely as *Take the Money and Run* was based on Dillinger. I was very surprised that there was any kind of to-do about it at all. It was innocuous—and insulting. It certainly wasn't terribly politically incisive or anything like that.

Q: My reaction when I heard that Herbert Ross was going to direct *Play It Again, Sam* was one of disappointment. Why didn't you direct it yourself? Or did you want to?

A: No, I didn't want to. I would never want to direct a play into a movie. I would only be interested in working on original projects for the screen. I was also already at work on this picture, and I didn't want to spend a year doing a project that I had done on Broadway. I wanted a director like Herb Ross who would do the job. I had never met Herb Ross, but as it turned out he did an ideal job. He got all the laughs in the play. What I'm hoping *Play It Again, Sam* will be, is a nice, solid, funny commercial picture, and hopefully entice a broader audience for me than I get with my own films. That's always a problem. *Take the Money* and *Bananas* and I think *Everything You Always Wanted to Know about Sex* at their most successful are special pictures in the sense that a certain audience follows them. I think *Play It Again, Sam* has a chance of being one of those Radio City Music Hall pictures. You know, clean and funny. It would be a big help to me in getting customers for my own movies.

Q: Did you adapt the screenplay yourself from your stage play?

A: Yes. It took me about ten days to do. It was so easy to do. I spoke to Herb Ross, who had definite ideas about how it should be done. The tough thing is always writing dialogue and that was all there. I'd played it about four hundred times. The transfer was so easy. And Herb had some very good suggestions for the screenplay. He has a surprisingly fresh approach. He suggested scenes and ways of doing scenes that never occurred to me. I was probably too locked into the play to think of anything new. Some of the nice laughs in the movie were never in the play. It couldn't have worked out better for me, and I was really delighted.

Q: While we're talking about collaborations, I'd like to ask you about Mickey Rose, and what his role is in developing your screenplays.

A: He's an old friend of mine from high school. Usually, I don't like to collaborate, and I only have on my first two pictures because he has a unique sense of humor—very close to mine. He really writes the same kind of thing. We just lock ourselves in a room together and start going.

Q: Have both of those films been from your original ideas?
A: Yes. *Bananas* and *Take the Money* were from my ideas.

Q: But your new film you've written on your own?
A: Yes, but I'll probably write with him again.

Q: Did you enjoy writing *What's New Pussycat?*
A: It was a crazy script, It was the kind of script like *Bananas*. But the people that made it—and I don't mean the actors, but the production people—didn't know how to do that kind of film. They just went out and spent a lot of money, hired the biggest names they could find.

Q: There's a lot of fun made of the psychiatrist figure in that picture, and I wondered if you would be playing a similar figure in your new film? Are you going to be playing Dr. David Reuben?
A: No. He doesn't appear. There's some reference to psychiatry in it, but minimal. But he doesn't appear. He hasn't even read the screenplay. He just sold the rights to the book. I never met him even to acquire it. The book actually was owned by Elliot Gould, and I acquired it from him.

Q: I'd like to ask you how you became involved with *What's Up Tiger Lily?* Why did you choose that particular film? Had you looked at a lot of Japanese movies? Did you have the idea first and then look for the right movie?
A: No. Someone else had the idea. A man who I eventually wound up suing, and winning—I always wind up suing—asked me if I'd look at a Japanese film he had bought. What he originally wanted was for me and my friends to sit in the background and make cracks while it was on. He didn't know what to do with the thing. He thought of getting a lot of comedians to dub voices. I saw it, and thought it might be a funny idea to put a different story in their mouths. I thought it was going to be easy, and where there was just a little bit of dialogue it would be even easier. I was wrong on all counts. It was very hard. I had to do it all with friends— Mickey Rose was one of the people, and Louise, who was in *Bananas*, and Frank Buxton, another friend of mine. We all got into a locked room together. We kept running loops all day long for weeks, and writing the story, making it up as we went along. And it turned out that what we really wanted was more dialogue, and the story would sag when there was less. But we didn't know that at first. We did it, and I turned it over to the producer.

Q: You also shot a little bit, didn't you?
A: We just shot that intermediary material. And then the producer changed a

couple of lines in it, and I sued him. It was very successful for what it was. I was surprised that it was so successful. We just thought that it was a little exercise, and that no place would play it or anything. But he distributed it well, handled it well.

Q: I don't think it played outside the States, perhaps because of the rights to the Japanese film. It certainly didn't play in Britain.
A: It played in Iceland. Someone's mother saw it there.

Q: What led you to become interested in making films?
A: Well, *Pussycat* was such an unpleasant experience for me. There was no one to sue on that or I would have. It sounds terrible. I was a nightclub comedian, and they asked me to do *Pussycat*, to write the movie, and we could shoot it in Paris. So I wrote it for Warren Beatty originally—he was supposed to do it. Then through millions of machinations they got Peter O'Toole. Beatty was on another project. I liked the director of the film very much, but the people in charge—

Q: Charlie Feldman?
A: Yeah, they just killed it completely. I fought with everybody all the time. I hated everyone, and everyone hated me. When that picture was over, I decided I would never do another film unless I had complete control of it. Then about six months later they asked me if I would appear briefly in *Casino Royale*. That I didn't mind doing, because I didn't have to write anything. I could just go over there and hope that it would turn out to be a good film.

Q: You didn't write your own part?
A: I ad-libbed lines of my own. I didn't even know what was going on. I just went over there. They paid me a lot of money, wasted a lot of time for ages. I sat around in London for about five and a half months on salary waiting to shoot. By the time they got to shoot me I was way on overtime in terms of my salary. The overage was enormous. They shot me for five or six days and that was it. I never bothered to see the film. I knew it would be a horrible film from what was going on there. It was a chaotic madhouse. I knew then that the only way to make films is to control it completely. Most of the people didn't seem to know what they were doing at all.

Q: There's a line in *What's New Pussycat?*—I think Clive Donner has said that it was a Peter Sellers ad-lib—when he says to O'Toole about Paula Prentiss, "Could I be the one who sees no one touches her for you." Something like that. It seems representative of your kind of humor. Do you remember that?
A: I don't, and I'll tell you why. I saw the picture once, fleetingly, years ago. I don't

remember much about it at all. I certainly don't remember any of the dialogue. I have no script of it any place. A lot of ad-libbing went on, which I like in the films I direct, but there was nobody on *Pussycat* to control the ad-libbing. Consequently it could be very funny, but sometimes it wasn't. But there was nobody in charge who knew how to winnow out the good stuff from the bad. They just slopped it all up on the screen.

Q: One element of your movies I admire are the throwaways. One that comes to mind is in *Take the Money and Run*, where through the prison railings there are two ventriloquist's dummies in the background.
A: I love those kinds of jokes. And I was thinking of doing a film with an enormous amount of that going on. The film I'm doing now isn't that—it's a different kind of picture—but I was thinking of doing a film where there are jokes constantly going on in the background, for the whole picture. You can imagine what it would look like.

Q: Do you feel visual humor any more difficult for you, coming from a nightclub background, where jokes were written? There are a number of completely silent sequences in your films.
A: It's no more difficult. It's just as hard to get funny dialogue. Actually, once you get on to it, it's probably a little easier to get funny visuals as to get funny dialogue. Dialogue is harder to do in films. I've always felt that if Chaplin had to use dialogue, it would have been a lot tougher for him. It's a big plus not to have to do dialogue. It would be easier for me to do a film where people said I couldn't use any dialogue at all. There's a big problem. You can make the film totally unbelievable, as with the Marx Brothers, where all the dialogue is gags; or you can make it believable. If Chaplin had spoken and played the same character, he wouldn't be doing gags all the time. He would have been speaking just as we are speaking now, and a lot of the picture wouldn't be funny, because you'd have to sit through a guy talking straight, or else he'd kill the believability of his character; whereas if he did jokes all the time, you'd never believe the other things. It's really a terrible problem to do dialogue.

Q: I think there is a related problem which you seem to have solved very well: the prominence given to the narrative. In the Marx Brothers' later movies, when the narrative became stronger the films became weaker. The same kind of thing applies to Jerry Lewis. You seem to have avoided that by side-stepping narrative. What about the film you are doing now?
A: Well, this one has more narrative to it, definitely. This is not a picture of gag, gag, gag. I like that form, because the less narrative, the more freedom. But then

you are obliged to be funny all the time, because you have nothing else going for you. In *Play It Again Sam* we can do a scene for two minutes, and people are interested in the story, so it doesn't have to be one gag after another. In *Bananas* if you don't have gags going for you, you've got nothing. The same thing in *Duck Soup*. Once the gags stop, you don't really care about the sitting room scenes, the love scenes and the harp solos. That's a good form if you can just get the right amount of narrative. Just enough, so that there is a bare story to follow. But not so much that you're locked in. It's nice to be able to stop and do a ten-minute scene on anything you want. You know Chaplin wasn't bad at that. I was looking at *Modern Times* the other day and he has just enough narrative. He'll suddenly have fun at the factory, and then he'll get the girl and go through a routine with her; he's telling some kind of story, but it's really told in terms of sketches. There's the factory sketch, and the sketch with the house, and the sketch where he's night watchman in the store. He'll just take five or ten minutes and skate around, do bits and pieces. That's really how you make a comedy film. You have to constantly stop and do sketches. Like in *City Lights* he'll suddenly stop and do two minutes in the prize-fight ring, then go back to the story, and then do two minutes on the statue. That's really what they're comprised of. He was very skillful at hiding that, to the degree where you can get that good marriage of narrative and gags. Then you can make it work.

Q: Have you ever come to the point where you've thrown out a bit of funny business because you thought it wouldn't fit the narrative?
A: No. I've thrown out tons and tons of material because I didn't think it was funny. In the past, if it's a choice between the narrative and what's funny, I always put in what's funny. I feel the audience will forgive it if they laugh. And they do. In this type of film, they'd rather have five good minutes where they laugh, even if it doesn't relate to the film and they have to say "Hey, what was that all about?" Nobody really cares. It's a very loose structure, that permits you to just stop and do two minutes on some completely different subject. What you suffer from is the lack of a suspenseful story. To a degree you can get both.

Q: The note-writing in *Take the Money and Run* is a good example of having both together. It's very funny, and it helps the narrative and the suspense.
A: That's hard to do though. A lot of times you come up with very funny ideas that have absolutely nothing to do with the story. It's a digression, and it's hilarious. I always think it's better to do it. You can always throw it out later.

Q: Do you think political satire is a more difficult thing to do, as in *Bananas* where you're making fun of actual people?

A: I don't think it's more difficult. I think you get more credit for it, undeservedly so. You know, *Take the Money and Run* was light and amusing, about bank robberies. If I had adapted it, using the same documentary style with the same narrative, about someone who worked in the White House, all of a sudden people would have said, "This is meaningful political satire." For some reason, you get a lot of credit when you touch on politics. But it's not tougher to do. It can be easier to do because there are so many good jokes. I just don't know enough about politics or have much of an interest in it. *Bananas* was coincidentally political.

Q: One of *Bananas*' strengths is that it doesn't take sides. You can satirize the left and the right, at the same time.
A: Yes, I really had no point I was trying to make in the whole thing. I was just trying to think of a funny idea. It could just as easily have been an idea about crime again, or bank robberies.

Q: There's not very much camera movement in your first two movies. I wondered if you had an antipathy towards moving the camera, if you preferred a static camera.
A: That's an interesting point. In the first picture there was more camera movement. It was my first film, and I was trying to discover when it's best to move it and when it's best not to. *Bananas* was purely experimental. I thought I would do almost the whole film without moving it at all, and see what that would be like. I think I found the answer, which is what I'm doing in this picture. There's quite a bit of camera movement in this one actually. In the first film it was hard to know when to move the camera and when not to, because I would always want to protect the joke. I found frequently in *Take the Money and Run* that I would ruin a joke by moving too much. I started the film thinking it would be visually more interesting to move the camera a lot. When I cut the film together I found out that it was better to use static shots, and just cut them. The truth is that it's a very safe way of working. In the picture I'm doing now I know that I could get all the laughs in the script if I didn't move the camera much. Comedy films are unlike other films: what's important in a comedy is the content of the shot, not the shot itself. The fact that a shot swoops or zooms just doesn't mean anything. What's funny in a Keaton film or a Chaplin film is that they set the camera up, and they let the comedian do what he does, record it, and that's what you laugh at. If you've got two guys tearing up a contract, you just want to see it lit nicely, bright. In this picture that I'm doing now I've tried to disregard the safe route, and make a picture that's visually appealing with a lot of moves in it, and try to call on what I've

learned so as not to screw up the jokes. I think it's working out. I think you'll find that this picture will look totally different from my two other films. Completely different, and, I think, much better. There'll be a lot of movement in it, and I think all the jokes will be there. Maybe I'm wrong. Perhaps when I start editing the film I'll wind up cutting those moves down a lot.

Q: Who's the cinematographer?
A: David Walsh.

Q: He hasn't worked with you before, has he?
A: No.

Q: Does he understand what you're wanting to do?
A: Yes. We had about two weeks of experimenting together. This is the first picture where I've cared about anything but the jokes. Well, maybe not. In the very first picture I did I cared about some things other than the jokes too. I cared about the shots, the compositions, and I found that when I got down to editing it, nothing mattered at all except the jokes. Every time there was a pretty shot and the joke wasn't funny, the joke went out. And the ugliest shots in the world, if the joke worked, stayed in the picture, and people laughed and loved it. So in the second film, *Bananas*, I subordinated everything to the joke. I kept the camera there, it was light and you saw it, and that was the end of it. On this picture I wanted to do something where the color was really pretty, and contributed, and the moves contributed, and everything worked—and also not screwed up. It took us about two weeks of working together to figure out what we were going to go for in color, what type of photography, of lighting. We shot tons of material because I didn't like the lighting in a shot, or shadows, subtleties that are possibly not that important to an audience. Because if the picture's funny, that's all that really counts in a comedy. I'm giving myself a double problem, in trying to make it funny and visually arresting. I don't know if it's going to work. I don't know if I'm hurting myself or not. It sure is visually arresting. It's going to look great. I hope I haven't screwed up the jokes.

Q: It seems like the right direction to move in.
A: Yes, it is. It's not the easy way out. The easy way out would be to make it funny, do it simply, and figure the jokes are going to carry. And they do carry. We did take a few weeks of reshooting. We'll finally be about a month over on this film when we finish. We'll have to go back and do some scenes over. Many times doing them over not because the joke isn't funny, because the joke will work, but doing it over

because the color's not right, the composition's not interesting enough, the time of day is wrong.

Q: It's good to know that you care that much.
A: I hope it pays off. If the jokes aren't good enough, the people will say, "Well, it isn't as funny as *Take the Money*." That's all they care about, and I understand that. Why should they care that we are experimenting with lenses, and all kinds of things where we might just be technically pleasing each other? When you see *City Lights* you just go in and you see him do it. The business in the prize-fight ring doesn't have interesting close-ups, and good angles. It's just simple, and that's it. And that is a very safe and good way to work. It gives you speed too. In *Bananas* we were able to go much faster—I mean cut faster, not shoot faster—because we never panned or dollied anyplace. We always cut over. It's all speed, and that gives you pace if you are cutting everywhere. Whereas in a picture that's done pretty, like, hypothetically, *Elvira Madigan*, you glide everywhere, and compositions change. It becomes very interesting. And it's very hard to do that in comedy. I used to notice that on the stage a lot. When you'd see a play directed by Mike Nichols—it would be simple, clean, bright, sets would be light, the lights would be on, you could see all the action and it would move fast. Then you'd see something directed on the stage by Kazan. It would have all kinds of pinspots, schmaltzy effects, lights dimming. It would look wonderful. The temptation when you direct is to want to do that kind of thing. That's where all the fun is. Just to turn the lights up bright, and have everybody talk fast and loud, is not so much fun, but often it's the right way to do comedy. I'm just hoping that I'm not getting too arty in my shots, and ruining jokes that would play fine if you just did them simply. That's the big challenge on this picture.

Q: How accommodating have Messrs. Rollins and Joffe been? Presumably you've got a bigger budget this time.
A: You see, they're my managers. They're producing because the more friends and close people we have on the project, the more control we have.

Q: So it's UA that's putting up the money?
A: Yes.

Q: Have you had any difficulty with them?
A: I've had no difficulty at all. When I made *Take the Money and Run* I decided I wouldn't make films unless I could get total control of the project. Therefore, on that picture, on *Bananas* and on this one—all the films I've done for UA—and two more that I owe them—I have absolute control. They don't have approval of

the script, they don't have casting approval, they have absolutely nothing. Not that it ever gets belligerent, but if it ever came down to it, I'm legally protected. But it never comes down to it. They might say to me, "Listen, do you think he's a good actor for the part?" Once in a great while they'll say something, I always try and give them the courtesy of listening, and talking with them. It never comes to anything. They always ask for permission just to come to the set.

Q: They want to save themselves a lawsuit.
A: No. It isn't like that. It's a real friendly relationship. If I handed them a script and said "I want to make this movie," they are obligated to make it, by the terms of our contract. But if they said to me, "We really hate this. We'll make it if you want, but we really don't want to," I might very well say, "I don't want to hold you to it." I probably wouldn't force them. But there's no problem, as long as I have a limit on my budgets, and as long as I don't exceed my budget.

Q: Are you going over on this one?
A: We're on budget on this one. At the very beginning, I tell them the idea that I want to do. Say, I want to do a picture about me working in a bank, and once they say okay, they can't ever see the picture—theoretically—till it's finished, totally finished, scored, cut. And then they have nothing to say about it after that. And it almost works out that way. They never ever see any rushes or dailies. They never see anything as it's being cut. They never ask to. Well, they did ask me once, and I said no, not out of any hostility to them, but only because it makes me uncomfortable for them to see it before it's finished. It's a very good working relationship. Although I'm legally protected, I'm sure that if we weren't all such good friends, if it wasn't such a friendly arrangement, they could be tough, they could say, we're going to take the picture away and sue us, and I could sue them and probably win after two years. But it doesn't work that way. It's done more on a personal basis.

Q: It's unusual to have that kind of freedom so early in your filmmaking career.
A: Well, UA is a pretty enlightened company. I'm not sure if I could get that anyplace else. I think they were the first people to give final cuts to directors.

Q: But *Play It Again, Sam* wasn't for UA?
A: No, for Paramount.

Q: Was there a different atmosphere prevailing there?
A: Yes, it's a different atmosphere. They were very nice, but everything worked so well. I don't know how they would have been if it didn't. Herb Ross was in total

control every day. He didn't go over schedule, he didn't go over budget, he knew what he was doing. The rushes were funny every day. He cut it together fast, the cuts worked very well, the screenings were good. There was never any moment where there could have been conflict. One hears stories, like *The Godfather*, where there's all kind of trouble, where Paramount intruded into the making of the film. I've heard that from other companies too.

Q: Is acting in your own films part of that idea of total control?
A: People always say that it's hard to act and direct at the same time. But the truth is that it's easy. For some reason they think quantitatively that if you're doing two things it's going to be harder. When I write scripts, I do it privately, home in my room. I wrote this one secluded in a room—it wasn't simple to write—but I wasn't doing more than one thing at once. And it was finished, and that was the end of the writing. Then we come to direct it. We go out on the set, we set up the camera, get the shot all set up, and it may take anywhere from five minutes to two hours to set it up. Then it's all set. Well, then it's nothing to walk around in front of the camera and do it. In fact, it's easier for me to do it myself than it is for me to go over to an actor and say, "Well, I want you to give me this, and I want you to be perturbed, but not too perturbed." I don't have the patience to do that, and I can't communicate myself to them well. But for me to run around in front of it and do it is the easiest thing in the world. Because I wrote it, I know what I had in mind when I wrote it. It's just simpler.

Q: Are there circumstances where you would direct a film you didn't appear in?
A: Yes.

Q: Or would you write a film without a part for yourself?
A: I would not just write a film. For instance, they asked me to do the screenplay of *Play It Again, Sam*. When *Play It Again, Sam* opened on Broadway the film rights were sold beforehand, before it even opened. It was sold to David Brown at Twentieth. It opened on Broadway, and they never asked me to do it. They didn't want to do it with me then, which I can kind of understand, because I wasn't really much of a star, and they had a big investment in it, and if they could get Dustin Hoffman, or somebody with more pulling value they would have been better off. I understood that. And they asked me if I would write the screenplay, for an awful lot of money. And I wouldn't under any circumstances write a screenplay unless I was directing it or acting in it. Just writing for the screen I think is a real dumb job. It's not a creative job at all. What's creative is directing and acting on the screen. Whereas on Broadway all the creativity is with the writer. On Broadway the script is 90 percent of it. So it's fun to write a play, but a screenplay is not

writing, it's not challenging. The movie is made by the director, the actors, and by the editor. So I would have no interest in just screenwriting. But if I had an idea for a terrific movie and it didn't have a part for me in it, I wouldn't hesitate to write it and direct it, and not appear in it. Actually, I always feel, like I felt about my first play, that once I write the thing, and it opens, they can treat me like a dead author. I sold *Don't Drink the Water* to films, and I couldn't care less if they made it into a musical, or made it into a terrible movie, which they did. I never went to see it. The same thing with *Play It Again, Sam*. When I sold it, I couldn't care less who they got to play it. As it happens, they got me. So I devoted a little interest to it. But as long as they pay it doesn't bother me for a second. I only wrote it as a play. I don't care if my plays are never made into movies. It wouldn't bother me.

Q: Had you ever seen the film *Che!*?
A: Yes, I saw *Che!*, but not in relation to *Bananas*. I saw *Che!* when I was doing *Play It Again, Sam* on Broadway, between a matinee and an evening performance. It was a terrible, terrible movie. Like *Bananas*, it was made in Puerto Rico. They had a lot of trouble with *Che!* down there. All those guys were very cognizant of that film. They knew all about the making of it. So they were very conscious of *Che!* all the time I was there. I was not aware of it.

Q: Do you stay close to your scripts while you're filming?
A: I don't stay close at all. I only care that the idea of a scene gets across. It doesn't matter at all to me if nobody does any of my dialogue. That's why I have no real respect for screenwriting. If a director comes on a set in the morning and says "We're going to film a scene at a funeral where the corpse gets up and runs away," I don't need dialogue for that. I can go in and tell the actors what I want, and have them make up their own things. They do it, and it's fine. It sounds real. All you need is one line for the day. You should know each morning where to show up and what your props are, and the rest of it can be improvised. So I don't really care that much about scripts. I follow them to a degree, because they are there, and we're geared to it. But any time an actor doesn't feel like following it or something, well, that's okay. It doesn't bother me. I have things I'm planning on doing in this movie with my ex-wife Louise which will be totally ad-lib. Pages of script exist on it, and if we feel like saying it, fine. In *Bananas* there were times we followed the script. The scene where she came to my house to recruit me for her organization—that was a written scene. We'd memorized the dialogue, and we thought "Why not?" Yet when she was breaking up with me in the park, we disregarded dialogue completely, we just ranted on and on. This time I'm going to shoot with two cameras when we improvise. That will make it a lot easier. In the

past I've improvised endlessly with one camera. Whatever I didn't like I would just jump out of the film. I didn't care about jump cuts, or anything like that. If the line was funny I wanted it in the movie, regardless of whether anything matched. That's fine for that kind of film. But this picture will be a lot smoother, and the improvisations will look a lot better, if they come off at all. We're taking care about matching angles this time.

Q: Did you ever improvise and then shoot something over again? To cover yourself?

A: No, we would always improvise, change the camera angle and then improvise again with different material, change it again. In *Bananas* I really hang on Louise for a long shot, because she was saying something that was good. If I had two cameras running, I would have one on myself so I could cut to me for reactions. But when the improvisation works you don't care that there's only one camera. Do you remember the scene in *Adam's Rib* where Judy Holliday is telling that story, I think it's to Katharine Hepburn, about how she shot the guy? They just put the camera down, and the two of them are across a table in the most unflattering position, just two profiles, and it goes on and on and on and on. And it doesn't matter. A really good director could have photographed that scene a lot more interestingly, but who knows that he wouldn't have hurt it? This way you hear what they're saying, you see them, everybody's clear. In comedy you are constantly aware of your whole body being seen. The Keaton, Chaplin, Marx Brothers, and Fields films were shot in the Academy frame. And that's a very big plus for comedy which we don't have today. The aspect ratio is different now, but it's still important to see the whole comedian. Now the screen is wider you can't compose to see the whole comedian as gracefully. It's very annoying. In 70mm it would be terribly hard. In *Mad Mad World* it's disastrous. You see exact jokes repeated from other movies where they worked—where the wheel rolls into the tunnel and then rolls back out, well, they're just not funny. It's because the screen size is very unwieldy. I would like to shoot a film in Academy aperture, but the trouble is that you can't get it screened in movie theaters that way. There was a tendency in old pictures to be closer and not show so much. The really interesting compositions are much tighter than you'd think. When you get wider, it's less interesting. You can put a lot of close-ups together and it would cut up nicely. But if you cut wide shots together, it looks wrong, and heavy. And yet where you see the comedian work best is in the wide shot. In *Day at the Races* where Chico sells Groucho those books outside the track, all you do is look at that thing. They could be playing it on a vaudeville stage. If I were shooting that for this picture, I would take three days to shoot it, make all kinds of shots and angles and moves and everything. And who knows if mine would work. I know that theirs works.

Q: What do you feel about physical comedy, and your use of your own body? Do you want to be a graceful physical comedian? In the sense that Chaplin and Keaton obviously were?

A: Yes, I'd like to be, but I don't know if I can be. Because of the nature of Chaplin's background and Keaton's background, they came to the screen with a tremendous training in acrobatics. There's nothing in my background that's like that. My strength, if any, is lines. I could probably deliver lines better than Chaplin can, because I don't think he talks very well. I would like to develop into a better physical comedian. I think that I have the instincts, but not the grace to do it. I know how to do it, and what's overdoing it. I might not ever be able to do it, but if I can, it will take me a few more pictures and hard work to learn those skills. In a sense, *Bananas* and *Take the Money* were writers' pictures. You didn't need a comedian to really make those pictures funny. When you do a joke like "For several hours he's turned into a rabbi," you can just hire an extra and have him sit there, and that joke works, because the writer has made it. You don't need a director for a gag like that. You just need to set the camera up. Both those films had material like that—they were essentially writer's pictures. *Play It Again, Sam* is much more of an actor's picture. That picture is only funny because the acting makes it funny. And this picture is a combination—still plenty of writer's jokes, but also some directorial gags, and some performing things. I've given myself some things to do here that are not funny on paper. Things that I've hopefully made funny in the performance. What I'd like to do in the future is to write pictures where the demands on me as a performer are enormous, where I don't protect myself with a lot of written gags, that will work no matter who does them. I want to write scenes that will only be funny because I make them funny. Chaplin did that, of course. In *Born Yesterday* the part of Judy Holliday is hilarious because she makes it hilarious. Another actress couldn't have done it.

Q: How do you feel about the almost slapstick stuff at the beginning of *Bananas* with the exercisers?

A: I wish I could do that over. I think my idea was right. My instinct was good. Those were my first two films. I didn't have the experience to know, from a technical point of view, what I wanted to do. For one thing, I should have had that machine built three months in advance. I should have spent a lot of money on it. I didn't. I figured, you know, it would work out. It was a big mistake, and I'd never make that mistake again. Another thing is, I would carefully work out my bits on that so I know I would have funny stuff. If I was going to have thirty seconds of it in the film I should shoot it for a week. But there I just got on the machine and winged it. From that point of view I feel bad about it. It was amusing enough to get by, but it's not what it should be. The idea was much better than I, as the director, knew how to exploit it. My first two pictures are full of areas ruined by my inexperience. By inexperience I don't mean lenses or things like that. I mean the inexperience of not knowing how to schedule a thing properly, how to shoot it right, to know when to say, "Don't break the set up. I want to look at it tomorrow," to know when to reshoot something a couple of times. These are the kind of things I'm doing on this new picture. I'll shoot something, and then have them keep the set up at great expense, rental expenses for the equipment, for the stage and all that. Then I'll look at it, and think about it and decide if I only had a few things here it would make it round out, and then go back, and schedule another day's shooting on it. I just didn't know enough to do that, on my first two films. When I started filming, all they said to me was, "You'd better not go over budget, so just keep moving." That's all I knew, so I just kept moving as fast as I could. I would keep saying, "Good enough. Let's go on to the next thing." Now I finally see the value of going very slowly. The next film I do, whatever it is, I'll put my art director on months before I begin, and meticulously go over every piece of wardrobe, every color of every book on every set. I started to do that here, and I didn't realize what an undertaking it was. I've done a lot of that in this situation. I've picked specific costumes for people, and specific colors and specific wallpaper. When I heard that Antonioni prepares a picture for six months I couldn't figure out what the hell is he doing for six months. I used to think if the shot was interesting, if you move the camera right, or set it up right, that that was more important, and that what you are shooting is of secondary importance. I couldn't figure out what it was that would capture my interest in the work of the really good directors. Finally I realized the importance of the content of the frame. The great directors spend ages on the set, on the lighting, on the color co-ordination, on the costumes. And then they would work on the shot. That's become very important to me. As I've been learning more and more about films, I've been going slower and slower and falling further and further behind. To think I could be a month behind on a picture, as I am now, is incredible. If I was a day behind on *Take the Money*, they would say to me, "You're a whole day behind, what are you going to do about it?" I'd say, "Well, I'm going to cut some scenes out of the picture and not shoot them at all." And I'd get my day back. And that's what I did. I actually cut material out of the picture. I'd just give up good scenes, because I couldn't bear the thought of being behind. I thought I'd get into trouble. They'd say to me, "You know it's costing us $20,000 a day to shoot." I'd figure out if I'm three days behind it's going to cost $60,000. Now it's different. I came to the set here yesterday morning, and we had a dozen extras for the day all ready to go. I walked on to a set that we had been working on for two days, an elaborate set which it took the carpenters hours to build. And I didn't like it. I wouldn't shoot on it. I had them chop it up and build it over from scratch. Up to a point you can do that. After a while you become crazy. I'm spending $2 million on this picture. I could do it a lot better for $4 million. For $6 million I could do it better still. But I didn't realize just how much latitude I had. Now I won't shoot a set unless it really looks good. I think you'll be surprised when you see this picture. It's not going to look in the style that I've worked before. Not a lot of handheld shots, not a lot of dialogue. There are scenes I've worked out with a tape recorder. For *Bananas* and *Take the Money* there were some scenes we did at Jack Grossberg's house, working them out on a tape recorder. All the stuff at the psychiatrist's office in *Take the Money* was shot in the production manager's living room. We didn't even have a set.

Q: What about the interviews with the parents? Were they shot as casually?
A: You know what we did for that? We rented an empty apartment in San Francisco. We shot the parents against one wall, the schoolteacher against another, and someone else against another wall.

Q: Perhaps we could ask you why you are being so tight on security matters regarding the script of this film? Is it because you've been hurt in the past?
A: No. I see no value in letting information out on the film. It can't possibly help the film. In fact, it could hurt the film. The film doesn't come out until August. You mention gags and ideas to people in advance, and you find a similar gag turns up on a TV show. Not intentionally. A guy hears it, and a couple of months later it will occur to him, and he might not remember where he heard it. He might use it without consciously stealing it. Finally, people keep on asking, "How are you going to make this book into a movie?" One of the publicity angles is to make people come and see how we change this unusual book into a movie.

Q: You've told us some things about the style of the picture. Is there anything you'd care to tell us about the content?
A: Let me tell you this much. It's a very personal approach to sex. I don't think anybody else would have made this same film. It's very far out. I hate to use that term because it's so innocuous, but the film *will* be far out—a unique and bizarre view of sex. Very.

Q: Don't you see all your films as personal?
A: I don't think anyone else would have made *Take the Money* or *Bananas*. I think that for all their flaws and immaturities, you can say that they weren't factory-made films. They were not the usual Hollywood product. I think those films will always be playing around, even fifty years from now, because they represent a certain kind of filmmaking. They're not great, but they're not machine-made either.

One of the things that helped *Take the Money* get off the ground was that it was not like everybody else's film. I do have a certain kind of style, it's my own. From a technical point of view it's not developed yet. There's a lot of areas where I still have far to go. One very important thing, as we were saying before, is developing myself as a physical comedian. But I think one of my pictures is recognizable as mine, even now. It's a one man thing—it's not that one guy wrote the script, and another guy edited it. For better or worse, you can recognize it as my picture. You can see all my mistakes, as much as you'd see any of the good things. They're all mine. Like with John Cassavetes, whether you like his films or not, the mistakes and the good things are all his.

Q: Another thing that applies to Cassavetes's films and to yours is that there's a certain friendliness and informality about them. They don't have the usual Hollywood gloss.
A: I think so. There's a roughness about them. I think this one will be a lot less informal. But I'm probably making a lot more mistakes on this film than I realize right now. It's only when you get into editing that you discover what your mistakes are. There should be enough mistakes in this one to stamp it as a Woody Allen picture.

Q: Are you conscious of an independent screen identity that goes from film to film, that your character is essentially the same in each; or do you feel like you're playing different parts? You mentioned Chaplin and Keaton, and you have a sense of a constant identity through all their pictures.
A: I think I'm the same, more or less. I've never tried to do a picture that was very different. Now I'm only thinking of the two films I've directed. In *Bananas* and *Take the Money* I think I play essentially the same character, but with a different occupation. In *Play It Again* I'm still the same character, in a different occupation, developed a little differently. And in this picture my part is also the same. More or less. I've never done anything like, say, Dustin Hoffman does, where I actually become a different character. I don't know if I could do that. It might be fun to try it sometime. A couple of the scenes in this one I do something different, but it's because you know it's really me doing it that makes it funny. If I played a Frenchman in a film, and I played it impeccably, it would still be the fact that it's me doing it that makes it funny. If you think of Marlon Brando in *Teahouse of the August Moon,* he got the guy's accent and got everything right, but not funny, he did a perfect characterization of an Okinawan; if you had had someone not as gifted playing that, but with a funnybone, maybe like David Wayne who did it on Broadway, it could be played for laughs. But Brando makes it so real, so perfect,

that the guy's not funny anymore. But if you put Milton Berle in that role, and of course you're aware that it's Berle doing it, as an Oriental, then it's got an extra quality of funniness to it. I think that it's important to comedy.

Q: Do you feel that you are playing yourself in your films, or is it a character you've created?
A: I think I'm playing myself. I've never consciously tried to create a character. I just get out there and do what I think is funny, and gradually something emerges. It's interesting how patterns emerge. People are always asking me about my masked parents. In this film the only shot of my parents is of my father, and he is masked. It's an interesting thing. I haven't done this on purpose. In *Take the Money and Run* they wore disguises to mask themselves. In *Bananas* they had surgical masks on. And coincidentally, in this picture, my father plays a scene with a face covering. It's nothing I consciously try and do. It never occurred to me. When I had the parents in a surgical mask it never for a second occurred to me that they were being masked. I just thought it was funny, at an operating table. So in the same way you don't really try and create a character. When I did my nightclub act, I just did whatever jokes I thought were funny, and then I'd look up six months later to read what people said about me in the newspapers, and they say things like "He's a little man at war with machines." I never thought to myself, I'll sit down and write some little man at war with machines jokes. Mort Sahl never said "I think I'll be a political satirist." He just said whatever he thought was funny, and people observed, "Gee, he's always talking about politics."

Q: Do you think that most of your future activities will be in filmmaking?
A: Probably most, but not by much. I'd hate to get too dependent on it, and I'd hate not to write for the theater. I've got some ideas for plays I want to do. But for some reason, and it's unfortunate, the theater is no longer vital. And if it is vital, it's not vital compared to film. The impact of a film can be so enormous. You communicate with such enormous impact, qualitatively and quantitatively; if the finest play opened on Broadway tomorrow you'd hear about it, and if you were in New York you'd want to see it, if you could get tickets. But if a movie opened that's important, like *Clockwork Orange* you know, bang, the impact is international and spectacular. So it's a very seductive medium to work in, because you really feel the reward when you score. If you have a hit play on Broadway, it's nice, but you know, you don't feel enough people are seeing it, there's no real hullaballoo about it.

Woody Allen Says Comedy Is No Laughing Matter

Kathleen Carroll / 1974

Published in the *New York Daily News*, January 6, 1974. Reprinted by permission.

He was wearing a battered Army surplus jacket and the receptionist couldn't help but stare. She is a movie company receptionist and is expected to know a star when she sees one, but this one she couldn't figure. She picked up the phone and called one of the executives. "There's a bum out here who says he wants to see you," she said. The bum? Woody Allen.

Woody has been having problems with receptionists for years. The first time I met him, the *News* receptionist mistook him for a copy boy and almost sent him out for her lunch.

The trouble is that Woody dresses like Woody Allen, a nice kid from Flatbush.

This particular evening (he was by now safely inside United Artists' executive offices, going over the ad copy for his new move *Sleeper*) he was dressed to go to the theater—in a shrimp-colored crew-neck sweater that exposed part of his undershirt, a brown cardigan, brown corduroy pants, and saddle shoes. "Nobody dresses for the theater anymore," said Woody. "I'll probably be the best-dressed person there."

Woody may still look like an errand boy, but he doesn't act like one. He used to be so timid that he would practically shrink into the wall if anyone so much as spoke to him. But success has brought him confidence.

Woody began the conversation by recalling our first meeting. "It's hard to believe that it was ten years ago," he said. I made the usual remark about water under the bridge. "A lot of things have gone under water," said Woody.

Not Woody's career. His movies—*What's Up, Tiger Lily?*, a Japanese-made film that he dubbed, *Take the Money and Run*, *Bananas*, *Play It Again, Sam*, *Everything You Always Wanted to Know about Sex*, and now *Sleeper*, which received an ovation in an East Side theater a week ago—have placed him in the ranks of Hollywood's greatest comic artists, the Marx Brothers, Buster Keaton, Harold Lloyd, and even Charlie Chaplin. What is sad is that he may be the last of the screen's great comics.

Part of the reason for the decline of film comedy is that comedy is such a delicate thing. "A fraction of an inch left or right can kill a joke," Woody said. A film comic must rely entirely on his instincts. He chooses what looks right to him. Whether it looks right to an audience is anybody's guess. As Woody observed, comedy audiences are especially unpredictable. They may see a movie one night and think it's hilarious and see the same movie a few nights later and hardly react at all.

Woody cited as an example *Everything You Always Wanted to Know about Sex*, an episodic film. "People would come up to me and say, 'I loved the fifth episode, but the third and first were the worst.' Some people said they adored it. Other people said it was in bad taste. There is no way you can think of pleasing people. Comedy is so ephemeral. It is so relational and so dependent on how the audience feels."

Sleeper was pure torture to do, Woody said. "I found myself working over and over on one particular scene, the kind of scene where I'm seen dangling from a ladder and, maybe out of incredible planning, I might get a minute of film."

With its futuristic setting (the year is 2173), *Sleeper* is like a cartoon to Woody, "a great big cartoon." He wanted the sets to be "cute and funny," but this wasn't easy to achieve. The hardest job of all was designing the robotlike butlers (Woody disguises himself as one during the film).

The robots wear full dress. "You can imagine—knowing me—how I felt about wearing tails. I'd like to do a film like I'm dressed now, a film based in New York. Anything so I don't have to dress. I have very low aesthetic ideals. Clothes are the things that motivate me. That's why I loved doing *Play It Again, Sam* on Broadway. I didn't have to dress at all. I could leave home dressed in my normal clothes and walk right out on stage just as I was. All I had to worry about was being neat. I was funnier because of it. When you're in a space suit in one hundred degree temperatures (as Woody was for *Sleeper*) you really suffer. You can't wait to get out of it, and so you only do one take. Consequently, you compromise your work."

What surprises most people is that Woody is so serious when he talks about his work. There is no suggestion of the zany neurotic he plays on the screen. He is very much the straight man.

"I'm amusing with close friends," Woody said, "but I'm generally quiet and serious. I'm the opposite of a cut-up. I do know comedians that are on all the time. They wake up in the morning and they're ready to go on stage."

To Woody's regret, "Television has replaced film as the mass medium. Moviemaking has become a high-pressure business with a low survival rate. I'm for turning out a comedy every year. Some of the other comedians could do it, too. I wish we could just keep turning them out. But you just can't work that way when you feel you are on the line every time."

Woody is troubled by the high admission prices, that five dollars, for example, being charged for *The Grand Bouffe*.

"I think you should be able to see a movie for a buck. That's what films should be. There should be a great many of them, and there should be room for experimentation."

More than anything, Woody regrets what is happening to the Broadway theater. He is sadly aware that Broadway has lost the glamour that it had when he was growing up. For that reason, he felt impelled to write three one-act plays for producer David Merrick. They are to be called *Sex and Death*. Sex and death, Woody said, are his "two favorite obsessions."

Woody is attracted to the idea of performing on Broadway again. "I would like to appear in the theater again because that is the most fun. You leave your house at seven o'clock. You go on stage and you get your laughs. The audiences are very nice. They don't drink like they do in nightclubs. The curtain comes down about 10:30, and you're free to go. It's very civilized compared to being in films. Films are strenuous, back-breaking work. You go from morning to night with bad hours, bad food. There is that wonderful story about Groucho Marx when he was doing *A Night in Casablanca*. He and Harpo were hanging from the back of an airplane. And he said to Harpo, 'Have you had enough?' And Harpo said, 'Yup.'"

Right now Woody will do anything as long as it means staying in New York and not spending time in Los Angeles. "I'm a big New York lover despite all its problems. The city has so much going for it. I enjoy the country only if I'm with nice people. Here you don't have to be with nice people to enjoy it. You can be with the muggers."

It was getting late. There was a knock at the door. Woody looked slightly alarmed, as if he expected a mugger. It was a cleaning woman.

Woody put on his Army jacket and the rest of his "disguise," a soiled rain hat, which he pulls down so it all but covers his ears.

He took a few steps to demonstrate how well the hat fooled people. The press agent accompanying Woody said: "I saw you one night at one of the Knicks' games (Woody is an avid Knicks fan) and I knew when I saw that hat that it was you." Woody looked discouraged.

I left him in the lobby of the building. Would he be safe? "I'm going to go and stand next to those uniformed guards," Woody said.

A Conversation with the Real Woody Allen

Ken Kelley / 1976

Published in *Rolling Stone*, July 1976, 34–40, 85–89. Reprinted by permission.

Though I had prepped myself carefully, I was altogether unready for what I found when I finally met the real Woody Allen, after weeks of delicate negotiations which finally culminated in his agreeing to be interviewed. First there was the matter of his size—he stood 6'6", weighed 245. Kind of broad at the shoulders and narrow at the hips. I was ushered into his presence by a bevy of midgets, who constantly surround him and on whom he depends for everything. Before I could see him, I had to put on a pair of weird emerald green glasses.

Then there was the matter of his voice—a pronounced South Topeka twang. And, most disturbing, his penchant for pulling practical jokes. Through his big corn-fed teeth he grinned a "Howdy, podna," and his huge hammy hunk of hand gripped mine, viselike, whereupon an electric buzzer on his index finger sent me into jangled paroxysms. "Har, har, har," he said, just as the red boutonniere on his lapel sprayed my startled physiognomy with lemonade. Then one of the ubiquitous midgets set my socks on fire, while another crept up behind me and knelt. With split-second timing Woody Allen pushed me over the midget, landing me in a ruffled heap on the floor. He then proffered the aforementioned hand to help me up and, sucker that I was, the buzzer jolted me once again. "Shucks, this is just our way of sayin' welcome, boy," he drawled, slapping me so heartily on the back that my phlegm sank to my ankles.

At this point I was sufficiently discombobulated and miffed to chuck the whole thing—I wasn't getting paid enough to put up with the antics of this big bumpkin. Then I noticed that one of the midgets—one who stood head and shoulders above the others, actually—had an appreciably different air about him from the rest of the pack. A slight, boyish-looking human, perhaps 5'6", with thick, black-rimmed glasses, eyes that were limpid pools of paranoia, a self-deprecating half frown on his face. He was sitting off in a corner, staring idly into space, rather obviously contemplating the answers to life, then carefully jotting down the questions in a loose-leaf binder.

After conversing with him for several minutes while the madcap frivolity swirled around us, I decided I really liked him. He was the kind of really decent, kind, thoughtful, thrifty, brave, clean, and reverent guy you'd be proud to have your sister marry. He saw a copy of Woody Allen's latest book under my arm, *Without Feathers*, a compilation of Allen's humorous essays culled from the *New Yorker* and other magazines, which was ten weeks on the best-seller list, and said with a poignant sincerity, "I hope you didn't have to pay for that."

When I told him I had lifted it from Brentano's he smiled wistfully. This man's name, it turned out, was Allan Stewart Konigsberg. He was forty years old, he said, and with a subdued modesty he told me he was the "éminence grise" (which translated loosely from the French as "grizzled antler") behind Woody Allen.

I had an important decision to make. After fully five minutes, I had made it.

Though still wracked with doubt, I decided that I would interview this chap instead of the real Woody Allen, whose churlish ways were so boring. After six hours I knew I had made the right choice, though when Konigsberg claimed to be the reincarnation of Kierkegaard, Nietzsche, and Freud, I turned the tape recorder off. During the entire session he smiled three times—an event tantamount to the arrival of Halley's comet, I later learned—and cracked not a single joke.

What a relief. "Sic semper" cerebrum.

Q: This may sound like a funny question, but do you consider yourself a comedian?
A: Yes, definitely. I had great trepidation about calling myself that years ago when I first switched from writing to comedy. But now unequivocally I call myself a comedian.

Q: As a comedian, then, the opportunity to make movies is a rare one—to have complete control. Have you broken any new ground?
A: I've never had any ulterior motive in terms of style or content or breaking new ground or anything like that. The only interest to me was making people laugh.

Q: Which movie have you had the most fun making?
A: None of them have been any fun at all. They've all been terrific anxiety and hard work. And for my own goals, I would consider all the movies that I've done failures. It's very hard to get a conception and transfer it in that idealized form right to the end. It takes an enormous amount of concentration and luck. And it's always been beyond my capability up to this point. I always finish and say, "Ugh— I only got 60 percent of that idea that worked and what a shame." Then you put it out and you hope the critics will like the picture. You hope they like it because you're involved in an economically burdened art—for me. I write for the *New Yorker* magazine strictly as a hobby now—I don't need the money. And when my

books come out I couldn't care less about it—it's strictly for my own enjoyment. But a film may well cost $2 or $3 million, so I do care that they are well received. But I don't think what the critics say about them necessarily bears any actual relation to any objective reality about them in any sense whatsoever. I think it's totally subjective. And somewhere in the equation, that fact gets lost, because they appear in print, and that has objective charisma.

Q: Did you see Russell Baker's criticism of *Love and Death*—that Woody Allen once again plays the poor schmuck, but the guy who nevertheless gets the girl at the end?
A: Right. There's just no way to please people. Now some people say to me, "You should never get the girl," where others say, "You should get the girl, we root for you to get the girl." If I was actually to look at all the things written about me from very respectable people who have not been hostile but who have tried to be constructive—it's all so utterly disparate that I just wouldn't know what to do.

Q: So you only try to please yourself.
A: First myself. I want to please an audience—to make an audience laugh—that's the idea. If I write a joke and after a couple of time nobody laughs, I take it out of the movie—I don't want to indulge myself that much. If I have the slightest doubt, I leave it out. I've left out many, many very good jokes. But I never put anything in a movie that the audience would like that I don't like—I would never do that. Sometimes there will be a bad thing in my films because I've either guessed wrong or judged wrong. Or for some reason or other, every conceivable alternative was bad and this is the best one I have. You really have to make an effort not to judge critics, because one's natural bodily impulses are to react positively to praise and negatively to criticism. But in the true scheme of things it means nothing, nothing at all, except possibly in economic terms. I've been lucky because for the most part I've done very well—economically that is, not in my own personal terms. But if I open a film and the basic critics that send people to movies—the *New York Times*, *Time*—all didn't like my movie, I would feel the reverberations economically and that makes it tougher to put the next movie out. That's what bothers you. Comedy is like playing the drums. Every guy in the world comes up to the bandstand during the breaks on Monday nights when I'm playing clarinet with a band at Michael's Pub in New York, and each guy thinks he can play the drums better. And, everybody thinks he's the expert on comedy. It's totally subjective.

Q: "But subjectivity is objective."
A: That's what throws you all the time.

Q: If you don't enjoy making movies, why do you make them?
A: I know this sounds facetious but I do movies because I have the opportunity, and I'm living in a world where everybody wants to do movies. And I'm in, through no fault of my own, through a series of bizarre quirks, a position where I write, direct, and star in my own films. I have total control over them, final cut. No one approves the script. I have everything going for me. And it all happened so accidentally—had you told me fifteen years ago that I was going to be the lead in a movie I would have thought you were crazy. It's the funniest thing in the world to me. So I make movies because I feel if I don't make them, someday I'll look back and think to myself, "They were dumping this stuff in my lap and I didn't take advantage of it." So I do it.

Q: How did *Love and Death* do commercially?
A: It was probably the greatest commercial success I've had, which is not saying very much because I'm not an enormously commercial filmmaker. I have to get terrific reviews to be a decent hit, which happened with *Love and Death* and *Sleeper*. I rarely see any money on my percentage arrangement with United Artists—my films just don't make enough. I'd need a *Graduate* or something to really get it. I could make a lot more money if I worked as a comedian in clubs—I get very little, either to make them or for salary. I make less to write a script, direct a movie, and star in it than what a star gets just for starring—about two-thirds less. So I'm not out to take the money and run, I'm in it for the chance to make pictures. But I'm sure that *Young Frankenstein* made an enormous amount more than *Bananas*, *Sleeper*, and *Love and Death* all put together. And that *Blazing Saddles* made more than all my movies put together.

Q: Did you enjoy those movies?
A: I saw *Frankenstein* on a plane. It was very amusing. I'm a very good audience for comedy and a good audience for Mel Brooks. He's an old acquaintance of mine. I enjoy him, I'm an easy laugher at his things.

Q: I guess his 2000-Year-Old Man is the comedic masterpiece.
A: I had written with Mel at the Sid Caesar show. I had been writing for Sid and someone said that Mel was going to be writing for Sid now and "he's just going to eat you alive, he's so difficult to get along with and he's so high-pressured." And I girded myself for a really unpleasant experience. And then he came on the show—he had written for Sid before and he was just as nice, amusing, intelligent as could be—he was *so* nice to me. So I've had very good experiences with him. And, of course, he's obviously funny—that combined with my liking him so much, I laugh at his movies.

Q: Was Sid Caesar your favorite comedian?
A: Sid was my favorite—no fun to work with at all but a brilliant comedian. Jackie Gleason I liked, and the Marx Brothers—my favorite overall was Groucho.

Q: Do you watch a lot of other people's movies?
A: In spurts. I go for a while and then I don't see any for a while.

Q: What other director do you really admire?
A: Really the only ones I have any interest in at all are Bergman, Antonioni, Renoir, Buñuel—basically serious stuff. I don't have an enormous interest in comedies.

Q: Do you learn a lot technically by watching their stuff—camera shots, lighting, that kind of thing?
A: No more. A move from zero to one is the best learning experience. Then your rate of progress slows down enormously. So mine is really slowed down. I learned a lot going from a non-filmmaker to a filmmaker with the first film or two. I've gotten more proficient at not making as many mistakes.

Q: You jumped from a futuristic treatment in *Sleeper* back to nineteenth-century Russia in *Love and Death*. What's next—Jane Austen?
A: I'm almost through shooting it, but I don't want to talk too much about it, because I always keep these things secret. It's a much more realistic, contemporary story. It's a comedy and for laughs. But it takes place in New York, now. It's not a costume or surrealistic kind of story— it's more romantic and more understandable.

Q: You worked for Caesar in the early fifties?
A: Right.

Q: Do you have a strong recollection of the fifties?
A: I have a very strong recollection of the forties—those were my formative years. I remember the fifties without any great feeling

Q: Yet you're in a movie right now that deals with a very important aspect of the fifties—blacklisting in Hollywood. In fact, *The Front* is the first picture you've been in since you started directing where you didn't write the script and didn't direct. Why did you decide to do it?
A: You know, the blacklisting was really after World War II, all the anticommunist propaganda was at a high point then. I remember hearing about blacklisting when I was in public school—not really understanding the implications of it at all. But

in retrospect, what I know now historically, it was a horrible time. The script expresses me politically even though I didn't write it. It was one of the best pieces of material offered to me. People that offer me material to do generally offer me comedies and I'm not interested in them because I write my own—I don't need them. Also, what they offer me is terrible. Usually they are much further out than anything I would write—people have a conception of me like they have of Salvador Dalí—that I'm *so* far out, which I'm not. And the other kinds of comedies I get from people are dirty, really filthy scripts and they are *always* stupid. It's very rare that anybody offers me anything decent at all. This was a very substantial political script, so it was fun to try and act in something seriously and, of course, something with a political position that expresses me. I would not do a film that didn't express me politically.

Q: You mean it presents your point of view generally?
A: Yeah. You know, this is no revolutionary position to take. I hated McCarthy, I hated blacklisting, the whole concept of it. So to that extent it expresses me politically. Also, the script is very interesting because both the director, Marty Ritt, and the writer, Walter Bernstein, were blacklisted then—it has a real ring of truth to it. If this picture comes off, I think it will be a picture about a very substantial political subject.

Q: It's hard to believe that such a handful of idiots could have exerted enough pressure to destroy people's lives and strangle a whole industry, indeed, a whole country. How did we move to the point where Jane Fonda can go to North Vietnam in the midst of the war and still get an Oscar, or that Jack Nicholson can talk about taking LSD in *Time*, whereas when Robert Mitchum was busted for pot in 1948 he declared publicly that his career was over?
A: Well, liberals, in my opinion, are always more correct. And the trend of progress is always the liberalization of things. What happens is the more phlegmatic people and totalitarian people eventually come around to points of view that are apparent to more sophisticated people at an earlier date. People have now come around to what the enlightened people were saying at that time. But blacklisting is a very vague notion to most people, something they are only vaguely aware of. It was one of these special phenomena that occurred in show business and in colleges—certainly not the brunt of the country was involved. It was an issue of bitter concern to a small amount of people, really. And as it filtered to a wider audience, it dissipated. It will be curious to see how people respond to this movie.

Q: It certainly portrays very graphically how people's lives were ruined.

A: I hope so. I know the John Henry Faulk thing on television got a very low rating. That was with George C. Scott, too. So . . .

Q: People who come to see Woody Allen jokes or Zero Mostel gags [Mostel plays second lead] will be surprised.
A: I think we have to dispel that myth up front because I think it will be disappointing to those people who pay their three dollars to hear jokes.

Q: What's it like for you starring but not directing?
A: I don't love that. I happen to like Marty Ritt very much—I know I'm in good hands. But I want to say, "Let's put the camera here, let's use this take," and he gets to say that. I miss it and would not want to do this much anymore. Maybe once in a great while, but it's not my idea of a great time.

Q: What kind of things were important to your political development?
A: Well, first of all, I'm not a very political person. I hate politics and don't believe in political solutions as long-term things. I don't think they work. The US has never been able to admit a realistic perspective on itself. It's never been able to transmit to students and citizens a sense of wrongness about some things, horribleness about some things, and sometimes terrificness about certain things. And there's an enormous hypocritical sense of self-righteousness about it that I don't like. And of course the US government is prey to all kinds of repression and pressures and I've always hated that—but I've hated politicians as long as I've known them. I don't approve of them. I don't like them. I have a very negative view of politics in general.

Q: And all politicians?
A: I have supported certain campaigns. I supported Lyndon Johnson, against Barry Goldwater quite actively. I played the Eiffel Tower—I was one of the people in Americans Abroad for Johnson because I was overseas at that time, and I did a show in Paris to raise money for Johnson. I am one of the few comics that can say he's worked the Eiffel Tower. And I supported McGovern, Eugene McCarthy, and John Lindsay. I thought they were outstanding in certain ways. Even then, they're basically politicians, but they were such enormous cuts above who they were running against.

Q: Okay, you don't believe in political solutions—to play Philosopher King for a moment, how would you effect change and what kind of change would it be?
A: I don't think there can be significant changes until there's an enormous restructuring of thinking in terms of philosophy, religion, and issues that are

deeper and more central—psychoanalysis rather than politics. Political functioning is always symptomatic treating—you have to treat the disease right alongside the symptoms. And politicians never do that. So it's always sort of a patchwork thing—it gets down to power groups. There's no coming to terms with life in the universe individually, so consequently political solutions express themselves in a very superficial way. Like the person who suffers from a depression, he thinks that by moving from New York to San Francisco that his life is going to change, when actually the problems go with him. The problems go with you from socialism to communism to democratic government. As Mort Sahl used to say, the issue is always fascism anyway. It's always fascism under different titles against a basically humanitarian type of approach under different labels. It has nothing to do with countries or parties. What we need is an impulse toward humanitarianism that has got to arise in each person noncoercively. People have to be made to realize the obvious worth of honesty and integrity. And until that happens nothing is really going to happen.

Q: But history is nothing but a chronology of oppressors oppressing the oppressed.
A: That's economic rather than political. I see it this way—if the humanitarian impulse exists, then it's irrelevant what economic system best expresses the needs of the community. It couldn't matter less to me, from a functioning point of view, whether I was living in a capitalistic society or a communistic society if the basic thrust of the people, their impulses are humanitarian—whatever works best for your community to keep it going in a livable economy where it minimizes the poverty or eliminates it. What usually happens, though, is that "communism" and "democracy" easily become expressions not of democracy or communism but of totalitarian mentality.

Q: What did Richard Nixon do for America?
A: He was a disgraceful criminal and I have only the worst feelings about him. He expressed in a certain way many of the feelings that the public had themselves. I think that when he won that election with that enormous majority in 1972 that the public somewhere down deep knew that they were voting for a guy that represented the worst impulses of the United States and their own worst impulses. That goes back to the cliché that the people get the government they deserve. They did. That was a very unhealthy period for the United States. It was obvious to me that Nixon was only really pressured heavily when it looked like people who had things to gain were going to lose them because of the embarrassment he was causing. And Ford was the guy who I remembered being on the wrong side of every issue—utterly unqualified to be president of the United States by any stretch

of the imagination. All the talk that he's a decent guy—I don't see it that way. He's decent to the extent that he's not as overtly totalitarian as the Nixon group. But his impulses are not generous—and I think it's important for a president to be *overly* generous.

Q: Were you active at all in the antiwar movement?
A: To the moderate degree a performer can be. But nothing approximating the genuinely courageous behavior of draftees who refused to serve.

Q: How did you beat the draft?
A: I was 4-F. I was psychologically unfit to serve. I took the physical—it was strange. I had all kinds of notes from all kinds of doctors, including an analyst, because I loathed the Army and wanted to do anything to get out. Every single doctor that I went to at the draft board would say "no evidence" to everything—claims to have asthma, flat feet—"no evidence." When I went before the psychiatrist, oddly enough, he asked me to hold my hand out. I wasn't trembling or anything, but my nails were so bitten—this is the exact truth—he said, "Do you always bite your nails like that?" I told him yeah, which I did, I wasn't faking. And that got me out. That was it right there in a nutshell. That was the end of it—it was the happiest day of my life.

Q: Do you regard yourself as a cynic?
A: Totally. You can tell from *Love and Death*—it's a totally cynical movie.

Q: Do you think cynicism and idealism can coexist in the same psyche?
A: Well, I do think they're two sides of the same coin, like sadism and masochism. One gains the upper hand at a certain point. You're possessed with a sense of idealism. Then it gets shattered and you go through a valley of cynicism.

Q: It's kind of the American schizophrenia—there's always the hope that you can change it, and at the end there's the same old shit.
A: Exactly. It's tantalizing. America, of all countries, has had the potential and *has* the potential to really achieve tremendous ends. It's right at our fingertips and all we have to do is make a little effort—but we get waylaid by the temptation of greed and fear.

Q: Who are your heroes?
A: I have a lot of heroes, but they're all unconventional. Sugar Ray Robinson, Willie Mays, Louis Armstrong, Groucho, Ingmar Bergman. . . . I'm such a great fan of the Marx Brothers. I guess I like anarchy down the line. I like anarchy and

I like that the individual is responsible totally for his own choice of behavior. One hopes that the individual is so educated and so mature they will choose, all the time and under no compulsion, the humanitarian course. The anarchy of the Marx Brothers was exhilarating. My heroes are all pure heroes. They're not diluted with the problem of politics.

Q: Have you met or wanted to meet any of them?
A: I don't like meeting heroes. There's nobody I want to meet and nobody I want to work with I'd rather work with Diane Keaton than anyone—she's absolutely great, a natural.

Q: When you were growing up, who were your comedic influences? Kaufman and Hart, or Thurber, or . . .
A: Yes, Kaufman and Hart—George Kaufman, basically. I was a great fan of his when I was growing up. I've started to outgrow that style a little, but I thought he was an enormously amusing commercial playwright. And S. J. Perelman—all the time.

Q: You have a touch of Perelman's wryness.
A: I adore Perelman's work. And Benchley. I appreciated Thurber but not really with great heart. But Perelman was just a knock-down-drag-out, hilarious writer, and still is to this day, relentlessly hilarious. When I was younger I got a real kick out of Max Shulman's books, but he and Benchley were writing just for laughs—I appreciate that enormously. When I write for the *New Yorker* now, basically, I'm always trying to just be funny.

Q: How about Lenny Bruce?
A: I met him twice, I wasn't a friend of his. I caught his show in the latter part of his career. I've heard some of his albums. I saw him a couple of times on television. He was not my taste. I have nothing against him or anything and I certainly thought that he was far, far finer in what he was going for than the people who were persecuting him, and in that sense I took his side. But as a creative comedian he wasn't to my taste. I didn't find him particularly funny, and I certainly didn't find his insights and ideas interesting, original, or particularly intelligent. I just didn't enjoy him. Whereas someone like Mort Sahl I enjoyed enormously. I thought he was quite brilliant and hilarious and fresh, an interesting thinker. Also at that time I thought Nichols and May were a brilliant comedy team, very perceptive and gifted. I just got no kick out of Lenny, though.

Q: What about Richard Pryor?

A: I haven't seen him in years—six or so. I'm sure I would like him because I'm a great audience for comedians. I find Jonathan Winters to be very funny—a great, great funny man.

Q: Lily Tomlin?
A: I caught part of her TV special. I was not crazy about her on *Laugh-In* because I didn't like that program—I didn't like what they made her do. But I liked her very much on her special. I thought she was quite brilliant and very attractive. She is funny and also very sexy and appealing.

Q: Does the kind of contemporary material Pryor and Tomlin do make you feel old-fashioned?
A: Without making any value judgment, it would be impossible for me to do the type of material they do. I think they're lucky in one respect because I think that what they're dealing with is more commercial. And I think that is in a good sense a tribute to them, that their concerns are social concerns and everyday life concerns and personal concerns. They communicate with people very well. Mine are more cerebral, and consequently less communicable and less commercial. There's just nothing you can do. It's the difference between innocent college kids with typical social petulance—as Fellini said, "I'm too old to change." Fellini is obsessed with those issues that obsess him, Bergman has his, the ones that interest me just interest me and that's it.

Q: When you write, do you write constantly, or piece by piece?
A: Both. Sometimes I'll have a terrific idea for a comic piece and I'll write it the second I get a free minute. And then other times, if I haven't been writing for the *New Yorker* for a few months, my guilt bothers me so much I could be happy doing nothing but writing for them.

Q: Do you ever suffer from writer's block?
A: Not a block, not even remotely blocked. I have times when I can't think of anything because, simply in the creative process, I can't come up with it. I strike out just like anybody else—but no block, there's nothing psychological about it. I think if you're a legitimate writer and you have something to say, a good creative impulse, you can't not write. You experience it the other way—you can't wait to get back to the typewriter, even though it's hard, and not fun. You spend hours and days when nothing comes. But your impulse is to do it rather than avoiding doing it.

Q: Have you ever gotten any flak from the way you portray women in your movies?

A: I haven't had any problem at all—I think I portray everybody equally cynically. The funny thing about *Love and Death*—while I got the girl, I also died at the end.

Q: What about the women's movement?
A: Pretty much everything women are saying has made sense—they have been shabbily treated. There has got to be a change of the relations of the sexes. And sexuality has nothing to do with the way anyone's been brought up to feel about it. Everything you've been told about sex up until this point is wrong.

Q: Is the rise of bisexuality a product of confusion or liberation?
A: My instincts are—I could be wrong; I'm not making any pronouncements—that it's a negative thing. But I'm much too ignorant on the subject to be confident of that. I'm just giving you my first reactions. I guess obviously a bisexual's first reaction would be one, and a heterosexual's another. But my instincts say that bisexuality is not an advancement. Now I do feel, naturally, in the case of homosexuality and bisexuality—as in all issues, such as the legalization of marijuana—that it should be an absolutely effortless thing of total free choice by anyone, with no kind of stigma legally or in any way at all. I *do* see it as symptomatic of negative forces, unhealthy forces. But I have an open mind about it.

Q: You ever smoke pot?
A: Yeah, once or twice.

Q: It didn't do anything for you?
A: It did, but that's not why I don't smoke it. Alcohol does something for me, but I don't drink it. I just don't like the idea of marijuana or drugs, or pills—any of that stuff. I occasionally have wine, but not too often, usually when I'm with a girl or something.

Q: The strongest you go is milkshakes?
A: Malteds. Sometimes I also have wine with dinner.

Q: Is it a sign of further decay that so many people are into so many kinds of drugs?
A: I think so. I think marijuana is a bad sign, that drugs are certainly a bad sign, just as alcohol is. Of course, I do admit it's to degrees, but to the lesser degree it's not as bad a sign.

Q: So how do you relax?

A: If I can't relax naturally—watch a basketball game, play or listen to jazz—if I can't relax normally, I'd rather not relax.

Q: You have a narc who plays in your band, right?
A: Yeah, I shouldn't say anything about it but it's true.

Q: Have you played for a long time?
A: I've played clarinet since I was fifteen.

Q: What kind of jazz do you listen to—Coltrane?
A: I've got a lot of Coltrane, an enormous amount of that kind of jazz—Miles, Charlie Parker, Monk. Also avant-garde stuff, Ornette Coleman, Cecil Taylor. But I'm not as interested in that stuff as I was—I love all those guys—but I'm more interested in New Orleans–style jazz.

Q: Like Kid Ory?
A: Yeah, all the time. I met Kid Ory once. In New Orleans. He thought I was a girl. He wanted to tell a dirty joke and I had long hair at the time and he said he wouldn't tell it with "her" in the room.

Q: You never listen to rock 'n' roll?
A: Never.

Q: What is love?
A: I don't know. It's a very tough question. There are many different kinds of love and the only love I'm really interested in is the love between a man and a woman. So that's the one one concentrates on. That's the most difficult one.

Q: There's a line in *Love and Death*—"Don't forget love between two women. That's always been one of my favorites."
A: That's right. There were a lot of references to that. It was pointed out to me that there were several references in that movie to that kind of sexuality, but it was inadvertent. I just don't know anybody that has a good relationship for any length of time. I just don't. That's another area where I'm very cynical. Everybody is dependent on love. Love is the result of the best kind of luck in the area of relations with the other sex. But strictly luck. There's an enormous human conceit that we can influence things much more than we can. Hence, a guy is dressing for a date, he'll say, "I'll wear the brown jacket," and then. "No, I'll look better in the gray jacket." Actually thinking that the difference is going to create an effect. Meanwhile the girl has decided a long time ago whether she's going to bed with

him. And the same, vice versa. The girl's thinking. "I won't appear too anxious." And they're all laboring under the conceit that you can influence things when actually those decisions are unconscious. People flounder around—it's a very complicated subject that nobody has shed any light on, really.

Q: I guess fifteen years ago you never thought you'd be idolized by millions of people.
A: Not only did I not think it then, I see absolutely no evidence of it anyplace now. It's been said to me numerous times and there's not a shred of evidence of it. My record albums have never sold, although the three albums I've come out with are among the best things I've ever done. I played college audiences when I was coming up strongly as a comedian, and I never drew. And my movies don't get such an enormous audience. They get decent size, just moderate. I honestly don't know who my audience is. I don't think they're necessarily college kids or New York people—it's just a disparate group, not enormously large, that's all I can think of.

Q: Surely, though, you suffer from the perils of fame—you know, walking down the streets getting accosted by little old ladies.
A: Sometimes that happens. I'm not too crazy about that. It's not an enormous problem. I disguise myself, I wear my hat down over my ears. It depends. Some days I get recognized, other days not at all.

Q: Isn't it a drag to be recognized?
A: Yes, it's a drag, for me. Other people I know range from not minding at all, being very grateful for it, to actually liking it. I'll go out with another actor and he won't wear a hat or anything. It's amazing. And I'm walking around with a brown paper bag on my head.

Q: It seems to me the worst curse anyone can have is to be recognizably famous.
A: To have inoperable brain cancer is a bad one, too. Actually, we have a tendency to make enormous problems out of these things. I walk down the street and see a guy that's blind, or a paraplegic, and I say to myself—what does he say to himself at night? I'm always whining and complaining about this guy's bothering me or it's raining, when there's quite a few people who cope with utterly insurmountable problems, and I don't know how they do it. It's unfathomable to me.

Q: Do you get upset when you see winos bleeding on the curb?
A: Sometimes. Sometimes living in New York you pass winos without seeing them and sometimes I've had genuine feelings of compassion. I go cover somebody with a newspaper—it depends on my mood of the day. You experience a

sense of impotency. I get up in the morning, I have my coffee, I have to get down here to shoot the film, and on page one of the *Times* there's news of a cholera epidemic in Bangladesh or something. And your heart is wrenched. You don't know what to do. And the next thing you know the downstairs bell is ringing and it's off to work. At times it's occurred to me that the only life of any consequence would be a missionary life.

Q: You should have been a Catholic. Say, were your parents atheists?
A: They were kosher. They sent me to Hebrew school for eight years.

Q: Do you speak Hebrew?
A: Yes; I can read and write it.

Q: [*Kelley speaks a Hebrew phrase.*]
A: That's very good. I don't understand what you said.

Q: It means, "After you finish the ice cream continue straight toward the seashore."
A: That's very funny. How often do you use that?

Q: You'd be surprised. Over the years I've found all sorts of ways of working it into conversation.
A: We never learned words like ice cream. It was all anxiety phrases. I hated every second of it. It was awful. My neighborhood was real religious.

Q: Do you identify at all with Philip Roth's Jewish characters?
A: I've read Roth and I've enjoyed him. I don't personally relate to them. I don't have that Jewish obsession. I use my background when it's expedient for me in work. But it's not really an obsession of mine and I never had that obsession with Gentile women.

Q: You never wanted to be a rabbi?
A: Not in the remotest way. I've always found it a silly occupation.

Q: Did your parents want you to be one?
A: No, they wanted me to be a pharmacist or a doctor, that kind of thing.

Q: What did you want to be?
A: I never had any serious plans until my senior year. I wanted to be a baseball player. I was a Giants fan, but I came from the Brooklyn Dodger area, not far from Ebbetts Field. I wanted to play second base for the Dodgers very much. I

wasn't bad. And I wanted to be a magician—that fascinated me. I practiced for many, many hours. I can do a lot of it now, but then I used to practice for six or seven hours a day. And I thought of being a cowboy, an FBI man, a crime reporter. Then when I was about fifteen I realized I could write jokes. I was always kidding around—I liked comedians and was interested in them. One day after school I started typing jokes out and looking at them. And I immediately sold them at ten cents a crack to newspaper columns. I was just making them up and guys were printing them. And very briefly after that I got a chance to write for the Peter Lind Hayes radio show. I was working immediately so there was never any doubt about what I was going to do.

Q: Was there ever any doubt about the existence of God?
A: I never thought about it seriously until I was a teenager, and then all feelings were negative from the start. I think the most important issues to me are what one's values in life should be—the existence of God, death—that's real interesting to me. Whether it's a capitalist society or socialism—that's superficial.

Q: So what happens after death?
A: Most likely, nothing. Or something that's utterly unfathomable to the human mind.

Q: Do you believe in reincarnation?
A: I certainly don't *believe* in anything. It's conceivable, but I don't believe in it. Perhaps we come back as a deck reshuffling itself. Maybe we turn into birds. Who knows?

Q: What, then, is the meaning of life?
A: The meaning of life is that nobody knows the meaning of life. We are not put here to have a good time and that's what throws most of us, that sense that we all have an inalienable right to a good time.

Q: It's in the Constitution—"life, liberty and the pursuit of a good time."
A: The pursuit is all right. We can pursue it, but we were not put here to have one. That anxiety is the natural state of man, and so I think it's probably the correct state. It's probably important that we experience anxiety because it makes for the survival of the species. It doesn't bother me that I'm not having a good time because I know I'm doing something right. Most people who are having a good time are paying an enormous price for it in some way.

Q: Can't you have a good time not having a good time, though?

A: Not a *very* good time, no. Because you're always aware that the basic thrust in life is tragic and negative.

Q: Did you ever go to college?
A: I was thrown out of NYU and then thrown out of CCNY the first year for not attending, bad marks. So I have no real college education. I don't even have a year of college. But I was a motion pictures major—I failed my major. I was not good in college.

Q: Was that traumatic?
A: For my parents, not for me. I loathed every day and regret every day I spent in school. I like to be taught to read and write and add and then be left alone. I regret all the time I spent in public school. It was a blessing to be thrown out of college.

Q: So who did you read?
A: Kafka, a lot I like. And Camus, Sartre, Kierkegaard. Anyone who's got a basically hard line. I sometimes think that some of those French intellectuals like Sartre are just as crazy as the French film critics, and that in the end the unromantic English philosophers are much less interesting but much closer to the truth. It's hard to argue with Bertrand Russell. The more you learn about life, the more you feel able to challenge what I consider romantic existentialist philosophers in the same sense that one challenges French film critics very easily because film is a simpler subject to understand. I'm also a great fan of Ionesco—I found his plays very amusing and imaginative. And I thought Genet's *The Balcony* was a brilliant play and I think Beckett is super-intelligent. I find him intellectually interesting, but I don't like his plays. Though he is able to communicate a sense of absurdity and despair that resonates within me. Kafka, on the other hand, just gets to me totally—he's the best reading.

Q: Do you ever grow small warts in strange places?
A: No. I never had any excrescences on my body or skin at all. I'm physically great—perfect.

Q: Is there anybody you really hate?
A: I hate all the standard villains. Hitler.

Q: Simon Legree?
A: Yes, Simon Legree. I think probably if you start me thinking on that I could come up with an enormous list of people I hate.

Q: Including Woody Allen?
A: I have, I think, an appropriate amount of self-loathing. And I think that's important for everybody. I don't trust people who are too confident about themselves. If it gets to be too much, you're wallowing in self-pity, and then it's no good. But to not take yourself seriously is important, to not think you're so hot—because you're not. The trick is to keep a very critical eye on yourself and not get upset if someone says you're terrible, and not think it means anything at all if people say you're dynamite.

Q: What are you afraid of?
A: Sickness and death more than anything. My other fears are subsidiary to them—they cover a tremendous amount. I'd be much calmer if I didn't have to face those things. The world would be better off if I didn't have to face those things.

Q: Are you a paranoid person?
A: I have a pessimistic view of people. Consequently, I have that view of myself. I think the worst in any given situation, so I think the other person is thinking the worst. The point is that paranoids are right a certain amount of the time. I guess that comes from my own feelings of hostility. I'm suspicious and negative. I feel others have to prove themselves to me, and I don't make it any easier on myself. I feel I'm not accepted and that I have to prove myself in any situation, that one can't take decency for granted, that you have to keep proving it to me.

Q: How has psychoanalysis helped you?
A: It hasn't helped me as much as I'd hoped. I've had three analysts, all Freudian. The only thing it's helped me do really is to gain a slightly calmer perspective on things. I don't get side-tracked on obsessional issues as much. I tend to question my feelings for various meanings rather than just accepting them at face value automatically.

Q: Do you ever try and crack up your shrink?
A: No, I'm serious all the time. I practically never make jokes in general, anyplace.

Q: No kidding. What are your long-term goals?
A: I'd like to keep growing in my work. I'd like to do more serious comical films and do different types of films, maybe write and direct a drama. And take chances—I would like to fail a little for the public. Not just for myself—I've already done that. I know I could make a successful comic movie every year, and I could write a comic play that would do very well on Broadway every year. What I want to do is go on to

areas that I'm insecure about and not so good at. This next movie I'm going to do is very different than anything I've ever done and not nearly a sure thing. It will be much more real, and serious. The alternative is to do what the Marx Brothers did—which is a mistake for them, and they're geniuses. That is, they make the same movie all the time—brilliant, but the same one. Chaplin grew, took chances, and failed—he did the right thing. That's very important. Comedians fall into that trap very easily—they just hit a formula that works and they cash in on the same thing time and time again.

Q: What's your ultimate fantasy?
A: On the possible side, to make very interesting serious movies, as I said. On the impossible side, I fantasize playing guard for the Knicks and being black—if I had my life to live over again, among the things I'd like to be is a black basketball player. Or a concert pianist, a conductor, a ballet dancer—I'm a big fan of ballet and modern dance.

Q: What's your favorite color?
A: I like autumnal hues a lot—you can tell from *Love and Death*.

Q: The photography in that movie was incredible.
A: My grasp of photography is getting better. That movie required it. You know, in Paris you get that weather all the time—foggy and gray. If you shoot in California, it's sunny and it doesn't look so nice.

Woody Allen on Woody Allen

Gary Arnold / 1977

From the *Washington Post*, April 17, 1977. © 1977, Washington Post Company. All rights reserved. Used by permission and protected by the Copyright Laws of the United States. The printing, copying, redistribution, or retransmission of this Content without express written permission is prohibited.

Annie Hall, Woody Allen's new film, is a sentimental comedy that loosely chronicles the romance between Alvy Singer, a comedian played by Allen, and Annie Hall, an aspiring actress-singer played by Diane Keaton. Evidently hundreds of titles were discarded, including "Woody Allen's Anxiety" and the unthinkably esoteric "Anodynia"—the psychological state characterized by an absence of pain—before Allen settled on plain, unprepossessing *Annie Hall*.

"You're in such a vulnerable position when you make a film," Allen remarked last week after completing an unusually long stint in the publicity spotlight. "You do what you have to do, then hope people will be responsive and that the movie will bottom out somewhere profitable enough not to embarrass United Artists at the next Transamerica board of directors meeting. All my films have gotten into profits, but they're modest successes. They don't seem to get beyond a certain plateau—they cost around $3 million and make around $10 million.

"The $3 million is an informal ceiling, and I feel perfectly comfortable with it. In fact, it began as a $2 million ceiling when I made *Bananas* and has gone up because of the cost of living more than anything else. I'd just be creating problems for myself if I tried to exceed that level. The box-office receipts would have to increase by some staggering amount to justify a budget in the $4–5 million range. My own personal feeling is that my films have a limited appeal, and I don't mind that at all. I'm always surprised that they seem to appeal to as many people as they do."

The nature of *Annie Hall*, which departs from the headlong farcical style of *Sleeper* and *Love and Death*, probably influenced Allen's decision to do a bit more promotion this time around. The new film, which opens April 27 at the Jenifer 1 and Roth's Tysons Corner 4 & 5, reflects a desire to be romantically affecting rather than persistently, outrageously funny. It's also a tentative step in a direction Allen feels compelled to explore, even though he's aware it may lead up a blind alley taken by many funnymen before him.

"I was consciously trying for a more sentimental kind of film," Allen said. "The earlier ones were just for laughs, and I realize I might be safer sticking with that approach. There's always a danger when comedians feel the need to express pathos, because they can push into masochism too easily. To avoid that I think I should maybe not do a comedy occasionally. I would never want to get pathetic, because I don't like that in other comedians' work.

"I think *Annie* may be a mild turning point. I began the script after *Sleeper*, but the fact that it didn't have as many laughs as I'm used to scared me off. I put it aside and wrote *Love and Death*, which was full of laughs. Even if I continue making nothing but comedies, I'd like them to be more dimensional. I couldn't do many of the sort of jokes I'd done in *Bananas* or *Sleeper* or *Love and Death* without risking involvement with the characters. I'm used to looking for laughs in the dailies. Here there weren't nearly as many laughs to go by. I had to trust to the relationships to carry the film. People kept telling me not to worry, and I hope they were right.

"Very few people can write really amusing comedy, but I don't value it more because it's rare and hard to do. What I hope to do next is a straight dramatic film. If the script works out, it would be a very serious no-laughs psychological drama without a part for me. I would really like to move in a more serious direction. I realize it may be a total mistake, and if I fail, I'll come back to comedy and resign myself to the fact that I may be limited to it. But . . . but if I were to succeed at a dramatic film, I think I'd find it far more satisfying."

Asked to compare modern film comedies with the silent classics, Allen replied with characteristic thoughtfulness. "The contemporary playing area for comedy has shifted," he said. "Chaplin and Keaton operated in a very physical world where people worked and struggled to cope with tangible obstacles and frustrations. I think the conflicts are interior now. They're psychological conflicts, and it's difficult to find a vocabulary to express those inner states, to make them visual.

"Bergman has discovered ways of doing it in a serious way. I'm trying to do it by talking directly to the audience or showing things like Diane's mind stepping out of her body, but it's all very tentative. I've never gotten anything close to a feeling of satisfaction from any film I've been associated with. For me they're all failures, but an audience, not knowing the grandiose plans I've had for them, may be spared the same disillusion."

Allen wanted to put a few technical finishing touches on *Annie Hall*. He was headed for the lab "to remove two points of yellow" that had bothered him in one sequence. Allen has made a conscious effort to stylize the look and color schemes of his films. It's important to him even though he doubts if many people in the audience care or notice.

"I think it's true that only a small percentage of viewers are really concerned with the look of a film," he said, "and perhaps it's just as well. It's always a shock to filmmakers if they pick up their old movies in some out-of-the-way place months later and see how the prints have deteriorated. A friend and I made the mistake of trying to catch 2001 in revival not so long ago. It was at an older revival house, but still a supposedly reputable place. Kubrick would have had a seizure; he's such an obsessive about the visual side anyway. The movie had been pretty much reduced to streaks and flickers.

"We're probably living at the end of an era. I think it's only a matter of time until home viewing is made as easy and economical as is desirable. That's one of the things I noticed when we were doing the L.A. locations for *Annie Hall*. So many people there were hooked on Home Box Office. It won't be that long before their thirty-inch screens will be six-foot screens. At that state why expose yourself to the inconveniences of going out to a theater, especially if the projection is habitually bad and the image isn't much larger than what you could have at home?

"I retain a certain feeling that you should go out and expose yourself to a little inconvenience, but it's nostalgia. It comes from the fact that I grew up going to the movies every weekend and associate it with so many pleasurable experiences. Now a lot of people have lost the habit of going, and movies are more of an art thing than a general, democratic form of entertainment. You couldn't blame people for getting even more selective about what they see and where they see it.

"Now that I've learned a little something about making movies, I'd hate to see too many changes on the technical side. I don't see any reason why movie comedies can't also look pretty. David Walsh and I worked very hard to get a streamlined look on *Everything You Wanted to Know about Sex* and *Sleeper*. I was hoping to work with him continuously, but Walsh didn't want to leave the West Coast. The idea on *Love and Death*, which was shot by Ghislain Cloquet, was soft, autumnal colors. *Annie Hall* is the first film I've done with Gordon Willis, and we plan to work together as often as possible. I didn't mind at all that some scenes were supposedly 'too dark' for a comedy, and I found that Gordy's style doesn't retard laughs.

"All the rumors about Gordy were highly exaggerated: that he was difficult and uncooperative and all the rest. Better yet, he's faster than anyone I've ever worked with and skilled in all sorts of ways that speeded up production. Shots like Diane's mind leaving her body are not opticals. Gordy knows how to get special effects like that in the camera."

Allen seems to inspire a special measure of affection among executives and publicists at United Artists. When *Love and Death* was released two years ago, it was apparent that UA personnel valued it more than *The Return of the Pink Panther*, which opened at about the same time and went on to enjoy more commercial success.

"They may appreciate *Return of the Pink Panther* more by now," Allen remarked dryly. "But it's true that UA is a more agreeable outfit to deal with. It's an unusually stable operation for this business. The guys are older, a little more cosmopolitan, and they stick around for a while. At the other companies there's a constant turnover of sharpies, so you can never be sure who'll be running the joint the next time around. UA doesn't interfere with you. They have something called 'concept approval,' but they'll usually trust me even if a concept doesn't particularly excite them. I usually show them the scripts voluntarily. The status quo wouldn't last too long if my pictures didn't pay for themselves. Since Transamerica owns UA, I might have a little difficulty if I ever tried to make a wild comedy about corruption in the insurance business. I think it's part of the general understanding that that situation will never arise."

Scenes from a Mind:
Woody Allen Is Nobody's Fool

Ira Halberstadt / 1978

Published in *Take One* 12 (November 1978): 16–20.

I worked with Woody Allen last year on Interiors, *and when we finished the last reshoots in early spring asked if I could interview him. He was busy cutting the film, then I was out of town for several months on another film. We got together in mid-June when* Interiors *was pretty much in finished form (the sound was being re-mixed) and Woody was in preparation for his next movie, to begin shooting in July. I started the conversation by asking about Joey (Mary Beth Hurt), a character I thought more foreign to his personal experience than Renata (Diane Keaton). This carried him into a discussion of courage and the importance of human relationships.*

Renata speaks for me, without question. She articulates all my personal concerns. You see there's the type of people that never question life in any way, they run their elevators and drive their cabs and they come home and do what's expected of them and they have a mindless existence. Then there are those people that luck out, and have talent, and it's pure luck, it's like being born beautiful or something. You know, they have ears and can play music or can draw. Much is made of it in society, and it's very pleasurable for the audience and for the person, but it's nothing like having courage or something, where an act of volition or bravery is required.

Then there's that middle ground of person that really is screwed. They do question life, they are sensitive and intelligent and all of that and they have no talent. They know they don't want to work in an office, they know they don't want to just junk their lives being a housewife raising kids or a guy working for an insurance company. But they're not going to be Nureyev and they're not gonna be a Michelangelo, so they're in bad shape.

If a guy has a great ear for music or can paint or something, he's lucky. He's born with a certain gene for that and probably some environmental thing when he's very young. I don't find any comparison between the two. The real act of courage for me is the guy who acts in spite of an almost paralyzing fear.

There are some people, I don't think of them as courageous. I think of them as naturally, mindlessly brave. They're heroes in the war or something. But for instance, if it's true exactly as she explained it to us in *Julia*, I would consider Lillian Hellman's action very brave, very courageous. I mean, if someone said that to me, carry this money beyond Nazi lines, or Communist lines under certain circumstances, that would be an act of *extreme* bravery. You can't get much more extreme than that. If it comes to torture, to shattering people who rise to the occasion in a concentration camp, and hold out information—you know, that's remarkable.

Sure, there's show business courage. There's stuff people talk about as courageous within a certain context, but it's courageous in the flimsiest little meaningless way. There is more courage for me to get out on stage than to sit in my room and write, but the whole scale of things is down. You're not talking about meaningful courage. It's gotta be where you risk your life. It's fine and it's important to work creatively, and to try new things, and not stagnate, and strike out a couple of times and stuff, but it's within a very safe framework. I mean whether my picture makes $1 million or $10 million doesn't mean anything in terms of bravery. It's great, but on a little scale.

The comedy that I'm making now—the issue again is comedy, which gives it a completely different treatment—revolves around what I started to do in *Annie Hall*, but this is darker than that. It's got to do with how a person can maintain his lifestyle and integrity, a decent life, in the face of the onslaught of contemporary society, all the temptations and all the terrible stuff that you have to go through. And so again, it's comedy, but on a more serious level. In addition to integrity, bravery, and courage, what interests me the most personally is more existential. Religious stuff for instance. Why are you here? What's the purpose of life? Spiritual meanings.

I tried to dwell on that to a degree in *Interiors*. Probably the picture will be perceived, and rightly so, as a psychological family drama. Anything on that level ... but I think there's also a certain amount of religious thought in it that probably will not be apparent to people, because I either failed to do it skillfully enough or it'll be too subtle, or the other things dominate the story so much. The mere domestic relationships will be so either likeable or unlikeable to people.

Renata (Keaton) has come to the conclusion that having a great talent or having talent of some sort, expressing yourself, to create things that will live forever, in the sense of her mother's perception ... dealing with vases and things, that doesn't mean anything. It's all jerk-off, it's all fooling around. You have a sense of immortality, that your work will live on after you, which is nonsense. Art is like the intellectual's Catholicism, it's the promise of an afterlife, but of course, it's fake—you're only doing it because *you* want to do it.

Originally I wanted Geraldine Page to have a religious character, to have believed in Christ and be very involved with that, and my feeling about that sort of involvement is that it's crazy. Yes, you can get a feeling of immortality, but it's crazy. There's no rational thinking. Renata comes to realize in the movie, if it's successful, that the only thing anyone has any chance with is human relationships. Unless she's closer to her sisters or her husband, or whoever, she's lost: no amount of artistic self-importance and disdain for philistines is going to do anything for her.

Richard Jordan seemed to me the failed artist who invariably turns to intellectualism, cerebralism, criticism, teaching, stuff like that. The kind of person who vents his personal hostility under the guise of high standards, but it has nothing to do with standards. When he discusses the play with Maureen Stapleton, she's saying that it's simple. He's saying, well, it's more complex than that, which is an intellectual posture. Intellectuals' positions are very complex, and that's all junk, you know, because they build structures for themselves. To her, it isn't at all complex. She's right. I mean, she may be right because she's mindless, because she's not a thinker, but she is right. She's not befuddled by all the intellectual constructions.

The other guy, Waterston, never deals with his own personal problems—goes on living with this girl, doesn't exactly know why, has feelings of love for her, but he only loses himself in abstractions—you know, the masses, as he says in the thing, "What is the life of one person over the life of thousands of others?" But the thousands of others are always vague and faceless. E. G. is just the father trying to do the right thing.

Flyn (Kristin Griffith) in the picture was to me the person who avoids the issue by dehumanizing herself. She goes to California, she's a pretty object. As Richard Jordan says to her when he's trying to rape her, she only exists in other people's eyes, she only feels that she exists in the comprehension of another person, and she's just a pretty object. She doesn't want to know from the family really, she lives out there, is involved in her pursuit of TV projects, and her grass, and her flirtations, and she is flirtatious with Richard Jordan. She's focused her mind, she chooses to live her life on one level completely. What she has going for her she pushes, and she's like an object, no real concerns.

Joey (Mary Beth Hurt) is, in a certain sense, the healthiest one at the beginning. She's got a terrible problem, but what probably happened I would imagine, was that years ago, when her mother cracked up, her father was most affectionate with her, and closest to her, because of the nature of the others, and because of that, she does have a few personal resources. She is trying to express herself in some way and just doesn't have the talent, and has to deal with a sister who does have talent, and another one who's attractive and successful. But Joey at least had the advantage of real indulgence from her father. Renata never had that advantage.

My feeling is that what I think is going to happen is that Joey is going to have a calmer life than her mother. There is some feeling between her and Keaton, though Keaton isn't quite ready yet for a rapprochement.

And I think Joey will feel the influence of Pearl (Maureen Stapleton). I don't know which philosopher it was that wrote that the natural person, the brave person, the good person, will always be perceived as a vulgarian by the other people. And this is what I think is true with Maureen. Maureen is far more natural and flexible and decent than all of them, but she'll always be perceived that way, as a vulgarian. Of course, she probably is a little vulgar, but I want people to be on her side, which I think they will be.

The film was originally, clearly about Joey, but in the editing and rewriting and shooting, it's become a little more ensemble. Still, I feel that Joey's the central character. I thought about Keaton as a possibility for Joey, with a completely different direction, and then I thought of Keaton's part being played by Jane Alexander, and it's just a different set-up. Keaton felt that she could play Renata better. If she had said, "Joey is perfect for me," I would have gone that way. I gave her her choice, who she wanted. Mary Beth, I had never seen, or anything. She came up to this office and the second she walked in (I don't think I spent more than sixty seconds with her), the second she walked in, I knew she was perfect for Joey.

I had seen Kristin Griffith before. I felt she reminded me of Keaton's actual sister in life. She looked like Keaton, and I thought she was sexy, an attractive girl, and would be the perfect girl for the part.

I never envisioned Geraldine Page at any point. Keaton saw her the second she read the script, said Geraldine Page, and I said I didn't see Geraldine for that part. I looked at every woman in town. I looked at cassettes, and movies, and was enamored of several, all terrific actresses. I was just going to touch that base and check Geraldine. In fact, that morning I was gonna tell Norma Lee (Allen's assistant) to call Geraldine and tell her not to bother. She said, it's too late, she's not home. So, she came in. The second she walked in, she was . . . I mean it was absolutely on the nose. She was absolutely perfect. I couldn't have done better with that part. I mean, she was born as that character, beyond my fondest expectations. I can't think of it any other way, it's simply impossible. It's a definitive playing of that particular role. She was born to play it, and I just have never seen that. I've always loved Geraldine Page as an actress.

I was very intimidated by the cast in general, just as intimidated by Maureen (Stapleton) as by Geraldine, and having to direct them, and Jordan, you know, who I always thought was a powerful actor—I was intimidated. First of all, I was lucky, in a sense, that they're all enormously pleasant and professional; Geraldine's a miracle to work with because she does it different every time, always busy doing something. I could say the worst things to her, I could say God, that was so phony, it was so soap opera, and she'd say oh, yeah, I guess you're right, and do it again brilliantly in another direction. So I was wrong to be intimidated, because they proved to be terrific together, and they were as sweet as can be. I thought they were gonna be, you know, a snake pit, but they turned out to be all nice people, so that was a big help to me.

People like Maureen and Geraldine, their tradition is theatrical, and they master this brilliant sense of emoting onstage, and then when you put them in films you always have to watch and make sure that they don't do those things that make them so great onstage. I was always telling them to play smaller, don't do so much, that was one thing. Whereas in a comedy film, it's always louder and faster: "Speak a little faster, please talk faster, please talk louder and faster." You're always saying that—and here, I was always saying, "Could you do it more real, could you not be so big, could you take that down, play it very simply." I said this in the most tactless way sometimes and none of them ever took any kind of offense. I would say, let's not do "Love of Life," and they would always laugh. I think they accepted basically that I think, and everybody thinks, that they're great to begin with, and it was a question of whether they were gonna be good or great or very special. They're not insecure about whether they can act or not. So it was not a big problem. But I anticipated a big problem, and spent a lot of time worrying about it.

The first film, the first two that I made, I was thrilled just to make them funny and that's all I cared about. I just wanted to survive, and to make them. I didn't care about anything else, everything was coordinated with the joke, everything. Then with *Everything You Always Wanted to Know about Sex*, I was trying very hard to develop as a filmmaker. I pushed that further in *Sleeper*. By the time I did *Love and Death*, I was very concerned with the filmmaking aspect, and with wanting to do darker things, not deal with a lot of conventional stuff. On *Annie Hall* we just pulled out all the stops and we did scenes that you would never think would be in a comedy, a very dark picture. *Love and Death* was my favorite picture. *Annie Hall* to me was a very middle-class picture, and that's why I think people liked it. It was the reinforcement of the middle-class values. The picture that expressed me the most, and certainly my funniest picture, was *Love and Death*. But most people didn't feel that way. The new film (currently in production) has a straight, black and white story. Straight narrative. There's no screwing around in time, and there's no special gimmicks, there's no dream sequences, no fantasies, no voiceovers, nothing. It's a very spartan kind of story. (Allen, Keaton, Michael Murphy, Mariel

Hemingway, and Meryl Streep are in the film.) In a joke film, the cutting rhythm helps with the jokes. It helps the illusion of speed and it helps with punching things around. One of the things I learned from my very first movie (*Take the Money and Run*) is that when you're making crazy comedy, don't do dolly shots. Tie down the camera and make the movie with cuts. It makes all the difference in the world. When I got to *Annie Hall*, which is a slightly more serious picture—that is, with no narrative and more story and everything—you can make dolly shots, because relentless speed is not what you're after. You can't get that speed with dolly shots. There's something inherent in the movement of the dolly that won't do it. So, in *Interiors* you can dolly forever. But there's no arbitrary movement in *Interiors*. Gordy (Gordon Willis, director of photography on *Interiors*) was very conscious of that. His feeling about it always has been that the actors meet the camera, and you almost never, ever in any picture he does, see the camera, because it's always done with the actors.

I had been looking for a New York cameraman to shoot *Annie Hall* when someone said Gordy Willis was free. I had loved his stuff but I had heard how difficult he was, angry, all kinds of awful things, and I didn't want to use him. I said to Bobby Greenhut, let's sign a contract but let's make the budget, so if we have to fire Gordy we can get another cameraman. Gordy was wonderful in *every* way. He was friendly, charming, intelligent, helpful—*absolutely*. Then I realized he'd come to have a bad reputation by working among people who had bad artistic instincts and were trying to force him to do things he didn't want to do—studio heads and so forth. I mean, he was just *wonderful* and I couldn't wait to work with him again in Southampton doing *Interiors*. While we were up in the Hamptons doing *Interiors* we both thought it would be great to do a black and white picture together. I wrote the script for the new film to accommodate the concept of black and white.

What usually happens is we talk over the script, he says we could do it like this or this, or I say do you think the scene could play all in a master so we could see the background. Sometimes it will be my idea, sometimes his, sometimes we bounce off one another. One great contribution of his was to shoot day for night out there (at Southampton for *Interiors*). I had never thought of that. I had thought of shooting night for night. He said no, if we shot day for night, it would have a more mystical look. This was very connected to content. He wouldn't shoot day for night if the film didn't have that poetic intention to it. He's an intellect; he's a mind. I can talk to him about it. He's smart. He reads the script and he reads and reads it again and we meet at my house and we make many decisions.

Also, I love and am very, very mindful of cinematography as a contribution to the script. It seems it should go without saying, but it doesn't. People don't realize photography is the medium, it's film! To them, perhaps, it becomes a necessary evil to tell the story. When I sit with Gordy, we go over all the alternatives, and many times I accommodate the scenes and the dramatic action to get better production, to give him chances to make better character changes or plot changes, situation changes, because I know it would give me great opportunity for photography, because I do think that part of what you're responding to up there, a big part, is film, you know, and I greatly appreciate that. I think Gordy likes to work with me. One of the reasons is my responsiveness. I'm a great audience for him, and I'm willing to go with him.

I hope we don't lose him to the world of directing. I know he'll be a good director, though he says he doesn't want it as a steady job.

To me, a film grows organically. I write the script, and then it changes in casting. I see people when they come in and then I decide . . . the story changes there. It changes if Keaton doesn't want to do these lines, and I don't want to do these—we shift around. And then when we're shooting it, it changes for a million reasons. Some creatively, sometimes we get ideas. Others because we can't get into a police station, so could I please make that scene in Zabar's? And the same thing in editing. In *Interiors* we took a scene with E. G. Marshall, which is written to be in the last twenty-five pages of the thing, where we're talking about his wife. And it's the first speech of the picture. And I've been doing this *constantly* with all my pictures, because they also grow in the editing.

You can't be married to what you set out to do, because film takes on a different quality when it becomes film—when you shoot it, when you put a frame around it, when you edit it. Stuff that was highly significant before becomes flat, and stuff becomes very meaty when it wasn't. I find with Ralph (Rosenblum, Allen's editor), we edit and the picture becomes very different, the picture assumes a different shape. I mean, it always assumes a different shape, but in the editing it becomes even more different. And I always find because of that there's a gap here on the scene, there's no ending here, because we've used the ending for the beginning, and every single picture I've done I've had to shoot more material. And now I budget for it. Now I just know that my first cut of the picture will be missing bits and pieces, I just know. There's no way to make a picture straight through.

I shoot very long. *Everything* was about fourteen weeks, *Sleeper* was twenty-nine weeks, *Love and Death* was twenty weeks. *Annie Hall*, *Interiors*, were sixteen weeks, which is what the new picture is budgeted at. So, considering that, I'm always told that Paul Mazursky or someone else could make the same film in nine weeks. And they probably can. But that was the one thing I learned, that the only mean device that I require is to be able to show up on the set and think two or three hours when I want to plan a shot, and if it doesn't work, go home that day and not think "Oh, God, every day I've gotta put footage in that can, and the meter's running." It's important not to feel rushed, talking to actors, or talking to Gordy, or not to force it if I'm tired at the end of the day, especially if I'm acting.

I remember showing up on the set and the production manager saying, "Jesus, it's 10:30," and the truth is, often those guys feel the important thing is the money and the budget, and the film is a necessary evil for getting the budget right.

It's better for me to have my guys as the producers. They've (Rollins and Joffe) always been my managers. Greenhut will be with me, this will be my third picture. Conceivably, I can see myself working with Greenhut forever.

They don't have to look for the writers or the guest stars, so there is nothing like that for them to do. I go in and I argue for the amount of stuff done on the ads, the credits, for what theaters we're going into. I do all that stuff. Charlie (Joffe) is there, though, on a rare occasion when something is needed. A guy that I can sleep nights knowing that he's in my corner, that I can trust.

I was hoping that people wouldn't take *Interiors* as depressing, as I think they will. I was hoping they would feel at the end of the picture there's a glimmer of hope. I spent a lot of money on this picture. Of course, it's not going to make a dime. There's no way that it's going to do good. Because, I mean, I've *seen* the picture. And I know. Obviously, it's not *Jaws II* or *Grease* or that kind of film. It's not the level of *Unmarried Woman* or *Dog Day* or *Cuckoo's Nest*—a serious picture, but with *entertainment*.

An Interview with Woody

Frank Rich / 1979

From *Time*, April 30, 1979, 68–69. © 1979 Time Inc. All rights reserved. Reprinted from *Time* and published with permission of Time Inc. Reproduction in any manner in any language in whole or in part without written permission is prohibited.

It is not the largest apartment in Manhattan, but it may be the airiest. Woody Allen's penthouse duplex is high above Fifth Avenue, and its glass walls provide an illusion of floating. Outside, in foreshortened perspective, like Saul Steinberg's popular poster, stretches much of the city: the lakes and woods of Central Park, the skyscrapers of midtown, the rococo parapets of the West Side. This is literally and figuratively Woody Allen's *Manhattan*: the movie's opening sequence, a montage of romantic cityscapes, was largely shot from the director's own terrace.

Last week, just before the film's premiere, Allen sat on a comfortably worn couch with his back to the view. He had caught the flu and was huddling over a bowl of chicken soup ("the mythological panacea," as he called it). Between his upset stomach and the details of *Manhattan*'s opening, Allen's normal routine had been disrupted. When he is not shooting a film, Allen usually gets up at seven, writes all day, and then goes out for a late dinner at Elaine's with a few pals (actor Michael Murphy, *Saturday Night Live* staff producer Jean Doumanian, his frequent collaborator Marshall Brickman).

Last week not much writing was being done. His home phone—a large console with pushbuttons to direct-dial friends and associates—was ringing, buzzing and blinking like a pinball machine. Earlier, Allen had checked out the theaters where his movie will play and found some of them wanting: new screens and projectors had to be ordered to "keep *Manhattan* from looking like *The Day the Earth Blew Up*." Equally unsatisfactory was the typeface in a full-page Sunday *New York Times* ad for the film: a new mock-up awaited his inspection. The most annoying problem was the Motion Picture Association's decision to slap *Manhattan* with an R rating because of a few four-letter words. Allen was not pleased: "People say that the industry has a ratings board to keep the government from invoking censorship—as if that's some big deal. It's censorship no matter who does it." Just the same, Allen would not dream of calling the ratings board himself and giving it a piece of his mind. That is not his style. "I have a tough time expressing anger to people," he explains. "Sometimes I wish I could raise my voice a little, but I just get quiet or become amusing. I can express anger to objects very, very easily, though. If the Cuisinart doesn't work, I have no trouble slamming it."

Such trivial bothers aside, Woody Allen seems content these days. Or at least as content as he can be. Rather uncharacteristically, he even seems tentatively pleased with his own work. "I wanted to make a film that was more serious than *Annie Hall*, a serious picture that had laughs in it," he says. "I felt decent about *Manhattan* at the time I did it; it does go farther than *Annie Hall*. But I think now I could do better. Of course, if my film makes one more person feel miserable, I'll feel I've done my job." He is only half joking. It is no wonder that his original title for *Annie Hall* was *Anhedonia*, a psychoanalytic term that means "incapable of experiencing pleasure."

Allen has his own misery, which is sincere and lifelong. It cannot be dissipated by the success of his movies. A shy workaholic who avoids the show-biz whirl and is never "on" in private, he not only talks about death in his films but spends a great deal of time thinking about it. "My real obsessions are religious," he says. "They have to do with the meaning of life and with the futility of obtaining immortality through art. In *Manhattan*, the characters create problems for themselves to escape. In real life, everyone gives himself a distraction—whether it's by turning on the TV set or by playing sophisticated games like the characters of *Manhattan*. You have to deny the reality of death to go on every day. But for me, even with all the distractions of my work and my life, I spend a lot of time face to face with my own mortality." In order to distract himself, Allen has spent his entire life compulsively mastering talents with fierce concentration: just as he spent hours practicing magic tricks as a child, he later set out to learn gag writing, performing, poker, sports, clarinet playing, and finally filmmaking. He also deals with his anxiety by seeing an analyst, but says, "That's only good for limited things—it's like going to an optometrist."

Manhattan, Allen feels, deals with the problem of trying "to live a decent life amidst all the junk of contemporary culture—the temptations, the seductions. So how do you keep from selling out?" Like Isaac Davis, his alter ego in the film, Allen tries to avoid selling out as much as possible. "I try not to do those things that will be successful at the expense of things that will be artistically more fulfilling. When I was young, I was always careful not to get seduced into TV writing. I was making a lot of money and knew it was a dead end; you get seduced into a lifestyle, move to California, and in six months you become a producer!

"At the personal level, I try to pay attention to the moral side of issues as they arise and try not to make a wrong choice. For instance, I've always had a strong feeling about drugs. I don't think it's right to try to buy your way out of life's painful side by using drugs. I'm also against the concept of short marriages, and regard my own marriages [five years to Harlene Rosen, two years to actress Louise Lasser] as a sign of failure of some sort. Of course I sell out as much as anyone—insidiously. It's impossible not to be a sellout unless you give away all your physical possessions and live like a hermit."

Allen has considered that, at least in a limited way. "I have talked seriously with my friends about giving 75 percent of all my possessions to charity and living in much more modest circumstances. I've rationalized my way out of it so far, but I could conceive of doing it." He adds, laughing: "I could not conceive of leaving New York and becoming monastic, like in *Walden*. I'd rather die than live in the country—in a small house or even in a nice house." (His friend Dick Cavett says, "Woody is at two with nature.") Even now, Allen does not live up to his means. His home is attractive, but not opulent, containing more books and records than anything else. His wardrobe of plaid shirts, jeans, and beat-up jackets is the same he wears in his movies. "Mariel Hemingway just saw *Annie Hall* again and called me up, amazed that I wore the same clothes she sees me in all the time," Allen recalls. "Actually I wear some of the same clothes in both *Annie Hall* and *Manhattan*. I'm still wearing a shirt I wore in *Play It Again, Sam* on Broadway in 1969." The only true indulgences he allows himself are a cook and driver, as well as a compulsion to pick up dinner checks. His isolation from financial affairs is so complete that he gave his producer-manager, Charles Joffe, the power of attorney to sign all his contracts and even his divorce papers.

Allen places no more of a premium on intellectual prowess or talent than he does on money or status. "I know so many people who are well educated and supereducated," he explains. "Their common problem is that they have no understanding and no wisdom; without that, their education can only take them so far. On the other hand, someone like Diane Keaton, who had not a trace of intellectualism when I first met her, can always cut right to the heart of the matter. As for talent, it is completely a matter of luck. People put too much of a premium on talent; that was a problem of the characters in *Interiors*. Certainly talent can give sensual, aesthetic pleasure; it's like looking at a beautiful woman. But people who are huge talents are frequently miserable human beings. In terms of human attributes, what really counts is courage. There's a speech I had to cut out of *Manhattan* and plan to get into the next film, where my character says that the metaphor for life is a concentration camp. I do believe that. The real question in life is how one copes in that crisis. I just hope I'm never tested, because I'm very pessimistic about how I would respond. I worry that I tend to moralize, as opposed to being moral."

Allen first began to grapple with these issues on film in *Interiors*, and he plans to make more serious films in the future. "I have always felt tragedy was the highest form, even as a child, before I could articulate it. There was something about the moodiness, the austerity, the apparent profundity of Elia Kazan's films then that sucked me in. With comedy you can buy yourself out of the problems of life and diffuse them. In tragedy, you must confront them and it is painful, but I'm a real sucker for it." Allen did not have a role in *Interiors* and will not act in his serious movies. "I can act within a certain limited range," he says, but notes that while making *Manhattan*, he had to resist a "real temptation" to play a sad drunk scene for laughs. "I could never see myself sitting in an analyst's chair in a film, talking about my mother and shock treatments and gradually crying—not if my life depended on it."

If Allen has a favorite actor, it seems to be Keaton. Talking about her always cheers him up: "She has no compunction about playing a lovable and gangly hick in *Annie Hall* and then very neurotic and disturbed women in *Interiors* and *Manhattan*. That's the mark of an actress and not a movie star. Keaton also has the eye of a genius, as you can see in her photos, collages, silk screens, and wardrobe. She can dress in a thousand more creative ways than she did in *Annie Hall*. When I first met her, she'd combine unbelievable stuff—a hockey shirt, combat boots, some chic thing from Ralph Lauren." Though Allen and Keaton have not been romantically involved since 1971, they remain close, and he hopes some day to create a musical for her.

Another actress Allen admires is his *Manhattan* co-star, Mariel Hemingway, who is seventeen. "I wrote the part for her after seeing her in *Lipstick* and stumbling across her photo in Andy Warhol's *Interview* magazine. She met with me, and after two minutes I knew she was right. When we were making the film, she always stayed in character when we improvised. Even when I went off in an unexpected direction, she could always go with the scene."

Allen will be in his new film, which begins shooting in September. He hopes the movie will go "deeper in both comic and serious directions" than *Manhattan*. "I want to make a film that is stylized and very offbeat. I want to try being funny without jokes, to rely less on dialogue and try to tell the story in images more." Once again, audiences will see some emulation of Ingmar Bergman, his favorite director. "Bergman amazes me in part because he tells intellectual stories, and they move forward for endless amounts of time with no dialogue."

Not that Allen has forgotten about laughs. While in the thick of making *Manhattan*, he spent dozens of hours watching Bob Hope movies to compile a one-hour film tribute for a Lincoln Center gala honoring the comedian. "I had more pleasure looking at Hope's films than making any film I've ever made," Allen says. "I think he's just a great, huge talent. Part of what I like about him is that flippant, Californian, obsessed-with-golf striding through life. His not caring about the serious side at all. That's very seductive to me. I would feel fine making a picture like *Sleeper* tomorrow, but I get the feeling the audience would be disappointed. They expect something else from me now. But I wouldn't let that prevent my doing it. It would be just too much fun to make a real out-and-out junk kind of thing." With some regret, Allen found himself having to cut jokes out of *Manhattan* in the editing. "They were very funny—not just one-liners, but sight gags—but in the context of the film, they looked like they had dropped down from the moon."

With *Manhattan* behind him and his new film partly written, Allen is taking the first vacation of his career, a week in Paris. "I made plans to go on several occasions," he says, "but I always called up my travel agent and called it off at the last minute. It got to be a big joke among my friends. But I like Paris. It wouldn't kill me if someone said I would be forced to live there the rest of my life." In Paris, Allen plans to do "the exact same things" he does at home: drift around, eat, and go to movies. Or maybe he won't. "If I get my predictable anxiety attack," Allen adds, "I'll get on the next plane and come right back to New York."

Creators on Creating: Woody Allen

Robert F. Moss / 1980

Published in *Saturday Review* 7 (November 1980):40–44.

One of the most prominent names in American comedy for over twenty years, Woody Allen began selling gags to professional comics when he was a teenager, and he later worked as a staff writer for Sid Caesar. After making a successful transition to stand-up comedy himself, he turned to filmmaking. Between 1968 and 1976, he co-wrote, directed, and starred in *Take the Money and Run*, *Bananas*, *Sleeper*, and several other hit comedies. In the Academy Award–winning *Annie Hall* (1977), *Manhattan* (1979), and his current film, *Stardust Memories*, he deepened his comedy with drama, and in *Interiors* (1978), he abandoned humor altogether and created a Bergmanesque essay in gloom. Away from the camera, he has also demonstrated a literary bent, publishing three collections of humorous essays and short stories. Born forty-four years ago in Flatbush, New York, he now resides in Manhattan amid the health-food addicts, street people, psychiatrists, literary mavens, pseudo-intellectuals, and random neurotics whom he has satirized so often in his films. He lives in a duplex penthouse on Fifth Avenue and produces his films from an office on West 57th Street.

Q: You've been characterized as a workaholic. Is this accurate?
A: If people saw the way I lived, they'd realize that I spend a huge amount of time just relaxing and goofing off, watching baseball on television, going to movies, taking walks, playing jazz, and practicing my clarinet. I don't work around the clock at all. How productive is my output? A film every year at most, probably even a little longer than that, and occasional magazine pieces and that's really it. It's not all that much work. If you work only three to five hours a day, you become quite productive. It's the steadiness of it that counts. Getting to the typewriter every day is what makes for productivity.

Q: You don't try to create anything in a single burst of inspiration then?
A: No. For me, it was a bad habit to do it that way. When I was much younger

the impulse was always to finish the thing immediately. It was very hard to put it aside and come back to it the next day. You become very obsessed with it. I just learned that that was a bad habit. You know, I like to get up pretty early in the morning and work and then put it aside and come back to it the next day.

Q: Do you have any eccentricities that spark your creative powers?
A: I prefer to write on a bed, more than anyplace else. I also can't stand any noise. I read that Tennessee Williams could turn on music—Bach, Vivaldi, or whatever—and still write. I couldn't do that in a million years.

Q: Does your work go through a lot of drafts?
A: I'm a compulsive rewriter. I usually do a half-dozen drafts. When I've shot a film and I'm working on it in the editing room, then I work the other way. I don't do a rough first cut of the film. I work very, very slowly and very meticulously so that the first cut is quite close to the film that comes out. I could almost show my first cut to an audience. When I used to edit with Ralph Rosenblum, his impulse always was to get a first draft of a film up on the screen and then fine-tune it from that point. But I could never do that.

Q: Rosenblum has remarked that you're extremely disciplined about your work, that you'll almost punish yourself by cutting good material if it doesn't contribute to the characterizations and the story line.
A: It's not so punishing; it's really a matter of survival. You look at that stuff with an audience and no matter how superbly you've conceived and executed the material, it may not work. They just sit dutifully through it and wait for the film to go on. Taking material like that out is a mercy killing.

Q: You test your films with an audience very carefully?
A: Certainly with comedy, your relationship with your audience is very close, very vivid. You can tell when you're dying and so you take things out.

Q: Do you find that your essays are harder to do than your films?
A: No, much easier. I don't have to face the sort of pressure that Benchley did or Russell Baker or other journalists who write on a regular basis and have to be funny all the time. If I don't have a funny idea for a magazine article, I just don't write anything.

But with a film, it's not really written beforehand. It's written during the filming. Let's say I decide I want to do a scene in a pet shop. All I need is a note that, say, Diane Keaton and I meet in a pet shop. I don't need the dialogue at that point. Then we find the pet shop and decide how we're going to shoot it. Then the whole scene is written there. Not just improvised but actually written there. The tone and atmosphere is determined, the amount of noise—everything. By contrast, the text of a play bears a very direct relationship to what you see on the stage. If you look at a film script and the movie itself, the movie is often nothing like the script. If you gave this pet shop scene to me and to Bergman and Fellini, it would come out totally different. It would be like three different movies. So writing for film is not exactly writing. You're just sort of making notes and you're constantly anxious about what it's actually going to be like and where is the thing going to be shot. You can't actually write it until you know about the location and what actress is going to play in it and so forth.

Q: What about the remarkable wit in your films? You don't just improvise that. Do the funny lines come to you at the typewriter or on the set?
A: Both. Sometimes I'll get a good run on dialogue when I'm writing, and other times not. Sometimes I'll just think of one joke and I'll try and set it up in the film. For example, I did a scene in *Annie Hall* with Paul Simon. We improvised and I just said to Paul: Try to get to the word "mellow" eventually because I have a joke I want to tell.

Q: Do you get different creative rewards from your different artistic endeavors—writing essays, making movies, playing the clarinet?
A: I'm glad I don't have to try and make a living playing the clarinet. I'd starve to death. As for the personal satisfactions that you mention, I think that when you're writing literary things the fun has to be in the writing of them because there's very little feedback on them. I'm never around when anyone reads them after all. But with a play or a movie you can actually hear the audience laughing. It's a more vivid response. You're constantly meeting people who've seen it. It's a lot less fun to make a movie than to write a story, because the undertaking is too fraught with peril and anxiety and hard work.

Q: And at the end of a day's shooting you can have three minutes of film.
A: Three minutes is a lot for a day's work. You accumulate the movie in little smears, little bits and pieces, which you store in canisters in your office. Say, I started shooting in April; now it's Christmas and I still haven't seen anything. I have no idea whether the thing is coherent or not. It's just a dot here, a dot there—not in any order. The first rush of depression comes when you put your first cut together and you realize how different the picture is from what you conceived. It's such a shock. There are all sorts of complex things that you just can't know until you step back from the camera. My own solution to that has always been to budget another three or four weeks of shooting to go back and fix things.

Q: Have your working habits changed since your early films?
A: Not too much. The only thing is that as you learn more, you become more and more obsessive. I just finished a film that's meticulously wrought, with months of pre-production, and I actually turned the cameras for thirty-one weeks; that's a long time. I work much, much harder at filmmaking today. I'm much more involved with sets, costumes, photography, all aspects of the picture.

Q: You're not really a "movie brat."
A: Not at all. To this day, I can't thread a Movieola or splice two pieces of film together. I have no interest in movies from that point of view. But regardless of the limited technical background you start with, you quickly begin to make distinctions between good and bad lighting, good photography and bad, sophisticated and unsophisticated editing. For instance, if I were filming a conversation with you and when I cut to you, maybe you're a bit on the blue side; then next time we see you you're a little bit on the yellow side. That wouldn't bother me in the old days as long as I got a laugh. Today we would make sure that you're lit perfectly. If what we had wasn't just right, we'd call back the actors and actresses, from Europe, if necessary, and reshoot.

Q: Do you show your work to anybody before it's finished?
A: Never prose. No one's ever seen any of those pieces before I sent them out. Films, yes. I always show a draft to people, usually supportive, loved ones, so that even if it's a disaster they won't go out in the street and tell anyone about it. I'm referring to close friends like Diane Keaton. They give me constructive criticism. Then I show it to an audience of maybe a hundred people. The best thing to do is just listen in the back. You assess people's reactions very well that way. They're going to laugh or be fidgety or attentive, and you can tell. You can sense when the thing is dying.

Q: How autobiographical are your films?
A: My films are only autobiographical in the large, overall sense. The details are invented, regardless of whether you're talking about *Annie Hall*, *Interiors*, or *Manhattan*. For example, I never had a friend who was married and having an affair, then broke it off, and finally went back to the mistress when I was dating her. I never had an affair with a sixteen-year-old girl. My father didn't work in bumper cars in Coney Island. I didn't grow up in Coney Island but in Flatbush. I didn't meet Diane Keaton that way and she didn't leave and go with a rock singer.
I think people will regard *Stardust Memories* as very autobiographical because it's about a filmmaker/comedian who's reached a point in his life where he just doesn't find anything amusing anymore and so he's overcome with depression. This is not me, but it will be perceived as me.

Q: Do you worry about the sources of your inspiration drying up?
A: Not at all. Quite the opposite in fact. I worry about not having enough time to develop the ideas that I have. I wish I could press a button and have a film come out because I have ideas for six or seven movies in the future. I just can't do them fast enough. What's difficult is when you're ready to make the film, you've got to choose one of those ideas and sustain your interest in it for a year. It's a funny thing, but as soon as you've committed yourself to one of the ideas, the others seem better. Just before Marshall Brickman and I wrote *Annie Hall*, we had decided to do a comedy set in Victorian England. We spent two months on it, structuring it to our satisfaction, not writing but working out the shape. We got it all structured, we had our last meeting, and I was going to start writing it the next day. But something came over me, some compulsion that told me we should do a story set in New York, a contemporary story. And we switched, the very day I was supposed to have started the other script.

Q: Do you feel you achieved the balance of comedy and drama you were after in *Annie Hall* and *Manhattan*?
A: Frankly no. I was disappointed in both pictures because neither turned out the way I wanted it to. It's very hard really because when you're trying to do that kind of work you fall into a trap—Chaplin fell into it certainly. Neil Simon and I were talking once and we agreed that we both succumbed to the same pitfall with our first plays—his *Come Blow Your Horn* and my *Don't Drink the Water*. The pitfall is the temptation to do comedy, then stop and do something serious, then back to the humor, then some more drama. The trick is to truly integrate the comedy and the drama, to intertwine them. I've decided that the only really effective way to mix the two modes is to do drama and interpolate comedy into it.

Q: A lot of people think you've been quite successful, artistically speaking, in your last few films.
A: That's because they don't know what I really had in mind. Also, a guy pays his $5 to get into a movie, and in general most American films just insult his intelligence completely. If he sees anything that's at all thoughtful or sensitive, he's very grateful.

Q: You're one of the few filmmakers in this country who get any sort of authentic sensibility into their work.
A: Well, I think I'm one of the few who are trying. And I have a big struggle because the quality of my stuff is not as high as I want it to be. And to be honest with you, the number of people who come to see my films isn't that great either. I have an audience, a public, but it's just not as large as you might imagine. I'm

not saying that my movies don't make money—even *Interiors* showed a slight profit—but I've never had a real blockbuster. I've never had a film that did anything near the business that Mel Brooks's movies do or *Airplane!* or *Animal House*. *Annie Hall* made less money than any other Academy Award–winning film.

Q: How do you react to criticism?
A: I read most of the reviews of my work with great interest. I'm very grateful to the media because I've almost always gotten a good press and it's helped my career enormously. I can't really say I learn from notices in any artistic sense because they don't affect my work. They do, however, affect the size of the audience that goes to see my work, so I look at them with the hope they'll be mostly favorable.

Q: There have been at least two major attacks on your work, one by John Simon in the *New York Times* and the other by Joan Didion in the *New York Review of Books*. How do you respond to critical broadsides like these two?
A: When a critic really doesn't like my work, I feel I've let him or her down. That's my honest feeling. I believe that the burden of entertaining people is on me, and whether it's a professional critic or a guy off the street who comes into the theater, I want him to like my movies. Sometimes a cab driver will tell me he didn't like my most recent movie, and I have the same disappointment.

Q: The commonest criticism is that sometimes you're pretentious.
A: I think that's correct in that I do have pretensions, I do want to create serious drama, and if I fail at that I would indeed seem pretentious. But I believe I have to try at all times to reach the highest possible level that I can, whether I'm doing comedy or drama.

Q: *Interiors* was the only one of your films that was generally not well received. Do you feel that the film was a mistake?
A: I don't think it was a mistake to make it. I think it was very important that I make it, that I face that kind of creative challenge. Still, I have to agree with the critics that the movie was a failure. I set myself an enormous task and I was just not up to it, at least not at that time. If I made the film again now, I'd do a lot of things differently and I feel it would be a better movie.

Q: Many people say they have noticed the influence of Bergman on *Interiors*. Were you consciously attempting to model your film on his work?
A: I was consciously trying to avoid it. But it was not easy—because he's my favorite filmmaker and obviously the subject matter lends itself to a Bergmanesque

treatment. I wanted to make a serious drama about human relationships with no jokes at all, no comedy. I picked the hardest sort of movie to do.

Q: Your most recent films concentrate on the neuroses of a small, affluent, well-educated class of people in Manhattan. Do you feel this work suffers at all from parochialism?
A: On the contrary, I think it's quite universal. It must be because people identify with my characters and situations throughout the world. My last three movies have made more money in Europe than in the United States. If I were parochial, I don't see how people in Rio, Buenos Aires, and Vienna could respond to my films, but they do. You could make the same charge about, say, Tennessee Williams: He only writes about sick people in the South. Or you could attack Chekhov because his characters are all indolent do-nothings, procrastinating and complaining.

Q: Do you see yourself as a distinctly Jewish filmmaker?
A: Not really. I draw my ideas from everything I've done and everything that interests me. It's only one element. It seems to me that certain subjects, like Jewishness, are unusually vivid; they have a disproportionate resonance. You can have six hundred jokes in your film and if two of the gags are Jewish, the picture will be perceived as a Jewish comedy. This is a false perception, I think.

Q: Do you have any long-range creative goals?
A: You mean like playing *Hamlet* someday? I don't think I ever want to do that. My goals are general rather than specific. I want to continue to grow and develop as a filmmaker and keep my hand in where theater is concerned as well. As a serious artist, I feel that I have a long way to go, but I thrive on creative challenges. I like to stretch myself. I want to make better movies than I have, with the hope that someday I might create a film that I'm totally satisfied with myself.

Allen Goes Back to the Woody of Yesteryears

Charles Champlin / 1981

From the *Philadelphia Inquirer*, February 15, 1981. Copyright © 1981 *Los Angeles Times*. Reprinted with permission of the *Los Angeles Times*.

Woody Allen's next film will be a broad comedy in the style of his first works.

Like a delayed punch line, these tidings seem to pay off the advice some of his fans were laying on him within *Stardust Memories* and seem as well to confirm the message he appeared to be giving himself (in the chipmunk voices of some extraterrestrial visitors) at the end of that movie.

But the return to early Allen is not a reaction to the rather sharp reaction to *Stardust Memories*.

"We know there was an enormous chance that that would happen," Allen said the other afternoon in his apartment on upper Fifth Avenue, "but I still wanted to make that particular film. But I also remember driving by shopping malls with theaters, on the way to locations when we were shooting *Stardust*, and saying to myself, 'Lines of people waiting to get in to see this picture on a Saturday night? Gee, I dunno.'"

Allen concedes that he was surprised, even so, that anyone would feel personally affronted by the film. "But from the time of *Annie Hall*, people regard anything I do as autobiographical, so I guess they look at *Stardust Memories* and say, 'Is that what you think of us?' I can't always sit with people and tell them to think of it as a fictional film about a filmmaker going through a crisis in his life. It's hard for them to dissociate him from me."

It was easier, Allen says, when he was less a celebrity. We also, he says, "live in a culture in which gossip has grown to huge proportions, so that any portion of a film that can be construed as gossip, even if it's all made up, is fascinating. It resonates with part of the audience."

(Gossip surrounds Allen's present friendship with Mia Farrow. They have never discussed nor contemplated it, he insists, but the press had had it impending, and a few days ago a New York newspaper printed, as fact, that they had eloped to Connecticut. "All made up, by people sitting around in rooms," Allen says.)

Allen stresses that nothing in *Stardust Memories* ever actually happened. "I never had a girlfriend who was in an institution. I was never about to marry a French woman with children. I never had any trouble with studio executives, and my driver was never arrested for mail fraud."

Still, the customers can be forgiven a certain amount of trouble making the dissociation, partly because Allen is always playing the character and partly because it is quite clear that what we have here is a spiritual autobiography even if it is not a factual one.

"You have to use the trappings of the things you know," Allen says. "It's hard for me to do a movie about a nuclear physicist who lives in Akron. It's more useful to deal with what I've observed. Writers like Faulkner and Hemingway were always throwing in things they knew about; yet they're not regarded as the guys in their stories necessarily."

Stardust Memories is for Allen the problem of a man who on the basis of his achievements should be both fulfilled and accepted and who finds himself spiritually bankrupt.

"It's about a malaise," Allen says, "the malaise of a man with no spiritual center, no spiritual connection. Nothing works. The love of his life is mentally unstable. The whole picture occurs subjectively through the mind of a character who is on the verge of a breakdown, who's harassed and in doubt and who has a fainting fit at the end from his imaginings about all these dark things. He has a terrifying sense of his own mortality. He's accomplished things; yet they still don't mean anything to him."

Allen does not deny that he is dealing with a particular kind of person and particular brand of trouble. "My interest isn't in losers or the downtrodden. It's the problem of spiritual emptiness.

"Some people can't understand a man with money having problems. I'm not saying that anything is as bad as not having food to eat. That's the worst thing there is. What people won't accept is how bad spiritual emptiness can be.

"I play clarinet on Monday night at Michael's Pub. I've been doing it for eight years. I don't get paid a dime, never have. That would change everything. But people ask me, 'How come you keep playing there? You don't need the money anymore.' They can't seem to understand doing something not for money."

To a degree, the harassment of Allen's filmmaker-hero derives from his success and his fame, but Allen regards the matter of fame as such as "secondary, subsidiary, and obvious." What is not quite so subsidiary is the ambivalent relationship between the public and the artist.

"You've got a guy in an early scene who comes up to the filmmaker and says,

'You're my favorite comedian' and then in a later scene shoots him. My God, I thought I was doing that symbolically, metaphorically, and then it was borne out tragically with John Lennon. It was just like Lennon. Even before Lennon, I don't think people wanted to hear that kind of thing. But it's true that the artist has this ambivalent relationship with an audience. He's dependent, but it also vitiates his privacy."

Allen is now working on the script of the new comedy, scheduled to go into production in June, with Gordon Willis once again his cinematographer.

Allen has also written a new play for a nine-week run at the Vivian Beaumont Theater of Lincoln Center. Rumors—all of them inaccurate, he says—have clustered about the play, *The Floating Light Bulb*. It will be directed by Ulu Grosbard, has six characters and one set. Allen will not appear in the play, which he describes, not especially helpfully, as a comedy-drama. He and Grosbard are consulting on the casting now. The play will open at the end of April.

Allen grew up consuming (ravenously) all kinds of movies, the American entertainments—Westerns, musicals, gangster films—and the stylish European introspections. He could have fun with the European style, as he did in *Everything You Always Wanted to Know about Sex* and in the brilliant train sequence that opens *Stardust Memories*.

But it is clear that his deepest affinities as a filmmaker are with the Europeans and their explorations of the dark side, reflected in the bittersweet feeling of passage and loss in *Annie Hall*, the still more somber mix of celebration and isolation in *Manhattan*, the almost unrelieved intensity of *Interiors*, and then the self-abrading portrait of a man at the edge in *Stardust Memories*. By no coincidence, Allen's films have grown successively more popular in foreign markets. *Bananas* was a success in France, though not elsewhere abroad. *Annie Hall* was, he says, the breakthrough—very successful abroad. *Interiors* was a success in Europe, and *Manhattan* did better in Europe than in the United States. *Stardust Memories* is doing nicely in Europe, and he has also acquired a following in South America.

"I do better now in Milan than in Moline," Allen says. "It's crucial for me, because I don't spend much on my films, but they don't gross like *Stir Crazy*, either. You can't keep people away from *Stir Crazy*. I don't have that problem. As a matter of fact, there was a news story that said *Stardust Memories* had gone over budget and cost $20 million. May I tell you that *Annie Hall*, *Manhattan*, *Interiors*, and *Stardust Memories* together didn't cost $20 million?"

When Ingmar Bergman was in New York a couple of years ago, he and Allen had dinner at Bergman's request. Allen found him not at all mysterious nor intimidating but "a charming, middle-class work-ethic filmmaker."

"We commiserated about the same trivial frustrations, like the distributors who call you after one showing and tell you it did $900, which was $200 more than

Annie Hall in the same situation and therefore you're going to gross $19 million domestic. They're invariably euphoric, followed by invariable disappointment; then they get mad at us."

The two filmmakers share, among other things, an ability to evoke superb and sympathetic performances from women. Allen concedes that he is quite proud of his work with Diane Keaton in *Annie Hall* and with Geraldine Page and Maureen Stapleton in *Interiors*.

Two of the roles in *Stardust Memories* were written for American actresses, but Allen confesses he could not find them and chose Marie-Christine Barrault and Charlotte Rampling for the qualities he sought. "I wanted a woman who was earthy and maternal, womanly without being matronly. That was Marie-Christine. Charlotte, of course, has a quality, a charisma, that's unique. She reeks from neurosis. She also has a lovely vulnerability—in real life, too."

In *Stardust Memories*, Allen wryly quoted many of the criticisms of his films, including the cry of self-indulgence.

"Self-indulgence," he says, "that's one of those catchphrases you hear a lot. It's because you're dealing in popular culture, and some catchphrases come easily. I thought I had a little fun with that in the Marshall McLuhan scene in *Annie Hall*. But you can call Shakespeare self-indulgent. You can call anyone self-indulgent. I had it with *Interiors*, too. People said you can't have drama without comedy. What about *Persona*? "They said it was just some characters sitting around talking all the time. I say, 'What's Chekhov?' They say, 'Chekhov's a genius and you're not,' and I certainly buy that. But that's not the point.

"I never quarrel with anyone who doesn't like a film of mine. Where I run into trouble is when someone tries to tell you what's wrong with it. They should just not like it. It's hard to explain why something is wrong. Just say you don't like it, and leave it at that."

Some of those who didn't, overall, like *Stardust Memories* were nevertheless touched by a quiet scene, the key scene I suspect of the film, in which Allen's voiceover remembers a particular Sunday when he and the woman he loved had been out for a stroll and a meal and were back at their apartment, she sprawled on the floor, reading the paper, he simply looking at her in gratitude and pleasure, while Louis Armstrong's "Stardust" filled the room.

"Oh, yeah," Allen said, "That was all the characters had to hold on to. Those moments, those memories. I've known those moments, sitting here"—he gestured at the living room and at Central Park below, bright and vivid in the winter sun—"with a girlfriend, and some wine, and with Louie, or Mozart, on the hi-fi. It's perfect.

"Oh, yeah, it's perfect. And then the doorbell rings, and it's a guy with a subpoena."

Woody Allen, Inside and Out

Gary Arnold / 1982

From the *Washington Post*, July 16, 1982. © 1982, Washington Post Company. All rights reserved. Used by permission and protected by the Copyright Laws of the United States. The printing, copying, redistribution, or retransmission of this Content without express written permission is prohibited.

Looking ruddily fit at forty-six and clad in comfortably rumpled tan slacks and jacket, Woody Allen arrived straight from a dental appointment ("Everything's fine; just my regular oral prophylaxis"). He offered a pressureless handshake, gallantly obliged a photographer by posing outside his business manager's office, eleven stories up, on a tiny, crumbling terrace ("Portrait of a coward—I'll have bad dreams about this tonight") and launched into an extended discussion of his new picture, his previous work, his lifestyle, his artistic expectations, and his attitudes toward peculiar nuisances like the press and the Academy Awards.

Breaking press silence for the opening of his new movie, *A Midsummer Night's Sex Comedy*, Allen had agreed to conduct the interview in advance of today's national release. The site was a bleakly functional little sitting room, adapted to double as a videocassette screening room on West 57th Street in Manhattan.

A boudoir farce about three fickle, turn-of-the-century couples, *A Midsummer Night's Sex Comedy* depicts a weekend of infatuation and flirtation at the country residence of an amorous, whimsical inventor, played by Allen, and his shy, suspicious wife, played by Mary Steenburgen. Their houseguests who join them in games of romantic hide-and-seek are Jose Ferrer and Mia Farrow and Tony Roberts and Julie Hagerty. *Sex Comedy* is the tenth feature Allen has directed in a directing career that began thirteen years ago with *Take the Money and Run*. It also represents the first installment of a new three-picture contract with Orion, the distribution company formed by Allen's original executive mentors at United Artists, Arthur Krim and Eric Pleskow. Allen has completed the second film of the deal, a comedy costarring Mia Farrow scheduled for release at Christmas. He begins shooting the third, a comedy intended for release next summer, within a month.

Q: Exactly where are we situated in your new movie?
A: We're situated in 1906 in upstate New York, actually at Sleepy Hollow. That's pretty much where the thing would have been. That would have been a feasible automobile drive out of the city with cars going at low speeds.

Q: When did the idea of doing a stylized period comedy pop into your head?
A: Well, I had written another comedy—the script for the movie that's coming out at Christmas-time—and thought of doing a serious film as a companion piece. I thought I wanted to do a film about poignant relationships, a film about a guy who missed an opportunity and was haunted by the thought and a girl who was about to throw in her lot with a much older man, not really the right one for her. The genesis was not a comedy but a kind of serious Chekhovian story, in the style of *Interiors* almost. That serious a thing. Then I started to think, God, it sort of cries out for a comic treatment—a group of people at a summer house on a weekend and the silvery moon in concert with the animals and flowers. Why not take a comic approach to it? Let the seriousness be a subtext. So I started to write it, and it worked very rapidly for me. I started to take delight in it. You know, I hate the country, but I began wanting to create the country, not as I experience it but as I would like to.

Q: A lyrical country.
A: Yeah. Where you could tiptoe out of your bed at night and run down to the brook and there would be a trysting spot. If all went well, if you got back with your wife, or if you met a girl you loved, you might see some intimations of immortality. You might see some forest creatures or spirits or something. The more I did that, the more I got away from the serious idea and kept making it a comic piece.

Then I had two scripts on my hands. I had the original, black-and-white, surrealistic comedy and this, the pastoral romantic thing that needed soft, warm colors. I thought, I'll wait a year to film this. Then I thought, no, why don't I film them together, because that way I could take advantage of the nice weather. In New York I can't film in the cold months. So I started to structure them and film them together. They're completely unrelated stories. The other one takes place in the 1920s in New York.

Q: Are the casts identical?
A: No. Mia and I carry over, but no one else. The production team was exactly the same, of course. So I shot them together, and, interestingly, it's economically feasible to do that. There was some slight saving by doing them together. Sometimes, you know, it takes all summer to get that maximum summer day look. We

shot fourteen weeks of summer to get a usable weekend. If you want two women in a swing musing about getting older, for example, and the sunlight dropping, you've got to shoot the scene between 4:00 and 4:45, when the sun figures to be casting just the right illumination. In order to take maximum advantage of our scheduling, not just sit and wait all the time for the sun to be in the right place at the right time of day, we could shoot other things for the black-and-white movie.

Q: You've chosen Mendelssohn's Wedding March as the main title theme for *A Midsummer Night's Sex Comedy*. Should this be taken as confirmation of the rumor that you're getting married?
A: No, no.

Q: That's just a bum rumor?
A: It's just a pure fiction that the press made up.

Q: Wishful thinking?
A: I don't know. The oddest things are made up about me in the press. I mean, some things are grounded in truth but other things are just made up out of left field like that.

Q: For example?
A: One thing was that I purchased a home on the beach, which is not true; that Mia Farrow and I were moving to Connecticut—this is, of course, not true. That we got married, then that we were getting married. There was an item about the movie in Liz Smith's column . . . that I was feuding with Orion when in fact I had just gone to lunch with Orion and we were talking about a new deal. I like them very much. It's been a good arrangement for me, as close as you could get to family. I don't ever have a problem with them. They've proved out over the years, been very supportive, very nice.

Q: As I recall, you originally worked within a budget of about $2 million to $4 million.
A: Right.

Q: And inflation increased that range to, where? Maybe $5 million or $6 million by the mid-seventies?
A: The late seventies. Now it's like $7 million. If I did *Annie Hall* today, frame for frame, without any changes at all, my production expenses would be at least double.

Q: While your working conditions have remained essentially the same?
A: Exactly the same.

Q: What about *Stardust Memories*? Remembering your fiscal conservatism, I was shocked by stories that had it costing in the area of $20 million to $25 million. Were those also fabrications?
A: Let me tell you: *Annie Hall* and *Manhattan* and *Interiors* and *Stardust Memories* put together cost less than $20 million. So that was, again, just a total lie.

Q: Hasn't a contradictory perception of you been spreading in recent years? At one time you were depicted as the most celebrated recluse in New York.
A: Uh-huh.

Q: Then we were led to believe that you were really a sneaky gregarious sort, always out on the town. . . .
A: No, *that* I don't know—that image I don't know. What I still read is that I'm at Elaine's every night, but that's perfect reclusivity. That's the one restaurant in town where you can eat and people are not allowed to ask for autographs and photographers are not allowed into the place. That's the fun of eating at Elaine's. I'm only surrounded by the same sixty or seventy people that seem to eat there every night. At a different restaurant, just an arbitrarily picked restaurant, people come up for autographs, the management calls the newspapers and the *Post* and says he's down here, come and get a picture of him. But *never* at Elaine's. I don't go anywhere. I'm not as reclusive as I'm made out to be, but certainly not gregarious. I've never had that problem.

I mean, I'm working most of the time. On the average day I get up and write or film or something. I come back home at night, get Mia, go up to Elaine's, have a bite to eat, and go to sleep early. I'm usually asleep by 11:00 or 11:30 every night. I see the same people I always have. I just came back from my dentist, who's been my dentist for thirty-one years. I see Marshall Brickman. I see my friend [producer] Jean Doumanian. I see Mia, Diane Keaton, Tony Roberts sometimes, Michael Murphy sometimes, but that's about it. That may be the only group of people I really see with any regularity. I did two pictures simultaneously. I'm about to shoot another picture. I spend my weekends writing. I enjoy it; it's not out of any frenetic drive. I like to keep working, I look forward to it. If you hear the press, you'd think that I slink around town with my hat jammed down over my eyes. I mean, sure, I wear my hat because I'm recognized by less people with a hat on, but many people will wear dark glasses for that reason. I just don't wear them. Things have not changed a great deal for me since I saw you last.

Q: Speaking of that occasion, which was right before the release of *Annie Hall*, did you ever collect your Academy Awards?
A: No, no.

Q: They're still someplace out in Hollywood?
A: Someplace, but I don't have them.

Q: Shouldn't they be sent to you? Or do you inquire about such things?
A: I don't have the vaguest idea. If you were at my house, you would see I'm not a memorabilia person. I don't collect clips and photographs and programs and that kind of stuff. It doesn't mean very much to me.

Q: I remember five years ago we got talking about the Oscars, and discussed how rarely straight comedy received proper recognition by the Academy. You said emphatically that you'd never be nominated.
A: I didn't think I would be.

Q: Famous last words. That was your year.
A: It was a total surprise to me. I never thought I would be nominated. I'm not saying anything negative. The award was fine—it made more money for the picture after the Academy Award came out. The picture suddenly did better financially than it did originally but the whole thing to me is . . . I didn't even watch it. I went to Michael's Pub, where I play on Monday nights.

Q: And if the awards had been on a Tuesday night?
A: If it had been a Tuesday night, I probably wouldn't have watched it anyhow. I didn't want to see Diane and Marshall and those people I knew sitting in the audience like this . . . [*he hunches down into the sofa, suggesting maybe cringing anticipation*] but I never got a chance to watch it. I went to Michael's, I played, had a very nice time.

Q: What about Michael's? They didn't have a television set?
A: No, no, they didn't.

Q: Nobody was really paying attention?
A: Uh, yes, there were a couple of newspaper photographers outside, but I go out the back way, so they didn't get me. I was there and I played jazz and went home at twelve o'clock. I had my milk and chocolate chip cookies, as is my custom after Michael's. Then I took the phone off the hook in my bedroom and went to sleep

and had no idea what happened. The next morning I got up, put the phone back on the hook, went downstairs (I live in a duplex), got my *New York Times*, made my breakfast, and when I opened the *Times*, I noticed on the bottom of the front page, "*Annie Hall* sweeps Oscars" or wins four Oscars or something. I thought, great, that's so nice.

Q: So you've got two statuettes gathering dust on a shelf somewhere in Hollywood?
A: I suppose so. And other awards are gathering dust too in other parts of the world. *Manhattan* won many foreign awards—a French Oscar, an English Oscar, a Spanish Oscar, South American awards. I don't know what happens to those things; I think the studio probably picks them up and gives them to the rep from Honduras, and he ends up with all the awards on his mantelpiece.

Q: Your former editor, Ralph Rosenblum, described your association in great detail in his book, *When the Shooting Stops*. Among other things he pointed out that you began shooting more routines, more sketches than you'd actually have screen time for, after *Take the Money and Run*, in order to protect yourself in the editing room with a wealth of material.
A: Right. I could do that up to *Annie Hall*. I could take a scene out of *Annie Hall* from the front and put it in the back and it would still be a coherent picture, because the time frames were so jumbled. Certainly pictures like *Love and Death* and *Bananas*, you could play around. But in a more tightly structured, dramatic comedy, like *Manhattan* or *A Midsummer Night's Sex Comedy*, you can't do that. There's no point in accumulating that kind of material because you can't use it.

Q: As a method of working, is one way more fun, more satisfying, than the other?
A: No. What happens is it goes in cycles of personal taste. It was fun this summer to do a tightly structured picture and a pastoral picture. Now, it would be fun for me to do something else—perhaps just a joke comedy from start to finish, or a very serious picture. It's important for me personally to mix up the stuff. I've been lucky because my films have consistently made a profit, almost all of them have made a profit. Never a huge profit, but nobody gets hurt. And therefore I get a lot of freedom.

Q: How do you assess your filmmaking career after fourteen years now? Has it been satisfying? Do you think you've achieved as much as you could have under the circumstances?
A: I think I'm working to the best of my ability. I'm not dogging it. I wish I was able to do better, and I hope that as the years go by, I will continue to grow and do

better films. But I've never done anything cynically, something calculated because it was the path of least resistance.

Q: What are your perceptions of the mistakes made on *Interiors*?
A: I should have brought Pearl, Maureen Stapleton's character, in earlier. I thought the audience would be entertained before the nub of the conflict emerged. I thought that it was entertaining enough before Pearl entered, but it wasn't. It should have been. I should have started it with Pearl coming in right away and the whole thing would have flowered right from the start. And, I should not have been quite as overtly didactic as I was. It was just from lack of experience and lack of skill, that's all. I think if I did a drama, a serious drama, the next time that I could correct some of those mistakes. I could start the conflict earlier and I could try and get my messages not so much in the dialogue as in the behavior of the people.

Q: Where did *Stardust Memories* go wrong?
A: Here's what I must say in defense of that film: I feel it was a misunderstood film. Now again, it may have been my problem that I just didn't have the skill to make it clearly understood. A certain amount of people understood it, so I always felt down deep that I had made it clear at least to some people. But I'll admit a lot of people saw that film and came away thinking, well, this is a film where Woody Allen is saying I hate my fans; they're dumb and they're grasping and they're gross-looking. Now, of course, there's nothing further from the truth. I don't feel that way. I don't *have* that many fans, and they're *not* grasping. What I wanted to do there was make a film about a totally fictional character—and I'll explain that in a second—a guy who had all the outer trappings of success—a penthouse, a limousine, a chauffeur, fame, an entourage, all of that—and yet, he was having a breakdown, he was completely unhealthy.

None of these things have happened to me, incidentally, but what happened was that people thought the character was me. Not only did those things not happen to me, I do not have those problems. I play a character who's a filmmaker because I'm familiar with the outer trappings of a profession like that. I can write about them. I'm not going to make myself a nuclear physicist who's having a nervous breakdown, because I just don't know what he'd do in the course of a typical day. So many people who saw the film felt that this Sandy Bates guy is Woody Allen and he hates all of us. And who *is* this guy to have a penthouse and a limousine and this contemptuous attitude? But I wasn't having a contemptuous attitude. I was having an attitude where I was taking the audience very seriously. I think they're at least as smart as I am, if not smarter. I didn't want to give them another formula picture.

Q: So separating the identities is an acute problem in your case?
A: Interestingly enough, this is a problem that the American public has had—not just the American public but the public in general—with their movie actors since the beginning of time. They think John Wayne or Humphrey Bogart is a kind of hard-hitting tough guy. If Cary Grant was ever at a loss, if they saw him act clumsily . . . Well, the same thing occurs in some distorted way with me. *They* think I am the guy I portray, and *I'm* playing a character. For some reason people felt betrayed by me in that film. They put their faith in me, they thought they knew me from all those other films, and suddenly I turned on them. But I didn't turn on them. I was coming off a very good experience with *Manhattan*. I had no bad feelings. My life was not threatened.

Q: Are you still in analysis?
A: Yes.

Q: What did you make of the psychiatric testimony in the Hinckley case?
A: Well, you've got to have insanity as a defense. I think that's got to be a defense, but the whole legal system in America is so screwed up. The fine points of law in the United States are so ridiculous. They're like laughable from an Italian movie. They'd make a good Italian comedy, you know. Obviously, this was not the correct outcome of that trial. It shouldn't have come out like that. Nor should he have been treated in any way except as a sick man.

Q: Did you bring up the topic with your analyst?
A: No. I've learned not to do that generally, because my analyst won't answer me.

Interview with Woody Allen

Robert Benayoun / 1984

From *Positif*, no. 279 (May 1984): 23–25. Recorded in New York, January 24, 1984, at the Filmways Studios. Reprinted by permission. Translated by Kathie Coblentz.

Q: *Broadway Danny Rose* has just opened, and already you're shooting your next film, *The Purple Rose of Cairo*. I was even tempted to give this tape the title *Broadway Danny Rose of Cairo*. Is there a connection between the two?
A: None. It's simply a coincidence between two films, one of which, *Broadway Danny Rose*, was more or less improvised on an impulse, while the other one had been contemplated for a long time.

Q: Why this preoccupation with roses? Danny Rose, in the film you've just finished, sends a white rose every day to his muse Tina Vitale (played by Mia Farrow).[1] And you've had a very close collaborator, your best friend for a long time, whose name was Mickey Rose.
A: I saw him again a few days ago—he lives in New York. He was my collaborator on *Bananas* and *Take the Money and Run*. Journalists are claiming that after a blue period, I've entered a rose period. I don't know, I must have a recurrent image of roses somewhere.

Q: The title *The Purple Rose of Cairo* suggests some exotic false memory like the one you used to get when you heard the word *Casablanca*.
A: My story doesn't have anything exotic about it, it's set during the Depression, and my heroes are out-of-work actors who go to the movies to kill time and go several times in a row to see an imaginary movie called *The Purple Rose of Cairo*.

Q: You've stated that you wanted to stop making Jewish comedies for a time. Why?
A: That was a statement I made under the influence of fatigue. I had just been working on *A Midsummer Night's Sex Comedy*, *Zelig*, *Broadway Danny Rose*, and *The Purple Rose of Cairo* back to back and I thought I could take a breather. A few weeks

later, I had recovered all my energy, and right now I certainly don't run any risk of taking a breather for a long time. Besides, I've never thought of a single one of my films as a "Jewish comedy." It's other people who generally pin this label on me. It's just that my comedies always speak of what I know best.

Q: *Zelig* was a harmonious fusion between the visual and the verbal; doesn't *Broadway Danny Rose* mark a return toward the verbal? For you, language has always been both a help and a handicap. It's what made you, and some people think it limits you. Isn't *Broadway Danny Rose*, which was shot in a very free style and also includes some very visual sequences, a way for you to harmonize both those aspects?
A: You know, it's important not to confuse visual with physical. All my films are visual, including *Interiors*, which was meant to have a dramatic content. As soon as there aren't any more physical gags or slapstick, people stop being aware of form in my films, but actually I've always been preoccupied with the visual aspect, even in my most talkative films.

Q: *Broadway Danny Rose* is a hilarious film, even though it contains moments of emotion. Isn't it a way for you to give in to the reproaches of all those false friends who are constantly asking you, notably in the dialogue of *Stardust Memories*, to go back to the "good old Woody Allen comedies," in short to renounce all your ambitions?
A: They will be fatally thrown off balance, because *The Purple Rose of Cairo*, for example, which I'm shooting just now, takes place in a very oppressive, even dramatic context, the great economic crisis of 1929. Still, it contains a good deal of humor. But the script of the following film, which I'm writing now, is entirely serious. In fact, what I enjoy the most is to constantly alternate between comedy and seriousness. I refuse to plan out my career, and more than ever I want to make my films according to my imagination, without listening to the menacing "good advice" or the wishes of anyone and everyone about what the real Woody Allen ought to be.

Q: Obviously you don't have anything in common with Broadway Danny. In *Manhattan*, you frequent Third Avenue or the hills of Central Park rather than Broadway. Danny Rose, even though he was familiar with the Borscht Belt, isn't Alvy Singer. His jokes are rather out of date, and if the customers in the Carnegie Delicatessen admire him, it's because he reminds them of what it was like in the Catskills in the old days.
A: It's true that Broadway has changed a lot since my father brought me there for the first time in '41. I was six or seven years old then, and the ambiance was very

different. You could meet bookies and horseplayers there more easily, it was, so to speak, an ambiance closer to Damon Runyon. Manhattan was more livable than today. I went to the movies in 42nd Street, which is now a shrine to drugs and prostitution. The film is set in a given era, and Danny Rose lives in the era when the Mob already reigns on Broadway.

Q: Since *Stardust Memories*, you seem fascinated by successions of unusual faces, sometimes grotesque ones. You see quite a few of them in *Broadway Danny Rose*. Is it true that you have a regular "Casting Task Force," as some people say, and that you recruit or summon people the way Fellini does, as soon as you find someone with an interesting personality?
A: Yes, I have a casting staff, which I ask for some very precise types of faces, and they spread out all over, handing out casting cards. Some of them have been working with me for almost ten years—I have a team that's virtually stable. On *The Purple Rose of Cairo*, the only one missing is Mel Bourne, my usual art director, who was working on another film, but he sent us over one of his protégés, because I've got a lot of construction—in this film, the scenery plays a major role.

Q: *Broadway Danny Rose* would be described as a small, quickly made film, in comparison to *Zelig*, which took a long time to shoot.
A: *Zelig* cost me two years of strenuous shooting and unceasing technical experimentation. Gordon Willis and I were fumbling around with complicated and rigorous special effects. *Broadway Danny Rose* is a spontaneous film, the way I like them. I didn't have to keep an eye on the sun—we wanted a visual style without artifice. And I worked in the European way, shooting in exteriors and in real interiors. You can't do that in Hollywood, where everything demands lengthy preparation, an unchangeable shooting script and continual retakes. Here, I can film on a moment's inspiration, call up friends on the phone and shoot quickly in familiar places with people who will have left the city the day after. I have my little group of favorite actors, or I'll recruit big stars for bit parts. On *Broadway Danny Rose* I used Milton Berle and Sammy Davis Jr.—I mingled them in with the non-professionals. On *The Purple Rose of Cairo*, I almost had Diane Keaton, and she's someone I'd like to get anyway to act alongside Mia Farrow sometime soon—it will be very funny to have the two of them together, they are so different! But I was able to put together some very different people, like Van Johnson, Milo O'Shea, Jeff Daniels, and Margaux Hemingway, and Danny Aiello who acted in my last play *The Floating Light Bulb*.

Q: On *Broadway Danny Rose*, did you improvise a lot?
A: The whole film, you mean! I like to grab hold of an idea on the fly, and work it

out without delay, like when I was leaving a restaurant with Mia, and she mentioned something she'd like to do. We'd noticed at the neighboring table one of those wig-wearing Latin women, talking a blue streak, loud and insulting, with dark glasses planted on her face, and Mia told me that it would be funny for her to play a role like this, at the opposite pole from the skinny ingenues she's all too often made to play. I took her at her word, writing the role for her at one go and shooting the film right away! Of course, I asked her to put on a few pounds and finally, I rounded her out with a little padding!

Q: In short, you practically never stop? While you were finishing the filming of *The Purple Rose of Cairo*, you finished this new script. With all these films being shot back to back, do you ever still find the time to read, to write for the *New Yorker* or for the stage, to go to the movies?

A: I am going to edit *Purple Rose* for a year and work on my script. I have several theater pieces in my drawer, I'm thinking about my first novel, and three weeks from now I intend to resume my weekly jazz sessions at Michael's Pub. You know, I shoot every day of the week including Saturdays and Sundays, but I only do five hours a day, which leaves me a little time to think, but not enough to see movies. Aside from that, I don't have any problems: my agents take care of absolutely everything. The transfer of power between United Artists and Orion turned out to be in my best interests. My next five films will be made for Orion. I lead exactly the same kind of life, I see the same friends, the same collaborators. All I have to worry about is creating. I consider myself eminently privileged. I work as an independent, without being accountable to anyone. If an idea strikes me as the beginning of an interesting film, I get to work with a small team, without arousing too much curiosity, and if a scene turns out wrong, I can reshoot it without causing a commotion. That's why I love New York, and that's why I'm going to stay there.[2]

Notes

1. Actually it's the character Lou Canova (Nick Apollo Forte) who sends the roses.—Translator's note.

2. Some portions of this interview were published in a different form in *The Films of Woody Allen*, by Robert Benayoun, translated by Alexander Walker. New York: Harmony Books, © 1986.—Translator's note.

Woody on the Town

Joe Klein / 1986

"Woody on the Town" © February 1986 by Joe Klein. This article originally appeared in *Gentlemen's Quarterly* 56, no. 2 (February 1986): 172–75, 242–43. Reprinted by permission of the author.

I asked Woody Allen what he would do if a doctor told him he had to move to Dayton, Ohio, or die.

"Dayton?"

"Akron . . . anyplace out there."

"I think," he said, giggling, "I'd die . . . I mean, you would need a *car*, right?"

"Don't you drive?"

"Oh, sure," he said. "It just doesn't come up very often in New York. I walk out of my building, and everything is there."

And then, a cascade of reasons—none of them very surprising—why he could never leave the city. He would miss the art galleries, the foreign movies, the restaurants. . . . What *was* surprising, as always with Woody Allen, was the intensity of his devotion. "I think," he said, "I probably eat out in restaurants 360 nights a year. No kidding. It's something I really love to do."

"What about the other five nights?"

"Well, you're left with pretty basic things like Thanksgiving and illness. I have a housekeeper who can cook, but I'd rather go out. I don't think I could live beyond a thirty-minute radius of the Russian Tea Room."

When Woody Allen says he could *never* leave the city, he is not only serious but fairly literal as well. The man does not cross bridges lightly. He will leave Manhattan, but never for long and only for a very good reason. In recent years, he has left for the following reasons: to shoot outdoor scenes (some exteriors in *The Purple Rose of Cairo* were shot in the Hudson River town of Piermont), to scout locations for future films and, several times a summer, to visit Mia Farrow for a weekend at her country place in Connecticut. "I like to go over to Paris for three or four days," he said, "but I haven't done that in several years."

Aside from that, he stays home.

"I like to sleep in my own bed," he said. "I know it sounds funny, but I just couldn't see going off to some location like Texas or Montana for weeks on end, living in a hotel room. That's why I make all my films in New York . . . and also, of course, because I love the city."

Woody Allen is fifty now. He looks the same—exactly the same—but *seems* older somehow, a curious presence: someone entirely familiar, yet not very well known. He has spent the past thirty years living on Manhattan Island, which he loves as only someone who spent the first twenty years of his life in Brooklyn can. The Manhattan that he loves and inhabits, though, is a rather remarkable place: prettier, cleaner, more romantic, and less dangerous than the city most people know. He created it in his films, and—while he acknowledges, sadly, that the other Manhattan exists—he somehow seems to have found a way to live in his creation; he is the only permanent resident, although visitors wander through from time to time.

"I know I've romanticized the city," he said. "I constantly run into Europeans whose only sense of New York comes from *Manhattan* and *Annie Hall*. I'd say about 75 percent of the people who see me play at Michael's Pub—which I've been doing for thirteen years now—are Europeans who are enticed to the city by the images in those films. If that's what they're expecting to find, I guess they're disappointed."

Still, Woody Allen's "New York" does exist. It coexists with the real thing, just as Woody Allen's "Woody Allen" (the character he plays in his films) does. In both cases, the lines blur. Woody Allen is often seen around town doing the sorts of things that one might expect Alvy Singer or Sandy Bates—or any of the names he's given himself in films—to do: playing the clarinet at Michael's Pub, eating dinner at Elaine's, watching the Knicks at the Garden, ducking into the Thalia for a revival or a foreign film. His habits, neuroses, and prejudices are as well known as his black-framed glasses, and so is his diffidence.

His notion of celebrity seems to stem—as does his sense of the city—from the 1930s and '40s, a time when stars were glamorous, "seen about town," and duly mentioned in the gossip columns, but not poked or prodded, as they are now, or expected to reveal intimacies. He will not talk about his life. He doesn't talk about his work either, which may well be the same thing. He is, however, more than happy to talk about both New Yorks, his and the less charming one . . . which is *almost* the same as talking about his life and work, since both revolve around the city.

We started talking on the Monday before Labor Day, one of those flannel-aired late-summer days when most everyone with a choice had left town. The city seemed drugged and muffled by the heat, the posher neighborhoods deserted. But Woody Allen was hard at work, as always, in a cool, dark sound studio on Broadway (in the Brill Building, once the home of New York's music publishers—the heart of Tin Pan Alley). He was completing work on his new film, *Hannah and Her Sisters*, in which he shows off the city more lovingly than in any film since *Manhattan*. The next day, without fanfare or vacation, he would start preproduction work on another one, which also would be set in New York.

"The city always surprises me," he said. "It's not nearly the place it used to be—from the twenties to the forties it was sensational, there was no place like it in the world—but I keep finding astonishing places when I walk around, which is something I do constantly. I've got enough locations to last five films."

It was early afternoon. He took a Snickers out of his pocket and asked, "You want some lunch?" Woody Allen first visited the city of his dreams in 1941, a time—there can be no real debate about this—when New York was the most glorious city on the planet. He was six years old. His father took him to Times Square, which was brash and exciting and vaguely naughty (it has since, of course, become a sewer). They visited the Circle Magic Shop on 52nd and Broadway. "It still exists," he said, "but it's been refurbished soullessly." (Recently it was torn down and made into a hotel.)

Brooklyn, despite the Dodgers and the colorful accent, might as well have been Iowa in those days; not much happened there, it was a suburb. Woody Allen grew up in Flatbush, a particularly staid community of attractive streets and fervently middle-class people. "We had one or two movie theaters in the neighborhood," he recalled. "But you'd come up out of the subway on 42nd Street in New York and there would be a whole street of movies, wonderful movies. There was the Laff-movie theater, which played only comedies. I saw Chaplin, Laurel and Hardy, W. C. Fields, and the Marx Brothers there. There was the Globe theater, which played only Westerns—Monte Hale, Lash La Rue, Hopalong Cassidy. Around the corner, on Broadway itself, you had the big theaters like the Paramount, the Capitol, and the Roxy, which had movies and live shows. I saw Duke Ellington *and* a movie at the Paramount for fifty cents. I saw Jackie Gleason there, and Gypsy Rose Lee. . . . I couldn't stay away from Broadway."

He played hooky regularly, he claims. He would pretend he was going to school, duck his books in a bush and get on the subway. The subway cost a nickel and was safe. "What we'd do is go to one of the big theaters in the morning—the performers would play all day, six shows a day—then we'd hang out in the big Automat for a while (it's a Burger King now) and maybe go to a movie on 42nd Street in the afternoon."

There were other attractions. Times Square was filled with skiball parlors, magic stores, tango palaces, and carny-sleaze. There were places like Ripley's Believe It or Not and Hubert's Flea Circus and Museum. "I saw a hermaphrodite at Hubert's," he said. "It lifted its skirt up, and you could see what it had. I never saw the flea circus there: What could fleas do? Go from point A to point B, I suppose."

His fascination with Times Square never faded. It's one of the more important neighborhoods in Woody Allen's New York, the place where agents have their offices and comedians hang out. It reeks of corned beef and cigar smoke.

"I read Damon Runyon when I was a kid, and that really influenced me—Runyon and Cole Porter defined New York for me. I really wanted to be part of that Times Square world, the gamblers and entertainers who'd go out nightclubbing every night, you know, with show girls and trade them around," he laughed. "I was talking to Eve Arden about it, and she said it was pretty safe in those days, too. After a show, she could go out with a girlfriend, have dinner someplace, go to an all-night movie. There was the old Madison Square Garden, and people like the sportswriter Jimmy Cannon, whom I really admire, who actually *lived* on 42nd Street. All that was pretty much gone by the 1950s, when I was old enough to start hanging around."

Broadway Danny Rose was his salute to that scene, a film that would have been more aptly set in the 1940s, "but you can't find any period locations in Times Square anymore," he said. "We looked, and there wasn't a half block that hadn't been ruined, junked up. It's too bad. I would've liked to have been around in those days when all the show-business people got together at restaurants and clubs late, after their shows. . . . The only thing I ever experienced that came close to that was in the late 1960s, when the Knicks were hot and everyone would go to the Garden to watch them play; every game was an event, you'd see everyone you knew, and then we'd all go out to dinner at Frankie and Johnnie's or '21.' That was something really exciting for the city—19,000 people exiting the Garden together, into the night. That's a great feeling."

The Knicks remain a passion. "I'm glad they got [Patrick] Ewing," he said. "I'm sure he'll help the team. But I would have been much happier if they'd gotten [Detroit guard] Isiah Thomas, who's my favorite player. I'd rather have a team with more charisma than a faceless but efficient entity."

Indeed, the Knicks are the only team he'll actually go out and watch, since you have to cross a bridge to get to either of the baseball stadiums in New York. "I've watched a ton of baseball on television this summer, though," he said. "I used to go to games at Ebbets Field when I was a kid. Arky Vaughan once kicked me when I asked him for an autograph. No kidding. I was with a friend, and we asked him, and he just kicked me. You know, 'Get out of here, kid.' Later, I heard he drowned."

Woody Allen may have been the only kid in Brooklyn who didn't root for the Dodgers. He liked the Giants, Manhattan's team. "I rode the subway to the Polo Grounds, where they played. I rode the subway to the Bronx for dates."

"That's pretty far," I said.

"Well, she was a very attractive girl," he said quite seriously.

Woody Allen's New York—the city in his movies—has peculiar geography. It ends at 96th Street, where Harlem begins. It extends south to SoHo, but not as far as Wall Street. It allows, grudgingly, for one outer borough: Brooklyn. In fact, there are only two *crucial* neighborhoods in his New York: Times Square and the quiet, elegant Upper East Side, where he and the characters he plays usually live.

Most of the romantic moments in his films take place on the Upper East Side—near the East River, or on the improbably peaceful, tree-lined streets of eclectic townhouses. "Annie Hall's apartment was on 70th Street between Lexington and Park, which is my favorite block in the city," he said. "Great architecture, and it hasn't been ruined."

Manhattan's two other main residential areas—the Village and the Upper West Side—exist primarily as foils for his humor. The Village (and SoHo, in *Hannah and Her Sisters*) is where silly, trendy, artsy things happen; the Upper West Side is where the insufferable intellectuals hang out. His low opinion of that neighborhood has been modified in recent years, however, by events that are reflected in *Hannah and Her Sisters*.

Mia Farrow lives on Central Park West, as does the character she plays in the new film (indeed, Farrow's apartment was used in the shooting). *Hannah* mirrors a softening all around of Woody Allen's various prejudices. Again, he plays a version of himself—but this time he grows, changes, and finds love; this time, too, the notion of "family" is celebrated as something other than claustrophobic; this time, most remarkably and wonderfully, he rejects isolation.

Actually, the West Side *has* changed . . . but in ways not reflected in *Hannah and Her Sisters*. It has been overrun by quiche eaters, an invasion that—oddly enough—hasn't yet manifested itself in Woody Allen's New York. The characters in his films tend to be generic New Yorkers or, like Annie Hall, refugees from the hinterlands. There are none of the preppy young suburbanites who have "rediscovered" the city, driving up rents, driving out the old shopkeepers, gentrifying Columbus and Amsterdam Avenues.

"I suppose it's better over there now," he allowed when asked about the invasion.

"Do you ever wonder if your films lured a lot of those people who grew up in the suburbs back into town?" I asked.

"God, I hope not."

There aren't very many yuppies in the East Seventies near Central Park, where Woody Allen lives, and which he mined for locations in *Hannah and Her Sisters*, using everything from a hideous modern synagogue to a local hamburger shop. It is a quiet, moneyed area where elderly couples totter together down Madison Avenue, the women wearing decades-old designer outfits with matching shoes and purses; their husbands, Palm Beach casual. The avenue hasn't changed much in the years he has lived there, although gelato-mongers and other outposts of urban cutery have begun to sneak in amid the art galleries, antique dealers, and understated little shops that have been there forever.

"It's changing," Woody Allen admitted. "Fashionable clothing stores are moving in, but I still know most of the shopkeepers in my neighborhood—it's a real neighborhood. I've had a relationship with many of them for more than a decade. I was the youngest person in my building when I moved in," he said. "People are always surprised that I live on the East Side. They have a strange conception of me. Because I don't dress up, and I'm a street person and like sports, they expect me to live in Greenwich Village or the Upper West Side. But when I moved to the city, the Village was kind of honky-tonk; I played a lot of clubs down there. The Upper West Side wasn't in too good shape, either. That's changed now, and almost all my friends live on the West Side. As a matter of fact, I can look out my apartment window—I live on Fifth Avenue—straight across Central Park to Mia's apartment on Central Park West. Diane Keaton and Marshall Brickman also live over there. I tried an apartment on the West Side for a brief time, maybe six months, but it just wasn't the same."

In August, Woody Allen commuted on foot each morning from the East Side to Times Square, where he was completing postproduction work on *Hannah and Her Sisters*. One day I walked with him, a beautiful day—one of those times when his New York and the real one overlapped. We walked for forty-five minutes, and he wasn't stopped once by a fan. There were a few shy waves, some eye contact, but no requests for autographs, no guys named Cheech recognizing him from television. In fact, at one point an art student walking in front of us dropped her portfolio; we stopped to help her gather it together, she said thanks and continued on, without recognizing him.

"From the very first time I came here from Brooklyn with my father, I wanted to live in New York," he said, "and I wanted to live in the elegant, Cole Porter part of New York, which is why I live on the East Side. That vision of the city was as important to me as Damon Runyon. I love Park Avenue, and Fifth Avenue. There is something wonderful about the way the streets feel here, it hasn't been ruined the way other parts of the city have—although you'll find things like. . . ."

He began to search for a certain block of Fifth Avenue he had used in the new movie. "There's a lot of talk about architecture in *Hannah*, and we used this," he said, turning onto Sixty-Second Street, a block of incredible Beaux-Arts buildings interrupted by a modern synagogue that looks something like a giant cheese grater. "Isn't that incredible?" he said.

"You know, Dick Cavett used to ask, 'Is there anything about the city that's better now than it was five years ago?' . . . and I think it's very hard to find anything that is. I don't know if I'm glorifying the past; I don't *think* I am," he said.

"The New York in my films is the way I'd like it to be. I know the city isn't really like that, and I feel terrible about what's happened here. It's like there was a dark cloud over New York—the fear, the dirt, the graffiti and junk. When we were working on *Manhattan*, we kept trying to find locations to romanticize the city. We tried hard, we were really looking—but everywhere I looked there were problems. We couldn't find a place in Central Park where there wasn't litter and bottles and graffiti."

Still, *Manhattan* was made, and the city seemed wonderfully romantic. In *Hannah and Her Sisters,* he even manages to make Central Park seem the gorgeous, idyllic place it can be at stray moments when the loose-joint salesmen and ghetto blasters are taking a break. His city commingles with the real one, especially on warm, sunny days in autumn and spring, on West Side movie lines, at parties where someone is talking too loud, in delis and in cabarets where standards are sung. The rest of us notice it from time to time—"This is a Woody Allen kind of moment"—but it is his fantasy, and, one imagines, he inhabits it as fully as the heroine of *The Purple Rose of Cairo* inhabits hers.

I asked Woody Allen if any of the really terrible things that can happen in the city had ever happened to him. "You walk around a lot," I asked. "Have you ever been mugged?"

"No," he said. "In fact, no one in my family has ever been mugged. We're very careful. . . . Actually, I *was* robbed once—my apartment."

"What happened?"

"Well, this is going to sound funnier than it actually was," he said, "but the thieves had obviously been to another apartment before they hit mine, and they must have been scared by something, because they dropped what they had and left. They left me a television set. That was my one experience with crime in New York."

Woody Allen

Alexander Walker / 1986

Published in *Cinema Papers* (Australia), no. 58 (July 1986): 19–23.

In New York, by the late spring of this year, the one solidly established new film in town, taking in money from the bawdy lights of Times Square to the sedater reaches of the East Side, was Woody Allen's *Hannah and Her Sisters*. Not since *Annie Hall*, nearly ten years ago, has Woody Allen so rewardingly hit that popular nerve which receives the vibrations of New York life and turns them into a representative pattern of people.

In this case, the people are all members of one Manhattan family. Hence the unusually large cast for a Woody Allen film. As usual, Allen wrote and directed it. And, as nearly usual, he appears in it, playing Hannah's ex-husband, a self-harassing, hypochondriac TV director, who has no sooner been cleared of the brain tumor he suspects he's got, than he rifles through several different religions trying to find the one that offers hope. Ultimately, he concludes, salvation lies in being able to laugh in the cinema.

But *Hannah and Her Sisters* is not a comedy, so much as a group portrait of people trying to shake a meaning out of their busy-busy lives. It opens at one Thanksgiving dinner and closes, two years later, at another. In between, we follow the ups and downs of three daughters from a show-business family, their husbands, lovers, parents, and offspring, all against a New York backdrop which Allen presents like a photo album of his favorite places and seasons.

Besides Allen himself, the cast includes Mia Farrow as Hannah, Michael Caine as her second husband, Dianne Wiest and Barbara Hershey as her sisters, Max von Sydow as Hershey's surly, live-in lover, Carrie Fisher as Woody's girlfriend, and veteran players Maureen O'Sullivan and the late Lloyd Nolan as Hannah's parents.

Part of the success of *Hannah and Her Sisters*, I suspect, is the feeling that people—or at any rate New Yorkers—have been taking away from it: namely that it presents, if not a happy ending, then a *happier* view of existence than is customarily offered by Allen's comedies of urban desperation. In this instance, the group seems to produce its own therapy. Whether or not this is intentional is, of course, something Woody Allen himself is best placed to answer. So, on a visit to New York, I made my bid to see him. It was just over five years since we had last met. At that time, the meeting was in the duplex penthouse he still occupies, which was seen in the 360-degree shot with which his favorite cameraman, Gordon Willis, opened *Manhattan*. It looks out on Central Park—and, coincidentally, towards the Central Park West apartment of Mia Farrow, who is Woody's closest off-screen companion. It is Mia Farrow's apartment that turns up in *Hannah*.

I was better prepared on this visit to encounter a Woody Allen who, as the years pass, adds up less and less to the comic Little Guy grabbing at one-liners like lifelines. Since our last meeting, I had translated Robert Benayoun's big, coffee-table book on Allen, *Beyond Words*, which comes out this summer. And, in it, a far more complex Woody Allen emerges than the usual Anglo-Saxon newspaper and magazine profiles present. He responds to Benayoun's Gallic interrogation with unwonted seriousness, revealing the breadth of his literacy (which, of course, shouldn't surprise anyone who has read his *New Yorker* stories), and also the reach of his ambitions. Neither the breadth nor the reach seems characteristically American: on the contrary, Allen's spiritual and literary baggage appears to have been freighted from Northern Europe and pre-revolutionary Russia. And, in this sense, *Hannah and Her Sisters* reveals itself as a film far closer in denseness to the social and cultural fabric of Czarist Russia than of Reagan's America.

This time, my meeting with Woody Allen was at The Beekman, an apartment house on Park Avenue which also houses the screening theater and cutting rooms of the Manhattan Filmmakers' Cooperative. The Beekman's solid old entrance hall has, unexpectedly, a Norman-arched ceiling, which gives anyone passing through it the impression of entering an Anglican church. The monastic feel is heightened by Woody Allen himself: polite, considerate, articulate, but obviously seeing sand run through his hourglass, as these questions eat into the time available to him for seeking answers to his own dilemmas, never mind making confession to critics who aren't able to grant absolution.

Q: I believe you've just finished your new film—the one after *Hannah*?
A: No, I'm *finishing* it. We're going to shoot again next week, because I'm not happy with a couple of scenes in it and we're going to do them over.

Q: Is that usual with you?
A: Uh-huh. This is my fifteenth film. I've never had a film that I didn't do extensive reshooting on. Most of them are made in the reshooting.

Q: Is it *that* extensive?
A: Uh-huh. We budget for reshoots to begin with, and my first eight or ten weeks' shooting are a "first draft." We look at it on the screen and, you know, it would be like asking someone to write a novel in one draft and say: "This is it. I'm not going to rewrite it." The same with a film. It's just that, with a novel, it's inexpensive and not cumbersome; on the screen, it's expensive and cumbersome to reshoot. It's not like erasing! But there's no other way to do it.

Q: So how much of the film is in the shooting script?
A: Well, I try and get as close as I can. I'd love one day to finish the first shooting and say: "Great. I don't need any reshooting"; or "I need only one day." But it's never close to that.

Q: Let me ask you first about *Hannah and Her Sisters*—Who or what came first in it? Was it an "idea" or a "character," or a set of characters?
A: Actually what happened was, I was re-reading *Anna Karenina* one summer, and I thought, "Gee, it's really interesting to do a story where you go from small groups of people to other groups of people and back to the first group." I thought it would be fun to do a movie with that technique. There were certain themes that were reverberating, that I had never really worked out fully. One was, I always thought it would be interesting to do a story about a man who had fallen in love with his wife's sister. That always interested me. Another thing that interested me was: What happens to someone who gets the news that he has to go in for X-rays and tests and that sort of thing? Because I see it around me so often. I've been guilty of it myself! When the doctor says: "I just want to check this next week" or "I want to take a little biopsy" or something, people get plunged into re-evaluating their lives: they get so frightened over that. So, these ideas were just roaming around, and I was able to coalesce them in a film where I could go from story to story.

Q: It's a very prodigal film. It throws up ideas, scenes, and sequences that, with elaboration, could themselves have made a separate film.
A: Right. You could elaborate on some of those and do them separately. But, to me, the fun was to try and interweave them. That was based strictly on having read *Anna Karenina* and thinking: What fun it is to work like that!

Q: In Robert Benayoun's book on you, he asks you some interesting questions about your predilection for Russian literature. *Hannah and Her Sisters* has, almost in its title, a Chekhovian overtone, hasn't it?
A: I guess it does and, interestingly enough now you mention it, *Hannah and Her*

Sisters, without my having any idea of what the story was, was really the very first thing that came—the title. It's hard to make that relevant. Once, years ago, I was sitting home working on another script—working on some names or something—and the title of *Hannah and Her Sisters* came to me. I had no idea of the story or anything. I just thought: That's an interesting title for something. And I filed it. So that was really the first thing that came.

Q: Now, Hannah and her two sisters: are they examples of womankind in general, or specific New York womankind? Hannah is a very serene character in the film—
A: Uh-huh.

Q: —as indeed Mia Farrow was in *Purple Rose of Cairo*. And her two sisters represent other aspects of women, and perhaps New York women?
A: They're three very different types, actually. As you say, Hannah is very serene and seems to have her hand on the wheel, though there are some hints in there that there are problems, too. One is, apparently, that her husband is not getting something from her that he needs, which causes him to drift a little to her sister. And then, in the scene with her sister in the dress store, when her sister says she's going to do a singing audition, Hannah is not exactly supportive. She *is* so on the surface, but not underneath. So, you know she's less than perfect. But of those three sisters, she's the one able to keep her life together, whereas the other two have had much tougher times.

Q: Such as?
A: Well, Dianne Wiest, who plays sister Holly, is completely neurotic. She's had a bad relationship in her life, and she switches from job to job. She's got a creative streak in her, but she has no control over her emotions. Hannah *has* control over her emotions. Holly is all over the place and any whim that happens . . . well, happens. She thinks she can write, she thinks she can act, she's gone from job to job, floundering completely. But she's also competitive with Hannah, because she wants to achieve success in the same area that Hannah did, although she's not suited to it at all. The other girl, Lee, played by Barbara Hershey, is the pretty younger sister, and kind of lost. She was an alcoholic for a while—I mean, not a genuine, falling-down-in-the-street alcoholic, but enough of a problem to be sent to Alcoholics Anonymous. And she has been living for years in a tutorial relationship with an older man who's really teaching her. In the end, she winds up marrying her teacher from college. So she's obviously in need of that kind of dependent relationship. It works for a while with a much older guy, but he is obviously too damaged himself, too difficult, and so it has to break up.

Q: There's a feeling about this film that there isn't in, I suppose, the films it may be compared with, like *Annie Hall* and *Manhattan*. It's a feeling of mellowness, even of happiness, at the end of it.

A: It's deceptive. I think that people are reading that into it. It's not intended. If it's true, it's an accidental success. I didn't want it to be a *depressing* film but, if you ask me, I wouldn't say it was happy. I'd say, first, Michael Caine has this inexplicable yen for his wife's sister in the film that causes him a lot of pain, that causes his wife some pain, because she senses he's drifting from her. It causes the young girl some pain, because she leaves the artist she's living with and is in one of those relationships where the guy loves her but won't leave his wife for her. It causes suffering for all those people. And, in the end, it does not *really* resolve itself in any tremendous way. Lee finally ends up with another "tutor," and Michael Caine drifts back to his wife, never really understanding what it was all about. The character I play is mortally afraid because of his hypochondria, and it causes him to quit his job and realize how trivial all the tension of his television show is, all the fight for ratings. He goes off on a quest to try and find answers to some of the deeper questions of life and, floundering in an amusing way, doesn't succeed in getting at those answers. He even thinks of shooting himself at one time—and then, finally, figures: "It's pointless to shoot myself. I'm never going to *know* any of this, I'm just going to have to hang on to that slim reed of 'maybe'—maybe there's more to life, maybe not." So, he gets no answers and just decides to hang on, have sleepless nights and anxiety; but *maybe* there's more to this than meets the eye. . . . So, I'd seen the film as not at all a *happy* thing, but as a slightly mature experience—or at least, content within great limits of resignation. The characters sort of *resign* themselves at the end. But people see this as great happiness!

Q: Would you say it's an optimistic film, *despite* yourself?

A: I don't see it as optimistic: I see it as vaguely hopeful. Not suggesting that there is more to life than we see, and not suggesting that the human heart is ever going to be fathomable or that we're ever going to understand our emotions or get control. We're all going to flounder around and hurt people and never understand why we fall out of love with people or why we love them, and never understand if there's a God out there or if there's not . . . just go on in a quasi-humorous sort of way.

Q: In *The Purple Rose of Cairo*, Mia Farrow finds that the movies are the consolation in her life. It's touching at the end, when she sits there watching Fred and Ginger dance on the screen—

A: —because of the way she played it.

Q: Of course . . . and the way it was directed. And, in this film, when you see the Marx Brothers and you realize that, well, maybe laughter is a sort of consolation that you're bringing to people, with the sense of contentment or resignation that accompanies it—do you see this as the male equivalent of the female character in *Purple Rose*?

A: In one respect only: that is, both characters seem to get sidetracked by a distraction. With Mia, real life in the film is an incredibly painful thing, and we're all forced to choose between reality and fantasy—and, of course, you can't choose fantasy, because there lies madness. You *must* choose reality. If you do choose reality, then things are not perfect and you get hurt. People betray you, things don't work out for you. She gets badly hurt. And then, at the end, the best she can do is kind of go back to these little distractions, because that's all the movie house offers her. Neither she nor a million other Americans were ever going to go out to Hollywood during the Depression and marry movie stars. She's just got an hour and a half of forgetfulness from the pain of everyday living. The same in *Hannah and Her Sisters*. You see the Marx Brothers and you say to yourself, "Well, not every second of life is torture." I mean, there are some moments that are pleasurable, and you may as well hang in for them, for they're the best you get. But I never found a sense of optimism in *Hannah and Her Sisters*—just a sense of reasonably healthy resignation . . . that, you know, you opt not to shoot yourself. . . .

Q: Or at least you miss when you pull the trigger.
A: Exactly.

Q: Tell me something about the casting. It's interesting to see Michael Caine in a Woody Allen film. It's also amusing to see Max von Sydow in a Woody Allen film.
A: Michael was originally an idea of mine, because I've always been a great fan of his. He's one of the few people around who can play serious *and* comedy. There's not a lot of us around! There are some great actors around, but you give them anything amusing to do and they can't do it. And vice versa: there are some wonderful comedians, and you give them something serious to do and they can't do it. But Michael seems to have a bigger scope than most actors: he just *can* play those things. I wanted a normal man—you know, not Marlon Brando or something: just a regular man who could play both serious and comic, where you could see him suffer a little and he could also get some laughs. . . .

Q: And Max von Sydow, who plays the touchy, rebarbative artist in the SoHo loft whom Lee lives with: whose idea was he? Yours too?
A: Someone else suggested him. We were sitting in this room, this viewing theater, pitching names, and someone said: "What about Max von Sydow?" The

second she said it—it was my casting director—it was, like, for me, nobody else in the world could play that role: he just seemed as right as could be for it. Yet he never occurred to me. When I was writing it, I had in mind someone naturally American, and *gruffer*—I mean, more like Ben Gazzara, someone like that: Lee was living with an angry artist. As soon as someone said "Max," it felt perfect. It was a pleasure he was available: he was certainly fun to work with.

Q: He also has that apocalyptic feeling he brings over from an Ingmar Bergman film.
A: Right: he's truly a larger-than-life character.

Q: And Maureen O'Sullivan as Hannah's mother?
A: Maureen was the natural choice: she was available, she's Mia's mother in real life, and she can act. That fell in naturally. It would be hard for me to cast the part of Mia's mother without casting . . . well, Mia's mother, who's an actress and right there! Lloyd Nolan, who plays Mia's father in the film, was one of the many names that came through. Actually, Lloyd was not the first choice for that part, because he lived in California and, you know, the film was not a high-budget film and we were fighting the budget. Wherever possible, especially in smaller roles, you try and hire people whom it's easy enough to fly in and put them up and all that. There was another actor we chose in New York, but we couldn't get insurance on him because he was elderly and they'd just had some health problems. So we went to Lloyd. I didn't know it at the time—none of us did—that Lloyd in fact was dying. He would come in and, very quietly, he'd lie down in the other room in Mia's house, which we were using for filming, or the make-up room; and then, very quietly, come on the set and *full out* do his thing beautifully, and then retire to the other room and husband his strength all the time. You didn't know what was really at the back of it. You just thought, "Well, he's an elderly man, into his early eighties," and you felt, "Well, the guy's tired." We didn't know he was dying. He was wonderful. I'd seen him in so many movies when growing up.

Q: We all had. A question with a figure in it: when you mention a budget for a Woody Allen picture, in what area does the budget lie?
A: Like $8 million, which is not a lot of money by American standards. *Annie Hall*, for example, cost $3 million to make and, if I made the same picture today, frame for frame, it would cost $8 million—you know, with no improvements at all—just because of the huge inflationary rise over the years. The unions and the cost of shooting in New York has gone up, up, up. I was talking to Jean-Luc Godard the other day, and he said: "Why do you make so many movies?" And I said, "Well, you know, I don't know what else to do. I finish a movie and then I have another idea. So, that's what I do for a living: I make movies." Then it turned out, on closer

examination, he's made about forty-five movies or thereabouts. I mean, he's got a *huge* oeuvre.

Q: I should have thought he was the last person to criticize you for your output.
A: He said: "Yes, I sometimes think I've made too many." But I don't think he's made too many. I always look forward to them.

Q: You like Jean-Luc Godard movies?
A: Yes. I think he's a brilliant innovator. I don't always love *every* film he's made. I think he's very inventive, but sometimes his inventions are taken by other people and used better. But he's certainly one of the innovators of cinema.

Q: There are scenes in *Hannah and Her Sisters* that look as if you said to yourself: "I must get this aspect of life—or this particular event I've seen happen—into a movie." For example, the two girls being driven back home at night by the man, and each one trying to make sure she is dropped off last, which is a very funny sequence; or the scene where the client comes into Max von Sydow's studio in order to purchase his painting by width and breadth to decorate his new home.
A: Both of those things I'm familiar with in real life: exactly right. I've been present at the first, where you wonder who's going to be dropped off first because you want privacy and thus you want to be dropped off last. And I know someone who was decorating a beautiful home and was buying paintings to fit in with the decor of the home. Those are true-life incidents, yes.

Q: Could I revert to what you mentioned at the beginning: how you have a built-in part of the budget for the reshooting and, in fact, how quite a lot of the creative things happen during the reshooting stage? Could you give me any specific examples?
A: Oh, sure. I can give you some big examples. In *Hannah and Her Sisters*, the whole of the second Thanksgiving party—there are three Thanksgiving parties in the film: at the start, the end, and in the middle, marking a two-year time-span—was an afterthought. In the original script, there were only two parties: one at the beginning, one at the end. But, as I saw the story on the screen and saw where I needed character development and where I needed climaxes to occur and all that, I went out and shot the entire sequence. When I say "reshooting," I mean some old scenes and some brand new scenes. So, the entire second Thanksgiving party, which is a big climactic chunk of the picture, was never in my original script and only became apparent to me that I needed it after I saw what I had on the screen.

Q: At what point does this become apparent to you? During the rough assembly?
A: No. What happens in reshooting, first you see the dailies. I sit here in this

screening room and look at the dailies the day right after we shot them and, if the scene looks good, we file it and go on. If the scene doesn't look good, I shoot it again the next day. I don't feel comfortable accumulating scenes I don't think are good. Then I finish the picture with all—presumably—good scenes and cut the picture together and it's usually a miserable disappointment. I don't say that facetiously: it is. I look at it with the editor, and we talk and sometimes I bring in the casting director, who's a friend of mine, or one of the players in the picture, like Dianne Wiest. And we sit and chat and look at the film, and take some scenes and put them in a different order and trim certain things out and then, finally, we come to a point where we say: "We've done what we can with this existing material."

The problem here is you need, say, a revelatory scene between mother and daughter, or you got to see the exploding gun here. . . . And then, I go out and shoot those things and put them in and, if I've guessed right, I've helped the film enormously. Usually, you tend to guess much more accurately in those situations, because it isn't going from zero to a film: it's going from an existing film where the gaps show you more palpably what's really required. Then, usually, I go out and shoot again. I can say to the producer: "Well, we've solved 80 percent of the problem, but we're still missing a scene," or "For some reason my idea for a scene with the girl at the end didn't work." We go out and shoot again . . . and again . . . and again, if necessary, until it's finally done. But I don't have to go over budget for that. I *have* a budget for that.

Now, there is a great tendency, when you're sitting with people watching dailies . . . they all want you to love the dailies because, you know, the producer doesn't want to hear: "I've got to go and do that again tomorrow!" So, the lights go on and all the heads turn back to me and it's, like, thumbs up/thumbs down on the thing. They want me to say "I love it!" and go on. But you have to have the courage to say it was no good. Because one doesn't realize that if, say, I shoot five scenes a day in a five-day week—between twenty and twenty-five scenes—and let's say just one shot is bad, and the other twenty-four are fine. You figure: "well, it's a great week: one out of twenty-four is nothing." You can live with that, and you go on. Then you find, after your twelve-week shooting schedule at that rate, that you've got *twelve* shots that don't work. You don't think it's much at the time, but it slowly accumulates. When you actually have to cut the film together and you're sitting in front of the editing table, you're stuck with twelve scenes that don't work. Let's say it's *two* out of twenty-five: then you've got *two* dozen scenes that don't work. The cost is huge in terms of the effectiveness of the film.

So, you really have to be nasty about it. You've got to say to the folks: "I'm sorry, it is not a good scene. You all love it, but for me it doesn't work," and you go and get it to be happy with it. Even at that rate, all the pictures come up imperfect. Even at that meticulous rate of shooting them over and over again, they still come out flawed. None of them is close to being perfect. Some are better than others, some are very entertaining to the public—but *flawed.*

Q: Creatively flawed.
A: Sure, because the public doesn't know where you're aiming. You're aiming for the stratosphere and you fall. You hope you fall successfully enough to give audiences a good time. But sometimes you fail abysmally.

Q: That must be rare.
A: It's been rare, fortunately. And it has to be rare in the film business, otherwise they don't give you the $8 million.

Q: Which film has been a disappointment to you?
A: For me, I've been disappointed uniformly down the line. I conceive the film—I sit home and write it—and, when I conceive it, it's brilliant. Everything is *true* Chekhov or Shakespeare: it's *great*! And then, you start work, and the truck with fresh compromises drives up every day. You can't get the actor you want, the set doesn't really look the way you envisioned it.... When you said in the script: "He comes in, hangs up his coat and kisses the girl," the guy's got to come in, walk across the room, take the coat off... and suddenly, it's taking forever. It doesn't happen on the screen the way you conceive it. So, you keep changing and compromising. And, when the picture comes out, it's, like, 60 percent—if you're lucky—of what you wanted to make. You don't get the 100 percent. So, for me, they're all *such* disappointments. They're so far removed from all the great masterpieces I felt I was conceiving.

Q: It must surely be a powerful consolation when you read the reviews?
A: It's not so much a consolation: it's a lifesaver. There are some filmmakers who are not dependent on reviews and some who are. I happen to be one that is. An extreme example: you could say anything you wanted about Sylvester Stallone and they'd come. But, when I make a film, if the critics don't support it, then I don't get much of an audience for it. So I trade a lot on the critics. Over the years, the critics have been very supportive of me, so I feel very relieved when that happens. But I feel I'd still like to get some of the nice critics who've been supportive on one side and say to them: "I'm sorry I let you down. If you could have only seen what I had in my mind's eye: I had nothing less than *The Bicycle Thief* or *Citizen Kane!*"

Q: Very likely, De Sica or Welles were saying the same thing about *The Bicycle Thief* or *Citizen Kane* at the time they made those films.

A: It's possible that that kind of thing happens. Bergman once told me that he'd been very surprised at the reception that *The Seventh Seal* got. It had been something they "went out in the woods and shot," so to speak, and he was very surprised at how Americans had taken to that film and how interested they were in it—those who saw that it had greatness written all over it. But, to him, it was just a film based on a play he'd written quickly. So, you may be right about that in certain cases. I'll run into someone who'll say to me: "Gee, *Annie Hall* is the best movie I grew up on!" And I'm thinking to myself: "Oh, I missed so many good depths and so many bright ideas in the original script!"

Q: Can you say anything about your new picture?

A: I can only say this: that I'm not in it, and it's deliberately nothing like *Hannah and Her Sisters*. I didn't want to make another picture like that right away. That's to say, an *intimate* picture. It's a big, colorful, comic cartoon, with a lot of music in it—almost a musical. But it isn't a musical: it's a nostalgic comedy about a plot, just sort of a part-documentary, part-plot account of certain years of my childhood—unrelated little incidents that I happen to know about second-hand or that I remember first-hand. It's got a very large cast, but tiny parts. Mia Farrow has a tiny part, so has Dianne Wiest, and Jeff Daniels and Tony Roberts and a lot of people I've worked with. Diane Keaton sings a song in it. It's meant to be a nostalgic memory-film for an hour and a half, and I hope it works as such. I'm writing my *next* film now, and I want to get back to more serious, intimate stuff. But I did want to take a break from that: I wanted to make something broader and less about suffering.

Q: When you say "more serious," how much more serious? Serious in the way *Interiors* was?

A: Yes. I'd like to start to clear the decks before the next series of films I make. I want the next few films to be of quite a serious nature. Yes, as serious as *Interiors*. Hopefully, I'll be able to improve my technique. I think I have improved since then.

Q: Have you ever thought of making a film in a foreign country?

A: I have thought of it. It would not bother me at all. Of course, right now, the world is in such a mess. I don't dare even go to the airport to meet my parents coming back from Florida! But, yes, it's not a bad idea to make a film abroad. Many of the great cameramen are abroad. They're *all* abroad, with the exception of Gordon Willis—all the great ones are either British or Italian or French. Yes, it would be fun!

Husbands and Wives

Stig Björkman / 1993

From *Woody Allen on Woody Allen: In Conversation with Stig Björkman* (New York: Grove Press, 1994), chapter 23, pp. 244–54. Originally published in Sweden in 1993 as *Woody om Allen*. Copyright © 1993 by Stig Björkman and Alfabeta Bokförlag. Used by permission of Grove/Atlantic, Inc., and the author. Any third party use of this material, outside of this publication, is prohibited.

Stig Björkman: *Husbands and Wives* is in many respects quite a daring project. I like it precisely for its boldness, for its directness and for its raw and rough surface. How was the style for this film conceived? At what stage did you decide to make the film the way it was made?

Woody Allen: I've always been thinking that so much time is wasted and so much is devoted to the prettiness of films and the delicacy and the precision. And I said to myself, why not just start to make some films where only the content is important. Pick up the camera, forget about the dolly, just hand-hold the thing and get what you can. And then, don't worry about color correcting it, don't worry about mixing it so much, don't worry about all this precision stuff and just see what happens. When you feel like cutting, just cut. Don't worry about that it's going to jump or anything. Just do what you want, forget about anything but the content of the film. And that's what I did.

SB: But do you think that one has to reach this stage of one's career, with the experience you yourself have obtained after a little more than twenty feature films, to be able to work in this way? To dare to work in this way, to neglect all the accepted "rules" of filmmaking? To attain the assurance that this way of filmmaking is not only possible but also functional?

WA: Yes, I think you need a certain amount of confidence. Confidence that comes with experience enables you to do many things that you wouldn't have done in early films. You do tend to become bolder, because as the years go by you feel more in control of what you're doing. When I first made films anyhow—and I know this is true about a number of other people—you tend to, as we've already discussed, do a lot of coverage and protect yourself in many ways. And then, as time goes on, you get more and more knowledgeable and experienced and you drop all that and you let your instincts operate more freely and you don't worry so much about the niceties.

SB: When you discussed this new style with your photographer Carlo Di Palma before the shooting of the film, what were his reactions?
WA: He was interested, because he always likes it when there's something exciting and provocative photographically.

SB: Was his work in some ways easier on this film? Did he spend as much time as usual on lighting for the scenes, for example? Or was he less careful when it came to lighting of the scenes?
WA: Yes, it was easier, because he would light a whole general area. And then I said to the actors, go where you want, just walk wherever you want. Walk into darkness, walk into light, just play the scene as you feel it. You don't have to do it the same way the second take, just do whatever interests you. And I told the camera operator, get what you can get! If you miss it, go back and get it. If you miss it again, go back again. Find your way yourself. And we did no rehearsals with the camera or anything. We would come in, he'd pick up the camera and we would do the scene and he would do the best he could. And I was wondering after this film, if it's worth it to try and make films in the old regular way. Because this way it goes very quick, and all that counts is the end result. So I may try and make a few films in that style. Because it's fast and inexpensive and it does the job.

SB: Was this a quicker shoot as well? Compared to your previous films?
WA: Quicker, yes. And it's the first time in years—*in years, decades*—that I came in under budget. It was both cheaper and faster.

SB: Did you have a lot of reshoots on this film?
WA: Three days. Usually I reshoot weeks and weeks and weeks. You know, sometimes a month of reshoots. I was always a famous reshooter. Here I had three days only.

SB: How did you come to think of this style for the film? In a way it's congenial with the theme and the story of the film. *Husbands and Wives* is about disrupted relationships and disrupted lives so in a way the style also—
WA: —complements the story. But I think you could say that about a lot of stories. The style would work for a lot of stories. After the fact it looks like it's perfect for this story. But it's also perfect for many films that I've done

SB: Which of your films, do you think?
WA: I could have done *Shadows and Fog* like that, if I'd wanted to. I could have done *Alice* like that. Any number of them. Right down the line. Because what the audience comes away with emotionally, spiritually, is the content of the film. The characters, the substance of the film. The form of the film is just a simple, functional thing. It can differ in style, like baroque or gothic architecture. The only important thing is that the audience is moved or amused or made to think or something. And you can do it this way.

SB: Did the script for *Husbands and Wives* leave more space for improvisation, or did the actors follow a script similar to those you've written for your previous films?
WA: No, there was a script, and they basically followed the script.

SB: The film has also the character of an investigation into the lives of the characters. I guess this was present in the script as well?
WA: Yes, I was thinking that these people were living their lives and the camera is there and can just do whatever it wants; when I need the people to say what they feel about things, they just talk about them. I just felt there was nothing I couldn't do, that I wanted to do. I didn't have to make any concessions to any formalities.

SB: And who in your mind is this investigator, the interviewer in the film?
WA: I never thought of it. Just the audience. It's a convenient way of letting the characters explain themselves.

SB: These confessions or confidences given by the characters, were they all in the script? They are not ideas expressed by the actors in any way?
WA: No, the whole film is written. I mean, the actors add words here and there to make the dialogue colloquial. That's all. It's all written.

SB: *Husbands and Wives* is, in many ways, a more violent account of relationships than your previous films. Not least in the acting and, particularly, in the case of Judy Davis and Sydney Pollack.
WA: Yes, it's more volatile and explosive.

SB: One of the more dramatic scenes in the film is Sally's telephone conversation with her husband in the home of the opera lover. It's embarrassing and astonishing, tragic and at the same time dense with a very black humor. It's handled with great bravura by Judy Davis.
WA: Sure, I know that kind of situation, because I've been in it myself . . . as a

person calling having something on his mind. And Judy Davis is probably the best movie actress in the world today.

SB: The actor who plays her lover, Liam Neeson, was a new acquaintance to me.
WA: He's an Irish actor. He's been in a number of movies. He was in one with Diane Keaton, *The Good Mother*. He combines this mixture of masculinity and intelligence. He is a superb actor and is a "real person." There is never a trace of fraudulence about him at all. He is authentic, in every gesture and in every word.

SB: Why did you choose Sydney Pollack for the part of the husband?
WA: I was trying to think of who would be good for that part, of men that looked that age, and his name came up when we were discussing casting, Juliet Taylor and I. And he came to see me, and he was very nice about it. He read for the part. And I said to myself, God, I hope he is going to be able to read this, because I will be so embarrassed if he doesn't read it well and I will have to not engage him. And he read it, and I could see from the first reading that he was very natural and good. He was great!

SB: I've never come to think about it in the same way, when I've seen you act in your own films before—maybe it's due to the unseen interviewer in the film—but somehow I was more aware of your double role as director and actor in *Husbands and Wives* than in your previous films. Could you tell me something about your feelings when you are "directing" yourself in your films? Are there any kind of problems for you in that process?
WA: No, there's nothing to it. It's a misnomer. I mean, I don't direct myself. I wrote the script. I know what I want from me and I just do it. I don't ever have to direct myself.

SB: So then it's just an inner feeling for you? You know when you have to make another take, you know when your own performance is right?
WA: Yes, it's an inner feeling. If it feels good, it almost always is good. It's very rare that I'm fooled on that. It's usually the other way around. It doesn't feel so good when you do it sometimes, but it's better than you thought later. That does happen.

SB: There is a scene in the film between you and the young girl, Rain, played by Juliette Lewis, where you are walking in Central Park discussing Russian writers. You talk about Tolstoy and Turgenev, and then you make a vivid description of Dostoyevsky, of him being "a full meal, with vitamins and wheatgerm added." Now and then you come back to Dostoyevsky in your films, and some of your films have a certain "Dostoyevskian," novelistic flavor and quality, like *Husbands and Wives*, *Manhattan*, *Hannah and Her Sisters*, or *Crimes and Misdemeanors*. These films seem to have a certain link.

WA: Well, I think that among the films you name, *Manhattan* is not quite in the same category as the others, because it's more romanticized. *Manhattan* has one foot in nostalgia and romance, in a certain way. But *Crimes and Misdemeanors* and *Hannah* and this film are darker. They are definitely darker. I also like this novelistic idea, in general. That always provokes me. I love the idea of working in a novelistic manner on the screen. I always feel I'm writing with film. It's something about the novelistic approach that I like. And even though I stray from it now and then, in a movie like *Alice* or something, I always seem to come back to it. I like real people and real situations and human life unfolding. You can do in the novel what you do in the film and vice versa. The two media, physically, are very close together. Not like the stage. That's a different thing entirely.

SB: When you write the script for a film like *Husbands and Wives* or *Crimes and Misdemeanors* or *Hannah*, do you in some way make up a general pattern for the characters or do their dramas develop along with their interchanging relationships and so on?

WA: It's very instinctive with me. I think about it for a while and get a general idea of where it can go. I just like to think for a while and make sure that I'm not going to start writing with all my energy and then stop after ten pages. When I realize that there is room for development, then my first draft is exploratory. I write it and see where I'm going and often I don't know where I'll be going and I make it up at the time. And finally when it's over, I make a few corrections, and give it right to my producer and have him start budgeting it and get the production going.

SB: In the scene in the taxi between you and Juliette Lewis, the girl Rain is making comments on Gabe's novel. She abandons her previous overt and spontaneous appreciation of the book and displays a more and more critical view of it. Do you find this to be a common habit among critics or judges of art or even friends? They can start from a very positive attitude and then gradually withdraw from their original point of view.

WA: Yes, people's feelings about things change, and they are not always so candid with you. It has happened to me in my life where someone who had loved a film of mine is confronted by other people who don't love it so much, then they lose confidence in their own judgment and start to feel more critical about it.

SB: In the scene in the taxi you have chosen to concentrate your image on Juliette

Lewis and use jump cuts instead of conventional crosscutting to the other character—yourself. Were parts of the dialog cut out in this way?

WA: Yes, there were things cut out. That was the most difficult scene in the movie to do. The lens made us look ugly when we were both in the same shot in the taxi. And the shot from the side looked better than the shot taken flat on. So I looked terrible, the lens was disfiguring my nose. Then I tried doing singles, I tried everything, but we couldn't make it work. So then I thought, she looks pretty. Why don't I just leave the camera on her? I thought, okay, you can hear me, so, you know. . . . And now it looks more interesting.

SB: Yes, I think so too. Definitely. In a way we are put in your position and we are experiencing her in the same way as the character you play.

WA: Juliette Lewis is a wonderful actress.

SB: I agree. How old is she? In *Cape Fear* she is supposed to be fourteen years old, in your film she is celebrating her twenty-first birthday.

WA: I think she is nineteen or twenty or so. Something like that. She is young. And very gifted.

SB: Is she an actress with whom you would like to collaborate again? Like you've mentioned earlier about Diane Keaton, Dianne Wiest, and Judy Davis.

WA: I sure would. Sure. She is great.

SB: You use this jump-cut technique throughout the film. Even to the extent of leaving very, very brief glimpses of the actors and then immediately cutting forward into the next situation. In the beginning of *Husbands and Wives*, for example, we see a very brief scene with Mia Farrow in the apartment. The shot is maybe just a few seconds long, and then you cut to a conversation scene where she has moved just slightly from the position she was in before. Was this done with the intention of keeping the same feeling for the scenes throughout the film?

WA: Yes, to make it more disturbing. It's what we were talking about the other day, more dissonant, like the difference between Stravinsky and Prokofiev. I wanted it to be more dissonant because the internal, emotional and mental states of the characters are dissonant. I wanted the audience to feel that there was a jagged, nervous feeling. An unsettled and neurotic feeling.

SB: Do you think this would have been possible without us having seen and experienced Godard and his early films?

WA: A filmmaker like Godard invented so many wonderful, cinematic devices. It's very hard to say whether it just would have been something that came over me one day, or that he's part of the rich treasure of wonderful filmmakers that have contributed to the vocabulary of film. You know, very often you do something and it's stimulating and exciting, but it's coming from your heritage of film literature or film semantics. I can only speak for myself on this, but sometimes I will do something in a film that you just couldn't relate to anybody else ever having done. And sometimes it's in the tradition of the vocabulary that other filmmakers have given us. So I don't really know. But I do very much love Godard's contribution to cinema.

SB: Yes, so do I. I mean, Godard in his way just went out and made his movies and undauntedly proposed that from this day, from this film, this way of making films is also possible, is now permitted.
WA: Right. He is probably the original guy who made just the content count and who just did what he wanted, put anything in that he wanted. So I do think he is and was a fine contributor.

SB: When seeing *Husbands and Wives* there is, in fact, a film of Bergman's that came to my mind. The only thing these two films have in common is this investigative attitude and the attack on the audience. It's one of my favorite German films, *From the Life of the Marionettes*. It has, as well, this quality of being a deep investigation into the lives of unknown people.
WA: Yes, it's a very interesting film. I haven't seen it in a while. I saw it when it first came out. It hasn't played much here. It was not a commercial success at all. I ought to see it again. It's a wonderful movie.

SB: The marital dilemmas and the marital problems that the two couples in the film expose and unveil are dilemmas shared by many people today. There is a great amount of possible recognition in your story about Judy and Gabe and Sally and Jack.
WA: Yes, those dilemmas are common. I've observed them around me all the time.

SB: There is another small but funny link between *Hannah and Her Sisters* and *Husbands and Wives*: the relationship between the Dianne Wiest and Carrie Fisher characters and their mutual romantic object, the architect played by Sam Waterston, and that between the Mia Farrow and Judy Davis characters to the editor played by Liam Neeson.
WA: Yes, I see that as a not uncommon thing that people do. Somebody likes a member of the opposite sex and they fix that person up with their friend. But I don't know what they hope to gain by it.

SB: It could be a check-up. In *Husbands and Wives* Judy gets her friend Sally to check up whether this guy Michael really is the kind of romantic possibility she herself imagines him to be.
WA: Or else she really wants to do it for herself, but doesn't have the nerve. So she sublimates and does it for her friend.

SB: Do you think the secretive way that Gabe and Judy behave towards each other is common in many marriages? I am thinking about their hiding away their works. She doesn't want to show him her poetry. He gives his novel to another woman to read.
WA: I think that happens. There are private parts or there are private things that carry some shame with them or some aggression or some guilt that one doesn't share with one's closest person. And that always is a problem, that always becomes a problem. It grows.

SB: Why did you want to show us parts of Gabe's novel visually and act it out in actual scenes? Why didn't you just let him read the parts for us?
WA: I wanted you to know some of his observations very clearly on certain aspects of relations between men and women. And I thought that this was a way of doing it, rather than just have him reading it. It would be interesting for the audience. It would be amusing for them, a little interlude, just to clarify certain feelings Gabe had about human relations.

SB: When you started to work on the editing of *Husbands and Wives*, had you talked about and discussed beforehand this new technique, this new style with your editor, Susan Morse?
WA: Yes, I wrote it into the script. I explained in the description that we would just cut where we would want to, we'd just jump and wouldn't pay attention to anything.

SB: And did she find it exciting and enjoyable to work in this unorthodox way?
WA: Yes, she loved it. We both had fun. Everybody—from a physical point of view, from a technical point of view—had more fun on this movie than anything else. The actors loved it. They didn't have to block, they didn't have to think about where they went. They could do what they wanted. It was very good that way. For everybody.

If You Knew Woody Like I Knew Woody

Douglas McGrath / 1994

Published in *New York* magazine October 17, 1994, 41–47. Reprinted by permission of the author.

"There is no greater memory that I have in my life, no warmer memory or fonder memory, than getting up in the morning, having my big piece of chocolate cake and milk for breakfast, my parents still asleep, going out, presumably to Midwood High School, but"—he raises his eyebrows above the familiar black rims—"*not* going to Midwood High School, meeting my friends, getting on the BMT subway, going into Manhattan, getting off at Times Square, which was like being in Wonderland, getting something to eat at the Automat, and then, for fifty-five cents, going into the Paramount Theater for the first show of the morning, Duke Ellington rising out of that pit with his orchestra, comics coming on, and seeing a movie. It was total Heaven."

Woody Allen shared this memory with me in his apartment this past Labor Day. We sat across from each other on matching checked couches, he facing the huge windows that face Central Park. In a felicitous union of icons, the Manhattan skyline was reflected in his eyeglasses. That image was familiar to me from our months of collaboration on the screenplay of his new film, *Bullets over Broadway*. I would come over and, for several hours a day, we would work. By four, our energies dipping, we slouched in our seats. It was with the sun setting that the outline of the West Side replaced my view of his eyes. I could tell what time it was by Woody's glasses.

You may have noticed that in between all that sunsety poetry talk I slipped in the whopper that I collaborated with Woody Allen on the screenplay of his new movie. This happy development came about when we were introduced by a mutual friend. She included me in a number of dinners she and Woody had, and he and I got to know each other. At one point, he asked our friend if she thought I would like to write a screenplay with him. I hesitated when she asked me. I was, at that time, writing the remake of *Born Yesterday*, a production that would soon be hailed as a mistake on everyone's part. I told her to tell Woody that if he was trying to use me to get ahead in the movie business, I wasn't so sure I wanted to let him dine with me again. Then she hit me with a polo mallet and I said yes.

We began working together in January 1993, and he warned me, "I can be brutal if I don't like something." I said that was okay by me, knowing that however rough he might be, he would never ask me, as a film executive once had, to enliven a scene by giving it more "phonetic energy." As it turned out, Woody was supportive and nurturing.

What made our collaboration at this time especially interesting is that this was when he was being accused of child molestation, an allegation that publicly launched his titanic struggle with Mia Farrow. So I came to know him in two ways: not only as a writer-director, through which I received undreamed-of access to his ideas, dramatic philosophies, and style of work, but also as a man and father, fighting a terrible battle at what was undoubtedly the most difficult part of his life.

We began our work by trying to find an idea. I like to think we were well matched for this because Woody has more ideas than he knows what to do with and I have one, which is to work with someone who has a lot of ideas. Constructing a movie provoked much animated talk of old movies. His most alarming confession ("I've never been able to sit through *The Wizard of Oz*") so disturbed me that, in a rare act of assertion, I cut him off. "Please," I said. "I don't want to know this about you."

We often made lists, by which I mean I often asked him to make lists. Here is my favorite: "If you take out the Marx Brothers and W. C. Fields," he says, "there are only—what?—three truly great American talking comedies: *Trouble in Paradise*, *The Shop Around the Corner*, and *Born Yesterday*, with Judy Holliday." (He was polite enough not to add, "not the inane version you had a hand in.") He reveres the silent Chaplin but is "very unenthused" about the speaking one.

He loves George Stevens, William Wyler, and King Vidor, and thinks Orson Welles is by far the great American director of the talking period. He does not care for Laurel and Hardy. He very much likes Coppola and Altman and Scorsese, citing *GoodFellas* in particular as an example of superb filmmaking. The only TV shows I've heard him praise are from the fifties: Sid Caesar's, for which he wrote, and *The Honeymooners*.

We spoke of his movies as well, and he is as hard on himself as he is on others. "Most of my films are failures," he says, defining *failure* this way: "You get an idea, you work on it, it's exciting, and you make it into a film—but you find that some of your instincts failed you, you had to make compromises, other stuff you screwed up. So when the picture is finished, it's an accomplishment just to get it coherent. And you figure, 'Gee, I had this beautiful idea, and I completely ruined it.' For instance, when *Manhattan* was finished, I tried to buy the film back from

United Artists before it came out. I wanted my agent, Sam Cohn, to offer them that I would do another film for nothing if I could destroy this one."

Of the more than twenty movies he has made, Woody views only four as successful. (He defines *successful*, with typical modesty, as "I had this idea and we executed it.") The movies are *Stardust Memories* ("One of the most criticized pictures I've ever done—but we knew it would be when we were making it. Still, in my terms, it worked"), *Zelig*, *The Purple Rose of Cairo*, and *Husbands and Wives*.

His calculation of a film's success does not include its financial performance. Unlike most people in Hollywood, whose skill at describing the business their movies do usually involves a richer fiction than the material they have chosen to film, Woody makes no pretense about popularity. "That's why it was interesting when all this courtroom stuff was going on," he says. "People asked me, 'Did all this publicity affect your films at the box office?' And it didn't, because there was nothing to affect!" He laughs. "The films I made at the high point of the conflict did exactly as well as my other films had done, which is not saying much."

The exceptions were *Annie Hall*, *Manhattan*, and *Hannah and Her Sisters*. "By my meager standards, those did very nicely. But certainly not very nicely by Very Nicely standards." When I ask him to explain why he feels he has been allowed to make uncommercial movies in a system that values the commercial above all else, he says, "You know, I've wondered about that many times myself. Bobby Greenhut [a longtime producer of Woody's] used to walk around saying, 'I can't believe this. It's like we're working on a grant!' "

Before I knew him, I thought of Woody as an artist aloof from the dirty concerns of business. I was surprised to learn that he is acutely mindful of expense. When he finishes a script, he sends it to Greenhut, who goes through it and comes back to him with a budget. If the budget is higher than they want, Greenhut will point out the more expensive scenes and Woody will decide if they can be changed. Greenhut will "look at a scene," Woody explains, "and say, 'Look at this—there's a traffic jam and you have to have eight hundred cars and it's going to be $200,000 a day.' So we change it and make it a guy in a phone booth. That's a slight exaggeration, but that's how it works."

This happened in *Bullets*. *Bullets* is a period piece, which automatically makes it more expensive. We would think of a scene and he would suggest a location such as Central Park, because the park did not have to be altered to look old. (There are only young trees, not modern ones.) However, we once set a night scene in the park—the opening-night-party scene near the end of the movie—and had to change it; because of overtime costs, shooting outside at night is more costly than shooting during the day. Woody changed the location to a restaurant where he had the windows blacked out and paid the cast and crew their normal day rates.

The preproduction period is short, about two months, and it is then that

Woody interviews actors with his long-standing casting director, Juliet Taylor, and scouts locations around the city. Even though he has filmed here for more than twenty years, he never has trouble finding new locations. "New York is inexhaustible," he says.

Once filming begins, he never rehearses. "I'll go in and meet with Carlo [Di Palma, his cinematographer], and the two of us walk around and plan the shot. Then Carlo does a general lighting. After he's done, I bring in the actors and I tell them, 'Can you go over here and walk to that table and get a cigarette or whatever,' and 99 percent of the time, they say sure. One percent of the time, they say, you know, 'May I get an umbrella instead of a cigarette?' And I say sure. Then Carlo finesses the lighting, and then the actors come on and I shoot the scene without them having done it before. There are three variations that follow: It either needs a little finessing; it's way off and I have to direct them to make it right; or they get it and it's never as good again."

When he watches, he watches the actors themselves. He does not use, as many directors do, a video monitor. (Greenhut has been trying to get him to use one for years, but, as Woody says, "I can't adapt easily to things.")

Woody's manner with his actors is respectful. "When I direct the actors, I get them on the side quietly. I don't stand on the set and yell, 'More of this! Give me more of this!' I never even yell 'action' or 'cut.' Usually, the assistant director does it. Years ago, Jerry Lewis told me that he had a portion of money in his budget called fun money. It was for fun on the set, parties and buying presents—you know, to create a comic atmosphere. But you wouldn't think you were at a comedy if you watched me direct. It's chaotic but quiet." (Jerry Lewis, incidentally, was originally meant to direct *Take the Money and Run*. When the deal fell apart, Woody, who had wanted to direct from the beginning, took over.)

Though he is willing to do as many takes as necessary (he thinks the greatest number he did was fifty, in a scene from *Broadway Danny Rose* where he and Nick Apollo Forte are crossing the street), Woody likes to do two takes and move on. "Usually the actors get things right away, but if not, I correct them into it."

If correcting them doesn't work, "and I've explained it to them, I'll say, 'Let me see those lines. Maybe I've made a mistake in the script,' and then I'll read it out loud, presumably to myself but so they can hear it. And I'll play it for them so they can get the idea without my telling them to play it that way. Then, if they still don't get it—" He pauses and then laughs. "I think seriously about firing them. Usually that doesn't happen. When you hire the kind of people that are in *Bullets over Broadway*, they make me look good. I don't need to hire Tracey Ullman and give her lessons in how to be funny."

Sometimes, though, cast members have to be replaced. He is teased by colleagues that in Arlington Cemetery there exists a wall like the Vietnam Memorial on which are inscribed the names of the actors whose parts have been recast. He regrets the turnover but explains, "I would rather have a movie where all the actors are good than an anecdote later about why someone wasn't."

In each film, he budgets a generous amount of time for reshooting scenes that don't work. If he isn't happy with a scene, he tries to reshoot it as soon as possible. "It just bothers me so much to put something in the can that I know is junk. I like to feel I'm salting away gold. You do a number of shots a week. Say you do fifty. And out of those fifty maybe forty-nine are lovely and one is bad. But at the end of the picture, there's been ten weeks, and that means you have ten bad shots, maybe twenty. That you can't live with."

He gives his actors enormous freedom. "I have no respect for the script at all," he told me once—an unsettling thing to share with your collaborator. "I always tell the actors, 'Change what you want; all I need is character reality and sometimes information.'"

In *Bullets*, an actor playing a gangster asked Woody, "Hey, Woody, you mind if I say this when I give the girl my hat—" and he offered a line that sounded like something a gangster would say when handing a girl his hat. Woody said sure, and the guy said, "Great! I got it from a Jimmy Cagney movie!"

His directing technique has changed substantially since he started. There are very few scenes in any of his movies of the last fifteen years where he cuts within the scene; he resorts to it only when there is no other way. "I don't do all that cutting because it's cheaper my way—it's quicker and the actors like it. This way I can sit down with them, let them talk, put the camera on them, and live things happen. They can do it different every time. Nothing has to match; they can say what they want, walk out of the shot, improvise, overlap, and talk. It becomes more live."

Believing that everyone is as adoring of their faces as they are, actors are pretty much always ready for their close-up. Woody's use of a single shot for the whole scene can disappoint such expectations. "The actors kid me about it," he says. "Michael Caine told Gena Rowlands after he worked on *Hannah and Her Sisters*, 'Don't save your best stuff for the close-ups. He's not going to shoot any close-ups.'" In fact, there are close-ups in Woody's movies, but they are done as part of a continuing shot.

By the time of *Husbands and Wives*, the still camera and meticulous compositions were gone. "All I cared about was the people and the story," Woody says. "When I wanted to cut, I cut. I didn't care what they taught you in film school: who was facing what direction, what cuts could make it. When I wanted something out, I'd cut it out and just jump. I wanted to do nothing but concentrate on the content of the movie. Fortunately that technique was copacetic with the content of the film. Whereas if I had done that with *Bullets*, you wouldn't have liked it. *Bullets* is a period piece. You want the thing to have an old-fashioned quality. To do it handheld would give it too modern a feeling. You wouldn't associate it with anything of the period."

Once he finishes a film, he never sees it again. "The only value of a film is the diversion of doing it," he tells me. "I'm so involved figuring out the second act, I don't have to think about life's terrible anxieties. The value it has to other people is that it gives them an hour and a half of enjoyment in the movie theater. It becomes *their* distraction."

As it happened, when Woody asked me to write a movie with him, he needed a distraction on the level of the Olympic Games because his personal resources were being tested in ways now well known. From the time we met, these events transpired: Woody's romance with Soon-Yi Previn, Mia and André Previn's then twenty-one-year-old adopted daughter; the months of fruitlessly trying to negotiate a settlement in which he would be allowed to see his children; the allegation of molestation; the convergence of bureaucrats, quacks, self-promoters, martyrs, moralists, and lawyers inside and outside the courthouse for the custody battle; Judge Wilk's ruling, which not only punished Woody but punished the children as well; the difficult and costly appeals that have followed; and the unremitting press coverage.

Needless to say, it was an interesting time to write a comedy. One day we were in the living room in our familiar positions: he pacing back and forth coming up with good ideas, me slouched on the couch, hoping he'd keep it up. He was telling us the movie. This was a standard way to begin: We would describe the movie to each other as far as we had it and then would try to see what the next scene should be. He began by raising his arms in a sort of Zorba the Greek–like attitude and snapping his fingers as if to signal the start of a show. Then he began: "It's the Roaring Twenties, and there's this playwright who thinks of himself as a great artist—"

The phone rang. He lifted his finger, indicating that he would be just a second, and took the call. He spoke in low tones, saying things like "a long history of mental problems . . . tried every drug known to man . . . private detectives. . . ." Then he hung up and turned back to me. He caught his breath, smiled, lifted his arms, and snapped his fingers. "Okay, Roaring Twenties, playwright, great artist, and he goes to a producer seeking a production of his play, but he wants to direct it himself to protect its artistic integ—"

The phone rang, and before I could blink, he was back on the line saying, "intensely claustrophobic . . . two red eyes at the window . . . sent her child to the *Post* . . . hairs in a glassine envelope." When he hung up the third time, he didn't snap his fingers. He just smiled sheepishly and said, "Okay, let's get back to work on our little comic bauble!"

Even while he was denied access to his children, he sought to protect them from what he felt was terrible and purposeful damage. When the allegations of molestation were leveled, Dylan's therapist, Dr. Nancy Schultz, met with Dylan several times and concluded that nothing had taken place. She was instantly fired by Mia. At what must have been the most confusing time of her life, Dylan was taken out of therapy. Woody insists that that was why it was crucial for Mia to keep Dylan out of therapy until the false allegations could be imprinted on her. "A professional therapist would have blown the whole scheme, as Dr. Schultz nearly had before."

Since Mia would not get Dylan a new therapist, Woody implored the court to appoint one, but Judge Wilk refused to force the issue. "So Dylan went month after month after month during the crisis without help," Woody says. "Once the damage was done, Mia handpicked a therapist. The therapist never even called me. I finally called him, but he was frightened that Mia would fire him if he didn't toe the line. He just totally bought into everything. I said to him, 'Did you know Mia is changing Dylan's name to Eliza?' and he said, 'No, I don't think so; that's just a play name, because I would be against that.' A month went by and her name had been changed to Eliza. Mia called Brearley, her school, and told everyone her name was Eliza. I called the doctor, and now he was evasive. He said, 'I seem to remember she liked the name Eliza when she first came to treatment with me.'"

While we were in the middle of writing the movie, two things happened in quick succession. There was the release of the report of investigators from Yale–New Haven Hospital whom the Connecticut police had hired. The report exonerated Woody of the allegations and urged his and Soon-Yi's instant reunion with Dylan. (This was in March 1993; Woody had not been allowed to see Dylan since August 1992.) Immediately following its release, the custody trial began. I attended the trial, thinking I might write about it. From the beginning, Judge Wilk seemed inclined to rule against Woody. Wilk appeared unable to move past Woody's romance with Soon-Yi, feeling that whatever Mia did in retaliation, including the false charges of molestation, was permissible, a piece of thinking that Woody compared to this: "If a guy gets fired from his job and the boss withholds his last paycheck and stiffs him, and the guy takes a machine gun to a shopping mall and shoots sixteen innocent people, you don't say, 'Well, hey, the boss stiffed him.' In this case, the kids are the victims of revenge."

Wilk's ruling denied Woody everything he sought. Disregarding the testimony of Satchel's therapist, Wilk limited Woody's time with his son to six hours a week and then only under supervision. He disregarded the testimony and advice of Dr. Schultz, as well as that of the Yale board, and forbade Woody to see Dylan at all, though not a single criminal charge of any kind was ever brought against him. He apparently discounted the testimony of Dylan's schoolteachers, of the children's nanny of seven years, and of the court-appointed supervisors who testified to Woody's loving relationship with Satchel. Wilk focused instead on the testimony of Dr. Herman, a man hired by Farrow who had never met Dylan, Satchel, or Moses. Finally, Wilk patronized Woody by calling the suit "frivolous," though it was the only legal option Woody had that would let him be with his three children.

Rather than calm the situation, Wilk's ruling gave Mia the freedom to do what she wanted, a license she has indulged: She has moved permanently out of New York, Woody says, and changed the children's names. She has changed Satchel's name, first to Harmon and then, after a year, to Seamus. So far, Dylan is still Eliza.

Amazingly, I never heard Woody speak harshly about Wilk. He feels that "judges have a tough time and Mia is very convincing." He shrugs. "I went seeking Solomon, but I wound up with Roy Bean."

I asked Woody why he wasn't angrier at Wilk. He says, "I put myself in his position. He was confronted by two people he doesn't know. One is this very attractive, charming, fawnlike woman, a mother of a number of children, some foreign adoptees, some handicapped. Then he sees me, who is, you know, less than charming, and I'm in there with this position: that I began a relationship with a younger woman who is Mia's adopted daughter. She was not my daughter, though many people believe that to this day, just as they wrongly believe that Mia and I were married, or even living together. Nevertheless, the judge sees it and thinks, 'The guy must be diabolical.' But our lives were so much more complex than that. We were unable to show him clearly enough that Mia and I never had a traditional relationship."

I asked him what he would have done had he been the judge. Would he really have given himself custody of the children? He surprised me by saying no. "I would have said, 'Look, you guys have gone through some extremely acrimonious months. I want to calm things down and do what's best for the children. This is a father who wants to be a good father to the children and has been a loving father. This is a mother who has had them living with her. Miss Farrow, you will have custody of the children. Mr. Allen will have normal visitation. And I don't want to hear that either of you poisons the children against the other.'

"If he had done that, we would not be in the mess that we're in now. Because what's happened now is that Dylan has no father at all, when she could have a very loving father. Satchel sees me in a totally forced, preposterous way. There's a supervisor present every second, so none of the normal things you can do with a kid can be done. I can't even chase Satchel around the house, because the poor supervisor would have to run with us. And worse, the presence of a supervisor confirms for Satchel what he's constantly taught at home: that his father is a bad man who cannot be trusted with him alone.

"If the court had only said at the very beginning of this, 'Mr. Allen is innocent until proven guilty,' and then let Dylan see me, even with supervision, till they felt secure there was nothing to the molestation allegations, or if I was permitted to see her after Yale completed its findings, or when the police dropped the case, or when the custody trial ended. But keeping us apart for two years has created a difficult gap. First they say, 'You can't see her because you could be a molester.' When that argument crumbles, they quickly shift to 'You have a relationship with Soon-Yi.' When we point out that Soon-Yi is a twenty-four-year-old woman and that Dylan always knew I wasn't Soon-Yi's father and she's met Soon-Yi's father [André Previn] many times, they now say, 'Well, you can't see her because you haven't seen her in so long it might cause her stress.' When I ask about the long-term stress of losing her father, they don't have an answer. The longer we're kept apart just provides greater consolidation against me, and a dependency on a parent who refers to me as Satan."

It is interesting to note that in the case of Satchel, where the court ordered visitation, punitively limited as it is, Woody and his son seem to have a flourishing relationship. The successful growth of their relationship happens in the face of continuing hostility from home. Woody says that on a recent visitation, he opened the door to his apartment to let Satchel and the supervisor in. Satchel had thrown up on the car ride over. The supervisor had Satchel in one hand and a bag of vomit in the other. Looking very uncomfortable, she handed him the bag and said, "Mia wanted you to have this."

There were only two times I saw Woody lose his temper throughout the long ordeal. One was when Mia allowed the British celebrity magazine *Hello!* to photograph the children, an arrangement for which she was paid. (Farrow's spokesman denies that she received any money.) "That she sells our story doesn't bother me," he says. "The exploitation of the children sickens me." The other time was when he found out that Dylan had been sedated, with her mother's approval, so that she could have a vaginal exam in another attempt to substantiate the discredited charges. "That shattered and horrified me."

As much as he can, Woody concentrates on those whose support heartened him: "A hero in this thing was *60 Minutes* and Steve Kroft. While all the press was vilifying me, Steve Kroft and *60 Minutes* came to me and said, 'We want to help.' Another hero in this was John Miller, a guy I'd never met. An experienced police reporter [and now the Police Department's deputy commissioner for public information], he saw through the thing from the beginning, knew I was being hustled, and told the truth. Also, Dr. Susan Coates and Dr. Nancy Schultz put their own reputations on the line because they had treated the kids and cared about them in the most responsible way."

Woody perseveres and remains optimistic but has told me that if the children are not finally treated with the humanity and sympathy they deserve, he may make a nonfiction film about the events. He will wait to hear the result of his appeals as well as to see what Mia says in her upcoming book.

Through it all, Woody has worked. He finished *Husbands and Wives*; co-wrote, directed, and starred in *Manhattan Murder Mystery*; wrote, directed, and starred in a new production of *Don't Drink the Water* for ABC; wrote a play to be produced next year; co-wrote and directed *Bullets over Broadway*; and never missed a single Monday-evening jazz session at Michael's Pub. He is now filming his new movie, a romantic comedy set in New York, starring Helena Bonham Carter, Mira Sorvino, and Woody.

Bullets is now done. When Woody showed me a cut of the film, I told him how impressed I was with some of the actors who had played the gangsters. He said, "Yes, well, there's a reason some of them are so natural at it. It doesn't require a lot of Method work on their part, if you get my drift." I praised one guy in particular, and Woody said, "Yes, we were lucky to get him. He was just sprung."

One of the gangsters had gone to Woody's high school with him, though Woody didn't know him well. ("I was only on cowering terms with him.") When he realized they had gone to school together, Woody asked him about some of their old classmates. (Names have been changed.) "I said, 'How's Greg Mottola?' and he said, 'You mean Greg the Nutcracker?' And I'd say, 'What about Vinnie Spinelli?' and he'd say, 'You mean Vinnie the Snake?' He did this for everyone I asked about!"

Someone working on the film had a tic, which prompted Woody to tell a story about the writer Abe Burrows. "Abe Burrows had a highly pronounced blink: He would squeeze his eyes shut and hold them that way for a couple of seconds, and then they would open again. And once, believe it or not, he had a partner who had the exact same tic. It was okay for a while, but then they got out of sync and didn't see each other for two years."

He tells these so well that I ask him if he would ever perform live again. "I don't know if I'd ever do stand-up again because when I did it before no one ever came." When I tell him I thought we could probably cough up a crowd, he insists, "There have been three records of my stand-up. They sold, over the thirty years they've been out, in excess of six copies. When the first one came out, I plugged the hell out of it. Not only didn't it sell but the record company spelled my name wrong. On the spine of the album it says, WODDY ALLEN. Even when I was getting the greatest reviews, I was not a draw. When I played Caesars Palace in the sixties, they had to move the potted plants around so the room didn't look so empty. I offered to give them back some of the money, but they said no. Another time, I flew to DC to a religious college, and the father who handled this for the school was shocked by the small turnout. I offered to give him back some of the money.

He said yes. So, you know, back then, I was too small a name to be embarrassed by having to cancel, but now I would just embarrass the promoters and myself. If I really thought people would come, I wouldn't be against doing it."

It has gotten late, and the reflection of the skyline has come back across his glasses. I ask him if his life has changed and how the New York he lives in today is different from the one of his childhood.

"Oh," he says, "my life's the same, but the city is much worse. They can't keep law and order, there are panhandlers everywhere, they can't make it comfortable for people to walk, nothing functions. I can't with any conscience argue for New York with anyone. It's like Calcutta. But I love the city in an emotional, irrational way, like loving your mother or father even though they're a drunk or a thief. I've loved the city my whole life—to me, it's like a great woman."

"Would you ever move?"

"I've thought about it. Paris is much like New York in a positive way. It's full of action, of restaurants and movie houses and bookstores and streets to walk on. It wouldn't be like going from New York to Amarillo. But I wouldn't be able to hold out. I get a whiff of Madison Avenue and 57th Street and Madison Square Garden, and I just feel my roots and blood are here. You know, more than anything, I could never leave because my children are here."

He tilts his head, and I can see his eyes behind the reflection. They are clear. "I could have easily avoided this whole thing. It's everything I've hated. I don't like publicity or interviews, and nobody likes to be falsely accused of a crime. But when my children get older, I want them to know that their father didn't abandon them but gave it his all.

"More than anything else," he says, "that's what I'm fighting for: so that at the end of this, they'll know that I fought for us to be together with every fiber of my being." He locks his fingers, cracking his knuckles. He lifts his eyebrows and smiles. "And I'm very high in fiber."

Interview with Woody Allen: "My Heroes Don't Come from Life, but from Their Mythology"

Michel Ciment and Yann Tobin / 1995

Published in *Positif*, no. 408 (February 1995): 26–32. Reprinted by permission. Translated by Kathie Coblentz.

Q: The visual aspect of *Bullets over Broadway* is paradoxical. Although it was filmed on location, it gives the impression of a studio work.
A: It's true that it was shot on location—the theater, the nightclub, the apartments are authentic places—because we couldn't afford the studio! New York has a very rich variety of places and we scouted a lot of locations to find the scenes that corresponded to what we wanted. Then my artistic director added the minimum necessary to achieve precisely the desired effect.

Q: You've already made a film about the movies, *The Purple Rose of Cairo*, then one about radio, *Radio Days*. For this film about the theater, what was the primary reason for it, was it connected to your own experiences of the stage?
A: No, not really. I simply thought that the idea of a gangster who wanted his girlfriend to act in a play in exchange for backing the production could be a source of comedy. All the rest came out of that: the theme of aesthetics, the theme of compromise, of knowing who is the real artist, etc. But initially, there was this situation: a girl without talent who was pushed to play comedy. It could have happened just as well against the background of the movies, but the period I chose—the twenties—and the place—New York—seemed to me to be suited to the theater of the period, to Broadway, with its mixture of gangsters, chorus girls, nightclubs. I liked the ambiance.

Q: It suggests a film of the thirties about the twenties.

A: I see what you're driving at. For my part, all I know about the twenties comes from photos of the era and the movies that evoke the period.

Q: In connection with *Broadway Danny Rose*, the name of the writer Damon Runyon was mentioned. Did he also inspire you for this new film?
A: From one point of view, absolutely not—I've told you what the starting point was. From another, the entire conception that Americans have of this era in literature and in the movies comes from Damon Runyon. It's hard to imagine the Broadway of those years without going through him. Of course, showgirls and gangsters really existed, but the exaggerated, highly colored, extraordinarily vivid memory that people have of them comes from reading his short stories. So, in a certain sense, my film is a Runyonesque conception of the twenties.

Q: *Manhattan Murder Mystery* was in part an homage to Billy Wilder. Isn't the character played by Dianne Wiest, the actress trying to make a comeback, also an allusion to Gloria Swanson in *Sunset Boulevard*?
A: There again, we're talking about an American cliché. I needed to have cartoon characters, otherwise it would become a serious treatise about artists and art. I had to work in the register of exaggeration. My heroes don't come from life, but from their mythology, from the diva to the gangster, to the producer, to the idealistic dramatist, to the Marxist intellectual.

Q: Most of the time, you write your scripts alone. For *Bullets over Broadway*, you have a collaborator.
A: Usually, I do indeed write scripts solo, but after five or six years, I feel lonely and I like to work with someone. Then I call up a friend and give him a list of ideas, and ask him which one he would like to work on. That's how Douglas McGrath was seduced by the story of the gangster and the chorus girl. If he had liked another idea better, that's the one we would have developed. Then we talk together, we have dinner together, we go walking in the park, and when I have the feeling that our conversations are advanced enough, I isolate myself and I write the script. Finally I give it to him and he gives me his comments. It's always the same process when I collaborate with someone.

Q: You like to make fun of people, but gangsters are one of your favorite targets. You had already written a piece on "Albert (The Logical Positivist) Corillo" in the *New Yorker*.
A: I love gangsters in fiction, like everyone. In life, I'm afraid of them! I like *The Godfather*, Scorsese's films. I was raised on the performances of Humphrey Bogart

or James Cagney in *White Heat*, a classic! American mythologies are unbelievably colorful. If you live in the country, you like cowboys. Personally, I've never greatly cared for Westerns except for *Shane* which, for me, is a masterpiece. But all the others, *High Noon*, *My Darling Clementine*, *Red River*, I appreciate them, but they don't really concern me. But then, for city people like me, gangster films mean a lot, from *Key Largo* to *Little Caesar*. They're part of my heritage.

Q: How did you develop the idea of the role exchange between the gangsters and the writer?
A: I thought it was a funny idea to have the racketeer employ a bodyguard for his girlfriend to make sure no one will cut her lines from the script. Then I continued this idea by having the gangster propose changes in the play. In the beginning, the "dramaturge" was content to shut her up. Then, little by little, I warmed to the idea that he would make suggestions that would be adopted and that he would be the real artist. I also had another idea that I didn't use because it would have weighed the story down, but I liked it a lot. The film didn't end the way it does today. The premiere of the play was a big success, and Cheech, for one year, became the toast of Broadway. Everybody took him to dine at Sardi's, considered him a hero and wanted to collaborate with him. But he ended up finding all these show people so shabby, so horrible, that he went back to the gangsters! That's always the way it is: you have an initial idea and it opens up to all sorts of variations.

Q: Did Chazz Palminteri give you some ideas?
A: What's funny in his case is that I had never heard of him, because De Niro was directing *A Bronx Tale* when I was selecting my actors.[1] The casting director had made me a list of actors for the role of Cheech, and when Palminteri entered the room, I knew right away that he was absolutely perfect for the character I'd written. When I learned afterwards that he was a playwright himself, I couldn't believe it!

Q: When you're shooting a film, is your script fixed once and for all, or do you let the actors get involved?
A: I give them a great deal of freedom. When they arrive on the set, I always tell them they can change the dialogue, add or subtract things, as long as the idea of the scene is expressed. Chazz, Tracey, Jennifer improvised because they like to do it. Others who feel less sure of themselves thank you for the opportunity you're offering them, but prefer to remain faithful to the script.

Q: What happens in a scene when one actor improvises and the other says his lines as written?

A: Oddly, it doesn't ever seem to cause problems. Some actors like to ad lib, others stick to what they've learned. What is important is to avoid a kind of perfection. It's not bad that sometimes their lines overlap, that there are mistakes: it creates an air of freedom. For years, I've been shooting scenes in a master shot, so I don't have to be concerned with making cuts match up.

Q: Were the restaurant scenes that lead into the flashbacks in *Broadway Danny Rose*, where the actors are talking at the same time, filmed like this?
A: The scenes were written by me, of course, but I encouraged them to add things on their own. Since they were real comedians in this film, they liked to improvise.

Q: In contrast to *Opening Night* by Cassavetes, where the audience saw important fragments of the play the characters were acting in, you chose hardly to show the work they were performing.
A: For me, the play within the play wasn't the important thing. It simply had to have a satirical aspect to it—which would be seen in the fragments I showed of it—evoking a typical play of the twenties. My artistic director and I looked at books to see what kind of scenery you found at the time, and I referred to plays of Eugene O'Neill or Maxwell Anderson to suggest this genre of literature in the excerpts you see. What is important is that the spectator understands that Jennifer Tilly's character isn't a good actress and that the play is full of intellectual pretension. But the real story of the film doesn't play out on the stage.

Q: Does your cinematographer, Carlo Di Palma, scout locations with you?
A: No, but once I've finished, he comes to visit all the places with me. Most often, he's satisfied, but sometimes he makes some technical remarks, for example when a ceiling is too low for him to adjust his lights. It's my eighth film with him, and he's a marvelous artist. We have one quality in common: he is very free. I worked a lot with Gordon Willis, who is probably the greatest American cinematographer, but for him to get the effects he's looking for, he needs you to be very precise. You can't move the camera too much, because his lighting is so meticulous. If you move one inch, it changes everything. The look of his films is perfect, like in a canvas by Rembrandt. Carlo is different: he adjusts his lights in a more general way, and I can move very freely. With both of them, I look for hot colors because that's what I like. Sven Nykvist, the other cinematographer with whom I've collaborated a lot, is closer to Carlo, he's open and flexible. The astonishing thing with him was that he obtained his magnificent effects while working very quickly. We were all very surprised by his speed of movement.

Q: In contrast to *Husbands and Wives* and *Manhattan Murder Mystery*, one doesn't notice much camera movement in *Bullets over Broadway*.
A: And yet the camera moves a lot, practically in every shot. In *Husbands and Wives*, we used a handheld camera a lot. That's the difference. In this film, the camera moves with the actors, it mustn't be felt by the spectator because it would be antithetical to the atmosphere of the twenties. When I made *A Midsummer Night's Sex Comedy* with Gordon Willis, I used the same very quiet approach, because it was also a period picture. The nervous movement of the camera seems to me more tied to the contemporary. I consider Carlo Di Palma a master, and his best work on one of my films was probably his cinematography for *Shadows and Fog*. Like Cheech, he's a natural, he learned everything on the job. He had the very same freedom on *Shadows and Fog* with overall lighting. Of course, the fog helped us tremendously. Without that, the sets would have appeared artificial and the lighting more garish.

Q: You seem to prefer the darkness to light.
A: I learned that from Gordon Willis, whom I began working with on *Annie Hall* and who was my collaborator for ten years after that. He had a natural tendency to underexpose and people nicknamed him the "Prince of darkness"!

In the beginning I was worried, but he reassured me. I realized that people kept on laughing, even with dark cinematography, despite the cliché that says that comedy has to be shot with a lot of light. That's nonsense!

Q: Since *Interiors*, a number of your films have a dramatic dimension, such as *Alice*, *September*, *Crimes and Misdemeanors*, or *Another Woman*. But then again your latest films more overtly play the game of entertainment, of "Make them laugh."
A: I believe that's more true of *Manhattan Murder Mystery*. I wanted to have a good time and just make people laugh. In this last film, I was more concerned with the problem of the artist: how people imitate the outside appearance of an artist without really being able to imitate what happens inside him. At what stage do you make compromises, and are we aware of it? Can a person be an artist and at the same time an abominable human being? Can an artist go so far as to kill in order to create? All these philosophical questions interested me, but all the same I didn't want to lecture and bore the audience. That's why I chose to have some grotesque characters. But I believe that there's more serious substance there than in *Manhattan Murder Mystery*, which is more "pure fun."

Q: When the character of Cheech takes the reins of the story, halfway through the film, he makes the more serious characters seem ridiculous. The film changes direction.

A: Yes, it changes direction several times, that's intentional. And I hope that the audience will laugh at it, because if they begin to take notes on the sincerity of the artist and the true nature of art, it's a failure.

Q: Do you appreciate the theater of Garson Kanin? The character of Jennifer Tilly recalls the heroine of *Born Yesterday*.[2]
A: Yes, I think *Born Yesterday* is the best comedy ever written for the American stage. I don't know his other plays very well.

Q: The relationship between the gangster and the girl in your film evokes this play.
A: It's a classic. But the play itself was a recollection of *Dinner at Eight*.[3]

Q: It's well known that as a child you went to the movies a lot. How about the theater?
A: I didn't see a play on Broadway until I was about eighteen. And I liked it immediately, I wanted to write for the stage. At the time, the movies were still pretty immature: entertainment, cowboys, stupid comedies . . . All the serious authors were performed on Broadway: Tennessee Williams, Edward Albee, Samuel Beckett, Arthur Miller, William Inge. The theater was their place. In the middle of the fifties, I went to see all the plays and I wanted to write plays myself. Then American movies began to become more adult. And directors took on importance, there was no longer just the star system. They began to be recognized as creators. Suddenly, authors deserted the stage and began to work for the movies. And the movies became our national theater, they achieved maturity. During this time, Broadway tried to survive by producing mainly blockbusters, like *Cats* or *Miss Saigon* today. Serious plays began to disappear, or moved off Broadway. But when I was young, the theater was marvelous, full of good plays, whether they were comedies or dramas. . . . Not any more. That's why I couldn't set my film in the milieu of present-day Broadway. There aren't any chorus girls nowadays, the gangsters have all become dealers, it's sordid.

Q: But there were the ones in *Broadway Danny Rose*. . . .
A: They were very sugar-coated!

Q: Starting with your earliest writings, for example for the *New Yorker*, you've showed your taste for pastiche, for variations around a precise genre. In your films, you take the genres of the cinema as a topic of comedy.
A: I grew up adoring these genres, feeling more at ease in the world of films than in real life. I was constantly at the movies, and it was bound to influence me. I

believe that's enormously true of directors like me.... They end up making movies about the movies. Robert Altman makes *The Player*, Martin Scorsese *New York, New York*.... We all grew up loving the movies, and so we became directors! Then it's hard not to let it intrude on our sensibilities....

Q: That's why *Bullets over Broadway* is as much a film about a certain type of movie as about the theater.
A: As you've said, in this film, the conception of the twenties in general, the conception of these kinds of characters is based much more on fiction (theatrical and film) than on reality.

Q: Speaking of the theme of the artist and his honesty, we would like to come back to *Stardust Memories*, which was a critical and popular failure, but which seems to us an essential film. If you were to remake this film now, would it be the same, particularly regarding your relations with the media or your fans?
A: It's the one of my films that I like best. I would remake it without changing anything, but I would probably have Dustin Hoffman play my part! That would help me a lot, because the only problem with this film is that people made it out to be too personal. If they had seen someone like Dustin Hoffman or Tom Hanks in my place, they would have digested it much more easily. But it's one of my best films, that's also the opinion of some people who received it enthusiastically. The reviews were mixed, some loved it, others didn't, but the public didn't come.

Q: If you're not acting in one of your films, like *Bullets over Broadway*, do you change the way you shoot?
A: No. I was too old to play the part of John Cusack's character, a young idealist. But if I had played him, I would have shot the scenes in the same way, using a stand-in in my place for rehearsals, and replacing him for takes. It comes down to pretty much the same thing.

Q: You're very productive and you seem to want to constantly renew yourself. Does it ever happen that you make a film as a reaction against the preceding one, a drama after a comedy for example?
A: It happens from time to time. Sometimes it's a natural chain of events: I finish a film and I immediately have a new idea, or I pull one out of my drawer. But other times, I really tell myself, in reaction to the previous film: "My God, I've spent one year of my life on a very serious film, or on the other hand a very zany film, it's time for a change." I just finished a new film last week, and I made it partially in reaction to *Bullets over Broadway*. I told myself: "I want to make a quiet, romantic film, one that also takes place in New York, while I'm about it...." And it's more

serious, more ironic, because I had just spent a year working on an extraverted film, with exuberant characters. After the release of *Annie Hall* (1977), a light film, named best film of the year in America, I directed *Interiors* as a deliberate reaction, I didn't want to redo the same kind of film. It's happened to me on other occasions.

Q: In economic terms, how have you succeed in maintaining this constant productivity through the years, while keeping total creative freedom?
A: In order to work regularly, I never let my budgets go too high, I avoid getting carried away by grandiose ideas. When I have a commercial success, I don't use it to ask for more money from my producers. So when I lose money, they don't hold it against me: they lose $2 million, it's no big deal. And I keep working. It's very important for me to be under contract with a company. What happens when this isn't the case? You're someone like Martin Scorsese, or another great filmmaker like him. . . . You finished a script five years ago, you go to a studio and tell them, "I need $30 million. It's a big film." They answer. "Okay, you're a good director. . . . But you need Jack Nicholson or Dustin Hoffman." Then you call Nicholson, and you have lunch with him a month later. He thinks about it for another month before telling you no. Then you try so-and-so, and that goes on for months and months. And one day someone says: "Get another writer to redo the ending, because Dustin Hoffman's agreed to do it, but he wants to change the ending." Years go by, meetings, rewrites, before the filming begins. . . . I don't know this situation. I don't ask for $30 million. I need much less. As soon as I've written it, I give the script to my production manager, who's always there. He comes back two weeks later, with the estimate. That's given to the casting director, the cast is chosen, that takes one month, and we start shooting it. During this time, the other director is back in meetings and lunches again! So I have a perfectly oiled machine, my production manager, my team, my small budgets . . . and I continue to work.

Q: Do you think about the budget when you write?
A: Just a little bit. I need to remain rational when I write, otherwise I could let myself go and make a film that would cost more than $30 million!

Q: So you're always conscious of the cost of the film?
A: Yes. I knew that *Bullets over Broadway* was going to be my most expensive film, and that was the case. We didn't go over $20 million, but, for me, that's already five million more than usual. The only other expensive movies I've made were period pictures. *Husbands and Wives* cost around $12 million, *Manhattan Murder Mystery* about $14 million . . . that's nothing, right! But *Radio Days* or *Shadows and*

Fog, where I had to construct this whole city, were expensive movies. Of course, not as expensive as all that: between $17 and $19 million. If I wrote a film and it was estimated to cost $25 million, I don't have it and I have little chance of getting it; anyway, I wouldn't want to make it, the restrictions would be too onerous. It's a factor that counts when I write. I couldn't start making up a film like *2001*, with all those sets to build and those tons of special effects: I would never put together enough money to shoot it!

Q: You could make a marvelous satire about that! So you function a little like a producer-director.
A: Exactly. I'm there at the start of the project and it remains mine. I don't *need* a producer. I have producers who put their names in the credits, but their role is mainly in relationships with distributors, etc. You know, once the script is finished, the stars are my friends or myself, I'm the director, the artistic direction and the team are there, it's a self-sufficient unit.

Q: This one is a "big" budget film, but without stars.
A: Yes, because no one has oversight over the people I hire. They always want a big star. But no one had heard of Chazz Palminteri (Cheech). It's one of the good sides of my situation.

Q: Speaking of casting, do you spot new actors on the screen or on stage who make you want to work with them?
A: It happens. Most often, my casting director gives me long lists for every role. There are names that I know and others I don't, and she presents them to me. But from time to time, I see someone good in a film and I take him.

Q: And when you've made a film with an actor, do you think about offering him different roles to better explore his personality?
A: Absolutely. If I use an actor and he's bad, of course not! Otherwise I always think about going back to work with him. In the case of Dianne Wiest, I had already used her before three or four times, and she's a great friend of mine. She called me while I was writing, and told me, "You have to write a role for me!" So I created this diva for her, she read it and exclaimed, "But I can't play that! She's completely hysterical, I wouldn't know how to do it, you need a more comic actress." I told her, "No, no, I know you can do it. I've known you for years, we've made movies together!" She tried, and we shot the first day: it wasn't working. I called her and told her, "Come see the rushes. This isn't good, and you're going to see where the hitch is. You'll see your mistakes immediately." It was the scene where she's at the speakeasy with John Cusack, she's smoking. . . .

Q: And she orders the martinis?
A: Yes, the martinis. It's the very first sequence we filmed. She saw herself: "I see where the problem is." I told her, "You have to make a lot more out of it! More hysterical! Don't worry, don't repress yourself!" And she understood.

Q: In *Manhattan*, you have your character say that New York is a metaphor of the decadence of modern culture. What do you think about that, fifteen years later?
A: It's still true. New York is on the cutting edge; everything happens in New York first, before it spreads out to the rest of America. Everything that's going to be happening in American culture in years to come is already happening in New York! It goes so fast. We were the first to have drug problems, delinquency, homelessness. . . . And then suddenly all America is touched by them. But New York's the first.

Q: And yet you still love it?
A: I love it, it's irrational. But when you love, it's irrational. You love a woman, she drinks, she cheats on you, but you can't stop loving her! I adore New York, that's all there is to it.

Q: A word on your choice of music. I have the impression that you browse your record shelves and choose your favorite songs.
A: Precisely. It's as simple as that. When I've finished the editing, I have lots of records around. I think that such and such a piece could work, I try it and it's good, if not I try another one. In two days maximum, I have the score of the whole film. And it's very good music, because I borrow from Bach, Cole Porter. . . . It's so much better! I discovered that years ago. For my first films, I had a composer, Marvin Hamlisch. He sat down and played the piano—excellently—while watching the film, but that wasn't quite what I wanted. He was disappointed when I told him I didn't like it very much. He answered, "But I worked all night long on it! It's beautiful!" We had it recorded by an orchestra, and I still didn't like it; we didn't use it. . . . This way, I don't bother myself with anyone, I take George Gershwin or Beethoven, I edit it into the film and it works perfectly.

Q: You've made a film about the theater, after the movies and radio. Have you already thought about making a film on jazz, another one of your passions?
A: I have an idea for a jazz movie, I've always dreamed of it. But it would be a very expensive film, because it would tell of the birth of jazz in New Orleans. It would call for an entire recreation of this period, in Chicago and New York as well. It would be very expensive, with the pre-recording of music, etc. . . . But it's a very good jazz idea, and if one day a studio seemed to be prepared to put up

the necessary money, I would make it without hesitation, I believe that this film would have a universal power of attraction.

Q: A comedy?
A: In part, but above all a film about music, and about my affection for it.

Notes

1. Chazz Palminteri is one of the principal actors in *Bullets over Broadway* and also the author of the screenplay, based on his own play, of Robert De Niro's first film as director.—[Note in original]

2. Brought to the screen by George Cukor in 1950 (cf. *Positif* no. 339), with Judy Holliday, who won an Oscar for reprising the role she had created on Broadway, then by Luis Mandocki in 1993, with Melanie Griffith.—[Note in original]

3. Play by George S. Kaufman and Edna Ferber, also filmed by Cukor (1933, cf. *Positif* no. 397).—[Note in original]

The Imperfectionist

John Lahr / 1996

Published in the *New Yorker*, December 9, 1996, 68–83. Also published in John Lahr, *Show and Tell: "New Yorker" Profiles* (Woodstock, NY: Overlook Press, 2000). Copyright © 2000 by John Lahr. Reprinted by permission of Overlook Press.

In the television alcove of Woody Allen's book-lined and flower-filled Fifth Avenue duplex penthouse is a framed letter from Arthur Conan Doyle which mentions Houdini, the great escapologist. The letter was a paper-wedding-anniversary present from wife No. 2, the actress Louise Lasser, but to Allen its meaning is more than sentimental. Allen, who had a childhood fascination with magic—"To be able to perform a little miracle was such a heady feeling, something worth practicing endless hours for," he told me during a four-day conversation this fall—is also interested in great escapes, particularly his own. Like Broadway Danny Rose, Allen is "strictly pavement," and metropolitan to his marrow, but his airy apartment is a rustic cocoon: an open tiled fireplace, kerosene lamps, wicker baskets full of logs, polished pine floors, walls covered with Early American folk art. Even his writing room is not the unkempt, minimalist sump his movies might lead you to expect, but is dominated by a four-poster bed, under whose blue calico canopy he likes to sprawl and write, overseen on the bedside table by framed photographs of Cole Porter, Sidney Bechet, and Fyodor Dostoyevsky—all, like him, technicians of distraction and delight.

When he is not closeted at home, Allen is locked away about twelve blocks south, manufacturing the illusion of himself at the Manhattan Film Center, which consists of a three-room editing suite at the far end of a dusky marble corridor on the ground floor of the former Beekman Hotel, on Park Avenue at Sixty-Third Street. A large, low-ceilinged screening room, wallpapered in olive-green brushed velvet, with an olive-green carpet, and eight olive-green chairs pressed against one wall, serves Allen variously as audition hall, conference room, and clubhouse. At one end, behind a curtain, is a film screen; at the other end, on a little dais, is an old drab-green couch, whose left side, where Allen sits, has been worn through to its cotton lining.

At first, in this subterranean green-brown stillness, he is hard to take in. He is small, to be sure (he claims to be "tall" at five feet seven), and is dressed in his familiar unprepossessing tweed and corduroy, but there's a difference between the magician and his bag of tricks. Allen does not stammer. He is not uncertain of what he thinks. He is not full of jokes or bon mots, and when he is amused he is more likely to say "That's funny" than to smile. He is courteous but not biddable. He is a serious, somewhat morose person who rarely raises his voice, who listens carefully, and who, far from being a sad sack, runs his career and his business with admirable, single-minded efficiency.

Even when he was growing up, Allen was more formidable than he liked to show; the dissimulation of powerlessness appealed to him in the same way that the fantasy of being invisible gives a thrilling sense of power. "I didn't want to play Bogart," he says. "I didn't want to play John Wayne. I wanted to be the schnook. The guy with the glasses who doesn't get the girl, who can't get the girl but who's amusing." Allen admits that in fact he was never a nebbish, never that shlub in his classic stand-up routine who goes to an interfaith camp "where I was sadistically beaten by boys of all races and creeds." He was a good athlete at school (a medal winner in track, a lead-off hitter and second baseman in baseball, a schoolyard-basketball player). And, contrary to his stand-up role as a social nudnik, Allen "wasn't a guy who was totally devoid of feminine companionship or couldn't get a date." In a sense, Allen's fiction has succeeded too well: the public won't divorce him from his film persona. "I'm not that iconic figure at all," he says. "I'm very different from that."

The real Allen holds himself in reserve. He is, like all great funny men, inconsolable; there is a boundary he draws around himself to protect himself and others from his sense of absence, which is palpable in his weak handshake, in the mildness of his voice, and in his subdued mien. Allen's antidote to anxiety is action: he saves his energy for the distraction of work, and his work ethic evolved early. "As an aspiring playwright in my late teens, I would meet some comedians, and I was taken by the fact that they all seemed to have a million distractions," he says. "I thought to myself, The guy who's gonna come out at the end of the poker game with the chips is the guy who just focuses and works." He adds, "You have to just work. You can't read your reviews. Just keep quiet. Don't get into arguments with anybody. Be polite, and do what you want to do, but keep working." On-screen, Allen is a loser who makes much of his inadequacy; offscreen, he has created over the years the most wide-ranging oeuvre in American entertainment. He is a stand-up-comedy star, the author of three volumes of classic *New Yorker* casuals and five plays (including two Broadway hits), an actor, and, of course, a writer-director of movies. His newest film, *Everyone Says I Love You*, is a musical, and one of his most radiant works. (It opens at the Sony Lincoln Square Theatre, in New York, on December 6 and will run for one week in order to be eligible for the Academy Awards; it goes on general release in late January.) His next film, *Deconstructing Harry*, is already in production. This will bring the total of Allen's feature films to twenty-seven, which averages out to one a year since 1969, when he started making movies and mass-marketing his anxieties.

"I've never felt Truth was Beauty. Never," Allen says. "I've always felt that people can't take too much reality. I like being in Ingmar Bergman's world. Or in Louis Armstrong's world. Or in the world of the New York Knicks. Because it's not this world. You spend your whole life searching for a way out. You just get an overdose of reality, you know, and it's a terrible thing." He adds, "I'm always fighting against reality." Recently, however, reality got much uglier for Allen. In August of 1992, the news broke of his love affair with the twenty-one-year-old Soon-Yi Previn, one of the eleven children of his frequent collaborator and long-time companion Mia Farrow, with whom Allen has two adopted children—Moses, who is eighteen, and a daughter, Dylan, who is eleven—and one biological son, nine-year-old Satchel. Throughout the brutal war between him and Farrow, a scorched-earth campaign of unseemly primal betrayals on both sides which was played out in the tabloids in 1992 and 1993, Allen remained an omnipresent part of the culture's dreamtime. In the press, he was under siege; in his writing room, he was prolific. He finished *Husbands and Wives*; he wrote and directed *Bullets over Broadway*, *Manhattan Murder Mystery*, and *Mighty Aphrodite*; he starred in a television version of his first Broadway hit, *Don't Drink the Water*; and he never missed a day—"not a single Monday"—of playing jazz at Michael's Pub. "He's *very* intransigent—in the best sense of the word," says the director Sydney Pollack, who turned in a splendid acting performance as one of the self-deceived spouses in *Husbands and Wives*. "For all the mild-manneredness, the Mr. Peepers thing, I have always felt he was a very strong man." In the midst of his crisis, Allen didn't go completely underground. "He refuses to stay off the streets, no matter how many people recognize him," Pollack says. "It's a pain in the ass for him. But he needs to move around in life all the time." As Allen once joked, "I hate reality, but, you know, where else can you get a good steak dinner?"

In *Stardust Memories* (1980), the character played by Allen, a movie director named Sandy Bates, declared a moratorium on funny business. "I don't want to make funny movies anymore," Bates says. "I . . . you know, I don't feel funny. I—I look around the world, and all I see is human suffering." Allen had decided to serve up more serious fare to his moviegoing audience. He says, "I was gonna do films that had a harder edge, like *Husbands and Wives*. If I wanted to make a film like *Shadows and Fog*, I was not in any way going to live out my end of the contract with the audience. I was gonna break that contract. I hoped that they would come with me, but they didn't." In an essay about Allen, the film critic Richard Schickel suggests that the audience left Allen, but Allen disagrees. "I left my audience is what really happened; they didn't leave me," he says. "They were as nice as could be. If I had kept making *Manhattan* or *Annie Hall*—the same kind of pictures— they were fully prepared to meet me halfway." But Allen defiantly refused. *Stardust Memories* made the point in its penultimate moment, when a disgruntled member of the audience, an old Jewish man, exits from the screening of a Sandy Bates movie. "From this he makes a living?" he says. "I like a melodrama, a musical comedy with a plot."

Now, sixteen years later, Allen has made that musical comedy with a plot and, incidentally, put a big deposit in the karmic bank. *Everyone Says I Love You* is a capriccio—Allen's wry version of an all-singing, all-dancing "champagne comedy," played out on the elegant avenues of New York, Paris, and Venice, starring Goldie Hawn, Alan Alda, Julia Roberts, Drew Barrymore, Tim Roth, and the old Ghost of Christmas Past himself. Here, in the world of pure money, Allen re-creates the sense of escapism which is his most vivid memory of moviegoing as a youngster in Brooklyn in the forties and fifties, "where no one's ever at a loss for the right phrase and everything comes out right at the end." Allen goes on, "After the double feature, you'd walk out again at four o'clock in the afternoon and suddenly the horns would be honking and the sun would be shining and it would be ninety degrees, and it wouldn't be Fredric March and Douglas Fairbanks Jr. I personally felt I wanted to grow up, move into Manhattan, and live like that. I wanted to pop champagne corks and have a white telephone and trade ever-ready quips." The world of *Everyone Says I Love You*—where mannequins in shop windows dance, where love almost always finds a way, where even the dead rise in ghostly chorus to sing "Enjoy Yourself (It's Later Than You Think)"—is meant to be an anodyne for both the audience and the author. "I had a pretty tough time for a year or two in there," Allen says, referring to his recent domestic troubles, which give urgency and poignancy to the film's bittersweet but unrepentant gaiety about lost love and new love. "His heart is opening," Goldie Hawn, who plays Woody's ex-wife in the movie, says; she compares him to "an armadillo" emerging from his protective carapace. Even Allen admits, "Perhaps in some way my relationship with Soon-Yi has had a salubrious effect. I'm willing to play more or be more playful." He says, "I thought, I want to enjoy myself. I want to hear those songs from over the decades that I loved so much. I want to see these people on Fifth Avenue and Park Avenue. It comes from what I wish the world was really like."

The lavish world of the musical denies emptiness and loss, but as a child growing up in Flatbush, Allen, who was born Allan Konigsberg, was visited early by what he once called "the bluebird of unhappiness." Allen has joked about his family's values being "God and carpeting"; what dominates his memories of his "lower-lower-middle-class" family is his warring, volatile parents, whose unhappy vibes "were there all the time as soon as I could understand anything." (He was the firstborn; his beloved sister, Letty Aronson, who is a co-executive-producer of *Everyone Says I Love You*, followed eight years later, in 1943.) "They were surviving. They were people of the Depression. They had no time for foolishness," he says of his parents, who were not so much hostile to him as indifferent.

The feeling was mutual. "I spent my time in my room," Allen says. "I never felt that either of my parents was amusing in the slightest way." He rarely used his parents as an audience for his magic tricks and never for his jokes. "That would have been like serving tennis balls into the ocean," he says. "I loved my parents. I do love them. But I had no interest in currying favor with them. I had other fish to fry at a very young age." (Martin and Nettie Konigsberg are now ninety-six and ninety, and live close to Allen. "I saw them this morning," he says. "It's the same thing. I'm sixty years old and I'll be standing in front of my parents now, I mean now, and they'll still say, 'Oh, come on, get a haircut. You look terrible.'" He adds, "They've stayed together out of spite.") By her own admission, Nettie was "very strict." "I remember you would hit me every day when I was a child," Allen is recorded saying to her in a documentary interview that is excerpted in Eric Lax's 1991 biography of Allen. His mother replies, in part, "I was very strict, which I regret. Because if I hadn't been that strict, you might have been a more, a not so impatient . . . you might have been a—what should I say? Not better. You're a good person. But, uh, maybe softer, maybe warmer."

Everyone Says I Love You reverses the gravity of Allen's past and acts out the importance of illusion to psychic survival. "In the end, we are earthbound," he says, explaining humor's ability to "defy all that pulls you down, that eventually pulls you all the way down." He goes on, "The comedian is always involved in that attempt somehow, through some artifice or trick, to get you airborne. Being able to suggest that something magical is possible, that something other than what you see with your eyes and your senses is possible, opens up a whole crack in the negative." *Everyone Says I Love You* does just that; and, by my lights, it belongs in the canon of Allen's best comic work: *The Purple Rose of Cairo* (one of his own favorites), *Broadway Danny Rose*, *Annie Hall*, *Hannah and Her Sisters*. "Now, I'm gonna level with you," begins the narrator, a flirtatious seventeen-going-on-thirty-seven-year-old called D.J., which in this swank world is short for Djuna. "We are not the typical kind of family you'd find in a musical comedy. For one thing, we got dough. And we live right here on Park Avenue in a big apartment—a penthouse." On the contrary, the wealthy lawyer stepfather and his radical-chic wife with their household of bumptious and precocious kids, a gaga grandfather, and a Prussian cook are exactly the elegant folderol you expect to find in a musical. Here, carrying the well-written story forward, is a shrewdly chosen selection of standards, including "Just You, Just Me," "My Baby Just Cares for Me," "I'm

Thru with Love," and "Makin' Whoopee," all sung by the actors (except Drew Barrymore, who is dubbed). Allen, who says, "I never, ever sing, not even with my jazz band," here sings a few bars of "I'm Thru with Love"—an event that does for pessimism what Chaplin's speaking did for silence. "I've locked my heart/I'll keep my feelings there," Allen intones, in a stanza whose meanings speak beyond the film's moment. "I've stocked my heart/With icy frigidaire." Allen never looks into the camera as he delivers the words, but his cracked, reedy voice finds a perfect pitch for loss and isolation. "I used to tell Mia all the time that I wish everybody sang in life as in a musical," Allen says. "Because you get transported into a world that is a better world than the one I live in. There's a certain tenderness and affirmation."

Allen is naturally a fan of Chaplin, and Chaplin is honored in Allen's living room by a rare photograph from his vaudeville days. Like Allen, Chaplin created joy out of the morbidity of solitude; his Charlie, like Allen's Woody, was a metaphor for his era. Their behavior is informed by many similar qualities: both are self-educated, reclusive, melancholy, and meticulous; both are comic geniuses who give life without actually loving it. But the differences in their styles are instructive. Allen disagrees with the argument that silent comedy was harder to do because the comedians had to get laughs without the benefit of sound. "My contention has always been that silent films were easier because they were working with one simple thing—the visual," he says. "But once you got out of the visual with sound and it became less abstract and more realistic and you heard the comedian's words, guys like Keaton and Chaplin were not at all funny. It's much harder when you speak."

Allen tried speaking his words onstage for the first time in October 1960, in a one-night audition at New York's Blue Angel. "I had unusual stage fright," Allen says. "I didn't have vomiting, but I couldn't eat all day long from the thought that at ten o'clock that night I was gonna go onstage." For the previous eight years, since he was seventeen, he had progressed rapidly from writing gossip-column gags for a press agency to writing sketch material with such masters of this arcane craft as Danny Simon, Larry Gelbart, and Mel Brooks. Originally, Allen seemed to just read his jokes to the audience. His manager at the time, Jack Rollins (who had discovered and managed, among others, Mike Nichols and Elaine May), recalls that he and his partner, Charles Joffe, who are now Allen's co-executive producers, "would howl with laughter" when Allen read his material. "He would be deadpan. It just broke us up." He adds, "The absence of shtick." Rollins convinced Allen that for the jokes to go over they had to be delivered with personality, and that required a performance. "He had no—zero—experience as a performer," Rollins says. "He would recite his stuff like a child doing show-and-tell. It was mechanical, lifeless, bloodless, monotonous. But the material was brilliant."

In 1954, also at the Blue Angel, the nineteen-year-old Allen had been blown away by Mort Sahl and his conversational style. "It was the greatest thing I'd ever seen," Allen says. "People thought he was a great writer and not a great deliverer, but they're completely wrong. He was so skillful that you thought he was just talking."

Sahl created what Allen calls "the illusion of naturalness"; Allen created the illusion of haplessness. In his first night out, he stepped up to the microphone and, in his nasal voice, began to embellish on his short-lived student days at NYU, where he'd actually earned an F in English and a C-minus in Motion Picture Production. "A lot of significant things have occurred in my private life that I thought we could go over tonight and, um, evaluate," he said. "I was a philosophy major. I took all the abstract philosophy courses in college like Truth and Beauty and Advanced Truth and Beauty and Intermediate Truth and Introduction to God. Death 101. I was thrown out of NYU my freshman year. I cheated on my metaphysical final in college. I looked within the soul of the boy sitting next to me."

Allen, who now talks about the art of joke writing in poetic terms— "You do it by ear, the same way that a poet needs a certain amount of syllables to make things happen right: the stammering, the repeating, the repetitions are all an instinctive attempt to get the right rhythm"— had discovered something in his low-key delivery. By a combination of brilliance and good luck (what he calls "a shooter's bounce"), Allen had hit on a persona, much in the way that Chaplin had found Charlie when he put on the bowler and picked up the cane. "Keaton and Chaplin reflected an era where the anxieties and underlying vocabulary of people's longings were physical. It was a physical era. It was trains and machines," says Allen, whose stance onstage was physically almost frozen. "I came along after Freud, when the playing field had shifted to the psyche. It was interior. What was interesting to people suddenly was the psyche. They wanted to know what was going on in the mind." At the beginning of the century, Chaplin's kinetic tramp made a legend of dynamism; by its end, Allen's paralyzed Woody made a legend of defeat. "How can I find meaning in a finite universe, given my shirt and waist size?" he asked. Allen's jokes raised the promise of meaning, then flunked the task. A climate of retreat had asserted its hegemony over hope. The shrug had replaced the pratfall.

Allen kept up his burlesque nihilism in the *New Yorker* between 1966 and 1980 with twenty-eight casuals, which were collected into *Getting Even*, *Without Feathers*, and *Side Effects*. One of his pieces, "The Kugelmass Episode," won the O. Henry Award for best short story in 1978. In these jeux d'esprit Allen indulged his philosophical frivolity ("Eternal nothingness is O.K. if you're dressed for it") and sent up a variety of literary genres, like diaries, in "Selections from the Allen Notebooks" ("Should I marry W? Not if she won't tell me the other letters in her name"), and pulp detective fiction, in "The Whore of Mensa":

"I'm surprised you weren't stopped, walking into the hotel dressed like that," I said. "The house dick can usually spot an intellectual."

"A five-spot cools him."

"Shall we begin?" I said, motioning her to the couch.

She lit a cigarette and got right to it. "I think we could start by approaching *Billy Budd* as Melville's justification of the ways of God to man, *n'est-ce pas*?"

"Interestingly, though, not in a Miltonian sense." I was bluffing. I wanted to see if she'd go for it. "No. *Paradise Lost* lacked the substructure of pessimism." She did.

"When the contact is intimate between the mind and the emotions of the reader, you can just drop snowflakes," Allen says of the difference between jokes for the page and jokes for the stage. "The most gossamer things work. But when you're out there facing five hundred people, you've got to have a good joke line." Eventually, Allen stopped writing what he calls "little soufflés." "I did not want to look up after years and just have a number of collections of those kinds of things, like S. J. Perelman and Robert Benchley," he says. "If I was going to take the effort to write prose, then I should write a book, because I felt that a book would be more substantial and more worthwhile and more challenging."

In moviemaking, Allen has been writing books, but on film. He has found his bliss, and he has a very specific definition of the term. "Bliss comes from the success of denial," he says. "Moviemaking is an immense distraction, which is a godsend. If you weren't killing that time and you weren't distracted, you'd be sitting home confronting issues that you can't get second-act-curtain lines for." Allen exerts an almost occult control over his work. "I have control of everything, and I mean everything," Allen told me one afternoon in the crepuscular gloom of his screening room. "I can make any film I want to make. Any subject—comic, serious. I can cast who I want to cast. I can reshoot anything I want to as long as I stay in the budget. I control the ads, the trailers, the music."

This is another way in which Allen is like Chaplin: in the history of the American film industry he is the only comedian besides Chaplin to be allowed to control his product and to work as an artist. Chaplin owned an entire studio and employed a huge workforce that "stood in line, at attention" when he entered the studio gates, as a publicist for his operation once wrote. Allen, who doesn't have a real studio, and refuses such ceremony, has nonetheless engineered a way to be always in production. His dream deal evolved out of an early relationship with David Picker, the late Arthur Krim, and Eric Pleskow, the enlightened panjandrums of United Artists, whom Allen says he "was blessed by," and who had a hands-off policy during the making of movies like *Bananas*, *Sleeper*, and *Love and Death*.

"It was a bit of an uphill fight," Pleskow says. "But overseas he became very important. Italy was the first foreign country where Woody became a big hit. Then it spread to France, and the Germans took him to heart as well. We developed a kind of rhythm. We could count on a film almost every year from him." When agents and industry executives questioned the wisdom of setting such a contractual precedent with Allen or tried to get a similar deal for their clients, Pleskow would tell them, "Look, if you bring me another Woody, who writes, directs, and acts, then we're talking about the same playing field." He goes on, "Woody was also able to get enormous casts for reasonable costs, because people want to work with him." In 1978, Krim and Pleskow left United Artists to form Orion Pictures, and Allen, after satisfying his UA obligations with *Manhattan* and *Stardust Memories*, followed them there. Their laissez-faire policy continued from *A Midsummer Night's Sex Comedy* (1982) until they left Orion, in 1991. But Allen's carte-blanche arrangement still stands. His last three movies have been for Sweetland Films, a company of foreign investors, who retain foreign rights for themselves and allow Allen's friend and executive producer Jean Doumanian to sell the domestic rights to a distributor. Miramax took on *Bullets over Broadway* (which cost $16 million to make and grossed $20.5 million worldwide), *Mighty Aphrodite* (which cost $12 million to make and grossed about $11.5 million), and now *Everyone Says I Love You*. "Woody has sacrificed great sums for his creative freedom, and he couldn't be happier about it," Sam Cohn, Allen's agent, says. In the old days, before Sweetland, Allen took union-scale wages for his services as writer, director, and actor, and his aggregate salary, according to Cohn, was "less than three hundred thousand dollars." He then got 15 percent of a film's gross, from the first dollar. If the film did well, he did well. (*Hannah and Her Sisters*, for instance, which cost $9 million to make, grossed $59 million worldwide.) In Allen's current deal with Sweetland, he gets a cash fee "in the very low seven figures," and then participates in the profits after Sweetland has recouped its money.

What would happen if he didn't completely control his product? I asked him. "I'd be gone," he said.

Allen sees his extraordinary artistic freedom as a mixed blessing. "You have no one to blame but yourself when you fail or when you do bad work," he explains. "I've often said, 'The only thing standing between me and greatness is me.'" Although Allen never revisits his films once he's finished them, he has a clear sense of their merits and limitations. "I would love to do a great film. I don't feel I've ever done a great film," he says, listing *The Bicycle Thief*, *Rashomon*, *Citizen Kane*, and *Grand Illusion* as his standards of excellence. He adds, "I'm still in pursuit, and that pursuit keeps me going. If it happens, it'll happen by accident, because you can't pursue it head on." Indeed, the charm of work is its promise of forgetfulness, not of immortality. Allen's Herculean regimen—he sleeps seven hours a night, devotes one hour to the clarinet ("To maintain the low level that I play at, you have to practice every day"), and spends most of the remaining day at work—is awe-inspiring to those who know what an endurance test making a movie is. "I am both deeply depressed and exhilarated by what he does," Sydney Pollack says. "It gives me a *terrible* headache. If I'm *lucky*, in my wildest dreams I can make a picture every three years. I don't know how he does it." Of his prodigious output, Allen says, "It keeps you from the fear here and now." To a man like Allen, who is "hyperaware" of his finiteness, the medium of film offers certain exquisite properties. Movies not only stop time and kill time—they preserve time.

Comedies take Allen about a month to write, dramas about three months. Allen, who was practically writing before he could read, takes no pride in his facility. But he is unique among contemporary American filmmakers in having developed an uncanny ability to write complex, full-bodied female roles, and the actresses cast in Allen's films have won a disproportionate number of Academy Awards—Diane Keaton, Mira Sorvino, Dianne Wiest twice—and nominations (Jennifer Tilly and Judy Davis). "I was interested in women at a young age," Allen says. "When I was in kindergarten, I was trying to date them. I mean date them. I would ask them if I could buy them a soda or something." He goes on, "I remember in P.S. 99 they called my mother to school—this was in the fifth grade—and said, 'He's always in trouble with girls. That's all he thinks of.'"

"He loves women. He's not frightened of women. Thank God," says Barbara Hershey, who turned in a powerful performance in *Hannah and Her Sisters*. Diane Keaton remembers being "crazy about him" at their first meeting, when she saw him standing on the stage of the theater where she was auditioning for *Play It Again, Sam*. "He could always get the girls, you know," says Keaton, who got the part and, for a while, Allen himself. (They stayed together for about three years.) "Girls have always liked him and had crushes on him because he's so funny and talented."

"It's more of an affinity with women," Dianne Wiest says. "There's some kind of relish, some kind of cherishing. It's complicated, really." She goes on, "He comes alive when he talks about Diane Keaton or when he talks about Soon-Yi. His whole affect changes. I've seen it with Keaton, especially. The way he listens to her. The way he makes fun of her. The way he has pride in her." (The teasing continues to this day. Recently, Allen called Keaton to leave a message on her answering machine. "I saw you on a television interview," he said. "The collagen is working.")

By his own admission, Allen has "gone to school" on the women in his life, and the particular intensity with which he takes them in—his habit of listening to and apprehending them—perhaps accounts for the fierce loyalty of his women friends. (Allen does have male friends, too: among them are the actor Tony Roberts, and the writers Marshall Brickman and Douglas McGrath.) Allen includes Wiest and Farrow in his gratitude when he says that the women he knows "have made major contributions" to his work. He adds, "I've been able to make a contribution to them, but they are there to make me look like a hero." Wiest claims that "no one else that I've ever worked with has demanded of me things that I was absolutely certain that I could not do," and she explains the genesis of her prima-donna role in *Bullets over Broadway*: "I called him and asked him for a job, basically. He is a very loyal, loyal friend to me. He said, 'Of course I'll write something for you.' When I got the script, I called him up and said, 'Who the hell were you thinking about when you wrote this? Because it wasn't me.'" But Allen knew, before Wiest did, that she possessed the right qualities, and he found a way to get them out of her. Sometimes the situation has been reversed: for instance, Mia Farrow's hard-edged, wig-wearing blonde in *Broadway Danny Rose* was not a type that Allen would ever have thought Farrow capable of, until, after observing Mrs. Rao, of the Italian restaurant Rao's, in New York, she said to him, "I'd love to play that kind of a woman."

"When I started writing professionally, I could never, ever write from the woman's point of view," Allen says. "It was when I met Keaton that I started. She has such a strong personality and so many original convictions." Keaton showed Allen how to appreciate the beauty of industrial landscapes, of old people's faces and their eccentricity. "I became interested in her and interested in her sisters and her mother as people," Allen says. "I felt I had a lot to learn from her. So I started to try and write things that gave her an opportunity to get out and do her thing." He adds, "It became fun for me to write from the female point of view. I had never done it before, so it was fresh. It also didn't carry with it the burden of a central comic persona that had to see everything the way a wit sees everything." *Annie Hall*, for instance, celebrated Diane Keaton and memorialized her high style and her and Allen's high times. "There's no human that makes me laugh like Keaton," Allen says. "She took me over to meet her grannies. Her 'grammies,' that's what they were. She would say, 'Friday night, it's Grammy Keaton, and then I have to see Grammy Hall on Tuesday night.' She had me over to her house for Thanksgiving. I was sitting around with these grammies. I almost died. After dinner, they bring out a deck of cards and everybody plays penny poker. I'm sitting there with this enormous table of goyim playing penny poker. And they're all looking at me suspiciously, like I have a scheme to take them in the card game. It was a scene I eventually put into *Annie Hall*."

In his gleanings from the personalities of his female friends, Allen is aware of a curious sleight of hand that takes place. "I'll write something that I think is a true character," he says. "When you see it—if I've hit it—you think that I know more about the woman than I really know. It's an intuitive thing, from knowing the actress and knowing the character that I want to write for her. When it works, you can extrapolate truths from it, because it's inadvertent. If you write something from the heart, it's full of truths that you never had to cerebrally impose on it. Someone can look at it and say, 'Gosh, how can you know so much about this subject?' Well, you don't."

Casting is another area where Allen's method is "strictly instinctive." Over the years, his shrewd selection has proved to be the kiss of life to many a career. In *Everyone Says I Love You*, for instance, Allen gives Goldie Hawn an opportunity to be better and more varied on-screen than she's probably ever been. "I've never played a mother of so many children," Hawn, who has four children, says. "I've never been able to bring that wisdom—that connection to older children—to the screen."

The actual process of auditioning and casting people, however, is embarrassing to Allen. "Very often it approaches enormous awkwardness," he says, explaining, "I feel for these poor people." Over the years, according to his casting director, Juliet Taylor, Allen "has gotten socially more relaxed"; nowadays, he actually sees and "reads" the actors. There was a long time when he preferred not to hear them read. But Allen still keeps these encounters "embarrassingly quick"—just long enough to get "that first rush of what they are."

The Woody Allen casting call is something of a legend in the business. It is held at his screening room, and Allen, who rarely sits during an audition, usually tries to head the actors off on the threshold of the screening room before they can take up a beachhead and sink into a chair. Even prior to meeting Allen, they are primed by Taylor with a litany of caveats: "You shouldn't be offended," "He does this with everyone," "This can be very brief." Just how brief Allen demonstrates by going into his spiel: "We're doing this around September. There are a number of uncast roles. Juliet Taylor thought you might be right for one of them. I just wanted to see you. Just to take a look at you physically so I don't have to do this from photographs. We'll let you know about this. Thank you." By the clock, with pauses and a few cordial nods of the head, it's maybe thirty seconds. When Taylor and Allen were considering English actors like Sir Ian McKellen or Sir John Neville for parts in *Mighty Aphrodite*, Taylor had to take Allen aside. "You have to let him sit down," she told him. "He's a knight." She adds, "Somebody else would come in who wasn't a knight but was very prominent. Woody would say, 'But they're not a knight. Why do I have to let them?'" Goldie Hawn, for her first meeting, swept into the screening room and, because of her star status, was given the couch. "She was beautiful, she was full of energy, she was great, she lit up the room," Allen says. "After the first ten seconds, I didn't have to have any more of her, that was enough." But not enough for Goldie. "I was just eating the air in the room, because he was saying nothing," says Hawn, who launched into an extensive, buoyant account of her travels. Allen cut her off with a joke. "Could you leave the room, so I could talk?" he said.

Allen is always looking for what he calls "thrill capacity." "Any artist—you see it very clearly in jazz musicians—comes out there, and what differentiates the great ones from the lesser ones is that they can thrill you with the turn of a phrase, a run, or the bending of a note. This is true of acting." He goes on, "You never know what Diane Keaton's going to do or what Dianne Wiest is going to do or what Marlon Brando's going to do. The same with Judy Davis. If you do ten takes with her she'll do it ten different ways."

Allen preserves a kind of authorial detachment from the actors; he stands apart from them, watching, judging, mulling, and then, like a novelist scrapping and recasting a chapter, he has been known to dismiss an actor and reshoot the scene. "He doesn't want to stand there and beg a performance out of you," Pollack says. "So he watches, and if it isn't working you're fired." (There have been a couple of dozen casualties over the years.) Allen also doesn't talk much to the actors. This can be disconcerting and demoralizing for the ensemble. Barbara Hershey, whose "favorite thing is to put my head together with the director and create the character," got no joy from Allen in *Hannah and Her Sisters*. "I never wanted to tell her anything," Allen says of his laissez-faire approach. "I would tell her not to think about it. 'Just get out there. Do what you feel in the moment. Fight for your survival. If you're doing something wrong, I'll tell you about it.'" The method saves Allen a lot of time and boredom. "That would be tedious to me," he says. "To have actors come over, sit down, and to go over all that nonsense with them. You accept the part. When you read the script, I assume you have enough brains and common sense to know what you're getting into."

Many actors find the experience cold, but it is also freeing and—in Allen's hands, anyway—effective. Hawn likens Allen's directing style to good parenting. "We have a tendency with our own children to impose what we believe their life should be," she says. "We put in front of them all the do's and don'ts, shoulds and shouldn'ts. So we corral the spirit. Woody gives you the space to experiment with your creativity, to feel abandonment. Therefore, you start to discover what else you can do."

"Woody throws you into the Mixmaster and turns on the switch," Alan Alda, a veteran of three Allen films, says. "One of the things that happen is that the actors are so without their usual props—without the usual acting tricks that they can rely on—that they reach out to each other on-screen in an extraordinary way. You see wonderful relating in his movies. People really look like they're talking to each other. The other reason they look like they're talking to each other is that they really are listening, because they don't know what the other one's gonna say. They know the gist of it, but he seems to deliberately write it in a formal, uncolloquial way and asks you to make it colloquial. Most of the time he'll say, 'That sounds too much like a joke. Mess it up a little bit so it doesn't sound so much like a joke.'"

In *Everyone Says I Love You*, there is a scene where Alda and his family argue over breakfast about family matters, for which, Alda says, "he did more directing there than in the entire first movie that I did with him." Allen himself uses the scene to illustrate his "typical way of directing." "It would be one master shot—everybody'd be in it," he says. "I'd get the actors together and tell them, 'These are the points that I need to make. I want to know that you're going to Le Cirque tonight, that the mother feels that she's championing the ex-con, and that the right-wing son is against her. I want that to come out.'" Allen goes on, "I just want the whole family to have breakfast and talk among themselves. So I say, 'Step on each other's lines. If you have a line that you want to be heard, fight to get it out. If you have exposition that's important, get it in somehow.'"

Allen is not easy on his actors, or on himself. "He's a sweet man, but he is not sweet when he's working," Wiest says. "Working with Woody is sweating blood, because he hears if you don't hit the notes. He's got great musicality. It's about hitting the notes. It's precision within the feeling. You've got to put the bead on the string, but before you even get to the string with Woody the bead has to be precisely round. It has to be great." Wiest, who in *Bullets over Broadway* was made to descend a staircase about thirty times, knows Allen's look of displeasure—what she calls "a mild and gentlemanly disgust." She explains, "His head is tilted to one side. The left side of his mouth is up, the right side is down. His eyes are downcast. It's a thoughtful pose. But I know what's coming. I know it's not good for me." After the first day of shooting, Allen phoned Wiest. "You know, it's terrible. It's terrible!" Allen told her. "I told you so!" Wiest remembers telling him. "I think you should get somebody else." He said, "No, I think it's something to do with your voice. We'll reshoot it." Wiest, who has a high-pitched speaking voice, lowered it, and after the scene was reshot Allen said, "That's it." Wiest says, "That *was* it. That was the character. I'd be in the middle of a take and he'd go, 'Voice! Voice!'"

"It's just not good," he told Diane Keaton in the first week of shooting *Manhattan Murder Mystery*. She explains, "He just will think of another way if it doesn't work. But if you're not cutting the mark, you're gone. It's not about friendship. It's not about anything. It's about the work." Allen does not regard his judgments as ruthless; in fact, he sees his lack of ruthlessness as a weakness. "I'm the opposite of a perfectionist. I'm an imperfectionist," he says. "I'm uncompromising with what I want to do with my work, but I'm not ruthless. I wish I were more ruthless. I feel that my work would be better if I could bring myself to express feelings of impatience or anger that I have but don't like to burden other people with." He goes on, "A more mature person would not go through that kind of mental anxiety. He would say, 'I'm sorry, we agreed that the costumes would all have red feathers on them and I'm not shooting unless they have red.' But I'll say, 'Well, all right, we'll do it this way.'"

Not always. On *September*, Sam Shepard was granted permission to improvise a speech, and, according to Wiest, ended up talking about leaving Montana to go East to medical school. As Wiest and Allen were walking back to the dressing room, Allen turned to her. "Montana? Montana?" he said. "The word 'Montana' is gonna be in *my* movie?" It wasn't.

As a director, Allen gets what he wants, but when he gets in front of the camera he also—to some degree—must give the public what *it* wants. In *Everyone Says I Love You*, Allen plays a typical Allen schlepper—a lovelorn American novelist living in Paris, called Joe Berlin. Joe's girlfriend has run off with his best friend, and he's suicidal. "I'm gonna kill myself," he says on a New York visit to his ex-wife, Steffi (Hawn), and her second husband (Alda). "I should go to Paris and jump off the Eiffel Tower. I'll be dead. You know, in fact, if I get the Concorde, I could be dead three hours earlier, which would be perfect. Or w-wait a minute. It—with the time change, I could be alive for six hours in New York but dead three hours in Paris. I could get things done, and I could also be dead." But on a trip to Venice with his daughter, D.J., he finds and wins the object of his desire—the married but unhappy Von (Julia Roberts).

By the lucky coincidence of Allen's story, D.J. has eavesdropped after school on sessions conducted by her best friend's analyst mother, and Von is one of the regular patients; thus D.J. knows Von's intellectual passions (Titian), her problems (search for perfection), and how to manipulate her erogenous zones (blow gently between her shoulder blades). Joe, given all this advance intelligence, can't miss, and he doesn't. His uncanny powers are a deception, but Von sees him as a fantasy come true. "You know it's not that he's tall or handsome," Von tells her shrink. "But he's, um, magical."

Allen's art mediates between the need for illusion and the need to reach some accommodation with the real: Von leaves Joe—not because his magical-seeming con has been uncovered but because it has done its work too well. Her fantasy of perfection has been fulfilled; she is no longer tortured by the ideal and can accept the real. She decides to return to her marriage. Joe says, "Well, s-, but s-supposing I said to you that—that none of this was really true, that this is all a façade that I've been putting on. And I've been . . . playing this character just to . . . just to win you over, to get you to like me, make you happy?" Von counters, "I'd say you were crazy." Von can't accept the truth; Joe can't ever quite admit it. The moment demonstrates Allen's dilemma, which is that his strength is also his limitation: he's the spell-binder trapped by the success of his magic into a performance of someone he is not.

"The only hope any of us have is magic," Allen says. "If there turns out to be no magic—and this is simply it, it's simply physics—it's very sad." At the finale of *Everyone Says I Love You*, he finds a way of expressing this longing for magical escape whose search dominates his films and his life. Joe, now abandoned by Von, takes his former wife, Steffi, away from a Paris Christmas costume ball and down to a spot by the Seine where, decades before, their romance began. Hawn and Allen are in evening dress, reminiscing. It's romantic stuff, but with regret just below the surface. As "I'm Thru with Love" strikes up, they start to dance—a Gene Kelly moment in a Woody Allen body. "What is more ridiculous than a man singing or dancing, in a certain sense?" Allen asks. "It's the aspiration of your most intense feelings, musicalized. If you took the music away, it would look so silly. It's so vulnerable and so open." But the music is there, and so is the magic—in the form of special effects. As if levitating, Hawn glides weightless beside Allen, vaults over him, is lofted by one foot high into the air above him. Allen shows the audience the trick and at the same time plays it on them. Here, Allen, the overreacher, finds a way of expressing "that almost something"—a Romantic imminence of perfection, harmony, and transcendent grace. After the dance, they kiss; but, as Allen says, "the truth of the matter is, it isn't magic. You kiss her, and she goes back to her husband, and they go home."

Comedians are by nature enemies of boundaries. They live easier by the laws of joy which they create than by the laws of good behavior which society sets down. Their job description is to take liberties—something that the public applauds in art but abhors in life. Allen is not the only comic powerhouse to have come a cropper in this confusion of realms. Oscar Wilde was jailed, exiled, and ruined for flaunting sexual convention offstage as brazenly as his epigrams undermined social convention on it. Joe Orton was murdered in his bed for the sexual rapacity in private that made his comedies so successful in public. And Charlie Chaplin, throughout his career, consistently scandalized the American public, which called for his censure, his apology, even his deportation. Chaplin defied convention by wedding three teenagers: he was twenty-nine when, in 1918, he married a seventeen-year-old actress; he was thirty-five when he married the already pregnant sixteen-year-old Lita Grey; and he was fifty-four when he walked down the aisle with the eighteen-year-old Oona O'Neill. He also fought—and lost on retrial, against all evidence to the contrary—a paternity suit brought by the twenty-five-year-old actress Joan Barry.

Near the end of *Everyone Says I Love You*, at a costume ball where everyone is dressed as one of the Marx Brothers, the boy-crazy D.J. meets "a terrific guy—I mean, talk about sexy," and the camera angle widens to reveal that she, the daughter of Allen and his ex-wife in the movie, is dancing in the arms of a comedian, a Harpo Marx look-alike. The image echoes Allen's own transgression with Soon-Yi.

In a sense, the public knows too much and too little about Allen's domestic turmoil. The very source of Allen's comedy—his ability to compartmentalize anxiety and to escape his sense of absence by turning it into fun—is what he came up against in the brouhaha: his detachment, so often the source of his comic glory, became his grief. Even now, when he talks about Mia Farrow, it's the legal, not the emotional, aspect of the transgression which he acknowledges. "People think I fell in love with my daughter. They couldn't tell the difference between my real daughter and Soon-Yi Previn," Allen says. "People think I was married to Mia. I was never married to Mia. I never lived with Mia for one moment in my life. Mia lived across the Park and I lived here." He adds, "Mia spread the word that Soon-Yi was underage, that I had raped her, and that she was retarded. Now, she's twenty-six years old. She is in graduate school at Columbia." (In an affidavit, Allen pointed out to the judge that "Soon-Yi was as old as Ms. Farrow when Ms. Farrow first married.") Farrow has disagreed with Allen's characterization of her remarks, but doesn't Allen's explanation dodge the issue of his parental role in the Farrow ménage in any case? "Until Dylan was born, I had no contact or interest in any remote way with the children, none whatsoever," he says. "I lived my life. They lived their life. Mia and I went out and worked together and that was fine. The only reason I believe that we stayed together was because we achieved a kind of separate stasis. It was comfortable and very distant, I mean, very distant, uh, you know, in every way." Allen, one presumes, was present at the conception of their son.

"Artists are just like everybody else when it comes to moral questions and questions of human behavior," he says. "They're not entitled to any more leeway." But Allen, who has always gone his own way in art, has done the same in life— at a cost to himself, and sometimes, as he must know, to others. "He has great balls," Diane Keaton says, of the artistic gutsiness that also translates into Allen's behavior. "He's got balls to the floor." *Deconstructing Harry* was originally called "The Worst Man in the World"; in it Allen brazenly addresses what he perceives as the public's view of him. "I'm going right into the teeth of it," he says. "It's about a nasty, shallow, superficial, sexually obsessed guy. I'm sure everybody will think—I know this going in—they'll think it's me." When the furor first broke in the press, and Allen was accused by Farrow of abusing Dylan, his own view, he says, was "everybody's nuts. If it wasn't for a deeper pain in terms of children I thought that it was almost comical." He goes on, "The thing just kept snowballing and snowballing. People kept saying, 'This guy's career is finished.' I thought, You must be joking. My career can never be finished, because I will always write. Nobody can stop me. The stupidity of these allegations will fall by the wayside—if not in a week, in five weeks or ten, and of course eventually they did." After a fourteen-month investigation, which included a lie-detector test and a series of interviews at the Yale–New Haven Child Sexual Abuse Clinic, the Connecticut authorities terminated their investigation without filing charges against Allen. But he has still been tarred by the brush of child abuse.

"On many, many occasions, many occasions, over the phone and in person, Mia had said to me, 'You took my daughter, and I'm going to take yours,'" Allen told *60 Minutes* in 1992. (History is fable agreed upon, and, again, the two sides don't agree: Farrow denies ever having said this.) When the elevator door to Allen's penthouse opens, the first thing that meets the eye is pictures of the children, on the hallway wall, and when Allen walks into his writing room, he goes through Satchel's bedroom, past what looks like a life-size Tyrannosaurus rex standing guard over the bed. But the legal system has determined that it is not in Dylan's best interests to see her father, and Allen, whose supervised visits with Satchel are currently suspended by mutual agreement, has asked the court for more extensive visitation rights and is awaiting a decision. (Moses has chosen not to see Allen.) In the meantime, Mia has changed the children's names. Dylan is now called Eliza; Satchel was briefly Harmon and is now Seamus. "The children's best interests have not been served well at all," Allen says. "Murderers, dope addicts, people in prison—convicted people—are allowed to see their children. I wasn't even charged with anything, and I'm not allowed to see them." He adds, "I got a bad judge." Allen is thinking of turning the issue into a film. "We keep going to court, and every appeal is long and costly. I don't see the kid, and the kid doesn't see me. There's nothing I can really do about it legally, but I am going to do something about it publicly. I have a wonderful idea for a kind of documentary that's funny and sad and original. I will probably call it 'An Error in Judgment,' because they kept trying to pressure me into saying I made an error in judgment. I think there has been an error in judgment here, but it's been made by the judge."

Allen has no such qualms about his own decision. "I feel it's been one of the best relationships, if not the best, of my life," he says of Soon-Yi, who is thirty-five years Allen's junior, and whose presence is a reminder of life's bounty. "This was a poor girl who was an orphan in Korea, starving to death, eating a bar of soap for food and then throwing it up," Allen says (though he doesn't specifically credit Mia, who adopted Soon-Yi, with liberating her from all this). In his stand-up act, Allen used to joke that he was "breast-fed on falsies," and proper nourishment—emotional and otherwise—was an issue in his own childhood. "I always ate alone—lunch, breakfast, all meals. I never ate with my family," he says. "There were no books. There was no piano. I was never taken to a Broadway show or a museum in my entire childhood. Never." To this day, Allen needs constant stimulation. "When I go for a walk, I get a topic to think about, I never just go out casually," he says. "If I get into an elevator and I'm gonna go up more than three flights, or something, I'll buy a newspaper. I can't stand the unstimulatedness, because the anxiety sets in very quickly." Allen, who couldn't trust his family to meet his needs, fed himself. As he says in one of his evergreen lines, "I was the best I ever had."

This great joke admits Allen's loneliness in the kingdom of self, a loneliness that can be placated only by attainment—by the power to somehow redeem life and to see in the eyes of others the glow of the ideal. "Years ago," Allen told me, "I wanted to write this story where I would play a broken-down little magician in a cheap apartment or something. The girl downstairs would enter her apartment, and in some way she was going for some kind of psychological therapy. I would overhear her. I would follow her, then contrive to meet her and contrive to make her life what she wanted it to be."

Soon-Yi, it seems, has allowed Allen to live out this fantasy of omnipotence. "She gets a big kick out of all that I can provide for her, loves it. I love doing it for her," he says. "It's a wonderful relationship, because here's someone that I can really make happy and do things for and who appreciates it. There's just no hostility." In the eyes of the tabloids he is some kind of wolf in sheep's clothing, but to Allen "there's a genuine love between us." He says, "We underwent a crucible of intense terror tactics when this thing happened. The two of us were in the house. We'd be laughing that it seemed like the entire world was against us. Downstairs, we couldn't go out of the house because there were television trucks and paparazzi all over. The two of us would go up on the roof to get our fresh air for the day. We were housebound sometimes for a week. You know, it was quite romantic. She came through with flying colors for me. She stood by me in every way. She just wanted me to know that, whatever happened, she loved me." Soon-Yi now runs the house she has helped to redesign, and she and Allen have lived together for almost four years. In the den at the far-north end of their apartment, which overlooks the entire leafy expanse of Central Park, Allen has placed a gigantic refectory table, where Soon-Yi does her work: books, a computer, and papers are laid out as if at a banquet. It's life's banquet, which Allen himself, in his drivenness, can only peck at. His delight in providing for Soon-Yi is not unlike his description of doing a magic trick: "being able to do something that isn't of this routine, humdrum, cruel world." His reward is as simple as it is profound: to see his best self reflected in the accepting eyes of another. A similar chemistry is played out in his moviemaking. "There is that constant aspiration toward the magical moment," Allen says, "but in the end . . ." He stops and looks away. The sentence goes unfinished. The gloom of his mortality settles over him.

No one gets out of life alive; but the final surprise about Allen is that, for all his legendary negativity, he seems to enjoy his life and has worked hard at enjoyment. He "still gets a thrill" at the sense of blessing when, in the lush part of New York he inhabits ("the zone," he calls it), "I see those families take their kids to those private schools and their chauffeurs pulling up, and see the guys in tuxedos and the women coming down, and the doormen getting them cabs." It's the "champagne" world Allen dreamed of inhabiting in ice-cooled Brooklyn movie houses on the empty summer afternoons of his youth.

One Monday a few weeks after our conversation, Allen and I met again for dinner before going on to his gig at Michael's Pub, which has moved to the high-ceilinged elegance of the Parker Meridien, on West Fifty-Seventh Street. Allen usually plays only the first set, and there's most always a line outside the room, so he enters the building from the rear and comes up through the kitchen just in time to go on. That night, he was facing a full house of about a hundred fans who were paying the twenty-five-dollar cover charge to hear the band but mostly to stare at him.

Allen plays the antiquated Albert-system clarinet used by his jazz heroes, players like Bechet, George Lewis, Johnny Dodds, and Albert Burbank. He has a Buffet clarinet, which he assembles at his table, in the rear of the room, facing the bandstand. "I don't think New Orleans jazz means much to anybody, but to a small few of us it's great," he says, fitting a Rico No. 5 reed onto his mouthpiece. What ravishes Allen about the music is the "warmth and simplicity" of it. "The more primitive the better for me. The enjoyment is more direct," he says. "The feeling is completely uncomplicated by any kind of cerebration. It's as simple as can be. Sometimes it's three chords. The guys who play it, who can really do it, make it so beautiful that it's astonishing."

Allen takes the stage. Here, wedged between a beefy banjoist and a crew-cut trumpeter, he goes through the band's repertoire and into a straight shot of joy. He plays almost the whole set with his eyes closed and his crossed left leg pumping like a piston. He claims to have a love for the music but "no gift," which isn't exactly true. What he lacks in breath he makes up for in vibrato. As the band swings into its program, which tonight includes "You Always Hurt the One You Love," "Seems Like Old Times," and "We Shall Not Be Moved," Allen's delicate fingers and his body warm to the task. He wriggles on his chair, rolling his shoulders and his head as he teases his croaky sound out of the clarinet. It's as if he were shedding skin, shaking free of his body and his woe.

Sometimes, in the early hours of the morning, Allen practices upstairs in his bedroom, staring out into the night. His treat is to put on a Bunk Johnson record and play in with the band. "I play with all the great players without having to meet them," he says. "To me it's like real. It's transporting. It's like being bathed in honey." In music, in film—in fact, in everything he does—Allen has created a fantasy world so potent that some of his most far-fetched dreams have come true. After all, as he says, Willie Mays has flied out to him in a softball game at

Dodger Stadium; he has played clarinet marching in New Orleans parades and at Preservation Hall; he has supped with Groucho and with S. J. Perelman. In his comic routines, Allen painted himself as the prince of pessimism: "I wish I had some kind of affirmative message to leave you with. I don't. Would you take two negative messages?" Yet he has certainly seized life with passion and with gratitude. "As you watch comedians with joy, or watch films with joy, it becomes metabolized and you pay it out," he says. "You're eating this food endlessly, endlessly. Then you look up and it's part of you." There is something poignant in Allen's avidity for delight. "If I were to close my eyes and imagine Woody," Diane Keaton says, "something I would keep with me is just the image of him watching *Cries and Whispers*. Do you know what I'm saying? Him being swept away. I've seen it on his face. I've seen it. It's moved me. It makes me love him."

Woody Allen: "All My Films Have a Connection with Magic"

Michel Ciment and Franck Garbarz / 1998

Published in *Positif*, no. 444 (February 1998): 11–16. Reprinted by permission. Translated by Kathie Coblentz.

Michel Ciment and Franck Garbarz: Even though *Everyone Says I Love You* had moments of gravity, it was an exuberant and fundamentally happy work. *Deconstructing Harry*, which you directed immediately afterward, is written in a darker register and seems to present itself as the response, done in a tragic manner, to *Everyone Says I Love You*.

Woody Allen: The characters in *Everyone Says I Love You* are altogether representative of the kind of characters Harry could have created. It's a typical example of an author manipulating reality according to his will: the characters are rich and charming, they live in exclusive parts of town, they sing. . . . Of course, nothing of the sort exists in New York, and if I've transformed reality, it's because I'd like it to be the way it is in my film. In *Deconstructing Harry*, you're confronted with reality. As long as the protagonist evolves within his own reality, the one he manipulates, everything's fine; as soon as he leaves it—when he has to confront the real world where people don't sing and don't dance in the street—you can see his life is a total disaster: he's self-destructive, he makes everyone who's close to him suffer, he lives in a state of permanent excess, he's addicted to barbiturates, he drinks, he's a sex addict. That's what happens to the character when he can't keep on transforming reality according to his desire.

Q: The plot of *Deconstructing Harry* recalls that of Bergman's *Wild Strawberries*, in which an eminent doctor sets out on a journey to a ceremony organized in his honor. All along the way, the doctor meets up with friends and loved ones who reproach him for his selfishness. Did you have this film in mind while shooting *Deconstructing Harry*?

A: No. I wanted especially to show a writer that you'd get to know through his novels. I wanted to deconstruct his stories so I could draw out truths about his life, even if his life wouldn't necessarily be represented on the screen. The fact that the character has to go to an honoring ceremony was mainly to let me insert the scene where he kidnaps his son. I'd attempted the same sort of thing several years ago, with *Stardust Memories*, where you got to know the protagonist through his films. But that wasn't as obvious. In *Deconstructing Harry* I wanted to make it obvious and I wanted the audience to enter the character's life through each of his novels. That's how the film was born.

Q: However, *Stardust Memories* was more focused on the social dimension of the artist and the people surrounding him. *Deconstructing Harry*, on the other hand, concentrates on the intimacy of the writer.
A: Absolutely. Besides, in *Stardust Memories*, the filmmaker character was successful, and he wasn't such a bad person, deep down. . . . In *Deconstructing Harry*, the writer character isn't as successful. He's a good writer, but not a brilliant one, and he's a very difficult character to get along with. . . .

Q: In *Stardust Memories*, you evoked the "Ozymandias syndrome"— identified by Shelley—according to which the artist becomes aware that art is meaningless and that his work won't save him. At the end of *Deconstructing Harry*, it's exactly the opposite, since you hint that in a sense the writer survives thanks to his writing.
A: Yes, because Harry's demands aren't as great. Writing really does save his life, for a time. Whereas in *Stardust Memories*, the character is confronted with the question of immortality, it's his desire to still be remembered after a thousand years. When you see him in his New York apartment, he has a whole lot of mundane problems: his chauffeur, his accountant. . . . And when his cook comes into the room and sets down the corpse of a rabbit, the sight of the dead animal reminds the hero of his own mortality. Harry isn't preoccupied with his mortality, he's content to just survive in his own time, to get through life without difficulty, and he doesn't worry about knowing whether his work will survive him.

Q: But do you think that the fact that the character is saved by his art means that you yourself consider that art has contributed to saving you, more in any case than at the time of *Stardust Memories*? Are you more serene in relation to your art?
A: No, I've always had the feeling that, for me, artistic creation was a savior. If I didn't have it, I don't see what else I could have done. But it was never a solace to me, either. Because, when it comes to ponderings about the meaning of life and existential anguish, art never brings any answers—it's never brought me

personally any answers. But I've known moments of great happiness in my life thanks to art.

Q: In *Manhattan*, you had already portrayed a writer who was reproached by the women in his life with using the real facts of his existence in his books. In the end, moreover, they all desert him. Is there a direct link between this character and your character in *Deconstructing Harry*?
A: As a matter of fact, this is a character I feel within myself. I could never portray an astrophysicist or an engineer. I wouldn't know how to behave. Whereas I feel capable of portraying a writer or an actor, or anyone who expresses himself by the word and by recourse to fiction. The same thing happened with *Annie Hall*, where I played the part of an actor who was also a writer and who, at the end of the film, started writing a play about his breakup with Annie. Because the dividing line between life, my own life and art is so indistinct, so fine that it's an obsessional theme with me.

Q: But the existence of a child in your character's life is something we haven't seen since *Manhattan*, until your last three films: in *Mighty Aphrodite*, you adopt a boy; in *Everyone Says I Love You*, you are a divorced father; in your latest film, you also have a son. It's a recent phenomenon.
A: There are certainly several explanations for that. First of all, I've aged and the characters I portray today are at an age to have children. Then, because I've had children myself, I get new ideas. Earlier, I wouldn't have thought about that. The experience of fatherhood has given me enough maturity to tackle this issue.

Q: From what point have you felt sufficiently at ease to write about the very painful experience of the end of your marriage to Mia Farrow and your divorce, and to use it in your films?[1]
A: I've never written about it! I have never written anything about my relationship with Mia.

Q: Even indirectly. . . .
A: Even indirectly! When I'm seen on-screen with a child, it could just as well be anybody. There are millions of films where you see actors with children. Since my break with Mia, I've made *Everyone Says I Love You*, *Mighty Aphrodite*, *Bullets over Broadway*, and none of these films has the least connection to my relationship with Mia. This relationship was unique and very enriching because we were both in the movies at the same time, we worked together, Mia adopted a lot of children. . . . That was at the same time traumatic and completely exceptional. But,

in all these films, I've never touched on those themes. Maybe one day I will, but that day hasn't yet come.

Q: In your latest film, there's a return of the psychiatrist character; there are actually three of them in all. It seems that *Another Woman* marked a break insofar as you evoked psychoanalysis there as therapy, as a serious phenomenon capable of bringing help to those who need it. Since then, psychoanalysts had vanished from your films, and now, in *Deconstructing Harry*, they make a strong comeback.
A: It's because this movie, like *Husbands and Wives*, is fundamentally founded on the psychology of the characters. That wasn't the case with *Bullets over Broadway*, or *Mighty Aphrodite*, or my musical comedy, even though, in that one, there is a psychiatrist character who gets eavesdropped on through the wall.

Q: As in *Another Woman*. . . .
A: Yes, it's exactly the same principle. But, in *Deconstructing Harry*, during almost the entire film you're in the head and the imagination of the character, so that it would have been impossible for me to make the film without psychoanalytical references. All the more because the characters are New Yorkers who are in analysis most of the time; people who question themselves, neurotics who enjoy talking about their problems so they can understand them better and analyze them. And in an almost symptomatic manner, any one of these New Yorkers is susceptible to being in analysis.

Q: How did you get the idea of "defocusing"[2] the image? As a result, you never really see Robin Williams in the film. What was his reaction? Especially when you know that he's one of the better paid Hollywood actors and you never see him on the screen.
A: He reacted very well! When he read the script, he found the idea very funny. It came to me a long time ago, when I had had a feeling of being "defocused" myself, baffled in relation to society. I felt "blurry." Around me, society was clearly defined and I had the impression that I'd lost my points of reference, that I couldn't focus. I said to myself, that could make a great story; I wrote it and I didn't like the result. So I put it aside. Years later, when I was working on *Deconstructing Harry*, when I was looking for stories that could have been written by the character and would reveal his personality, I thought of that one, which gave me an opportunity to use it in my film. I had to appeal to ILM [Industrial Light and Magic, the special effect specialists—editors' note] in California and I asked them: "How can you 'defocus' one character without defocusing all the others?"

Q: You seem to like to make movies with big-name Hollywood stars, like Madonna,

Julia Roberts, Demi Moore, and, soon, Kim Basinger. How do these stars adjust to the way you direct actors? Do you make certain demands of them which aren't necessary with other types of actors, like Judy Davis for example?

A: The only thing that we ask of them is to understand that we can't pay them a very high salary, and we can't afford to satisfy their usual requirements and provide them a hairdresser or a personal trainer; so we ask them to come to the set, do their work, and go home. If they agree, fine, otherwise all they have to do is not sign! Afterwards, they get their name in the credits like everyone else, in alphabetical order. They're very satisfied with the situation, it's not a problem. I send them the script, they look it over—like Robin Williams or Billy Crystal; if they find it funny and think they can be funny in it, they accept the role. And afterwards, they go back to their careers as stars.

Q: On the set, there's no difference between the stars and the other actors?

A: No, on the set there's no difference at all. The actors come to the set and do their work; they're all very professional. Besides, I have the advantage of not depending on them to get financing, which means a lot. There are a lot of filmmakers who have to sign a star for their movies in order to get financed. As soon as the star accepts, they're afraid to offend him, because, if the star backs out, the whole film becomes a dubious proposition. I don't have any such problems, which simplifies things. And all these stars are wonderful. I haven't met up with any yet who are maladjusted or act like prima donnas.

Q: The title of the film, *Deconstructing Harry*, refers of course to the main character. But the film is also shot through with narrative elements of deconstruction, like in the opening credits scene, where you see, repeatedly, Judy Davis getting out of a taxi; or like the one between you and the psychiatrist, where you resort to elliptical editing and jump cuts that are very visible on-screen.

A: Exactly. Right from the writing stage, I had the idea of using jump cuts to give the film a nervous, jerky, and disjointed rhythm. On the other hand, in Harry's stories, I didn't want any jump cuts. His stories had to be edited in a very linear manner, and I didn't want anything to disrupt them, so you could appreciate the shift between a neurotic existence and an existence entirely controlled by art. I decided to open the film with the sequence with Judy Davis so as to familiarize the audience with this style. If I had gone about it otherwise, if I had placed a sequence like that in the middle of the film, I'd be running the risk of having people think it was a mistake. Also, I decided to begin the film that way so the audience would know straight off that we'd done something a little different with the editing.

Q: In comparison to most of today's American movies, your film is of an extreme density and complexity, not only by reason of the frequent passages from reality to the imaginary world, but because of the absence of chronology that characterizes the flashbacks relating your life. So there are three levels of narration: the present, the past, and the time of the fiction. And even the past is scrambled, so that you had to be aware that you were running the risk of losing the audience along the way. . . .
A: True, but I felt instinctively that the public would understand. You know, the present time isn't a great period for American movies. I think that things are going to improve, thanks to the young independent filmmakers. The emergence of all these independent films represents a tremendous reservoir of talent. But right now, movies are always short of inspiration, and mostly all we get are remakes, sequels, and blockbusters.

Q: You are one of the rare ones who venture to experiment with new modes of narration. It's truer than ever of your latest film.
A: True, but at the same time I don't belong to the mainstream of the cinema and my public isn't very numerous in the United States. My films aren't very expensive, so I don't really run risks and I can work in total freedom. I've been lucky enough to have always had an audience, certainly not a very big one, but loyal.

Q: How did the Jewish community react to your film and its deriding of the narrow-mindedness of religious extremists?
A: It's true of all religions, and I speak of the Jewish religion because it's the one I know best. When the film was screened in Venice, the Israeli critics reacted very favorably and I was even invited to Israel. Regardless, any one of my movies—any comic film in general—is capable of shocking a part of the public. Humor is a very complex factor to handle and all directors of comedy run up against the same problem. There will always be people who think what you've done is too daring, too religious, too politically committed. . . . One minute, you have feminists on your back, then African Americans, etc.; there's always a minority that will take offense at what I do.

Q: All the more so as we're in the middle of the "politically correct" era. It's even more obvious today.
A: Yes, but in the United States, people are beginning to pull back from that just now. They're tired of the politically correct and they suddenly feel pretty silly. Harry is a character completely removed from the politically correct, he's way too much of a loser for that.

Q: Besides marking a return to psychoanalysis with the film, you're exploring your Jewishness again, which is very present in the film through your ex-wife, your sister who becomes Orthodox, your brother-in-law. . . .
A: It's linked to Harry's character, the New York Jewish writer. I wanted to evoke all his problems, whether they were connected to women, his sexuality, his family, his religion, because those are the essential aspects in the life of an individual, and I tried to show that, no matter what aspect was being considered, Harry was badly adjusted to existence, a kind of dropout.

Q: In *Another Woman*, Marion, the protagonist, cuts herself off from everyone who's close to her and shuts herself into her writing. Is there a connection between this character and your character in *Deconstructing Harry*?
A: Yes, there is. These two characters—one of them in a much more serious register—are maladjusted, unbalanced. Marion also leads an existence of a vast emptiness, very cold, and she isn't aware that she makes people close to her suffer and that her behavior is self-destructive; just like Harry. Only the treatment of the characters is different, since the first is treated in a tragic manner and the second in a comic manner. But the two characters are very similar.

Q: And both are very lonely.
A: Absolutely. Harry fights against his loneliness with pills, alcohol, and prostitutes; Marion doesn't fight it, she only entrenches herself in total isolation.

Q: Speaking of prostitutes, you already maintained a very strong relationship with one in *Mighty Aphrodite*. In *Deconstructing Harry*, the only person who agrees to come with you on your journey is also a prostitute by the name of Cookie.
A: Prostitutes are interesting characters from a dramatic point of view, insofar as they are genuinely maladjusted socially and live on the margin of society. They've always interested artists, from Dostoyevsky to Lautrec, because they're highly colorful characters who evolve in a dangerous environment, one charged with a permanent sexual tension. They're excellent nourishers of artistic creation.

Q: People always invoke the comic dimension of your work, your neuroses . . . and omit to mention the imaginary. And yet everyone knows that you admire Bergman, Fellini, and Fritz Lang, and your films are very often marked by the imaginary and the fantastic, whether one thinks of *Alice* or *The Purple Rose of Cairo*, where actors step down from the screen. *Deconstructing Harry* has recourse to the imaginary again, sometimes in an extreme form, notably when you give a depiction of Hell.
A: It's a very important element for me. A woman wrote a book about that, in the

United States, a few years ago. When I was younger, I was an amateur magician, and magic and the occult still fascinate me. They are elements that constantly show up in my films: in *The Purple Rose of Cairo*, in *Alice*, in *Zelig*.

Q: In *A Midsummer Night's Sex Comedy*. . . .
A: Exactly. Deep down, all my films, if you look at them closely, have a connection with magic, including the sketch in *New York Stories*. It's essential for me. I don't like stories that are too realistic. I am very sensitive to that as an author and a film lover. I like stylized works that have something of magic about them. In my musical comedy, we both dance in the air. So magic has always formed an integral part of my work.

Q: How do you overcome the aesthetic problems connected with the depiction of the imaginary, like Hell in your film? Because, if the point of movies was originally to record the real, the intrusion of the imaginary has always posed problems. Some people, like you, handle it remarkably well, as the depiction of Hell in your film testifies.
A: You can be excessively realistic in film, even more so than in any other form of expression. On the other hand, in film you can allow yourself to give free rein to the imaginary, which is hardly possible in the theater or elsewhere. In film, you can actually have the best of both worlds. For Hell, I went to look at drawings and paintings of . . . Bellini, I believe, or maybe Giotto, anyway the painter who illustrated *The Divine Comedy*.

Q: Botticelli?
A: That's right. That's how I pictured Hell to myself. When I discussed it with my artistic director, he suggested that we depict Hell in the modern manner. That's not what I wanted. I wanted a classic vision of Hell, I wanted fire, people chained in sulfurous abysses . . . the real Hell.

Q: We've heard you are calling on the cinematographer Sven Nykvist once again for your next film.
A: Not the next one, it's already finished! It's a black and white film and Sven does a remarkable job with lighting for black and white. As you know, I've already worked with him on several of my films and I appreciate what he does a lot.

Q: Do you use him because you admire Ingmar Bergman?
A: That was the case at the outset. At the time, he was only known for work he'd done in Sweden. I found his work remarkable and I've shot three films with him. I've just finished the fourth.

Q: You say at one point in *Deconstructing Harry*: "Tradition is the illusion of permanence." That could be a quip, but I think that's what you feel deeply and that, for you, change is necessary.

A: Yes, I think that this tendency to want to create a permanent tradition is, how should I put it, deplorable. People strive to create something lasting, but it doesn't last and can't last. Certainly, traditions exist, as in the Jewish religion and, I'm sure, in other religions that have lasted for millennia. That's wonderful, but even they aren't permanent. Because two thousand, or even five thousand years is nothing in the absolute. Also, permanence is a concept devoid of sense, and tradition attempts to promote the idea of permanence.

Q: How did you get the idea to name the college "Adair"?

A: I'd read some poems I liked a lot, written by an older poet by the name of Virginia Hamilton Adair, that were published recently in the *New Yorker*. I never met her, but it was in homage to her that I named the college "Adair." Her poems have come out as a book in the United States, but the better ones were published in the *New Yorker*. She's rather old, she must be seventy or eighty years old, and she's only recently become known among connoisseurs of poetry.

Notes

1. Allen and Farrow, of course, were never married.—Translator's note.

2. Thanks to this trick, the actor Robin Williams appears "soft" whenever he is seen on-screen.—[Note in original]

Reconstructing Woody

Peter Biskind / 2005

Published in *Vanity Fair*, December 2005, 320–22, 326–27, 365. Reprinted by permission of the author.

For decades, Woody Allen could do no wrong. Then, in 1992, his luck turned, bringing personal scandal, legal battles, a front-page drubbing by the *New York Times*, and shrinking US audiences. But his extraordinary output never slowed, and this month's *Match Point*, starring Scarlett Johansson, may reverse the slide.

It's been a long time since Alvy Singer wooed Annie Hall: on December 1, Woody Allen will be seventy. But while that may make his boomer audience feel old, he himself isn't giving much ground to the Grim Reaper. You can still set your watch by his production schedule: almost every year for nearly four decades he has written and directed a new picture—the Joyce Carol Oates of the movies—and this year has been no different. He is set to release his latest in December, the excellent *Match Point*, a moral thriller, featuring Scarlett Johansson, Emily Mortimer, and Jonathan Rhys-Meyers, which he shot in London during the summer of 2004.

And on a dull August morning in 2005, he is in London again, on Craven Terrace in Bayswater, reshooting a scene from *Scoop*, his thirty-sixth feature as a writer-director, which will be released sometime next year. It's a newspaper comedy, also starring Johansson, along with Hugh Jackman, Ian McShane, of *Deadwood* fame, and Allen himself. (He won't divulge the plot, but says it's not based on the Evelyn Waugh novel of the same name.) The scene in question, first attempted some days earlier, was marred by a sentence of dialogue Allen doesn't like, and so the crew has returned to the street for another try. It's an extended walking-talking shot in which Allen is caught in animated conversation with Johansson, who is wearing an open white shirt over a gray tank top. The scene ends up inside a launderette. Switching back to director mode, Allen says "Cut!" and then, "Good take, but the mike popped out of her cleavage, so we didn't get sound. We have to do it again."

Dressed down and wearing spectacles, Johansson looks like an altogether different person from the bombshell she plays in *Match Point*. At the end of their second collaboration, she and Allen have achieved an easy camaraderie. Full of energy, she bounces up and down in front of him. He steps backward in mock alarm, muttering, "Watch it—I'm fragile." She even has an array of affectionate nicknames for him, variations on "Woody," like "Woodrow," and "Woodness." Despite his attempts to make her look like a normal human being, she radiates beauty and youth. Under a slate sky, her blond hair fairly shimmers and throbs; she looks like a visitor from another, better world, plopped down into this drab London neighborhood populated mostly by Middle Eastern immigrants. Allen blends into the street scene rather more easily, but that doesn't stop a considerable number of locals from recognizing him. They flock around him, requesting autographs and photo ops, which he grants with considerable grace. It is clear his appeal extends well beyond the borders of Manhattan, famously his natural habitat.

There are financial reasons this quintessential New York filmmaker has been shooting in London, but the move also feels karmically apt, a kind of symbolic exile. His American audience has dwindled over the last decade, the Hollywood studios that once treated him like a prince have turned cold, and even New York film critics, heretofore his staunchest allies—the hometown fans—seem to greet each new picture with a collective yawn. It's as if this filmmaker, who in the 1970s and '80s and well into the '90s seemed to connect effortlessly with an influential if rarefied slice of urban America, has slid into irrelevancy.

All of this was dramatized in an extraordinary and venomous front-page piece printed three years ago by the *New York Times*. The paper's culture pages had once functioned as a virtual Allen house organ, but on June 5, 2002, under the headline "Curse of the Jaded Audience: Woody Allen, in Art and Life," two *Times* reporters with no particular expertise in film drew readers' attention to the fact that "a grand total of eight people showed up yesterday for the matinee of Woody Allen's latest movie, *Hollywood Ending*, one month out of the box and now playing in exactly one theater in Manhattan, a $4.95-a-ticket discount house in Times Square." The ostensible occasion for the piece was a lawsuit Allen had filed against his former longtime friend and producer, Jean Doumanian, for an alleged $12 million owed him. But the article's prominence and snarky, gloves-off tone seemed to suggest a larger agenda: to take Allen down. The reporters quoted the opinions of various courthouse hangers-on—"His sense of humor is sort of frozen in the seventies. He appeals to an older crowd"—and even made fun of his physical infirmities. They concluded that "for Mr. Allen . . . after more than thirty years as the on-screen embodiment of angst-ridden, urbane New York, his long moment as cultural icon may be over." Within Manhattan's hothouse film and media circles—the world which Allen both lives in and often skewers in his films—this was the equivalent of a stoning in the public square.

Allen has become an artist without honor in his own country—not, unfortunately, an anomalous situation. Many of his heroes have shared this fate. Akira Kurosawa found it nearly impossible to obtain Japanese financing in the twilight of his career; feeling himself shabbily treated by the Swedish government for a few years in the 1970s, Ingmar Bergman refused to make pictures in his homeland; and in two of the most egregious American examples, Charlie Chaplin found it expedient to leave the country altogether in the early 1950s, one step ahead of Red-hunting squads baying at his heels, while Orson Welles in his later years was reduced to shilling for Gallo wine. Still, one would hope that in most countries a national treasure like Allen, especially one who toils in a profession wherein selling or burning out is an all too common occupational hazard, would be showered with distinctions, lionized, and fêted.

After all, Allen's body of work is without precedent in quality and quantity, not measured against just other American filmmakers but worldwide. At the risk of hyperbole, or of sounding like a lunatic, it could be said that there is no such thing as a bad Woody Allen film—weaker ones, certainly, pictures that do not work consistently from beginning to end, comedies that aren't quite funny enough, dramas that are solemn and lugubrious, but never a stupid picture, one that is begging to be walked out on. Even his aesthetically unsuccessful films are better than most of the pictures that come out of Hollywood. If you play the parlor game How Few Outstanding Films Are Necessary to Create the Reputation for Being a Great Director, you arrive at a surprisingly low number. Look at some of Allen's contemporaries: Bob Rafelson, one (*Five Easy Pieces*); Peter Bogdanovich, two (*The Last Picture Show, Paper Moon*); William Friedkin, two (*The French Connection, The Exorcist*); Robert Altman, four (*M*A*S*H, McCabe & Mrs. Miller, Nashville, The Player*); and so on. Even Allen's beloved François Truffaut directed only three masterpieces, all early in his career: *The 400 Blows, Jules and Jim*, and *Shoot the Piano Player*. By this standard, Allen is an auteur among auteurs. Among his thirty-five films, there are a good ten that can hold their own against any of those just mentioned: *Annie Hall, Manhattan, The Purple Rose of Cairo, Broadway Danny Rose, Zelig, Hannah and Her Sisters, Crimes and Misdemeanors, Husbands and Wives, Bullets over Broadway, Deconstructing Harry*, and now *Match Point*, not to mention a slew of very good second-tier films and one-offs, such as "Oedipus Wrecks," the only true gem in the anthology film *New York Stories*.

But perhaps it's all for the best that Allen hasn't been embalmed by the Kennedy Center or dubbed an American Master on PBS. He insists that although he doesn't read his reviews, good, bad, or indifferent, he's aware the ardor that once burned hot in the breasts of the *Times* and the national critics has at best cooled, and at worst been extinguished, but that he doesn't care: "All you can say about that is, when you're in the public eye, that's what happens. And you know, there's nothing you can do." Except, in his case, make another movie.

If Woody Allen is philosophical about the vagaries of his reputation, he's not so happy about getting old. His seventieth birthday weighs heavily upon him, although it's impossible to guess his age from looking at him. His once red hair is graying, and he has a bald spot on the crown of his head, growing, I imagine, like the hole in the ozone layer, but his face is unlined, and he looks a good ten years younger than he is, maybe more. In the early evening, after a day on the set of *Scoop*, he is sitting on a sofa in the living room of his rented home in tony Belgravia, just south of Hyde Park. It's an odd-looking place on the outside, perhaps originally a carriage house for an estate that no longer exists, a wide, low, white stuccoed building with a flat roof topped by a balustrade that looks as if it was supplied by one of those American roadside garden emporiums with plaster-of-Paris fountains and pink flamingos out front. It wouldn't be out of place on a back lot—some hack studio designer's idea of a Spanish or Italianate villa. Inside, though, it's light and spacious, with a swimming pool in the basement, an obvious draw for Allen and his wife Soon-Yi's two daughters, Bechet, six, and Manzie, five.

"Aging is a terrible thing," he says, dourly. "The diminution of options and opportunities. It's all just bad news. You deteriorate physically and die! I was an extremely good athlete as a child. I can't maintain that. I mean, my eyesight's not anywhere near as good. I've lost some of my hearing. All the crap that they tell you about—you know, dandling your grandchildren on your knee, and getting joy, and having a kind of wisdom in your golden years—it's all tripe. I've gained no wisdom, no insight, no mellowing. I would make all the same mistakes again, today."

Allen's own judgment of his films is probably tougher than his detractors would imagine. "I've made, oh, perfectly decent films," he says. "But not *8 ½*, not *The Seventh Seal*, *The 400 Blows*, or *L'Avventura*—ones that to me really proclaim cinema as art, on the highest level. If I was the teacher, I'd give myself a B." As late as 1992, Allen expressed the hope that he might still make a film that could hold its own with those of the great auteur directors. "One of the things that happens as I get older is that I realize that I'm not going to do it," he says. "That real, real genius is in very few people in any art form, in any business, in any area. Whether you're a surgeon, or a painter, or whatever. When you're younger, you've got decades to make films, and so you strive for greatness, because you haven't proven, yet, that it's not going to happen; the final results are not in. I'm going to be seventy, and maybe I'll get lucky, maybe something will come up that's really extraordinary. But I feel that level of greatness is just not in me. Because I see no evidence of it, after a very, very fair try. It may just be not in the genes, or I just don't have the humanity to do it—the depth of humanity to do that. But I'm resigned to the fact that it's not going to happen. And I can live with it because, you know, what can I do?"

"That's a depressing thought," I say.

"No, it's not a depressing thought. What happens is that—let's say I'm in a room with Bergman or Kurosawa, and they have achieved this [greatness], but ultimately they're going to the same place I'm going to. You understand that art doesn't save you. It doesn't save me. So then I think to myself, What's the value? After Kurosawa sits back and says, 'Yes, *Rashomon*—I did a very fine job there,' what happens? He still has to come home, you know, and eat his bowl of rice, and down the line, they bury him. It's not that I'm losing my passport to paradise. I'm not. There are a lot of things in life I'm not going to have. I'm not going to play like Michael Jordan. I also will not make films like Kurosawa or Bergman."

There was a time, which lasted a good two decades, when it seemed as if there were no limit to his talent. His success was aided and abetted by friends in high places: the group of studio executives—including the legendary Arthur Krim—who gave him complete creative freedom, first at United Artists, then at Orion Pictures; his agent Sam Cohn, once one of the most powerful in the business; and the influential New York film critics who used to dominate the national media and who framed the reception of Allen's early work. They squabbled about everything—except Woody Allen. Pauline Kael and Andrew Sarris, as well as the *Time* and *Newsweek* reviewers—all agreed that he was a comic genius, and they helped bring his brand of urban humor out of the New York art-house ghetto to places such as Toledo and Oklahoma City.

Chief among Allen's admirers was Vincent Canby, the influential lead critic of the *New York Times*. Unstinting in his praise, he never met a Woody Allen picture he didn't like. In fact, it's no exaggeration to say that Canby played a key role at the beginning of Allen's film career by making the first picture Allen directed by himself, the mock caper movie *Take the Money and Run*, into a modest hit with a glowing review. From that point on, Canby gave the filmmaker unblinking support. When *The Purple Rose of Cairo* came out, in 1985, Canby wrote that it "again demonstrates that Woody Allen is our premier filmmaker. . . . I'd even go so far as to rank it with two acknowledged classics, Luis Buñuel's *The Discreet Charm of the Bourgeoisie* and Buster Keaton's *Sherlock Junior*." Two years later, on the release of *Radio Days*, he added, "I can't think of any filmmaker of Mr. Allen's generation with whom he can be compared," and when *Husbands and Wives* opened, in 1992, after bracketing him with Bergman, Truffaut, and Fellini, Canby wrote, "The entire Allen canon . . . represents a kind of personal cinema for which there is no precedent in modern American movies."

Canby's enthusiasm was buoyed by Allen's romance with New York, expressed most lyrically in his valentine to the city, *Manhattan*, with its iconic shot of Allen and Diane Keaton sitting on a bench by the East River just south of the 59th Street Bridge, but present to one degree or another in almost all his movies. New

Yorkers loved him back. Not only had he captured the nervous rhythms of late-twentieth-century urban life, he had portrayed the city as New Yorkers wished it were, invested with the glow of nostalgia for a time that passed so quickly it was over before it really happened, leaving an ache of sadness in its stead.

Few cities—Fellini's Rome?—have ever belonged to a filmmaker as fully as New York has to Allen. To find a comparable relationship between place and artist, we have to look to the great nineteenth-century novelists: the London of Dickens, the Paris of Balzac, the St. Petersburg of Dostoyevsky. Allen was the closest thing New York City ever had to a poet laureate.

But in 1992 he abruptly fell to earth. His longtime companion and lead actress, Mia Farrow, found his nude Polaroids of twenty-one-year-old Soon-Yi Farrow Previn, one of her adopted children (with former husband André Previn), on the mantelpiece in his living room, and the subsequent scandal burst into the headlines like a nuclear fireball. Farrow accused Allen of sexually abusing their adopted daughter, Dylan, then seven. Allen indignantly denied her charges. "I never did anything. I would never molest a child," he said during a hearing. He was cleared by a panel of doctors from Yale–New Haven Hospital, but Farrow eventually won full custody of Dylan as well as the couple's biological son, Satchel, then four, and their adopted son, Moses, fourteen. The judge in the case accused Allen of being "self-absorbed" and decried what he saw as Allen's inability to comprehend the negative impact on his children of his and Soon-Yi's relationship. Allen was ultimately denied visitation rights with Dylan and allowed to see Satchel only under supervision; Moses, being older, was given a choice and declined to see his father.

Amid the scandalous headlines and the flurry of suits and countersuits, Allen, whose worst sin up to that point had been shunning the Oscar ceremony, was reviled and pilloried on all sides, although most of his close friends stood beside him. ("I love him. He's a very important person in my life," says his old friend and occasional collaborator Marshall Brickman.) He gave an interview to *Time* magazine in which he didn't help his cause, declaring, with seeming cold-bloodedness, that "the heart wants what the heart wants." Pundits predicted that his career was over. After all, for most of his films to work, audiences had to love him, and now they didn't.

Recalling his assertion that he would make the same mistakes all over again, I ask if this is true regarding Farrow. "I'm sure there are things that I might have done differently," he replies, soberly. "Probably in retrospect I should have bowed out of that relationship much earlier than I did."

"You must have discussed your problems with the relationship in your therapy."

"I did. I was a chronic whiner in therapy about everything in my life. I did certainly whine about that. I did."

"What do you think would have happened had you not left those pictures of Soon-Yi on the mantel?"

"I don't know. But it was just one of the fortuitous events, one of the great pieces of luck in my life."

"Didn't Freud say there's no such thing as luck? It was either intentional or one of the most flagrant Freudian slips in the history of the world."

"Right. Although Freud also said that sometimes a cigar is just a cigar."

"Or sometimes nude pictures are just nude pictures?"

"I feel this is a case of a cigar being a cigar. It was a turning point in my life for the better."

He answers every question readily, without blinking or dodging, his eyes unwavering behind his trademark glasses with their emphatic black frames. I ask if he ever sees his and Farrow's children.

"No, no."

"How do you feel about that?"

"Well, I feel terrible about it. I spent millions of dollars and fought in court for years to do it, but could not swing it."

Despite the Sturm und Drang in the tabloid press, the lurid accusations against him and so forth, in the scandal's immediate wake Allen carried on, professionally speaking, as if nothing had happened, which is to say that over the next year, he made two films, wrote a play, and never skipped his Monday-night gig playing his clarinet at Michael's Pub. "Having a stable family life is very nice," he says, "but I can work under unstable conditions, too, because—this is not a skill, this is probably a shortcoming—I'm a compartmentalizer. [While writing a screenplay] I'm thinking, Oh, this is a great joke, and God, if I bring [a character] in here, I screwed up the first act—I've gotta go back and fix that. The phone might ring, and it could be my lawyer saying, 'Do you know that they said that you smacked the kid on the top of the head with a ball-peen hammer? You didn't, did you?' And I say, 'No, of course not.' But I don't sit there and think, That bitch, she said I hit him on the head with a ball-peen. I ignore it.

"The height of compartmentalization was when I was making *Mighty Aphrodite*, right after [in 1994]. We couldn't think of an actress to play my wife. I needed someone who was slightly older, like in her thirties, and sophisticated. [Casting director] Juliet Taylor was saying, 'We'll have to use an English actress, because there's just no American actress available that's right for that.' And I said to her, 'Let's get Mia.'"

According to Allen, the rest of the conversation went like this:

Taylor: "What are you, nuts?"

Allen: "Why not? She's perfect for this."

Taylor: "You must be kidding."

Allen: "No. You know, it won't bother me at all. I mean, this is work. One thing has nothing to do with the other.... She's a very good actress. She'll be very professional. She'll know her lines and give a good performance, because she'll want to. I don't have to socialize with her. I don't talk to the cast, usually, anyhow."

Taylor: "I would never let you do that. I mean, that's the craziest thing—I wouldn't hear of that."

Needless to say, Farrow wasn't offered the part (Helena Bonham Carter got it), but Allen still insists the notion had merits. "Now, to me, I want to get the best casting. The fact that Mia and I had been terribly contentious and had a terrible experience—yes, that's true. But, you know, that doesn't mean that she shouldn't play the part. I'm just not the kind of person that thinks, Well, you did a terrible thing to me in my life, and so I'm not working with you. I'm not going to cut off my nose and spite my face. I mean, there's a line that you draw. I wouldn't put, you know, Hermann Göring in a part, but short of Nuremberg crimes...."

It's hard to assess the impact that the Farrow scandal had on his subsequent fortunes. During the next few years he made some of his best films, including *Bullets over Broadway* (1994), written with Douglas McGrath, which earned him Oscar nominations for directing and screenwriting and won Dianne Wiest an Oscar for best supporting actress (her second under Allen's direction, after *Hannah and Her Sisters*). But it's safe to say the scandal didn't help Allen's career. His longtime co-producer Charles Joffe admits, "It hurt him." As Allen himself puts it, "There are people that just were never crazy about me. Then, when I hit the newspapers with all of that, they said, 'See? I was right.' So now, whatever I do is bad. I could make, you know, *Grand Illusion* or *The Bicycle Thief* and they'll find fault with the movie."

In the wake of the scandal, when *Husbands and Wives* and its follow-up, *Manhattan Murder Mystery*, didn't perform as well as hoped for by Tri-Star—the last link in the studio daisy chain that had financed his movies for more than two decades (Tri-Star head Mike Medavoy had been a co-founder at Orion)—Allen just shrugged and seamlessly moved on to Sweetland, an independent production company run by his old friend Jean Doumanian, best known for her disastrous one-year tenure at *Saturday Night Live* in the early eighties.

At the same time, Allen's cozy relationship with the critics took a hit. Back in 1993, just when the director needed him most, Canby moved to the theater beat of the *Times*. He was succeeded by Janet Maslin, who liked Allen's films and treated the filmmaker with respect. But when she left the film page in 1999, she was succeeded by a troika that included two younger men, A. O. Scott and Elvis Mitchell. While they didn't have any particular agendas, it seemed like a generation gap had opened between them and Allen; they were not about to give him the benefit of the doubt.

The relationship with Doumanian came apart in 2000 when she reportedly told Allen, only a month before the start date for *The Curse of the Jade Scorpion*, that she was pulling the plug, giving him forty-eight hours to find alternative financing. Allen sued Doumanian later for unpaid profits, and they eventually settled, reportedly for a substantial sum. (Doumanian's office referred my calls to her lawyer, who declined to comment because the settlement remains sealed.) Nevertheless, Allen's suit triggered yet another avalanche of bad press, including the page-one "Jaded Audience" smackdown in the *Times*. (That piece was so vitriolic that even some people at the paper blanched. "I thought at the time, This is outrageous," says Maslin. "It was an unusually spiteful and vindictive piece. All I could think about was that if Vincent Canby had been alive, he would have gone berserk. . . . There are people who'll never forgive Allen for the Farrow scandal, who won't even see his movies anymore.")

Allen's probably right in his oft-stated conviction that drama has a gravitas that comedy, which comes more easily to him, doesn't. But the problem with his work, if there is one, may have more to do with the rate of his output than with the shallowness of his soul. Anyone who writes at the furious pace he does is bound to repeat himself, bound to get tired or stale. Which brings us to the sticky subject of his most recent group of films, the ones that have taken a drubbing from the critics, more or less starting with *Small Time Crooks*, in 2000, and followed by *The Curse of the Jade Scorpion*, *Hollywood Ending*, *Anything Else*, and *Melinda and Melinda*. He has had slumps before—every filmmaker has. The real problem with the recent pictures is not that they're bad—they're not—it's that they're slight. His truly great films are dense dramas or social comedies, alive with anger and irony. Most of all, they are how-we-live-now films that give you a shock of recognition; in his characters you see your friends or people like your friends or, if you're unlucky, yourself. They jump off the screen—the anxious lovers in *Annie Hall*, the conflicted family members in *Hannah and Her Sisters*, the broken middle-aged spouses in *Husbands and Wives*—and you find yourself saying, "Yes, that's how it is, that's how we are!" By way of contrast, many of the more recent films feel like cerebral exercises, extended stand-up routines that play out ingenious premises—"what if" pictures such as *Melinda and Melinda* (the same story told twice, as comedy and tragedy) or, more successfully, the underrated *Hollywood Ending* (a film director struck by hysterical blindness and hiding it from his producer). By Allen's own admission, he has been avoiding the richly hued tapestries that made his reputation: "I have not been attempting to do that kind of film. It has not interested me that much." Why this is, he will not or cannot say. Marshall Brickman offers one guess: "It could be that he got exhausted emotionally from all the things that happened with Mia, the new marriage, and so on. I can't believe that that emotional roller coaster doesn't take its toll. You can't write a movie like *Crimes and Misdemeanors* or *Hannah* without really pulling stuff out of your gut. At a certain point you need a rest."

It could be true, too, that he's tired of people reading his serious films autobiographically, usually to his disadvantage. For example, he often portrays artists of one stripe or another wreaking havoc on the lives of those close to them, as in *Deconstructing Harry* (in which he played the title character, a narcissistic writer) and *Sweet and Lowdown* (starring Sean Penn and loosely inspired by the life of the jazz guitarist Django Reinhardt). Allen invariably denies that these characters have anything to do with himself. But, says Brickman, "it's inevitable that people are going to identify his characters in his movies, especially if he's playing them, as *à clef* in some way, because that's the way he made his mark initially, talking about himself as a stand-up comic. He can deny it, but it's certainly true."

One reason critics and audiences mine his movies for scraps of biographical detritus is that Allen is so private. He doesn't—or hardly ever—make the talk-show circuit, doesn't open his home to *Architectural Digest* or *InStyle*. Even those who have worked with him closely don't pretend to understand him. Says Richard Brick, who co-produced *Sweet and Lowdown*, *Deconstructing Harry*, and *Celebrity*, "He's the proverbial enigma wrapped in a mystique."

There's also the question, raised by some reviewers, of whether Allen has lost touch with contemporary life and culture. His own private life has always been circumscribed. Unlike most of his peers, for instance, he never did drugs, even in the days when joints were more common than cigarettes. "I was in the thick of it, in the sixties, because I was a nightclub comic who worked with jazz musicians," he says. "I worked with acts that couldn't walk onstage, they were so high. I remember being with Jack Benny, who was much older than me, and a very staid, Beverly Hills, Jewish comic. And he was saying to me, 'I've got to try marijuana—I'm just dying to try it.' I've never had a puff of marijuana. I've never had cocaine. I've never had speed. I've never had heroin. I've never in my life had a sleeping pill. I don't have drug curiosity. I don't have travel curiosity. I don't have any curiosity. That's part of my symptoms. It's kind of a low-level depression. It's not the kind of depression that sends you into the hospital, or makes you want to kill yourself, or something. It's kind of like part of or half a depression. Maybe it would be better for me if I did feel extremes a little more, and I was irate, or a letter writer, or broken up when I was treated unfairly, or experienced great joy and fun when—but this has just not been my personality. My shrink said to me, a long time ago, 'When you came here, I thought it was going to be extremely interesting and kind of fascinating, but it's like, you know, listening to an accountant or something.' My life has been very dull."

It's so dull that around the time he started seeing Soon-Yi he finally ended the on-again, off-again psychotherapy that had run like a thread through most of his adult life and served as fodder for countless jokes, although he never did get rid of his celebrated phobias. He is still claustrophobic and agoraphobic. He won't go through tunnels. He doesn't like the country after dark, or showers with drains in the center of the floor. ("Who knows what's down there? I've seen water bugs come out of drains.") The way he describes it, in a manner somewhere between serious and ironic, there's a ritualistic quality to his behavior: "I don't like to change the pants that I wear when I'm working on something. I do it with great trepidation, only if I spill something really nauseating on them. I have the same breakfast, every day: skim milk with Cheerios, raisins, banana. I always cut the banana into seven slices. And I count them and re-count them to make sure that there's seven. Because my life has gone well with seven slices, and I don't want to tempt fate and have six or eight."

There's an abstemious quality to Allen's life as well. As one close friend says, "He lives to deny himself." If this is really true, it makes his string of great films all the more remarkable—they should give dullness a new cachet. But paring down his life is key to his preternatural focus on work. When he's not in production, each day is the same: he's on the treadmill first thing, takes his kids to school, writes much of the day in longhand sitting on his bed until he doesn't feel like it anymore, practices the clarinet, eats dinner at home or sometimes out at Elaine's, watches a ball game, and goes to bed early. This is at once his greatest strength and his greatest weakness; the price he pays for his intense focus—his ability to "compartmentalize"—is perhaps its flip side: tunnel vision. "You exclude things that might be helpful to you artistically if you don't open that door to new experiences," says Brickman. "There's no free lunch. What happened with Woody is that he needed to re-adjust his on-screen persona to stories and material that were age-appropriate, move on to the problems of middle and older age in the films he appears in as a character."

Despite the self-graded B, Allen defends his recent work, but he also acknowledges that there are themes he returns to again and again—like the paranoia about anti-Semitism his characters give vent to in *Annie Hall* and *Anything Else*, or the epiphanies about the consolations of art or love in the face of existential despair that have climaxed so many of his films—and that this can pose a problem for some viewers.

"I've been around a long time, and some people may just get tired of me, which I can understand," he says. "I've tried to keep my films different over the years, but it's like they complain, 'We've eaten Chinese food every day this week.' I want to say, 'Well, yes, but you had a shrimp meal and you had a pork meal and you had a chicken meal.' They say, 'Yes, yes, but it's all Chinese food.' That's the way I feel about myself. I have a certain amount of obsessive themes and a certain amount of things that I'm interested in and no matter how different the film is, whether it's *Small Time Crooks* here or *Zelig* there, you find in the end that it's Chinese food. If you're not in the mood for my obsessions, then you may not be in the mood for my film. Now, hopefully, if I make enough films, some of them will come out fresh, but there's no guarantee. It's a crapshoot every time I make one. It could come out interesting or you might get the feeling that, God, I've heard this kvetch before—I don't know."

Back in the USA, a few weeks later, we are sitting in Allen's screening room in an apartment building on the Upper East Side. He is dressed much the same as he was when I last saw him, in a pale-blue long-sleeved shirt and khaki pants. The room, done in muted greens and browns, with heavy velvet drapes, and a half-dozen or so easy chairs, settees, and couches scattered about, is a tad frayed around the edges, lending it a comfortable but funky look, like the lobby of the Algonquin Hotel before it was refurbished. Next door is a small editing room, where editing has begun on *Scoop*.

Allen, pleased to be back in Manhattan, is apprehensive about the movie's first cut, which he will look at in a day or so. "That's the time the cold shower sets in," he says. "That's when your heart says to you, My God, this thing is too long and too slow and this joke doesn't work, and that performance doesn't hang together. Then you have to do the real work, the real sweating."

We begin talking about finances, Hollywood's and his own. While Allen continues to enjoy a privileged, nearly unique place in American film—he doesn't have to brook creative interference from the suits—he now has to do what everyone else in the film business has done from year zero: chase the money. In the old days, his films may not have made a huge dent at the American box office (his biggest grosser was 1986's *Hannah and Her Sisters*, which took in $40 million), but his audience was passionate and loyal and he could rely on foreign grosses, often as much as or more than his American box office, to make up any shortfall and even ice the cake. Plus, for his longtime studio backers there was the bonus of being associated with a filmmaker of quality. But since *Deconstructing Harry*, which earned $10.6 million, Allen's grosses have dipped to about $5 million a picture, against budgets that have averaged about $20 million. Fox Searchlight, which had financed his previous movie, *Melinda and Melinda*, did not even bother to bid on distributing *Match Point* because of *Melinda and Melinda*'s numbers: $3.8 million domestic gross and $16 million foreign. Says another distributor who passed on the new film, "*Match Point* is wonderful, but they were asking $7 million for it and, as I recall, a lot of the foreign rights had been sold off." (Eventually, the film was picked up by DreamWorks.)

And so Allen has discovered that money, at least American money, now comes with a great many strings attached. "In recent years, the studios' attitude has changed," he explains. "It's 'Look, we're not just the bank. You can't just come to us and say, "Give us the money," and then we don't see it till it's finished. We'd like to have input.' I don't feel that they're qualified to give the input. They wouldn't know a good script from a problem script or how to cast a picture, not the first thing about it. That's not the way I want to make films. It would've been tough for me to go in and pitch *Match Point* to someone. They wouldn't make it, just as they wouldn't make three-quarters of my pictures." In England, on the other hand, the money, in this case furnished by a consortium of investors including the BBC, comes with no strings, or, more accurately, strings he can live with: a largely British cast and crew, and British locations. Allen likes working in the UK. "The stars don't deem it any kind of a comedown to do a three-line part. I'm able to work on a low budget there and it doesn't look like a low budget. If I made *Match Point* in New York, it would have cost me more money."

Like *Match Point*, the cost of *Scoop* is about $15 million, a bit cheaper than most of his recent films. According to Allen, he's always been frugal where budgets are concerned. "I've worked cheaply so I could have my freedom. If I needed two weeks of reshooting, if I wanted to get this actress, if I wanted to have that expensive Cole Porter song—I had to pay half of the costs from my salary. . . . There were times where I ate my entire salary up. I've never gotten rich making movies."

I bring up the duplex penthouse he used to own on Fifth Avenue.

"When I bought my penthouse on Fifth Avenue, in the 1970s, I was a nightclub comic and just starting to make films. I paid a song for it. It was like $600,000." Twenty years later, when he sold it because it was small for a family with two young kids, he got $13 million. Then in 1999 he and Soon-Yi bought a townhouse for $17.9 million in the Upper East Side's Carnegie Hill neighborhood—a big townhouse, 20,000 square feet, because of his claustrophobia. They put in twenty-nine telephones, he says. But it turned out to be way more space than they needed, so he turned around and sold that in 2004 for $24 million. The family is currently renting on the Upper East Side, pending the purchase of a new home.

"I made more money in real estate than I've ever made from movies," Allen continues. "Compared to my contemporaries, it's relatively nothing. Barbra Streisand could be in a movie, or someone could direct a movie, and make on one picture what I make in five. I wish I had more money. Take a look at my offices, for example, and take a look at Marty Scorsese's place up the block. I've got these two rooms, with rented editing equipment, and he's got—I'm not saying he doesn't deserve it, he does—he's got archives and screening rooms and conference rooms. It looks like an opulent law firm. It's beautiful.

"Now, I'm not crying poverty. By the standards of my sister, who worked for years as a teacher, or her husband, who worked as a principal, or my mother, who worked in a flower shop—forget it. Show-business salaries are so inflated that next to a normal salary it's like a pasha or something. It's unbelievable. But I'm not Hollywood wealthy. I've never taken advantage of the sellout opportunities I've had. I've never agreed to do *Annie Hall II*. I've never really cared that much about money." (He has in fact been approached "all the time" about doing an *Annie Hall* sequel.)

In recent years, Allen has become quite the family man, and he is uncharacteristically upbeat about it.

I ask him what it's like, at nearly seventy, to be married to a woman as young as Soon-Yi?

"If somebody told me when I was younger, 'You're going to wind up married to a girl thirty-five years younger than you and a Korean, not in show business, not having any real interest in show business,' I would have said, 'You're completely crazy.' Because all the women that I went out with were basically my age. Two years younger. Ten years was the maximum. Now, here, it just works like magic. The very inequality of me being older and much more accomplished, much more experienced, takes away any real meaningful conflict. So when there's disagreement, it's never an adversarial thing. I don't ever feel that I'm with a hostile or threatening person. It's got a more paternal feeling to it. I love to do things to make her happy. She loves to do things to make me happy. It just works out great. It was just completely fortuitous. One of the truly lucky things that happened to me in my life."

"There must be a Pygmalion-esque dimension to it? The way Alvy forced books on Annie Hall and dragged her to *The Sorrow and the Pity*?"

"No. I do not mold Soon-Yi into anything. She's very self-possessed and she runs the house and the kids and our life. She runs it better than I could ever run it because she's interested in it. She will check the accountant's statements, and she will deal with health issues, and she will structure the kids' lessons after school and their playdates. And I am free to work and have a great time with her and have a great time with the kids. As I say, it was like two people that you would have thought, Are you kidding? Forget it—it's the craziest thing in the world. And just by sheer accident, it worked out just delightfully."

The conversation returns to *Match Point*, which is a departure from Allen's recent films in that it is a thriller with a whiff of *Fatal Attraction* as well as a good dose of the usual existential angst. The main character is an impecunious tennis pro at a posh club in London who insinuates himself into the heart of a wealthy family and is then forced to make desperate moral choices when his new position is threatened. Generating good buzz, the film has already been hailed by the *New York Times*. A. O. Scott, who has been tough on Allen in the past, reviewed the new film last May after its premiere at Cannes and called it "first-rate" and "both a departure and a return to form." Allen says it is just the kind of movie his fans have missed: "It's a serious picture and I haven't done a serious picture in a long time. To me, it is strictly about luck. Life is such a terrifying experience—it's very important to feel, 'I don't believe in luck. Well, I make my luck.' Well, the truth of the matter is, you don't make your luck. So I wanted to show that here was a guy—and I symbolically made him a tennis player—who's a pretty bad guy, and yet my feeling is, in life, if you get the breaks—if the luck bounces your way, you know—you can not only get by, you can flourish in the same way that I felt Marty Landau could in *Crimes and Misdemeanors*, where he killed that airline stewardess he was having the affair with, Anjelica Huston. If you can kill somebody—if you have no moral sense—there's no God out there that's suddenly going to hit you with lightning. Because I don't believe in God. So this is what was on my mind: the enormous unfairness of the world, the enormous injustice of the world, the sense that every day people get away with the worst kinds of crimes. So it's a pessimistic film, in that sense. But I've always been accused of being either cynical or pessimistic—misanthropic, that's another one—and I never felt I was misanthropic or cynical. But I am definitely pessimistic."

"Pessimism, cynicism, and misanthropy. The trifecta of Jewish misery, neurosis, or whatever."

"Yeah. The realists' trifecta. I feel a cynic is what they call a realist—you know what I mean? Mark Twain was pessimistic. Freud was pessimistic. So what? That's just a point of view of life."

Match Point is indeed a pessimistic movie, shocking even, for the violence that shatters the veneer of its upper-class world, but it doesn't feel like it, because of the pleasure that a well-made movie conveys. And for all its Englishness, it seems pleasantly familiar, like a homecoming; the irony, of course, is that Allen had to go away so that he could return. My guess is that the audiences will embrace this picture; they're ready for him to return. As Brickman puts it, "Americans are unforgiving, but it's also true for Americans there is nothing that is as delicious as the cycle of redemption."

And Allen? Despite himself, he can't help but pierce the darkness of advancing age with a frail ray of light. He admits, "I'm kind of, secretly, in the back of my mind, counting on living a long time. My father lived to a hundred. My mother lived to ninety-five, almost ninety-six. If there is anything to heredity, I should be able to make films for another seventeen years." Maybe he'll join Kurosawa yet. But then he adds, "You never know. A piano could drop on my head."

Still a Working Stiff

Scott Foundas / 2005

First published in *LA Weekly*, a Voice Media Group publication, December 15, 2005. Reprinted by permission.

Not quite twenty-four hours before I arrived at the Park Avenue office he has kept for the better part of his professional career, Woody Allen celebrated his seventieth birthday. Well, maybe "celebrated" isn't the right word. "I spent the day fighting off morbid resignation," Allen says, sinking into one of the green-velour roller chairs scattered about his private screening room. It's early December, just after Thanksgiving, and New York is already alive with the signs of the season: The first chill of winter hangs in the air, the tree in Rockefeller Center has been lit — and a new Woody Allen movie is set for release. Only this time, and for the first time in the thirty years since *Love and Death*, Allen didn't shoot his latest picture on his home turf. Not one single frame of it.

That *Match Point*, which opens in limited release on December 28, unfolds against London's tony Belgravia district instead of Long Island's tony Hamptons (as it did in the original script) may be, as Allen himself says, little more than a cosmetic change. But there is much else about the film that suggests an extreme makeover, the latest shift of course in a career that has thrived on renewal and reinvention. The story of an ambitious, working-class tennis instructor, Chris Wilton (Jonathan Rhys-Meyers), raising himself up through the echelons of British high society, *Match Point* may be the youngest (and sexiest) picture Allen has ever conceived—of the four principal cast members, the oldest, Emily Mortimer, is a mere thirty-four. There's no role for Allen himself, nor even one he might have played (à la Kenneth Branagh in *Celebrity* or Will Ferrell in *Melinda and Melinda*). And both literally and figuratively speaking, we're thousands of miles removed from the New York Jewish intellectual life that is the nexus of the director's best-known films: The characters of *Match Point* are as WASPy as they come, comfortably inhabiting a world of upturned collars and sockless loafers, expansive country homes and nepotistic family businesses. And they're unabashedly middlebrow: They talk on their cell phones at the opera, their film viewing tends more toward *The Motorcycle Diaries* than *The Sorrow and the Pity* and, in one of the movie's most perversely funny sequences, a character rushes from the scene of a double murder to a performance of the latest Andrew Lloyd Webber musical—a grisly crime of a different sort. But what is most remarkable about *Match Point* is its vitality, how it bubbles over with life and filmmaking energy, arriving on the heels of several Allen films (*Melinda and Melinda*, *Hollywood Ending*, and *The Curse of the Jade Scorpion*) notable chiefly for their lethargy. To paraphrase the late Pauline Kael writing about John Huston's *Prizzi's Honor*, if you didn't know Allen had directed *Match Point*, you might think a fresh new talent had burst onto the scene.

Since its out-of-competition premiere at Cannes in May—where many speculated that, had it been given a competing slot, it would have walked off with a major prize—buzz about *Match Point* has been building to a head, and it's something that Allen, who once said, "The less I know about what people think of my work, the better off I am," is hardly oblivious to. "Look, I make a lot of films," he says. "Some come out fairly good. Some come out mediocre. Some come out poor. This one came out well. I could see it myself: When I finished the film, I felt, 'Oh, this is a good film,' and it doesn't surprise me that people are responding to it. I must say that I got every break a film director could want making this film. When I needed Scarlett Johansson, she was available. When I needed a rainy day, I got a rainy day. When I needed sunshine for a week, I got it. It was like I couldn't screw the film up no matter how hard I tried. It is indeed a better film than most of the films I've made before—just by coincidence, by happy luck."

As it happens, luck—happy or otherwise—is the driving concern of *Match Point*, a movie in which the fates and fortunes of the characters teeter precipitously over a moral chasm rather like the slow-motion tennis ball that drifts through the film's first frames, bounces off the top of the net and, for a moment, hangs undecided in midair. An opening narration intones, "The man who said 'I'd rather be lucky than good' saw deeply into life," and while some will no doubt construe those words as a statement of principle on Allen's own behalf in the post-Mia years, the moral ambiguity of *Match Point* is the one thing that doesn't feel new at all for the director—save for just how ambiguous it is. Like *Zelig*'s eponymous (and briefly fascistic) chameleon, Chris Wilton is a Highsmith-ian cipher who adopts bits and pieces of others' personalities as he goes and, like *Crimes and Misdemeanors*' Dr. Judah Rosenthal, he's a man who will ultimately kill to protect his position in life. Yet if Zelig had second thoughts about Hitler, and Judah was wracked with guilt over ordering the death of his mistress, there's barely a trace of compunction to be found in Wilton's steely, blue-eyed gaze and sotto voce Irish lilt. Skilled as Wilton is on the tennis court, his true athletic prowess has been in the game of life, meeting the wicked serve of blind chance with the mean backhand of free will. Until, that is, he runs up against the smoldering aspiring actress Nola Rice (Johansson), who's nearly as fast on her feet as he is.

"I wanted to do something on the subject of luck being a force that people are afraid to acknowledge in their lives," Allen tells me. "People like to boast and say, 'I make my own luck.' But the truth of the matter is we're all at the mercy of luck much more than we realize, and we've got to cross our fingers that nothing happens—that when those X-rays come back . . . well, you've just got to stay lucky. To some degree, it's in your control; you don't have to smoke. But non-smokers die too. You want to feel you can control things to some degree, because if you can't, life is scarier. So you give yourself the illusion that taking all these vitamins means something. You're always searching for control, and in the end you're at the mercy of the hoisted piano not falling on your head."

Woody Allen has had enough luck in his own career to make you wonder where all the bodies are buried. He has directed thirty-five feature films in thirty-nine years, writing or co-writing all of them and acting in most. He has been nominated for twenty Academy Awards—thirteen times as a writer, six times as a director and once (for *Annie Hall*) as an actor—and has directed fourteen performers (including himself) in Oscar-nominated roles. The former nightclub comic has also enjoyed total creative control over his work virtually from the beginning, as well as a series of generous patrons—most notably former United Artists head and Orion Pictures co-founder Arthur Krim—who've been perfectly willing to let Allen take the money and run. Notoriously secretive about his scripts (even prohibiting his own actors from reading scenes in which they don't appear), he shuns executive input into the casting process and refuses to screen dailies for anyone but himself. And if he's only occasionally been good box office, he's kept his budgets low, talked name actors into working for scale and brought an invaluable prestige factor to those who sponsor him. "It's been part luck, part dogged insistence, manipulation and negotiation," Allen says, freely admitting that his cherished autonomy has been harder to maintain in recent years—at least in America, where there are ever fewer Arthur Krims holding positions of influence in the industry. "It's the reason I made this film in England," he continues. "There were film companies [in the US] that were perfectly willing to work with me—provided I would let them read the script, they could know who's in the picture, they could see dailies. They didn't want to be, in their words, 'just bankers.' And my feeling is: Just be a good banker and we'll be thankful; you don't have to be a script editor.

"I figured out that I could have this situation more the way I wanted it if I got the money in Europe, because they don't have a studio system. It's a limited amount of money, of course—*Match Point* was a $15 million picture—and as long as I keep to that budget, they give me the money in a bag, they go away and I give them the picture." Even then, Allen says, it's plenty hard to make the movie you want. A famous tinkerer, he reshoots scenes constantly during production and has frequently reconvened his casts for additional reshoots during post. One entire project, *September*, was scrapped in rough-cut form and filmed over again from scratch; nearly one-third of *Crimes and Misdemeanors* met with a similar fate. Indeed, for Allen, nothing about a movie is set in stone until the prints have been shipped off to theaters. "Let's say in *Annie Hall*, he's supposed to live in a little house on a street in Brooklyn," Allen says. "Then I'm scouting locations for another scene and all of us are standing there—Gordon Willis and myself and the art director—and we see a house that's above a roller coaster. I go home immediately and change the scene. Then let's say I've written a part for an older actress . . . name an older actress . . ."

Elaine Stritch.

"Oh, I don't mean that old! Someone let's say in her thirties or so, like Angelina Jolie, and then I find that she's not available, but Scarlett Johansson is. Well, suddenly the character hasn't been married once and she's only twenty years old. So it evolves a lot before you do anything. When I start filming, I look at the dailies and I think, 'This is terrible. This is not going to work. It's drab. The scene is tedious.' I reshoot the next day; I don't wait. I like to know that when I'm finished with the film, I have everything in the can just the way I want it. Then I put the film together and screen it—that's really like taking a cold shower! Then you see where you guessed wrong in a serious way. I sit with the editor and we make a lot of changes and we look at it again, and eventually we realize this is as good as we're going to get with this material: It still lacks an important scene here; she never should have said this over here. So I call the actors and we get back together and I try to fix it. Sometimes the actors are in Africa doing a movie and I can't get them and I have to figure out some other way."

Or not. "I felt I didn't do as good a job as I should have on *The Curse of the Jade Scorpion*," Allen says when I ask him about the critical and commercial failure of his most recent films. "I felt that I did a very good job on *Hollywood Ending* and for some reason that picture wasn't appreciated sufficiently; I felt it was a really wonderful comic idea and that I executed it just fine and it should have been very enjoyable. Of course, this is totally subjective and I'm probably the worst person in the world to make these judgments. You know, in the course of doing films, I like to do some just for fun, and I know going in that people are not going to get the same full meal out of them. They're more like a dessert. What *Match Point* has going for it, which you can never really get in a comic film, is a certain impact that, since time immemorial, has always given you a deeper feeling than a comic piece. You can worship a comic piece and adore it, but the real impact comes from a dramatic hit.

"Comedy, by its very nature, defuses. The situation is tense, and Bob Hope or Groucho Marx says a joke. And it's pleasurable. Whereas drama confronts. Blanche DuBois comes into the room and it never gets defused. To me, it's always been something I've aspired toward. Having said that, my next movie, *Scoop*, couldn't be lighter. While I was doing *Match Point* I discovered that Scarlett Johansson is very funny and nobody is showing that. So I made a very light comedy. She's a college newspaper journalist in London who gets on to a scoop about a series of murders; I'm a small-time kooked-out magician who's playing in a vaudeville house there. She falls in love with Hugh Jackman who's an aristocrat. While I was doing it, I thought, 'Yes, this is fun and I'm having a good time. I'm getting to knock off these jokes and Scarlett's being funny.' But really my heart is in serious work and, since I am now getting older, I think I should devote myself to more serious work and do some serious films."

Is it possible for a filmmaker to have nine lives? Allen seems to be working on it. Such things aren't unheard of in the arts—Picasso had his blue and rose periods before venturing into cubism, Jackson Pollock his flirtation with representational forms. Reincarnation is a rarer phenomenon in the movies, though, where risk and reward almost always run in inverse proportion. But Allen has never been one to traffic in past glories, having navigated his way from the slapstick shenanigans of *Bananas* and *Sleeper* to the seriocomic romanticism of *Manhattan* and *Annie Hall* to the muted chamber drama of *Interiors* and *Another Woman* and the brutal dissection of marriage (complete with careening handheld camera and violent jump cuts) that was *Husbands and Wives*—the masterpiece of the second half of his career. And now there is *Match Point*, which comes burnished in the supine glow of a London summer, but may be Allen's darkest, most Darwinian portrait of human nature. (Earlier this week, the film scored four Golden Globe nominations, including Best Picture.)

Collectively, and for all its failings, it is one of the most singular bodies of work in American movies, and one that has seen its creator remain a relevant cultural figure at a time when contemporaries like Neil Simon and Mel Brooks have long since run out of steam. "I worked with some great comedy writers in my life—those two, and also Larry Gelbart—and they aspired to do great comedies and they have done great comedies," says Allen. "I was always more pretentious than they were. I wanted to be a dramatic writer. So I had someplace that I wanted to go that was difficult for me and challenging. I've also never minded failing. For some reason, that was not a sensitive thing with me. Now, I would rather succeed, of course! But I knew when I was making *Shadows and Fog* that there would not be a human being who would want to see it."

To be sure, Allen has had his ups and downs, personally and professionally, sometimes commanding a larger audience in the tabloids than in cinemas. Yet he's continued to make a movie a year (whether he needs to or not, some have jested), and the feverish work pace has ultimately served him well. "Jean-Luc Godard told me, sitting in this room, 'You make too many films,'" says Allen. "'You shouldn't make so many because that way they become more valuable.' But I don't think in those terms. I think more the way Bergman thought, like it's blue-collar work. You come in, you make the film, you put it out and you go on to the next film. With *Match Point*, right now I'm doing promotion for it because I have an obligation to DreamWorks to do that. But to me it's history. I did it two summers ago. It's out and running in Europe, I've made another film since, I'm lining up my next film. I don't really dwell on these things."

In other words, don't look for Woody Allen to slow down anytime soon. Even when his films have failed to capture the public imagination, he himself never has and probably never will. And at a time when seventy is the new forty, it could be that he's just getting his game on. "A guy who fixes sinks or installs television sets can't wait for the weekend so he can get on his boat and do his things," he says. "I don't feel that way. If I was working at a regular job, I would come home on the weekend and write, because it's fun for me. If no one would back my movies, I'd still be writing plays or books. What else would I do? I don't enjoy the beach or the country. I like the city, and in the city there's always time to work. And I don't work as hard as people think. It appears that way, because most people spend a lot of time raising money for films. They finish a script and two years down the line they get it on. I've never had that problem—I pull it out of the typewriter and bring it over to the office and they start budgeting it fifteen minutes later."

In person, Woody Allen looks like Woody Allen—black-frame glasses, white button-down oxford, baggy tan corduroys, and weathered burgundy lace-ups. Yet something isn't quite right, like a film that's gone slightly out of sync. The manner is graver; the voice lower-pitched; the hands that, on-screen, flail about in wildly expressive body language, rest quietly at his sides. It's hard to put a finger on it at first, but gradually I realize that the man sitting before me—this poised, serious, thoughtful filmmaker—scarcely resembles Alvy Singer at all. According to Allen, it's perhaps the biggest misconception people have about him. "The picture people have of me is the character that I play on the screen and I'm not that," Allen says with utter conviction, echoing claims of mistaken identity he's been making to interviewers for years. "They think that I'm a dysfunctional, New York Jewish neurotic intellectual. First of all, I have no religious connection whatsoever. I mean, I was born Jewish, but it's the last thing on my mind. I'm atheistic. I have no interest in any religion in a practicing way, including Judaism—they're all rackets. Secondly, I'm certainly not intellectual. I'm a middle-class person playing the part of a neurotic intellectual. People mistake that for who I am, but actually, I'm the guy who sits next to you at the ballgame or the movie house. I'm the guy who will be home tonight with a beer watching the Knicks on television. I'm not going to have my nose in my Kierkegaard."

To wit, the man who said "I'd rather be lucky than good"—the one who saw so deeply into life—was no highbrow philosopher, but rather the great New York Yankee pitcher Lefty Gomez, who helped take the Bronx Bombers to five World Series, where his 6–0 record remains unsurpassed. A very lucky man indeed.

But surely, I say, you've read Kierkegaard, and Freud and Marshall McLuhan. . . .

"But only because I had to to survive. I didn't read them because it's an instinct in me or because I liked it. I read those things because the girls I was dating wouldn't go out with me if I hadn't. It's not something that comes natural to me or which I find very enjoyable. I'm also not really neurotic, except to the extent that everybody has a certain amount of quirks. I lead a very normal life. I function well. I've always been productive. I've had ongoing relationships professionally for many years. I have, at this stage of my life, a good marriage and good relationships with almost all the people who've ever been a part of my life—not all of them, but almost all. I travel. I play jazz. If you spent a week with me, you would not think that I was neurotic. You would think just the opposite probably: You would come to me with your problems and say, 'You know, I'm at sixes and sevens about this, but you always seem to be decisive and calm about these things. You don't get ruffled or angry about them. Help me out.' And that's more who I really am."

Perhaps it wouldn't even take a week to see all that, but just a couple of hours, on the Upper East Side of New York, on a brisk December afternoon.

Interview with Woody Allen

Scott Tobias / 2008

Published in *A.V. Club*, August 13, 2008. Reprinted by permission.

It's hard to gauge Woody Allen's impact on American comedy and culture, because it's vast and still ongoing. Even setting aside his comedy albums, his writings for the *New Yorker* and other publications, his jazz band, and his appearances as an actor in other people's work, there's still his filmography as a writer, director, and often star, stretching to more than forty features. Beginning with *Take the Money and Run* in 1969—or the overdubbed 1966 lark *What's Up, Tiger Lily?*, if that counts—Allen has been the standard-bearer for New York Jewish wit, and a persistently insightful chronicler of human relationships. He's received an astonishing twenty-one Oscar nominations, and won three, for writing and directing *Annie Hall* (which also won Best Picture) and writing *Hannah and Her Sisters*. Other highlights from his long career include *Bananas*, *Sleeper*, *Manhattan*, *The Purple Rose of Cairo*, *Crimes and Misdemeanors*, *Husbands and Wives*, *Sweet and Lowdown*, and *Match Point*—all produced at a movie-a-year pace that continues four decades into his career.

After decades of being closely identified with New York, Allen has recently made a series of features in Europe. The latest, *Vicky Cristina Barcelona*, is one of his strongest efforts in many years. Scarlett Johansson and Rebecca Hall star as American friends with very different ideas about romance. While vacationing in Barcelona, they're mesmerized by painter Javier Bardem, who whisks them off on a romantic sojourn, but remains haunted by his tempestuous former lover, Penélope Cruz. Allen recently spoke to the *A.V. Club* about the elusiveness of romantic chemistry, salvaging mistakes in casting and writing, and how his beloved New York Knicks are better off losing pretty than winning ugly.

The A.V. Club: How does Barcelona affect the story in a way that another city, like Rome or Madrid, couldn't have?
Woody Allen: It doesn't. This picture could've been made in Madrid, it could've been made in Rome, it could've been made in Venice or Paris. There's a lot of cities

that it couldn't have been made in—what you need is a colorful, kind of exotic, cosmopolitan city that's got great cultural depth and enormous visual potential. There are a number of cities in Europe that have that. It wouldn't have been easy to make it in London, because that has a less exotic, slightly drier feeling, although it's a great city. But Barcelona is one among a number of cities that it could've been made in, and they were the ones that called me and said, "Would you make a film in Barcelona if we finance it?" And I said, "Sure." But if someone from Rome had called and said, "Would you make a film in Rome?" I very easily could've made the same film in Rome. Now, when I say the same film, I would not have had Penélope and Javier, and of course I may be underestimating—I'm sure I am—the enormous impact simply of their personalities, and how much they make the film. There may not be two comparable Italians and two comparable French actors that could've delivered what they delivered. So that is a factor.

AVC: Did the Whit Stillman film *Barcelona* have an impact on you? Both films, in addition to having the same backdrop, contrast American and European notions of love.

WA: No. I had no interest in it in relation to this film. I watched it and enjoyed it years ago when it came out, but it had no . . . I was just fumbling around for an idea that I could do in Barcelona amongst various notes I have at home, ideas on scraps of paper. And I came up with two girls going on a vacation. And then Penélope Cruz called and said she heard I was doing a film on Barcelona, and she'd like to be in it. After we met, I then started to think, "How could I accommodate Penélope? What does she suggest as a character?" And that led me to her character. And so the thing formed in a completely different origin.

AVC: Does that happen often, where you know who you want in the movie, and then you start to write it around them?

WA: It doesn't happen too often anymore. Years ago, when I was in all my movies, I always knew that it was going to be me and Diane Keaton, or me and Mia Farrow, or me and somebody else, and I could do that. But in recent years, there's been no one that I worked with too consistently. Scarlett Johansson and I have now done several pictures now, and it does help to know in advance that Scarlett's going to be the girl, or whoever else it may be. It does help to know what actor or actress is playing the part, because you can avoid what flaws they have in their performance range, and exploit their strengths.

AVC: There's a really critical scene in the film where Javier Bardem propositions Rebecca Hall and Scarlett Johansson and convinces them to travel with him. Could anyone but Bardem have pulled that off?

WA: That's what I was thinking before. There probably are not a lot that could. There are some that could, but you really do have to have that kind of brooding, complicated, charismatic personality to not come off like a boob, and for women to be provoked by his proposal and to think actually that it might be interesting. If I didn't have Javier to play that part, and I was making the film in Spain, I don't know if I could've found someone. I don't really know, because I'm not familiar with the Spanish cinema, so I don't know if there's another who knows enough English, and also has that kind of complexity to him.

AVC: It's a romantic film, but would it be fair to characterize it as being ultimately pessimistic about love? One woman desires stability and the other desires passion, but both seem to be heading for different kinds of trouble.

WA: I would say the film is quite a sad film. The basic cosmetics of the film, as you watch it, are not sad, and so as you watch it, you're seeing a beautiful city and hearing wonderful music, and seeing these beautiful women and this charming guy. So hopefully you would enjoy yourself, and there are some laughs and some moments you're interested in. [Mild spoilers follow and continue through the end of this exchange. —ed.] But when it's all over, and you tally up, you find that Javier and Penélope can't live with each other and they can't live without each other, so they're kind of tortured in their relationship. And Scarlett Johansson knows what she doesn't want, but doesn't know what she wants, and probably will never know what she wants. And she kind of goes through life and has a relationship no matter what it is, and thinks, "This is the one that's going to give me a sense of fulfillment." And then over time it palls, because there's a discomfort in her, there's an anxiety inside her that she attaches to every relationship sooner or later, and thinks that it's the relationship, when in fact the shortcoming is in her. And she'll never really find exactly what she's looking for. And Rebecca Hall would've loved to have some kind of exotic relationship with this person [Bardem], but in the end, she's just too scared and not the type, and she handles it awkwardly. And she is probably going to be some version of the marriage of Patricia Clarkson and her husband. Maybe not identical, but her husband will probably, as years pass, be the guy that plays golf and maybe gets the boat, and they will have a stable, functioning marriage that's not the worst in the world, but will never reach any great heights at all. So on the whole, I do feel that it's a very pessimistic picture, and sad.

AVC: So this romantic arrangement between Bardem, Johansson, and Cruz is the least conventional in the film, and also by far the most successful. Could a relationship like that ever last, or is it just a temporary chemical balance that's going to eventually dissolve?

WA: I don't think those relationships do last. The thing that's exciting about them is the volatility. It's like what Penélope says to Javier in the movie, "You like my mood swings, my inconsistencies." What's attractive to him is that she's unpredictable and capable of enormous artistic vision and enormous sexuality, but also capable of other passions that are really impossible to live with, and the chemistry between them is never going to work out. And he'll always feel that she's the greatest woman he's ever known when she was healthy, but she's so rarely healthy. And she'll always be enormously attracted to him because he's such a charismatic personality, but she's too volatile, too nuts to have it work out, and so it's sad.

AVC: As you mentioned before, you'll occasionally have actresses like Scarlett Johansson or Diane Keaton who repeatedly appear in your films, but your casts are otherwise always rotating, and you're always working with new people. Does it become tough to predict what that chemistry will be?

WA: I'm sometimes surprised by it. I usually get people that I know are good. When I was hiring Javier, I had not seen him in the Coen brothers film [*No Country for Old Men*], because that was yet to come out when I made this film. But I had seen him in Spanish films, and I knew he was wonderful. And I'd seen Penélope in [Pedro] Almodóvar's films, and I knew she was wonderful. And Scarlett, I was a fan of. So I'm not surprised in retrospect that these people were able to play off each other very well, but sometimes you get a surprise, and usually it's not a pleasant surprise. Usually, you hire people that you think are wonderful, and they are, but you've mixed the wrong ingredients, and you say, "Gee, this guy was so great in all his other pictures. What happened here?" Or some woman that's wonderful, and she just doesn't come through for you.

AVC: What do you do when it doesn't work out like you had hoped?

WA: Well if it's brutal, I fire the person, because there's an investment of millions of dollars of people's money, and I don't want the thing to be a disaster. But you try everything until you get to that point. That's your last resort, and you finally resign yourself to the fact that you're not going to get 100 percent from the scripts you've written: "This person will give me 60 percent, and this person will give me 60 percent, and it will still be a decent, watchable movie, but I'm not going to get an electrifying chemistry." But if it's not that, if it's "Oh God, this is brutal. I'm not getting anything, this is embarrassing," then I pull the plug.

AVC: Does it become upsetting to have 60 percent, to know that the movie isn't everything it should be?

WA: Yes, but more often, I blame that on myself. Once in a while, that will happen with acting, but 95 percent of the time, when something's going wrong, it's because the script wasn't really as good as I thought it was. If I had written a good script, it would have been hard to ruin it. If I had written a bad script, then you find out that there's trouble, and almost always, the trouble on these movies is the script. It's the acting once in a while, but 90 percent of the time, it's the script. And it's the directing also, once in a while. But it's rare that I'll say "Oh God, I directed that poorly." Because it's easier to direct. If you direct something poorly and reshoot it the next day, stage it better, make it work better, you have a lot of possibilities. You can edit it in certain ways so that it works, but there's no getting around weaknesses of the script.

AVC: Do you not really perceive those weaknesses until you're actually there filming it and looking at the footage?
WA: Yeah, usually, you start noticing it in the filming of the movie. It can be later. It can be after you put it together and you say, "Oh, uh-oh. Nobody's sympathizing with this guy's problem—actually, they hate him. I didn't count on that. I thought they would be in his corner." And then you have a lot of work to do. You've got to start editing and then reshooting. And you start struggling to make something that's survivable.

AVC: It's often said that directors make three different movies: one in the writing, one in the shooting, and one in the editing. Do you feel that's true, or do you have enough of a grasp on a production that it generally winds up looking like the one you envisioned?
WA: The movie is usually, for me, something organic that grows all the time. I sit home and write it, and I'm in an isolated, four-walled environment, and I don't know what's going on. I just write it, and it's appearing in my head in some idealized way where every single moment works, and every little thing is perfect, because it's in my head. Then you go out and start doing preproduction, and you find out you're not going to get Javier Bardem or Brad Pitt or whoever you want. So you're going to have to get somebody else, and you're not going to be able to afford that scene, because they've budgeted it at a million dollars, and you're not going to be able to get that location, because they won't let anybody shoot there, and you find by the time you're actually ready to roll the camera, you've made fifty compromises on your original script. And then you shoot the script and you hear them say the dialogue, and you start changing it because it doesn't sound so good, and you think of new jokes that are quite good, and things are changing all the time as you're doing it. And then when you edit it, you're constantly taking out dead material and throwing it away, and looking for clever ways to join the best of the material with the next-best of the material so that they don't notice you've dropped out two speeches or six speeches or something. This goes on and on and the thing just grows, and by the time it's over, it's either matured in a good

way and you've come up with something that's worth watching, or you've buried yourself.

AVC: You've said in the past that when that entire process is over, you're done with the movie. You don't look back. Is that correct?

WA: Once the movie's over, there's not much point. When the thing is edited, mixed, and color-corrected, and you've finished it. . . . In my case, I never read anything about it, I never think about it. *Vicky Cristina Barcelona* has not yet come out, and I'm already finished shooting and editing a film with Larry David, Evan Rachel Wood, and Patricia Clarkson, and I'm now working on another film. So I just keep going and don't look back. I work very hard on the film when I'm working on it, but once it's over, it becomes over for me. So the film *Take the Money and Run*, which was my first film, I finished it, I did the best I could, and I haven't looked at a frame of it for nearly thirty-nine years. I made it in 1969, and I haven't looked at a frame of that film since the day I put it out, and that was the end of it. That's the way it is with me. There's no point in looking back, because there's nothing you can really do to improve the film. You can only aggravate and wish you had done stuff better. And so I just put it out and move on, and as I say, I'm a couple of films ahead of the one that's about to emerge now.

AVC: So it wouldn't be a pleasure to look at them, like an old photo album or something, just to see where you were at a particular time?

WA: That's a pleasure I deny myself, because then you get into nostalgic self-involvement, and I don't think that would be good for me. I don't like to reminisce much, and my walls don't have photographs of me and the actors I was with, or any of that stuff. If you were in my house in New York, you wouldn't know I was in the movie business. It just looks like a regular house, like the home of a lawyer or something, and I try and keep that disciplined, and just work. There are so many traps you can get into, and looking back on your own work is certainly one of them.

AVC: In the late eighties and early nineties, you made a series of films—*Crimes and Misdemeanors*, *Husbands and Wives*, *Deconstructing Harry* particularly—that were dark and interpreted as personal. Have you backed away from that? Or were those films misinterpreted?

WA: No, my films are misinterpreted all the time. I don't mind that. Everybody's films are misinterpreted. But there's no malice or stupidity in the people that misinterpret them. You know what you do, but someone else sees it, and they want to talk about it or write about it, and so they misinterpret them. But those are not any darker than *Vicky Cristina Barcelona*, and certainly no darker than *Cassandra's*

Dream or *Match Point*. These are all quite dark films, and the films that I'm making at the time, contrary to what people might think, are not a reflection of what's going on in my life. People think that the way I feel in my private life at the moment reflects how I make films, but everyone who makes films, or does any kind of creative art, will tell you that that's not so, that sometimes when I'm feeling my happiest and everything's going well in my life, and my love life is wonderful and my health is wonderful, I'll make my darkest, most depressing kind of thing. And other times, when things are not going well for me and I'm having a hard personal time, I could be making my silliest comedies. I was not in a particularly happy state of mind or place in my life at all when I made *Take the Money and Run* and *Bananas*. This is not a good time in my life. There's no reflection in one's personal life, and I've heard this from other artists as well that people tend to think the product is a reflection of their personal feeling at the time, when in fact it isn't, really. It's just a matter of what idea they can come up with, or whatever strikes them inspirationally, having no relation to their personal mood.

AVC: Are you looking forward to the Knicks in a post–Isiah Thomas era?
WA: Well, I was looking forward to the Isiah Thomas era. [*Laughs.*] I don't think anything's going to happen. I think they're definitely going to be better. There's no question at this point, because there's been so much pressure on them to be better. I think Isiah came in and tried to make them better, but he was faced with a very, very difficult situation. It's not easy to just come in and take a team and simply make it better, and then the fans get impatient. You know it'll be wild enthusiasm at first, and then as soon as the results don't happen, the fans start to get impatient, and they want to tar and feather you. So he definitely tried. He came in and bought the players that logically would be exciting. As much as the fans got on [point guard Stephon] Marbury, they were thrilled to the nines when he joined the team. Everyone was excited, and I thought Isiah tried, but it was too tough to do, and I think [new coach] Mike D'Antoni is going to try, and I think with time and some sense, they'll gradually get better. But there's a difference between being better and being fun to watch. A workmanlike team that wins games is not necessarily a team that is fun to watch. What I'd like the Knicks to develop into is a team that's fun and that's colorful and that you really like to watch every night, which is the way they were many years ago. It was fun to watch them, because they didn't just pile up wins in unappealing ways.

AVC: Like the [San Antonio] Spurs.
WA: Yeah. I'd really rather be entertained and have them come in second than be bored stiff and see them grind to a first-place finish.

Interview with Woody Allen

Douglas McGrath / 2008

Published in Interview, September 2008, 252–57, and online at http://www.interviewmagazine.com/film/woody-allen-/. Reprinted by permission of the author.

Woody Allen started his career in show business as a teenager. He would send jokes in to the popular newspaper columnists of the day—men like Earl Wilson and Walter Winchell—who would print the jokes they liked and attribute them to Woody. He did not inform these big Broadway columnists, of course, that he was a student at Midwood High School in Brooklyn—that might kill the big Broadway sheen they liked their columns to have. One day, someone from a big PR firm asked Wilson, "Who is Woody Allen?" Wilson didn't know—the stuff came in through the mail. "Some guy in Brooklyn," he said.

The PR people located Woody and hired him to write jokes for them. When he showed up at their office on Madison Avenue, they saw right away that he was just a kid—he was sixteen at the time—but they didn't care; the jokes weren't going to be attributed to him anymore. No, for forty dollars a week, every day after Midwood High let out in the afternoon, Woody would come in from Brooklyn on the subway, and until it was time to go home for supper, he would sit at a typewriter and write jokes. The PR people would then send the jokes to the columnists, now attributed to one of their clients: "At El Morocco last night, Jimmy Cagney was overheard saying. . . ."

Very soon, Woody had one of the top jobs in TV, writing for Sid Caesar. But that was just a training period for him. He would go on to conquer nightclubs with his stand-up routine (if you've never heard the moose routine, you have not known true bliss), Broadway, and, of course, the movies. Depending on whether you count a couple of shorts and TV films, Woody has directed more than forty films, all of which he has either written or co-written—including *Bullets over Broadway* (1994), the picture that we did together.

Woody's latest film, *Vicky Cristina Barcelona*, stars his most frequent leading lady in recent years, Scarlett Johansson, along with Penélope Cruz and Javier Bardem. Shot in Spain, it's his fourth film in a row to be made in Europe—and outside his native New York, which has provided the backdrop for so much of his work. Along with the familiar hallmarks of his style, *Vicky Cristina Barcelona* has a new quality: there are dissolves in the film, for instance, and close-ups in a way he hasn't used close-ups for a long time. They give the film a sometimes dreamy, romantic quality. It's a quality that will probably be gone from Woody's next film—a comedy starring Larry David—because, again, he's changing subjects and genres.

He's seventy-two, but light on his feet, always looking, always open to finding new ways to explore the mess we make of our chances in this world.

This is just my opinion, of course, but of Woody's forty-plus movies, I think there are more beauties, more classics, more stop-the-channel-surfing films than any other director in American film history. Is that too grand a claim? Woody would surely have a heart attack to hear me make it, and would quickly offer what he feels to be superior choices. So, to make him happy, I'll just leave it that there are not many people who have helped both Sid Caesar and Scarlett Johansson do their best work.

Douglas McGrath: I thought I'd start by talking to you about something that you never seem to have a shortage of: ideas. Whatever your problems might be, writer's block has never been one of them. But when the time comes to start a new project, how do you decide what you're going to do? Do you base it on wanting to do something different from what you've done before? What guides the choice?

Woody Allen: It's usually that I just go into the bedroom and think and look at my notes to see if I have anything that seems interesting that's occurred to me over the year, or if anything is occurring to me at the time. The thing that is the most viable is what I do. So there's no real rhyme or reason. Theoretically, I could do two musicals in a row, or a musical and then a terribly dramatic picture or something. People think that there's more calculation to it but there isn't—it's really just chance. I consider myself lucky to get an idea, so I proceed ahead as soon as one emerges that seems to have a beginning, a middle, and an end.

DM: Do you keep a little notebook or a pad with you so that when things occur to you, as you're playing the clarinet or you're walking the kids to school, you jot them down?

WA: I don't keep a notebook, but I do jot. I have a drawer full of matchbook covers and napkins and little notes. And some of them seem sensational when I'm jotting them down and then later I can't imagine what was so exciting about them. And then others actually hold up and become films.

DM: What film took the longest to go from the matchbook or the napkin to the screen? Is there one movie in particular that you held onto and struggled with the longest before you found it?

WA: It wasn't a struggle, but the longest thing that I ever had like that was the idea for a film that I don't consider a masterpiece at all, *The Curse of the Jade Scorpion* [2001]. The idea of a detective who is hypnotized by an unscrupulous character, and made to rob, and then consequently becomes both the robber and the person who is looking for the robber, occurred to me forty years ago and remained in my drawer as an undone idea. I think it actually occurred to me as a sketch because I was just a sketch writer at the time. But it always had a certain interest to me, so I came back to it and touched on it many times. But I could never really figure out how to do it or if it was worth doing. And then, finally, I did it and made, I think, the fatal mistake of playing the lead myself when it should have been played by a more serious actor. I think as soon as I played the insurance investigator—and I probably made the character an insurance investigator because I wouldn't have been credible at all as a detective or as a policeman—it had a certain junkiness to it. There was a lack of substance and seriousness. Whereas if it had been someone like Jack Nicholson playing the part, then it still would have been funny, but it would have had a better spine, a better center.

DM: Is there a film that happened the fastest—an idea where you just thought of it and then sat down and wrote it through and shot it?

WA: A very quick one for me was *A Midsummer Night's Sex Comedy* [1982]. It happened while I was working on *Zelig* [1983]. We had a few weeks off, and I was looking for ways to kill the time, and it just occurred to me to try to do a movie set in the country. The idea was to do a movie that was kind of like *Manhattan* [1979], but where I extol the beauty and the charm of the country, which really doesn't come natural to me. I wrote it from scratch in about three weeks' time with no prior structural ideas or character ideas or anything, and then I decided I would shoot it while I was shooting *Zelig*. So I shot them simultaneously on some of the same sets.

DM: Really? Was that not a little confusing?

WA: It was emotionally confusing. Everyone said to me, "How are you going to shoot two films at once? You'll be exhausted. It's so much work." And I, of course, pooh-poohed that. The truth is that it isn't much work. But the real trick is that, emotionally, it's very hard to pull out of one film and then focus on the other. That I found very difficult.

DM: What in the world possessed you to write a movie set in the country?

WA: Inertia. I was sitting at home not doing anything and for some reason it just crossed my mind that Mia [Farrow], who I was going with at the time, had a pretty house in the country and wouldn't it be nice to do a little pastoral romance with the Mendelssohn music and the flowers and the moonlight? And so I did it. The film was hugely unsuccessful—nobody came to see it. But I enjoyed making it. It was fun to shoot the country in a pretty way.

DM: Your new film, *Vicky Cristina Barcelona*, is an interesting comparison here because, though it's set in a city, it has a less urban feeling than many of your films. How did you decide to make this movie? Was it based on an idea that you'd carried around for a long time? Or was it something that came more quickly?

WA: It's an idea that came to me. The people of Barcelona called and said, "If we put up money for the production, would you be interested in making a film in Barcelona?" And, of course, I was because, one, they were ready to put up the money, and two, Barcelona is such a lovely city that it's a treat to be able to live there for the months of shooting. I would not have accepted that invitation if it was the Gobi desert or something. So I accepted the offer, and then I was faced with having to write something for Barcelona. Just coincidentally, when it was announced that I was going to make a film there—before I had anything written—Penélope Cruz was in New York and her office called and said she'd like to come over and meet me. So she came by and said, you know, if I'm doing something in Barcelona, then she'd be interested in participating. And, of course, that was a godsend to me because she's so gifted and so beautiful—I couldn't get my mind around it when I was talking to her. And then they said that Javier Bardem would also be interested and was available, so I thought to myself, "Okay, I want to make a film in Barcelona." Then I had to think up an idea. I thought, you know, "I don't want the film all in Spanish, so it's going to be about Americans." And then I thought, "Well, a few girls visit Barcelona and they become involved in a situation. . . ." And, gradually, one thing piled on another and the story developed. I wrote it, and when I got over there to shoot, the locations dictated the ambient feel of the picture. So even though the movie is shot in Barcelona, it has a slightly more rural feel because Barcelona is an older city and it doesn't look like New York City or Paris or London. It's got quite a Mediterranean look to it—quite a warm, floral, easygoing look. So, you know, it has that quality. It was fun for me. It was, in a certain sense, the first really foreign film I've ever made.

DM: Tell me how.
WA: Because working in London [where Allen shot his last three films, *Match Point*, *Scoop*, and *Cassandra's Dream*] is kind of like working in New York. Everyone speaks the same language and the city is completely metropolitan, full of noise and traffic and bookstores and restaurants and theaters. It's just another version

of New York or Paris—they all are very, very similar. But Barcelona is really like Europe to me. Occasionally, Penélope and Javier would speak Spanish on the set, and the atmosphere. . . . When I look at *Vicky Cristina*, I see Scarlett Johansson and Javier riding bicycles in the country, and it looks to me just like the foreign films I used to see in the fifties and the early sixties. And because of that, I felt like all of the stylistic devices of the foreign films that I had grown up watching were fair game. It didn't demand the kind of journalistic, fast, traffic-y, nervous rhythm that you get in New York. It had a more slow, sunny, bicycle-ly feeling to it. And the story lent itself to being told that way. So I really felt like I'd finally achieved what I wanted to when I was a young man: I'm a foreign filmmaker. Of course it's not a foreign film—it's an American film. But it has that quality to it.

DM: The Spanish music that you use in *Vicky Cristina Barcelona* sets such a great mood right from the beginning. Was that music that you knew already?
WA: No, I didn't know that music. How I found the title song—the "Barcelona" song—was one of those show-business stories. I get a million things in the mail every day. People send me their résumés, their photographs, their DVDs, the songs they've composed. I can't handle all that stuff, so I give it over to my assistant, and we try to answer the people politely but nothing ever really comes of anything because I'm inundated. But in this particular case, I was bolting out of the hotel in Barcelona to go and shoot at seven o'clock in the morning, and there was this CD that had been delivered to the room with the song "Barcelona" on it. Normally, I just chuck the CDs in a pile and I never really hear them. But because I felt like I had a slightly longer car ride to the location where we were shooting that day, I brought this one along and stuck it in the car just to see what it was like. And, you know, the second I heard the song, I said to the producer who was in the car with me, "I want to get this song and use it in the movie. It's perfect for what I want."

DM: I think I know the answer to this, but do you believe that CD being in your hotel on that day was an act of fate?
WA: I don't. That's just a pure accident. The thing arrived, and I happened to be running out and I grabbed it. It's just a pure accident.

DM: This is the third film you've done with Scarlett. Did you have her in mind when you were writing *Vicky Cristina Barcelona*?
WA: Well, you know, I *always* have Scarlett in mind. [*Laughs*] I'm the president of her fan club. I wasn't thinking of her when I sat down to write *Vicky Cristina*, but as I got into it, I thought, "Oh, you know, Scarlett would be great to play this part

because it's that kind of neurotic, sexually free person." And Scarlett oozes that out of every pore.

DM: Over the years, I'm sure you've had all kinds of reactions from actors who work with you. But sometimes you'll find people—particularly younger people—who have grown up watching your movies and are quite nervous around you, sometimes fawning and obsequious. How would you describe what Scarlett is like around you?
WA: Ah, Scarlett. . . . She's not fawning and obsequious—*I'm* fawning and obsequious. [*McGrath laughs*] She's got a great sense of humor. Scarlett is one of the few people who always tops me. Whenever I say something amusing, she always manages to say something quicker—and funnier than what I've said—in return. So if you add that wit and that speed to those looks and that sex appeal and that talent, I'm completely overmatched. So she's not fawning. I will say that the other members of the cast on *Vicky Cristina* were not fawning either. You know, I'm the kind of director that, if you haven't met me and you believe the nonsense that you read in the newspapers, you might think, "Oh, he's cold and intimidating in some way." But the second people start to work with me, two words flash on my forehead in big neon letters: NO THREAT.

DM: I know we've discussed it over the years, but occasionally you hear that some actors are thrown by the fact that if you're happy with a take or a scene, then you don't really talk about it much because you're ready to move on. Do you find that some actors need a lot of verbal reassurance?
WA: I think, you know, that some actors would like that, even if they're too shy to really say it. But I always feel like I've hired the actor, so I must think they're good to begin with or else I wouldn't have done that. If I don't say anything, they should feel like, "Good, I did it. I knocked it off and we're moving on." If I have to say, "Come on, let's do that again," or "Let's have a talk about that," then that's where I would think they would feel a little less comfortable. I've never been a big one for all that, you know, well-meant *bonhomie*—that backslapping, double-cheek-kissing nonsense—on the set. I don't have the patience for it and I don't feel that any of that is necessary. But I'm not intimidating or biting or mean. I am, as I say, no threat. Clearly, everyone sees, when they come to the set, a person who is floundering. [*McGrath laughs*] And I'm not being facetious when I say that people must start to wonder, "Now, wait a minute. How did this guy get any type of reputation at all? Because he doesn't really seem to know what he's doing." And then they start to realize down the line, you know, "His mind is not on this. He's unfocused. He's not sure what he's doing. He's hunting-and-pecking

his way through this and I wonder if I did the right thing accepting this job for no money...."

DM: *[laughs]* Well, do you feel unsure when you're on the set? What's your level of confidence versus insecurity and doubt?
WA: My level of confidence is always high, but it's unmerited confidence. It's unearned confidence. I never do any homework whatsoever. I don't even know in the morning sometimes what scene I'm going to be shooting later that day. I've given it no attention, no thought. I just go to the set, and they give me the stuff that I'm going to shoot, and then I start to look around and figure out what to do and how to do it. So I feel complete confidence, but that doesn't mean that I should. I really do kind of flounder around. I'm not exactly sure what I want—I know more what I *don't* want. I know if somebody performs badly or if something is going to be too heavy-handed or stupid. But what I really want out of the thing, I find out as we go. Sometimes the actor does something and I think, "Hey, that's great. That's much different than I envisioned—and much better. This is a good way to go."

DM: Now, your next film after *Vicky Cristina Barcelona*, which you've just finished shooting, is set in New York. What was it like for you to be back shooting a movie there again? It's been a few films.
WA: It was great fun to be back in New York. I had a very interesting cast. I worked with Larry David in the starring role. Not many people know this, but it's the third film he's done with me—he was in *New York Stories* [1989] and he was in *Radio Days* [1987], both times in brief roles. But here he's got the major starring role of this picture. And in addition to being hilarious, he's quite a first-rate actor. And I worked with Evan Rachel Wood, who is just sort of a miraculous young actress—I mean, every instinct she has is sensational. And, of course, there's Patricia Clarkson, who I also worked with on *Vicky Cristina*, and she's one of our great actresses. So I was in great shape.

DM: I know that it hasn't been that long since you last shot in New York, but is there anything different going on in the city now for you as a filmmaker?
WA: Well, it's gotten more expensive. You know, since New York is such a wonderful place to shoot, many big-budget films have come into the city and a lot of money has been spent here on movies, so it's become more expensive. If you've got a budget of $40 million or $80 million or $120 million, this is a nonfactor. But if you're like me, and you have a budget of $15 million and you've got to make the whole thing work with everybody's salaries and the music and the song rights and

the titles and the opticals and everything, then it's a big deal. So I did find myself financially struggling.

DM: Will that affect whether or not you keep shooting in New York?
WA: I'd like to keep shooting in New York. I like to shoot in the big cities. You know, New York is my home and I have a particular fondness for it. I think it's a place where you can generate any kind of story wonderfully. But I also would be very happy to make a film in Paris or Rome. I probably will do a few more films in European cities—as my father would say, "for the simple reason that my wife likes to travel." In the summertime, when I shoot, the kids are off from school and she likes to spend the summer in Barcelona or Rome or London or something. And so I like to make her happy. That is one of the reasons that I think of shooting in Europe. Then, another reason is, of course, that these European countries invite me and they make it very appetizing. They put the money in the bank. And they're not film studios. They don't have the slightest interest in the script or the casting—they just want me to be happy making the film. So it's a very nice experience. On the other hand, I'm a creature of the New York City streets. I like to sleep in my own bed and I love the early mornings in the city and the sunsets here. So, you know, it's a toss-up.

DM: You mentioned your family. You're the father now of two little girls, and yet your films haven't dealt much with fatherhood or that aspect of your life. Is that something you might write about someday?
WA: Well, if I did write about it, my guess is that I would write about it in a serious way. It's hard for me to see between the extremes of fatherhood in *Long Day's Journey Into Night* [1962] or on *Leave It to Beaver* or something where you have these kind of wisecracking kids and they're cutesy and you take them to FAO Schwartz and it's the kind of movie that you just want to dynamite. So it's hard for me to think of a movie with kids that I would want to make that is not tragically serious. Because as soon as you introduce kids into a comedy, you're already in the domain of cute or warm—all those viscous, nauseating places.

DM: I think I have my answer. [*Laughs*] You work a lot. You're almost never *not* working on something. Why? Do you enjoy it? Or do you do it out of a different need?
WA: I enjoy working but, but I do it really to . . . it's good physical therapy for me—it's important to get up in the morning and to *do* something. My grandparents used to get up in the morning and they'd sit and stare out the window all day long and grow old and fat. That's what they did—they did *nothing*. And I don't enjoy that. I get antsy. I like to *do* stuff. I like to get up and practice music and

write something for the *New Yorker* or work on a script or direct a film. But what I do doesn't have to be movies. If my source of funding cut off tomorrow and I was never able to make another film, I'd be very happy writing for the theater, or if I couldn't do that, writing a book or a novel or an autobiography. I like to work because it keeps me occupied. What else do you do if you don't work?

DM: Well, I'm not recommending this but you could go to museums, you could go to the ballgame, you could go to—

WA: I do that. I live near all the museums so I go to all of them. I'm ubiquitous at the Knicks games. I watch a lot of baseball on television. I do all that stuff. I've got plenty of time to play with my kids—I bring them to school in the morning. I have time to do the treadmill. I have time to practice the clarinet. I have time to go on tour with my jazz band and take walks with my wife and still make movies, because none of this stuff is rocket science. None of it is that demanding.

DM: Is there any source of satisfaction that you get out of working? I mean, I assume it's about more for you than just staying busy.

WA: There is an inexplicable delight in the act of creating. In the sense that if a guy paints a canvas . . . you know, I've done this sometimes where I've gone and bought a lot of paints and just for the fun of it had an orgy of painting. I mean, I can't paint at all.

DM: What kind of things do you paint?
WA: Autumn fish.

DM: Autumn fish?
WA: Autumn fish, yes. I can paint the general shape of a fish in autumn colors. They don't look like fish—they're fish like either a retarded adult or an infant would paint them. But, you know, it's that thing where you're doing the activity and all of the sudden someone says, "Hey, you've been doing this for six hours." It's like that with any kind of work. There's a very pleasurable feeling that comes from making stuff. You get lost in doing it and you don't think about all the nasty things that life has planned for you.

DM: But do you take any pleasure at the end when you look at the finished product? Or are you already on to thinking about what's next?
WA: I do enjoy it but very briefly. I'm not a person who has any sentimentality about the past. You know, I don't really have any photographs of me with my actors or posters of my films or any of that stuff up in my house. I don't save any of that stuff. I don't read anything about me. When I'm through with a project, yes,

I feel, "Hey, this is good. It came out very nicely. I'm very happy," or conversely, "I'm so frustrated. I had such a beautiful idea and I screwed it up every inch of the way." But then we turn the film over to the people that paid for it and they put it out using some kind of voodoo system. They figure, "We'll do this much on advertising, and we'll put it out in seven hundred theaters during this time of year because if we put it out after Passover but before graduation...." They have this real voodoo system that never ever amounts to anything. And I don't want to hear about the film after that. So I give them the film, and then they ask me if I'll do a little promotion for it, and I do as little as possible because I feel like a person talking about his film does not induce anybody to see it. For me to say, "Well, it was very challenging making a film in Barcelona," or "It was incredible working with two beautiful women such as Penélope and Scarlett on the set every day. . . ." You know, it doesn't mean a thing to anybody. Nobody cares. People decide whether they are going to see the film or not based on whatever ineffable system their body uses, whether it's reviews or word of mouth from their friends or the smell of the picture to them. So I do a little promotion out of loyalty to the money people because I don't want to be a mean guy. But I have no interest in the picture. For instance, *Vicky Cristina Barcelona* is coming out now. I've already finished the picture with Larry David, and I'm working on a script for another new film. So I have no interest in *Vicky Cristina Barcelona*. If people love the film, then that is delightful. If they don't like it, then . . . hmmm . . . that's tough. They're either completely right in not liking it, or they're quite brilliant and they see flaws in it that I never saw, or they're philistines and they don't get it and I was right. But it's irrelevant because I don't really know or care.

DM: Was that always true?
WA: It was true after the first couple films because when you go into the business, all of your illusions are shattered right away. You find out that great success does not change your life in any meaningful way and failure doesn't change your life in any meaningful way. And then you find out that the reviews of your film—1,600 reviews from all over America, each one contradicting the other one—don't mean anything to you either. So finally you just give up. If you don't have fun doing the film, then the results of the film will never give you any fun. You find that your film wins some kind of award or is much extolled, but nothing happens. Your life is the same. You still get the sniffles, the toothaches, and all that. *Nothing* meaningful changes in your life. So I gave up on that idea decades ago.

DM: Did your parents ever tell you what they thought of certain films?
WA: No. They didn't think much. They were just delighted that I was quote-unquote

famous. But they couldn't discern between one or the other. They didn't get most of the pictures.

DM: They didn't have a favorite and a least favorite?
WA: No, no. My mother would have liked the ones that had strong stories, and my father used to just walk down and look at the lines outside of the theaters.

DM: Well, that's important, too—especially for parents.
WA: I know. Sean Connery told me the same thing about his father. He said his father used to walk down and look at the lines and come back home and tell him there was a big line at this theater, a big line at that theater. My father did the same thing.

DM: Do you think your parents shaped or contributed to your worldview? Can you point to parts of your personality that can be traced to each of them?
WA: Yeah. I think—and my sister would agree—that I've inherited the worst of each parent. I have my father's hypochondria and lack of concentration. I have his amorality. I have everything bad that he had. Then I have my mother's surly, pill-like, complaining, whining attitude. The only positive thing you could say is that my mother instilled in me—probably at a greater cost than it was worth—an enormous sense of discipline, and a feeling that the highest achievement that I'm capable of is not good enough. And so I'm always striving, and that has redounded to my benefit. I've earned some money doing that, and I've stayed on the straight and narrow for the most part, so that's been a help to me.

DM: This is an old-fashioned idea, but based on that, would you say that you've fulfilled your promise?
WA: I don't think that I've fulfilled my promise, no. I think that the sabotaging of my promise began in childhood because, you know, I was not led in the right direction by my parents really.

DM: Why? What direction did they lead you in?
WA: I mean, I never read a book until I was eighteen years old. I never read a single book. I was a smart kid and I was not understood by my parents.

DM: Were they encouraging you to be something other than what you were?
WA: They were like all Jewish parents. They hoped that I would be studious enough to become a doctor or a lawyer or some professional thing. They were creatures of the Depression—they would have been thrilled if I had been a pharmacist or something reliable. But I don't think that I've ever fulfilled my promise.

I think that I was born lucky with a very good sense of humor and a reasonably good native intelligence. But I should have studied and been bookish. I should have gone to college and become a philosophy major. I should have studied literature. I should have aimed much higher than I aimed. I mean, I was interested in show business and magic tricks and tap-dancing and joke-telling—these were, you know, the trivial, escapist activities of my childhood. I should have been interested in writing novels and serious plays and poetry and things like that. Had I been better directed as a child, those are things that I think would have stood me better in life. I could have utilized whatever natural gifts I had in a more profound and deeper way. Now, I don't know this to be true—it's just something that I think.

DM: Well, I know you don't believe in reincarnation, but if you were to have another chance or if you could come back, would you wish to be something other than what you've been?
WA: Well, you know, if I could just hope to have a major talent, then I would rather have it in music than in any other field.

DM: Oh, really?
WA: If you said, "Would you rather be the best film director in the world or the best painter in the world or a great musician?" then I'd rather be a great musician.

DM: You mean someone who plays the clarinet?
WA: No, no. I wouldn't want to play the clarinet. I'd want to play the piano. I mean, I would trade my talent right now, even up, for Bud Powell's talent. That would be just fine with me. And I know I'm not picking Glenn Gould or Vladimir Horowitz—I'm picking a struggling jazz musician. But that would be fine.

DM: And you'd rather be a performer as opposed to a composer?
WA: Yes, yes. I'd rather be a performing musician. But that's something that I don't have the talent for. I mean, none of the arts are any good unless you really are great at them. If you're Matisse or Picasso or Horowitz or Bud Powell or Louis Armstrong . . . I mean, you really have to be great. Otherwise it doesn't mean very much.

DM: What's the worst thing about getting older?
WA: Well, of course, your body breaks down and you're closer to death. So, you know, that's an unbeatable combination.

DM: Is there anything good about it?

WA: There's nothing good about getting older—absolutely nothing—because the amount of wisdom and experience you gain is negligible compared to what you lose. You do gain a couple of things—you gain a little bittersweet and sour wisdom from your heartbreaks and failures and things—but what you lose is so catastrophic in every way.

DM: Not a good trade.
WA: No. And, consequently, the whole thrust of science and the medical profession is to try and prevent it from happening, to try to prolong life, to keep you from dying, to keep you from getting older, to rejuvenate you. I mean, that's everybody's wish. The fountain of youth is everybody's sought-after thing.

DM: You've written a lot about death over the years. Have your feelings about it changed at all?
WA: No. It's a no-win proposition, because you know what happens? You die. Don't forget that I'm not a religious person, so you die, and you disintegrate in one way or another—either you're cremated or you decompose—and you're gone. That's it. There's no other at bat. It's one strike and you're out.

DM: Of all your films, is there one that represents what you think is the best of who you are? It doesn't necessarily have to be the best film.
WA: Well, that sort of changes from day to day with me. There's a small group of my films that I favor over the large majority of them, where I feel like I achieved, you know, something worthwhile in my own terms. There are a few of those films that I'm sort of proud to have done, and I feel that if you were to show them in a festival with Truffaut's films and Antonioni's films and Fellini's films . . . they wouldn't be the best, but they wouldn't be hooted off the screen either. They could certainly serve as the hors d'oeuvres or the warm-ups to the really great films.

DM: And which of your films are those?
WA: Well, I think *The Purple Rose of Cairo* [1985] is a film like that, and *Bullets over Broadway* [1994] is one, and *Zelig* [1983] is one, and *Husbands and Wives* [1992] and *Match Point* [2005]—I probably have six or seven that I feel are respectable pieces of work, where I don't have to run and hide my head in the sand. You know, I've got a lot of B material. I don't have a lot of failures—real abysmal failures. I mean, I've got some of them, for sure, but I don't have a *lot*. I've got a lot of B material. And a quantity of F material. . . .

DM: I guess what I'm asking, though, is if there is one of your films that tells us the most about your philosophy of life? You know, if someone couldn't meet you,

and wanted to know what Woody is really like or what gives us the most sense of his worldview—his fears, his optimisms, his anxieties, his hopes—is there one film that kind of best sums that up?
WA: Well, to date—if it's just that—I would probably say *Anything Else* [2003].

DM: Really?
WA: Yeah. You'd get it in a more abstract way in *Purple Rose,* because clearly I do believe that reality is dreadful and that you are forced to choose it in the end or go crazy, but that it kills you. So that film does sum up a great feeling that I have about life—I mean a *large* feeling that I have about it. But in terms of just me personally as a kind of wretched little complaining *vantz*, I think you would see that in *Anything Else*. There's a lot of me in there.

DM: Very interesting. You're full of surprises.
WA: Well, it is *me*. I'm not saying that *Anything Else* is my best film, although, I didn't think it was a bad film at all—I think that one is better than many films of mine that were more successful. I won't say that it's never the case, but very often there's no correlation between the quality of one's work artistically and its commercial success. *Everybody* knows that.

In Conversation: Woody Allen

Adam Moss / 2008

Published in *New York* magazine, October 6, 2008, 172–77. Reprinted with permission.

Few would argue that Woody Allen is the filmmaker most identified with New York, a distinction that has less to do with the settings of his movies (though most were shot here) than with a sensibility that is urban and anxious and obsessive, and often (still) very funny. Born in the Bronx in 1935, he grew up in Flatbush and had his first joke published in the New York *Daily Mirror* at age sixteen. His movie career almost exactly spans the forty years of this magazine's history—from *Take the Money and Run*, released in 1969, to *Vicky Cristina Barcelona*, his thirty-ninth movie, which came out this summer. When we met in early September, he was editing *Whatever Works*, a comedy starring Larry David that will be released next year—and that marks Allen's return to New York after filming his last four movies abroad. ("I can only tell you it's about a crabby character who lives in New York and has an experience with Evan Rachel Wood and Patricia Clarkson," he says, "a comic experience I'm hoping is funny. But for me to say it's funny doesn't mean anything.") We spoke in his screening room on Park Avenue, huddled close on two rolling chairs because, he said, he is hard of hearing. He was soft-spoken and voluble, his voice rising slightly only when the conversation ventured, in asides, into the present political climate, a state of affairs that clearly exasperates him. But mostly we talked about the city—both the one where he lives and the one in his imagination.

New York: Let's start with the opening of *Manhattan*, as ecstatic a valentine to New York as any four minutes in the history of movies. Over a series of iconic images of the city, the voiceover begins, "Chapter One: He adored New York City, he idolized it all out of proportion—no, make that, he romanticized it all out of proportion." How much of that is you speaking, and how much is your character, Isaac?

Woody Allen: Well, you know, for some reason I've always had an irrational love for New York. There's no reason that you would necessarily like it on paper. It's very expensive. Very little of it works. I've made films in many cities—London, Barcelona—where the people are very polite and courteous. You think to yourself, *Oh God, this is a pleasure*. And New York is nothing like that. But the city is so full of chaos, and the chaos is, for many people, pleasurable. Recently, I was living in a sublet on Madison Avenue, and every night you would hear ambulances and sirens. It was truly a lullaby. And I remember years ago once sleeping out in the Hamptons—

NY: You owned a house in Southampton—
WA: Yes, this is true. Many years ago, when everyone I know had houses in the Hamptons, I thought maybe it was for me too. I bought a very, very beautiful house in Southampton, and I spent over a year fixing it up. I put in trees, I changed the roof; I mean, I did an incredible job. Then I went out there one night and I slept in it, and I never came back.

NY: At the time you made *Manhattan*, the portrait of New York in the movies was pretty bleak. Films like *Death Wish* made it seem like a violent cesspool. Were you deliberately trying to replace that impression with a more romantic one?
WA: Well, I was raised on those movies that gave you an image of Manhattan, and that was the image of Manhattan that I fell in love with. I grew up in Brooklyn, and I wasn't privy to the parties and the people at the Stork Club with their ermines over their shoulders coming in at four in the morning and calling people on white telephones next to the bed. Where I lived, we ate on linoleum. So when I moved to Manhattan, I wanted the actual Manhattan to be like that. I wanted people to be able to go to the theater at 8:40 and then to a supper club, and to be able to walk home through Central Park. I didn't want them to have to fear for their lives. So I pushed my idea of it, and people always used to say to me, "Oh, you look at New York through rose-colored glasses." And that's fine, but I got my idea of New York from Hollywood.

NY: But if you were making a movie about your real New York, what would that movie look like? How different would it be?
WA: Well, because I've been successful, I've made enough money so that I can live fairly decently in New York—first in a very pretty penthouse on Fifth Avenue, and now in a very pretty townhouse in the Seventies, between Park and Lex. I have a driver. I eat at the good restaurants. I live, in a certain sense, in a bit of a bubble in New York. I don't live exactly realistically.

NY: In that same opening monologue to *Manhattan*, Isaac says, joking in part, that New York has become a metaphor for the decay of contemporary culture.

Back in 1979, people would have understood what you meant. Now maybe a little less so, because New York isn't in quite a state of decay. Have we lost something by losing the decay?

WA: We don't miss the decay, but we do miss the middle class. It's a shame that you can't live on this isle of Manhattan unless you have money. When I first moved here from Brooklyn, I moved into a one-room apartment, but it was right off Park Avenue in the Sixties. And it was $125 a month. I don't know how all these people who come to New York to seek fame and fortune do it. I guess they wind up living in Brooklyn and Hoboken.

NY: When you go to Brooklyn now, you must find it unimaginably different from the Brooklyn you grew up in.

WA: Yes, there are certain parts of Brooklyn that have become very, very desirable. My old neighborhood, as it turns out, became Hasidic. Which is, for me, the kiss of death.

NY: So many of the signature aspects of New York in your earlier movies—the independent bookstores, a grittier artists' Soho, Checker cabs, revival houses . . . they're all gone. Do you mourn that? Are you essentially nostalgic by nature?

WA: Yes, I mourn that, for sure. There are times where I'd finish a movie, like *Everyone Says I Love You*, and five places in the movie would be gone before it came out. Le Cirque would be gone. The bookstore on Madison Avenue would be gone. I couldn't keep up with the rate of change, and the change was always the progression, really, of opulence. I especially mourn the movie houses, because when I grew up in Brooklyn, you only had to walk three blocks to go to a movie theater. They were ubiquitous.

NY: Do you still go to movies in theaters?

WA: I don't, because I have this [*gesturing to the screening room*], and so it's much easier for me to call up and say, "Can I get a print of *The Women* sent over here?" and I can just come in here with a couple of friends on a Saturday night and see it. But when I drive down the street and I see a marquee and now it says Duane Reade, it's awful.

NY: Is there anything about the new New York that's better?

WA: Uh, well, it's safer. But, you know, I think change of this sort is almost always negative. Things degenerate.

NY: Always?

WA: Look, I thought movies got better. They're not now—

NY: I read an interview recently where you named your favorite movies in different categories. I think the most recent film you had on any list is *Airplane*.
WA: Yeah, I have a soft spot for that film. There have been other funny movies since, but that is a funny one. But I grew up in what they called the Golden Age of Movies. Really, it was the golden age of movie stars. William Powell and Fred MacMurray and Edward G. Robinson. The stars had some kind of charismatic hold that later stars don't have.

NY: And why is that?
WA: Because the screens were big and the world was not as small, and Hollywood was a distant place. They acted out myths. Now, it would be hard to find better actors than, you know, Robert De Niro and Al Pacino, but the public sees them as guys in the neighborhood. The world's gotten much more casual; it's not as dressy as it was. But the movies themselves, when you think back to the so-called Golden Age, were junk for the most part. When we started to get into the late sixties or seventies, though, there was a little rush when cinema moved away from centering on the star and started to center more on the directors. And suddenly, we started to have good movies. Of course, we've taken a turn recently when the studios realized that it was to their advantage to spend $100 million and up on a movie because they could make $300 million, and what is the point of making a fine movie that makes $15 million, which was good enough years ago? They want to gamble for bigger stakes, and who can fault them, that's the business they're in. So the films have taken a big hit.

NY: Do you think audiences are less sophisticated?
WA: People are always talking about the dumbing down of the country. Now, it's hard to believe that they could be dumber now than they were in my time. Theoretically that can't be. But when you look around at Broadway theater and films, it's hard to argue with the fact that we're going through a period of coarsened public taste. And yet you don't want to be caught saying that because then it seems like you're one of those people saying, *In my day, it was great*. You know, it wasn't that great in my day either. I'm sure if you went back to the 1800s and the 1500s and the Greeks, they would say garbage sells, too.

NY: Do you have a theory about why the culture keeps getting coarser?
WA: The country has, over the years, moved to the right. And it's possible that accompanying that move to the right, you also get a lessening of taste. But I don't know if what I'm saying is true, because I have shown some very good films—Bergman, Fellini—to kids from good schools like Yale. Bright kids. And they were not impressed. You know, it wasn't as though I picked out some kid from

the Midwest who's a churchgoing barbarian. Those same kids that you see in the movie house doubled over with laughter over fraternity toilet jokes are very often kids from Columbia and Yale. We might also still be feeling the fallout from the sexual revolution, when everybody just ran amok talking dirty and doing things that were forbidden and it became the mark of drama and comedy to be simply outrageous. Not necessarily dramatically interesting or particularly comic, but just outrageous.

NY: Is there a recent film about New York by another director that you think especially nails the experience of living here?
WA: No.

NY: Let's talk about 1968. You were still doing stand-up, and an amazingly fertile period for comedy was just winding down.
WA: Yes, it started in the late fifties. All of a sudden there were all those wonderful kind of Catskills-style comics—Jack E. Leonard, Phil Foster, Henny Youngman, Buddy Hackett, and they were hilariously funny guys. And then—see, Lenny Bruce I found artificial. I found him one of those guys who—without being a genuine intellectual or a particularly thoughtful person—saw an avenue to exploit and exploited it. I mean, he was fine. I think he towered over me. But then strange flowers started emerging on the scene that were different from the other flowers. There was Nichols and May. Jonathan Winters. And Mort Sahl. And they made the world of small, chic nightclubs and being a comedian not only acceptable but kind of snobby or stylish. And people that had ambivalent feelings about being a comic before suddenly found you could discuss intellectual matters.

NY: As you did.
WA: But I was not in that class. There was a whole group of us that were successful comics. Shelley Berman, Bob Newhart, Bill Cosby, myself. But the three great geniuses of the period were Nichols and May, Jonathan Winters, and Mort Sahl. I still find Mort Sahl funny. I was with him the other day, in California, and he's eighty-one and he's teaching at Claremont College. And he said they have a course out there that they offered him to teach, on the Holocaust, and he didn't take it. He said, "I wanted to see first how history judges the event."

NY: The persona you developed in stand-up and later in the movies was of an anxious, neurotic Jew. Do you feel like the anxious, neurotic Jewish archetype still has the same cultural meaning now?
WA: I don't know. I didn't set out to do it. I just went up and made jokes, and

people told me that I was an anxious, neurotic Jew. I didn't sit down and think, *This is a good side of the street to work.*

NY: Do you think the New York Jew has gotten too assimilated?
WA: No, I'm a big one for assimilation of everybody. But the basic problems remain the same. People still have existential anxiety, relationship anxiety. It just may not be expressed in Hebraic idiom.

NY: Do you know anyone who still goes to an analyst?
WA: I do, though psychoanalysis has gone through a lot of changes.

NY: As the world's most famous analysand, can you say whether you think analysis works?
WA: People always tease me. They say, look at you, you went for so much psychoanalysis and you're so neurotic, you wind up marrying a girl so much younger than you. You don't like to go through tunnels, you don't like to stand near the drain in the shower. But I could also say to them, I've had a very productive life. I've worked very hard, I've never fallen prey to depression. I'm not sure I could have done all of that without being in psychoanalysis. People would say to me, oh, it's just a crutch. And I would say, yes. It's a crutch, and exactly what I need in this point in my life is a crutch.

NY: For a long time, you enjoyed largely favorable coverage in the New York media—until you first started seeing Soon-Yi. The press—particularly the tabloid press—hit you hard. And certainly over the years, this has become more of a tabloid town. Do the tabloids amuse you or trouble you?
WA: I've always believed that thoughtful people don't really take the tabloids seriously. They're basically a form of entertainment. I enjoy them as much as the next New Yorker.

NY: But do you think New York has gotten meaner?
WA: When you travel around the country, you see what a tough town New York is: rude, competitive, a town where good, logical ideas are ignored in favor of unworkable ones. And yet, all these other towns are so dead and boring compared to New York.

NY: If you could live forever in the New York of one of the past four decades, which decade would it be?
WA: I can't go back earlier than that, right? Okay, 'cause I just want to add, parenthetically, the period leading up to World War II, that was really the time to be

here. But, I guess, the seventies. There were a lot of good movies in the seventies, and politically we weren't completely in the toilet.

NY: Were you in the city on September 11?
WA: Yes, I remember exactly where. Someone in my house—I lived on 92nd Street then—said, "A plane just crashed into the World Trade Center," and then we turned on a television set and then another one crashed, and we saw that. Two days later I was scheduled to go to Europe. A lot of people canceled going to Europe, there was a lot of fear. I wasn't afraid, not because I'm anything but a major coward, but I was flying privately. I didn't think that I could be hijacked. And because I went and I was a New Yorker, I became the spokesman for New York City and September 11. And I was on all the Sunday-morning news shows in France and England and Italy. I was suddenly on their versions of *Face the Nation*. And they were asking me, is this going to be the end of all humor? (They have a way of putting these things in European countries.) Is this the end of New York?

And I said no, not at all. Not for a minute. I feel I was completely right. If you drop a person in New York City now and you drop them before September 11 and they didn't know, they wouldn't know the difference. I felt New York would metabolize it, and it would go on. New York would be the same vibrant city. And it is.

Woody Allen on Life, Films, and *Whatever Works*

Terry Gross / 2009

Originally broadcast on *Fresh Air with Terry Gross*, June 15, 2009. *Fresh Air* is produced by WHYY, Inc., and distributed by NPR. Reprinted by permission.

Terry Gross: This is *Fresh Air*. I'm Terry Gross. My guest is Woody Allen. He has a new movie that's partly an old movie. Woody Allen wrote the screenplay for his new film, *Whatever Works*, in the seventies. The leading role was written for Zero Mostel, but Allen put the screenplay aside after Mostel died in 1977, the year *Annie Hall* was released.

Last year, when Woody Allen was ready to start a new film, he faced the possibility of an actor strike. He wanted to finish shooting a new movie before the threatened strike, but that left him no time to write a new screenplay. So he dusted off the one he wrote years ago for Zero Mostel and cast Larry David in the leading role.

Larry David plays Boris Yellnikoff, a former Columbia University professor who came close to winning a Nobel Prize in quantum mechanics. He's as misanthropic as he is brilliant. He hates most adults, and he hates children, which is bad news for the children who come to him for chess lessons.

In this scene, Boris is sitting in a cafe when he's confronted by the mother of one of his chess students.

[*soundbite from* Whatever Works]

Gross: One day, Boris finds a teen-aged runaway named Melodie, played by Evan Rachel Wood, sitting in front of his Manhattan home, begging for some food. He reluctantly takes her in, she stays, and they eventually marry, in spite of the approximately forty-year age difference between them and in spite of the fact that Boris thinks she's brainless.

At the start of the film, Boris states his philosophy of life, which is: Life is short, so take what little pleasure you can get in this chamber of horrors. It's a

philosophy expressed in several Woody Allen movies. Here's Woody Allen at the beginning of *Annie Hall*.
[*soundbite from* Annie Hall]

Woody Allen: [*as Alvy Singer*] Well, that's essentially how I feel about life, full of loneliness and misery and suffering and unhappiness, and it's all over much too quickly.

Gross: That basic philosophy is restated in Woody Allen's recent film, *Vicky Cristina Barcelona*. Here's Javier Bardem inviting two beautiful, American tourists, Vicky and Cristina, to spend the weekend with him.
[*soundbite from* Vicky Cristina Barcelona]

Gross: Woody Allen, welcome to *Fresh Air*. You know, it's interesting, at least three of your films kind of start with the same premise. I'm wondering why has this question framed several of your movies, that life is hard, life is full of pain, but life is short, so do what you can to get some pleasure.
Allen: Well, this is hardly an original thought with me. I mean, down through the ages, all the important writers and all the important philosophers have, in one form or another, come to the conclusion, the obvious conclusion, that you know, life is a terrible trial and very harsh and very full of suffering, and so whatever you can do with the stipulation that you don't hurt anybody, without, you know, ruining a life here or there or causing any damage, there's nothing wrong with it.

Gross: So when we talk about making movies, does that give you pleasure? Like what's the ratio of pleasure and pain in making a film?
Allen: Well you know, it's a different kind of pain. See, making a movie is a great distraction from the real agonies of the world. It's an overwhelmingly, you know, difficult thing to do.

You've got to deal with actors and temperaments and scripts and second acts and third acts and camera work and costumes and sets and editing and music, and you know, there's enough in that to keep you distracted almost all the time. And if I'm locked into what would appear to be a painful situation because half my movie works, let's say, and the whole second half of it doesn't work, or a character in my movie is terrible, you don't believe the love story or something, these are all problems that are, or generally are, solvable with reshooting, with editing, with thinking, diagnosing what's wrong. And they distract you from the real problems of life, which are unsolvable and very painful problems.

Also in the problems of moviemaking, if you don't solve your problem, all that happens to you is that your movie bombs. So the movie is terrible. So people don't come to see it. Critics don't like it. The public doesn't like it. This is hardly a terrible punishment in life compared to what you're given out in the real world of human existence.

Gross: So, may I ask, what are some of the real problems that making movies distracts you from?
Allen: Well, they distract me from the same problems that you face or that anyone faces, you know, the uncertainty of life and inevitability of aging and death, and death of loved ones, and mass killings and starvations and holocausts, and not just the manmade carnage but the existential position that you're in—being in a world where you have no idea what's going on, why you're here or what possible meaning your life can have and the conclusion that you come to after a while, that there is really no meaning to it, and it's just a random, meaningless event, and these are pretty depressing thoughts. And if you spend much time thinking about them, not only can't you resolve them, but you sit frozen in your seat. You can't even get up to have your lunch.

So it's better to distract yourself, and people distract themselves creatively in the arts. They distract themselves in business or by following baseball teams and worrying over batting averages and who wins the pennant, and these are all things that you do and focus on rather than sit home and worry.

Gross: So we've talked about how your characters try to find pleasure in a life full of pain. My impression of you is that you're the kind of person for whom pleasure is hard to come by, in part because you've said you're a claustrophobic, agoraphobic. *Annie Hall* was originally going to be named *Anhedonia*, which means an inability to experience pleasure. Is pleasure hard to come by, even when your work can find it?
Allen: I do—there are a number of things that give me pleasure. But you know, hanging over the pleasure is always the dark cloud of the human predicament so that I can get pleasure when I'm playing with my children, or I'm doing something with my wife or playing jazz.

I like to play music, and I do find it pleasurable, but these are transient oases in a vast desert of unspeakable gloom. But I do get pleasure like everyone else. It's pleasurable for me to go to a basketball game, or you know ... but always overriding it is the notion that it's ephemeral, very ephemeral.

Gross: Now your new movie, *Whatever Works*, was written a long time ago by you for Zero Mostel to star in. What year did you write it?
Allen: I don't remember the exact year, but it must have been the seventies. I mean, I wrote it years ago, threw it in the drawer, and then I took it out because I needed a script quickly because there was going to be, possibly going to be, an

actor strike. And so I had to—I couldn't work on a script. I had to have a script quickly to do a picture before that potentially imminent strike occurred.

So I took it out of my drawer, and I felt it was quite a good story, and unfortunately, Zero had been unique, and it was very hard to think of anyone to play that role, and over the years, decades, it occurred to us, Juliet Taylor and myself, that—

Gross: She's your casting director.
Allen: Casting director, yeah—Larry David could probably do this in a very, very funny way.

Gross: The character that Larry David plays is a real misanthrope, and unlike some of your other earlier characters, he's not self-deprecating. He's not insecure. In fact, he thinks he's a genius, a kind of superior being. And in that respect, you're almost leaving out the likable part because what we identify with in your earlier characters, and I mention the early characters because that's the period that you wrote the script, is that they had these insecurities. They were self-deprecating. So I guess I'm wondering why you made this character so condescending to other people, somebody who thinks he's a genius.
Allen: Well, this was supposed to be for Zero originally, and he was a big, fat, blustering guy who thought that he had all the answers and thought that everybody in life was inferior to him.

Gross: You think Zero Mostel himself was that way?
Allen: No, no, not Zero himself—

Gross: Oh, oh, okay.
Allen: —the character that Zero was playing. Actually, Zero was, you know, quite the opposite of that. But you know, he was a big, blustering character who had no patience with anybody. But of course when you look at the character, the character is full of self-doubt and full of anxiety and can't fend for himself and can't function in relationships. He's really no different, it's just that his façade is, you know, if I had written that years ago for myself, the character that I could play with my limited range was self-deprecating, and the persona that I always felt comfortable acting out was that kind of an intimidated, victim-style character. But at the time, that was not the story. The story was written not for me but for Zero, and so it was—it would be the difference between having someone like Groucho Marx or W. C. Fields play a character and Charlie Chaplin play a character. One is more persecuted and victim-like, and the other is—the other two are much more insulting and condescending and superior.

Gross: So why did you feel so at home playing the self-deprecating character and felt like that was your comfort zone?
Allen: Yeah, I don't know. I just—you're just born into it, I guess. [laughter]

Gross: Born into self-deprecation?
Allen: You know, I'm not an actor, and I don't have a big range. I mean, I could not play, you know, Shakespeare. I can—there's certain things I feel comfortable doing, and I just, I can't explain why. I just do. Yes, in life I think I am self-deprecating, and frightened of everything, and it's an area that I feel comfortable making jokes about because I'm always joking about my personal foibles.

Gross: My guest is Woody Allen. His new movie, *Whatever Works*, stars Larry David. We'll talk more after a break. This is *Fresh Air*. [*soundbite of music*]

If you're just joining us, my guest is Woody Allen, and his new movie is called *Whatever Works*, and it stars Larry David and Evan Rachel Wood.

In the movie, Larry David is in his fifties, and Evan Rachel Wood is still in her teens when she shows up kind of homeless on his doorstep. And he decides, kind of against his will, and against his better judgment, to take her in and give her a few meals and then to let her live there, and then they get married.

So forgive me for asking this because this is a little personal, but this was written before, like, long before you married Soon-Yi, but it means, let's be honest, that everyone's going to be looking for clues in this movie about your relationship with your wife.
Allen: Mm-hmm.

Gross: And again, let's be honest. A lot of your fans were really kind of upset when you married the woman who is the adoptive daughter of your long-time lover. So I wonder if you thought about that kind of thing when you were making the movie, that people would just be, like, looking for clues about the older-man-younger-woman relationship and how that applies to you.
Allen: People do look for clues in my movies all the time—

Gross: For who you really are.
Allen: —in all of my movies. They are constantly searching for clues in my movies. And no matter how many times I've told them over the years that, you know, I make these stories up, some of them I've made up with other writers. I've worked with Doug McGrath, with Marshall Brickman, Mickey Rose, they make up stories, you know, they make up half of the story with me. The people always look for clues in my movies, and they think, based on my movies, that they know me, and of course they don't know me.

And there are some things you could've learned about me over the years but not much, really. You know, I was never who anybody thought I was from when I started.

When I first started as a comic in Greenwich Village, people thought that I was, at that time, some kind of a little beatnik and someone who, you know, was a kind of mousy intellectual, and you know, none of these things were ever true. You know, I never lived in the Village. I always lived in a very nice neighborhood uptown in Manhattan.

I was never intellectual. I was never interested in intellectual things. You know, when I explain to people I'm the guy that you see in his T-shirt with a beer watching the baseball game at night at home on television, they find that hard to square with the characters that I played in the movies. But in the movies, I'm just acting.

So it doesn't bother me, but it is something that I've tried to be honest about over the years and explain to people, but they don't feel comfortable hearing it. They listen to it, and either they don't believe me when I say it, or they don't want to believe me because it diminishes their enjoyment, or it's important that they have some kind of image of me that's meaningful to them for some reason. I don't know why. But I've never been—I was always a very athletic little boy, always, you know, never a loner or a loser, always the first one picked on any team.

Gross: You were the first one picked on any team?
Allen: Always.

Gross: See, I wouldn't have believed that. [*laughter*]
Allen: I know. I was always a very—

Gross: Very counter to your image.
Allen: —very good athlete. I was interested even in playing professional baseball. I was, you know, won track medals. But nobody thinks of me that way. They think of me as some kind of little bookworm—because I have these big, black glasses, black-rimmed glasses—and they think of me as a bookworm and give me more credit for intellect than I have. And you know, I couldn't make it through college. I couldn't make it through my freshman year of college. And this was not because I was some artist or intellectual above it. I couldn't cut it. I mean, I wasn't—

Gross: You flunked out?
Allen: I couldn't get the—I flunked out. I was thrown out of New York University in my first year there—

Gross: What did you fail?
Allen: —because I couldn't get the marks.

Gross: In what subjects?
Allen: I was a motion picture production major, but now I had to take regular subjects, as well.

Gross: Don't tell me you failed motion picture classes.
Allen: English and Spanish and subjects like that. I failed those subjects. And I didn't do well in motion picture production, either.

Gross: Was this because you were busy writing jokes for other people and not studying, or—
Allen: No, no, I wasn't too busy. I wasn't too busy. I was uninterested. I mean, I— you know, I played ball. I was, as I say, I was athletic. I played cards. I liked to—I wasn't interested in erudition and education. Those were not things that—I was not brought up to be interested in that, and I wasn't interested. You know, I didn't see it in my home. And so I just—this is long-winded—but just to say that people have, you know, are constantly looking for clues to me in my work and seizing on things that are quite, quite unrepresentative of who I really am.

Gross: Woody Allen will be back in the second half of the show. His new movie, *Whatever Works*, stars Larry David. I'm Terry Gross, and this is *Fresh Air*. [*soundbite of music*]

This is *Fresh Air*. I'm Terry Gross back with Woody Allen. His new film, *Whatever Works*, stars Larry David in a role Allen originally wrote for Zero Mostel. Allen wrote the screenplay in the seventies. Back in the seventies, when Woody Allen starred in several of his films, you couldn't help but wonder how closely the screenplays resembled autobiography.

Can you describe the neighborhood you grew up in? A lot of people imagine you growing up under the rollercoaster in Coney Island [*laughter*]—like your character in *Annie Hall*.

Allen: Right. Right. People think that. No, I grew up in a very nice section of Brooklyn called Flatbush. And when I grew up there it was a lovely section. I mean there was a ball field, and playgrounds. There were many, many, many movie houses within walking distance of—no matter where you were dropped you'd be within walking distance of a couple of movie houses. And the school that I went to was quite a nice school. And the blocks were tree-lined, and safe, and you could go out and play ball all day long in the streets, and schoolyards, and it was a very nice neighborhood. It was—I was not deprived, and I didn't grow up poor.

Gross: What was your parent's relationship like? And what did it make you think marriage was like?

Allen: Marriage for my parents was kind of like what it was in all the other neighboring houses and friends' houses. It was a long truce is what it was. All the parents in the neighborhood, the men and women, they loved each other. There were people who were from the Depression, and so money was a big factor because nobody had any real money and everybody had to work. But usually what would happen is the men and the women would—the guys would work all day and they'd come home, and then on the weekends the guys would take bridge chairs out and play cards at a table and the women would keep with the women.

There was no sense that a guy was coming home on the weekend so he could take his wife and, you know, leave the son with the babysitter or the daughter with a babysitter and check into a hotel and have a romantic weekend or do something romantic. There wasn't that. The guys would be watching the ballgame or not watching so much, listening on the radio to the ballgames together. They'd be playing poker, or gin rummy, or pinochle together. And that's how it was even when there was a dinner or something, uncles and relatives would get together, and as soon as the dinner was over the guys would be in the other room around the card table and the women would be talking in their room about—you know, and you didn't get a sense, you didn't come away with the sense of romantic passion. There wasn't much interpersonal charm to it.

Gross: I know that your movies aren't your life. But there's a scene in *Annie Hall* that I—it's just so funny and I feel like I know these people. It's the dinner scene where you're at dinner with Diane Keaton, Annie Hall's family, and it's a much more kind of formal, you know, quiet, polite, everybody eating slowly kind of setting. And you compare that in your mind with the family dinners you were used to where people were shoveling down the food and hollering at each other and everybody's aggravated and talking about who has diabetes. Was dinner like that at home?

Allen: Dinner was not really like that at home. No, because I ate by myself at 5:30, and my mother ate at 6:30 after she had made dinner for my sister and myself, and my father got home at a quarter to nine, and he would have a—so no, that stuff was made up and exaggerated for comic purposes.

Gross: How come you ate alone?

Allen: I ate alone because I liked to eat alone, because I liked the solitude. I liked to eat and read a comic book or something and—

Gross: Your parents let you do that without accusing you of being antisocial and turning your back on the family? [*laughter*]

Allen: They were so happy that—[*laughter*]—that I wanted to eat alone, you know. . . . No, because we always lived with aunts and uncles and things. And my mother would have a better time eating with her sister. Or, if my father got home in time and she was waiting for him, with him. But you know, what am I going to talk about with my mother? I was ten years old or nine or eleven and out in the streets all day playing stickball and we had nothing to talk about.

Gross: Now you started in comedy by writing jokes and you were writing for an older generation. Were you writing jokes that you couldn't imagine telling yourself, but that you were writing for the comics who would be telling them?
Allen: Yes. I couldn't imagine being in front of an audience. I wanted to be a writer and I wanted to be, again, alone in my room, not bothered by anybody, not in front of an audience. And so I never saw myself performing.

Gross: What was the pay like? Did they pay you per joke or per joke that they used?
Allen: You know, the pay was a lot. I mean, at the time, when you think that my father and mother both had to work their whole life. My father drove a cab, and was a bartender, was a bookmaker, and was a—he ran a poolroom. My mother always worked for the flower market. And they had to combine their salaries. And I started working—and their combined salaries would be maybe less than a hundred dollars a week combined. And I started working and the, immediately I was making close to two hundred a week, just as—I mean I was seventeen years old and I was making that. And before long I was making fifteen hundred dollars a week. And in those days, I mean this was the early fifties—

Gross: That's a lot of money.
Allen: —you know, the fifties, and it was more than my parents, put together, would make in ages. So the show business salaries I always felt were way out of whack with reality. Now, I haven't made a big protest over that over the years you'll notice [*laughter*]—but I always did feel that they were—when you see what a school teacher gets and what some terrible comedian gets or some awful singer gets, you know it's shocking.

Gross: Did you say your father worked in a poolroom and he was a bookmaker?
Allen: Yes. He, my father had a lot of jobs. He was always scuffling to make a living. He sold jewelry, he was a waiter, he was a bartender, he was a cab driver, he ran a poolroom, he was a bookmaker for a while. . . .

Gross: You must've met a lot of colorful characters through him, unless you were not welcome in that world.

Allen: I was young to have met the colorful characters. But he was always bringing home stolen merchandise, and you know, that was fenced to him for no money at all. So he'd always be coming home with a fur coat for my mother, or a typewriter, or a tape recorder, or this—and picked this up for two dollars and this up for twenty dollars. And there was a lot of that over the years, a lot of stuff bought, I remember that, you know, fence junk.

Gross: Were you supposed to keep that a secret, that it was fenced?

Allen: It was never expressed that way. It was, you know, it was that he came home with a bargain and—

Gross: Right.

Allen: —you know, that—and you say my God, where did you get that electric typewriter for a dollar and quarter? [*laughter*] It's brand new. [*laughter*] And you know, but you never knew that. And my father was an inveterate numbers player. There was not a day in his life that he didn't play the numbers. And whenever he won, you know, it was money for everybody. I mean he just spread it around, like Jackie Gleason and *The Honeymooners*. I mean he just, everybody—it was such a pleasure if he came home and had hit his number. My sister and I and my mother all knew we were going to be rewarded with an extravagant bonus.

Gross: My guest is Woody Allen. His new movie, *Whatever Works*, stars Larry David. We'll talk more after a break. This is *Fresh Air*. [*soundbite of music*]

My guest is Woody Allen and his new movie is called *Whatever Works*, and it stars Larry David. Several of your characters have had, to one degree or another, a dose of hypochondria. And I'm thinking like, you've definitely reached the age where people get real symptoms. [*laughter*] And you know, as you get older, as we all know, there are certain insults to the body. And I guess I'm wondering what it's like for you to deal with the body's aging process?

Allen: Well first off, let me say, you know, you get insults to your body all the time. I mean—

Gross: True.

Allen: —you're always walking on the abyss. [*laughter*] And I was never a hypochondriac. I never have imagined that I get a sickness or a disease. My problem was being an alarmist. That is, if I get chapped lips I think it's brain cancer. [*laughter*] You know, so . . . it's that I immediately go to the worst permutation possible. And as I've gotten older, I so far, haven't really gotten any terrible problems that I know of. I want to qualify that. So I haven't really experienced much breakdown. I've lost some hearing and I have a hearing aid that I use. I don't have to use it all the time because I haven't lost that much, but I'm much more fun to be with if I have it on. But I haven't started to seriously break down yet, and I'm hoping that it either never happens to me, that science always keeps one step ahead of me, or that I just die in my sleep one evening, and then that I never experience some terrible breakdown of my body.

Gross: Now just one more question. And again, this is kind of personal, but it's really more about your movies I think. After you married Soon-Yi, I think a lot of people went back and re-watched *Manhattan* or thought about *Manhattan* because it's the story of an older man and a younger woman—middle-aged man and a teenager. And the ending of that movie was always ambiguous to me. I can never really tell whether you thought that the character you played, when he finally—after telling the Mariel Hemingway character to leave and go on a trip to Europe to study, and that, you know, she'd be better off doing that and leaving him. And then at the end he kind of begs her to stay. Like, was he doing in your mind the right thing? I mean like what did you think of that character, the part you played?

Allen: I had no idea. You know Marshall Brickman and I wrote that together and we tried to figure out some kind of ending for the picture. We would've been happy to write any ending on the picture that would've worked—that they stayed together, that they didn't stay together, that you couldn't tell. To me it didn't matter. I mean I had no—I had no special feelings about that. We were looking at the beginning of the movie for some rich areas to get comic scenes in. And one of the areas that we—we came up with a few. And one of the areas was the older guy and the younger girl. And, but that had no relation to my life at the time and it was nothing there that was of any particular interest to me or to him. It was just a good laugh gimmick and a good romantic gimmick, so I really don't know, you know, what happens at the end. I mean I remember the ending, but I don't . . . I never knew and we never cared. We knew we could end it that way and have an effective dramatic punch to the audience, and we moved on.

Gross: When people love somebody's art, they become very interested in the artist and that leads them to be interested in the artist's personal life or what they can find out about it. And it's like some of your fans felt just upset, and in some ways even betrayed maybe, because of your marriage to Soon-Yi. And they started reevaluating, well, do I see his films differently now? Do you think it's fair or wrong to have, to evaluate an artist's work by decisions they've made or what you think of decisions they've made in their personal life or do you think that that's . . .

Allen: I think you can evaluate an artist any way you choose to. You're free to evaluate an artist in any way that you want to based on anything that makes you happy.

Gross: And do you care what people think of your personal life? Or is that just irrelevant to you?

Allen: Well, you know, if I say I don't care, it sounds so cold and callous. But let me put it this way. How could you go through life, you know, taking direction from the outside world? I mean, what kind of life would you have, if you were—if you made your decisions based on the outside world and not what your inner dictates told you? You would have a very inauthentic life.

Gross: So you told us you didn't eat with your family when you were growing up, that you ate alone because you liked to be alone with your comic book at dinner—

Allen: Yeah.

Gross: — and your parents preferred the company of adults. Do you eat with your children now?

Allen: I eat with the children, yeah. But, because they like our company, and, you know, the generations are different. I'm much closer to my children than my parents were to me. I'm more of a friend to my children. My wife is more of a friend to my children than my parents were. When I grew up, the parents were much removed in the hierarchy of the social ladder, the family ladder. And so my parents were one thing and I was something else, and we had nothing in common to talk about.

But, my kids and I and my wife talk about the same subjects. And we're all friends. So, it's a different tenor to the relationship. But that's something that has evolved in general over the years. Younger parents are different with their children than the older generation parents of now. I'm an older parent, but I'm still a parent in a younger generation than the generation that I grew up in, obviously. So . . . I do eat with my children. And we like it.

Gross: One more question. Of all the movies that you've seen, what movie have you seen the most times?

Allen: What movie have I seen the most times?

Gross: Mm-hmm.

Allen: I guess I've seen—I have to name three movies that I've seen many, many, many times. I've seen *The Seventh Seal* many, many times. I've seen *The Bicycle Thief,* many, many, many times. And I've seen *Shane,* many, many, many times, because those are three of my favorites. Now I have other favorites that I like equally, but I haven't seen them quite as much as I've seen these.

Gross: Well, I want to thank you so much for talking with us.
Allen: Okay. Thank you.

Woody Allen: The *Film Comment* Interview (Expanded Version)

Kent Jones / 2011

Published in *Film Comment* 47, no. 3 (May/June 2011): 35–37; expanded version online at http://www.filmcomment.com/article/woody-allen-the-film-comment-interview/. Copyright © 2011 by the Film Society of Lincoln Center. Used by permission of the Film Society of Lincoln Center/*Film Comment* magazine.

Q: When you're in the editing room, do you think about getting into a groove, in a musical sense?
A: To make it move?

Q: I suppose.
A: Well, your instinct tells you as you're doing it. Just like if you're a stand-up comic, you're out there on the floor and your instinct tells you, "Don't do that next joke like you'd planned, cut right to the one after it." And so when you're editing, your instinct says, "Don't stop for what you thought you were going to show there. Cut it here, you don't have to show them going back to the apartment, just keep moving." It's something that you feel as you go along.

Q: Does it get down to a matter of frames?
A: Yeah, sometimes it does, particularly with comic stuff, because the *slightest* thing upsets comedy. I remember when I was making *Take the Money and Run*. We were cutting on a Moviola. And there was some kind of prison break or something, a lot of confusion, and the editor I was working with at the time, Jim Heckert, said, "Stop where you think the cut should come." So I was doing it, and I stopped it. We put a mark on the frame and we went on. And when he showed me the scene again, I stopped it and it was on the exact same marked frame, which I didn't see in advance. Your feeling has to be so true to it that the material demands that *this* is the place to cut. When it's comic.

Q: But does it really feel that different when you're dealing with something more serious, like *Match Point*?
A: It's not as critical. So you run a few seconds longer on something, or a second longer, or shorter—it's not *fatal*. But for a joke, you can actually ruin the laugh, and that's unpleasant.

Q: I can see where it would be. I wanted to ask you a general question about how you work out the movie with your DPs, because you've worked with a lot of great ones.
A: Usually, we have a chat about the film to begin with, and we get on the same page. I like the film, first of all, to be very warm. I don't like blues, I don't like sunny days. I like a warm, overcast feeling, I like rain. I don't like to shoot long days. I like to set up the shot myself, and then let the cameraman look at it. Now, sometimes he'll say, "Great, it's beautiful." And sometimes he'll say, "It's very good, I just want to make an adjustment here." You know, he'll suggest something that he thinks is better and I'll usually agree with him because I'm working with guys who are great and they're usually right and I'm not. Then they light, and we've talked about lighting—not of the individual shots, but the overall lighting, and I know their lighting from their other work and from having worked with them before. This is the second film I did with Darius Khondji, we're gonna do a third this summer. I worked for ten years with Carlo Di Palma and ten years with Gordon Willis, and you get to know them and talk the same language. They'll never show me dailies that are far off, because they know what I like and *they* like it. So it works out very well, and there's never a conflict.

Q: The opening of *Midnight in Paris* felt very mysterious to me. It's as if Paris is waiting for someone or something to inhabit it.
A: Well, I just wanted to put people in the *mood* of Paris. And Paris is a hard thing to convey because it's got so much going for it. You know, it's different in different seasons, in different weather.

Q: I'm sure that it's going to be compared to the opening of *Manhattan*, but it's very different.
A: It's different because the opening of *Manhattan* has dialogue over it. It has a more 1940s, detective story narrative to it. And we started the narrative right away there. Here, we go the entire length of the jazz recording without any dialogue.

Q: The music, by Sidney Bechet, also takes you to an interesting place.
A: Yeah, because he lived in Paris for so many years, and he wrote that song, and

the song *feels* French. And he's got that Edith Piaf vibrato in his playing, that real French café singer's vibrato.

Q: I felt like Owen Wilson brought something very surprising to the movie. Did he surprise you?
A: Completely surprised me. When I wrote this movie, I did not think of Owen Wilson. The character was an Eastern intellectual, who would have been more Ivy League. If I was younger, I would have played it—not that I'm intellectual, but I *look* intellectual. And I couldn't find anybody who was really right who was available and *Eastern*. And then I was talking with Juliet Taylor and Owen's name came up. I started to think, "I bet if I *rewrote* this"—because Owen seemed like a blonde, beachcombing guy with a surfboard—"and made it more of a *West* Coast problem, a *West* Coast character, he could really do it well." So I rewrote it, and we sent it to him, and he was eager to play it. And he just . . . I mean, I never had to give him any direction, he knew just what to do, and he played it *exactly* the way I wanted it.

Q: When he makes the "demented lunatic/right-wing Republican" remark, it seems like he kind of means it.
A: Yeah. He's a sweet, sincere guy, and he's being honest there, thinking, "We're two Americans, we can disagree and still respect one another." That's the Obama fallacy: that your opponent is going to have as much grace and dignity as you have. And they don't.

Q: I loved the scenes in the twenties. I loved the ease of them, the re-creations.
A: We were lucky. We got guys who were able to emulate the original people very well. The guy who looked like Picasso at that time was *amazing*. I was shocked.

Q: Buñuel was pretty good too.
A: It was very hard to find a Buñuel. It was a tough one. People know them older. At that young age, Dalí just had that little moustache, and Picasso didn't have the striped shirt and the bald head.

Q: You're revisiting something with this movie that you opened up with *A Midsummer Night's Sex Comedy* and *The Purple Rose of Cairo*.
A: It's a recurring, nagging feeling of mine that the reality we're all trapped in is, in actual fact, if you dissect it, like a nightmare. I'm always looking for ways to escape that reality. One escapes it by going to the movies. One escapes it by becoming involved in the trivial nonsense of "Are the Yankees going to win?" or "Are the Mets going to win?" When in fact it means nothing. But life means nothing

either. It means as much as the ballgame. So you're constantly looking for ways to escape from reality. And one of the fallacies that comes up all the time is the Golden Age fallacy, that you'd have been happier at a different time. Just as people think, "If I moved to Paris I'd be happier" or "If I moved to London. . . ." Then they do, and they're not. Even though these places are great, they're not happier, because it isn't the geography that's eating them up, it's the existential reality of how grim a predicament we're in. So, I've played around with that before, the notion of wanting to get out of the real world, get out of time. Here, Owen does get a chance to go back, and it's fine. But he realizes as he looks around that those people want to go back too, and that it doesn't matter where you go, that life is unsatisfying whether you lived in the Renaissance or La Belle Époque or now or one hundred years from now. It's an unsatisfying situation.

Q: You mean, because it's never going to be all-embracing, and you'll never have the perfect conversations and the perfect sympathy that you want.
A: You're always looking for some way to beat the house, but you can never do it. You get to Paris in the twenties, you see that everyone there is unhappy too and they want to be someplace else, and there's a lot of downside—you go to the dentist and there's no novocaine, there are a lot of negatives. So you have to eventually conclude that you're in a meaningless and even tragic predicament. Starting from these grim ground rules, you've gotta figure out how you're going to navigate through life and why it's worth it. This is all grim stuff for comedy.

Q: I remember when *The Magic Lantern* was published here and you reviewed it for the *Times* book review, and you were talking about the monologues in *The Passion of Anna*. You wrote something like, "It's great cinema, but it's also great showbiz."
A: Right! That was the thing about Bergman. He was always erroneously thought of as, "Well, this guy's some kind of cerebral intellectual, I'm not gonna understand this, I'm gonna hate the pictures, they're black and white, grim theme." But what made Bergman great—and there were guys who were working the same side of the street but who were *not* great—was that he was show business, he was an entertainer. When the death figure comes in *The Seventh Seal* or when those dreams occur in *Wild Strawberries*, that stuff is very theatrical and very exciting, and you're on the edge of your seat. The movie's not homework, where you're being taught something and you sit through it dutifully. There's suspense. You know, "My God, what's gonna happen?"

Q: Bergman deals a lot with magic and the supernatural.

A: Bergman's work is full of those kinds of touches. He just does them and assumes you're gonna go with them. And then you do. They're done with confidence.

Q: Did you like *Saraband*?
A: I did think that he was running out by then. But sure, I liked it, because I had a sentimental feeling for those actors, and I always like what he tries to do. I always feel that his failures are worth more than most people's successes.

Q: I recently took a fresh look at *Another Woman*, and I was wondering if Rilke has been important for you.
A: There's a conclusion that is arrived at all the time by artists but is frequently unearned—that in the end you have to love, and love is at the core of everything. When it's not earned by the artist, you pooh-pooh it. But with certain artists, like Rilke, that sense *is* earned. The sense of "You must change your life" is earned. And that's what was so overpowering to me about Rilke: fundamentally, love is the best you can do. He was a sufficiently deep enough and great enough poet that when *he* says it, you feel that he knows what he's talking about and that he's not doing it for feel-good purposes. I did that once and regretted it ever since.

Q: On what occasion?
A: In the original writing of *Hannah and Her Sisters*, Michael Caine continues to love Hannah's sister, and he longs for her at those family get-togethers just as much as ever, but he's grimly attached to Hannah. And my character never gets a really hopeful moment. But I found in the editing that my character's *unhappy* moments were unearned, because of my lack of skill, and those endings just fell off the table. They were unhappy in a way that, say, a Chekhov ending is not. In Chekhov, the endings are unhappy but exhilarating. You feel something positive through the unhappiness. I wasn't a good enough actor to earn that. And so in order to save the movie from utter destruction, I reversed course a little, and it worked, and the picture was very commercially successful. But I always regretted it. I tell myself, "But if I *didn't* change it, it would've been very unsatisfying to people." Not simply because it was a sad ending, because sad endings are often not unsatisfying at all, but because I wasn't skillful enough in the movie to move toward that ending, so that it became the inevitable, the *correct* ending. When Oedipus puts his eyes out, everything is moving in that direction, and it's just fine. You don't need him to say, "Well, I realized that life is unpredictable, and I now have learned two things." But I felt I needed to do that, and I've always regretted it. I've always counted that as one of my failures—not commercial, but artistic.

Q: Were you going to end the film with Dianne Wiest telling your character that she's pregnant?
A: Yes.

Q: Which is not sad.
A: No, it wasn't sad, but it didn't have the Marx Brothers positive moment in it: "Heck, life is pretty awful but there are some oases." It didn't have that bullshit in it. Throughout the entire film, he was unable to have a child, and it looked like he couldn't, but with the right woman, he could. And that was fine. That was, I felt, something that I deserved to be able to say. I didn't deserve to be able to do the Marx Brothers scene because it was tacked on, and so was Michael Caine adjusting back to Mia. I played around with it a little and sold out.

Q: Those moments really don't feel like they're tacked on.
A: Well, maybe because we did it skillfully, and it wasn't as egregious as I felt it to be. But as the author, with another intention, I felt it all the time.

Q: Do you feel like you corrected the mistake in another movie?
A: I've tried to never do it again. *Hannah* was a big success, but *I* wasn't getting the kick out if it that I wanted. If a movie of mine is a success, I like to feel proud and say, "Yes, I worked hard and it came off, and I appreciate that you appreciate it." But I wasn't able to have a clear conscience on *Hannah*.

Q: But the Marx Brothers moment in *Hannah and Her Sisters* is in keeping with the scene in *Manhattan* where you're naming the things that make life worth living. It also seems directly related to the end of *Sullivan's Travels*.
A: Well, I'll tell you an interesting thing. I only saw *Sullivan's Travels* after I made *Stardust Memories*. I had never been an enormous fan of Preston Sturges.

Q: Were you thinking of *Unfaithfully Yours* when you shot the scene in the detective's office in *Midnight in Paris*?
A: No, but I did love that movie, because it was Sturges, who was an urbane wit, doing an urbane movie. When he worked with William Demarest and Eddie Bracken and Betty Hutton, it was more bumpkin humor, and I couldn't warm up to that. I, personally, was a Lubitsch fan, because Lubitsch was cosmopolitan and sophisticated, and unsentimental to the end. And in that one movie, Sturges was cosmopolitan, and I thought it was wonderful. People thought I'd been influenced by *Sullivan's Travels* when I did *Stardust Memories*. Jessica Harper, who was in that movie with me, said, "You have to see *Sullivan's Travels*! It's just like this movie

and you'll love it." I did see it afterwards and I didn't love it. But I do think he was a great film director. I thought his pacing was great and he knew how to write. It's just that I personally was a Lubitsch man. I am a paleface rather than a redskin. I like the European material very much. I respond to it. When you get out toward the middle of the country and the West, I can appreciate things but I don't enjoy them as much. I've often said, not so facetiously, that when I was a kid and a film began with a pan of the New York skyline, I was right with 'em. But when they were rural, I could appreciate the movies, but I had trouble *personally* enjoying them. I still do.

Q: So I'm assuming that you think the end of *Sullivan's Travels* is unearned as well.
A: Yes, it's a commercial cop out, because life does *not* have an ending or a resolution. It's an unearned optimism.

Q: Do you find yourself looking to movies for inspiration?
A: Well, it happens automatically. I watch them for pleasure. I don't study them for the lighting or the camera angles or the blocking. I watch them strictly for the story and for pleasure. And they do influence you. You see good movies and you want to make a movie like that sometime, because it was so much fun and you got such a kick out of watching it. [*Door opens*] Oh, it's time for my band practice. [*Points*] That's my clarinet. I have to practice every day in order to be mediocre.

Woody Allen Interview

Scott Foundas / 2011

First published in *LA Weekly*, a Voice Media Group publication, May 19, 2011. Reprinted by permission.

The first time Woody Allen saw Paris, the year was 1964 and his first original screenplay, *What's New Pussycat?*, was being turned into a movie starring Peter Sellers and Peter O'Toole. "Like everybody else, I grew up getting my impressions of Paris from American movies," he tells me one recent morning, as he sinks into a green roller chair in the velvet-draped screening room of his New York office. "So before I ever went to Paris, I was in love with the city, because Hollywood was in love with the city, and whenever you saw Paris it was the city of romance, music, wine, beautiful hotels, *Gigi*. Then I went there, and the city lived up to its hype."

Allen lived in the city for eight months, playing a supporting role in *Pussycat* and remaining on call for new jokes and rewrites. "On the one hand, I was having a wonderful time, because I was living in this magical city all expenses paid," he remembers. "On the other hand, I hated what was going on with my movie, because I felt they were ruining it."

As the shoot drew to a close, two Americans from the wardrobe department, whom Allen had befriended, announced they would be making Paris their new home. "And I said, 'I love it too,' but I was afraid to stay. I thought, 'Gee, I'd love to stay, but . . . I just don't have the courage to uproot my life and move here.' Now, that is a decision that I've regretted many times."

Allen's love for the city is obvious from the first frames of his forty-first feature, *Midnight in Paris*, which opens with a three-minute, dialogue-free montage of Paris street scenes both iconic and ordinary, day slowly giving way to night as the expat saxophonist Sidney Bechet's "Si tu vois ma mère" plays on the soundtrack. "No work of art can compare to a city," notes the film's protagonist, a successful American screenwriter (wonderfully played by Owen Wilson) who, like Allen, lived in Paris as a younger man and now finds himself there once more, on vacation with his high-strung fiancée (Rachel McAdams) and her parents, while trying his hand at his first novel.

When French producers first approached Allen (who has directed five of his last six pictures abroad) about making a film in the City of Light, he happily agreed. "But I had no idea for Paris at all—none," he says. "So I asked myself: What do you think of when you think of Paris? Well, romance is what you think of—at least, it's what I think of." Then Allen hit upon the film's title but still had no story to go with it. "And I'm thinking to myself for months, well, what happens at midnight in Paris? And then one day it came to me that somebody visiting Paris is walking around at night, and it's midnight, and suddenly a car pulls up and he gets in and it takes him on a real adventure."

That adventure, which (spoiler alert!) has been carefully concealed from the *Midnight in Paris* trailer, is a journey through time, in which Wilson's character finds himself spirited away to the Lost Generation Paris of the 1920s, rubbing elbows with F. Scott Fitzgerald and Ernest Hemingway, soliciting writerly advice from Gertrude Stein (Kathy Bates) and falling in love with the muse (Marion Cotillard) of Picasso and Modigliani. It's a premise that might have seemed incredibly corny but in Allen's deft hands becomes something magical, as sublimely enchanting as any Allen film since 1985's *The Purple Rose of Cairo*, where a movie hero steps down from the screen and into the life of a Depression-era New Jersey waitress.

"A certain amount of people in the world become obsessed with magic, and as a boy I was one of them," Allen says of his recurring interest in fantasy and the supernatural, which also crops up to varying degrees in films like *A Midsummer Night's Sex Comedy*, *Alice*, and the "Oedipus Wrecks" segment of *New York Stories*. "I always feel that only a magical solution can save us. The human predicament is so tragic and so awful that, short of an act of magic, we're doomed."

"Nostalgia is denial," says the pompous intellectual hilariously played by Michael Sheen in *Midnight in Paris*, before going on to define a condition he terms "Golden Age thinking" as "a flaw in the romantic imagination of people who find it difficult to cope with the present." One such person is Wilson's Gil Pender, whose novel-in-progress takes place in a "nostalgia shop" and who longs to live in a time other than his own—at least until he discovers that everyone in the past seems consumed by a similar desire, yearning for the Belle Époque or even the Renaissance.

There are those, surely, who would peg Allen as something of a nostalgia merchant himself, from the number of films he has set in a rose-colored yesteryear to the jazz standards that routinely comprise the soundtracks of even his contemporary tales. Yet if *Midnight in Paris* is undeniably one of Allen's most personal films, it is also one as skeptical of "Golden Age thinking" as it is susceptible to it.

"Nostalgia is a trap, there's no question about that," Allen say matter-of-factly. "It's based on the idea that now is always terrible. So there's always a sense that if you could have lived in a different time, things would have been more pleasant. One thinks back, for instance, to *Gigi*, and you think, well, this is Belle Époque Paris, they have horses and carriages and gas lamps and everything is beautiful. Then you start to realize that if you went to the dentist, there was no Novocain, and that's just the tip of the iceberg. Women died in childbirth—there were all kinds of terrible problems.

"Naturally, if I'm sitting here now, and they're dying in Libya and the economy is going under and we have a terrible split in the country and they're patting us down in airports, I think to myself, 'God, wouldn't I be better off sitting at Maxim's in the 1890s?' But it doesn't really work that way, and that's how nostalgia trips you up. For movies it's great! In movies, you can create the past as you want to see it. But I do think that's the sad note in my movie, that everybody doesn't want to be where they are."

I ask Allen if he agrees with the lines he wrote for Gertrude Stein in the film, in which she states that the job of the artist is not to succumb to despair but to find an antidote for the emptiness of existence. "I don't know if I believe that myself," he replies. "That's all easy enough to attribute to a character in a movie, and one could make a case for that—that the job of the artist is to show why life, despite all its horror and brutality, is worth living and is a valuable thing. But one could also take the position that it's not the job of the artist to do anything at all—just to make the best art that he can, because art gives pleasure and pleasure gives distraction, and distraction is the only thing that gets us by, really."

At age seventy-five, with a career as a comic, writer, and filmmaker that spans a half-century, Allen himself has become an iconic part of American cultural lore—something that gives him more than a bit of pause.

"I was thinking with great horror the other day that, since I'm a known person, a hundred years from now someone will make a movie about New York in my time, and I would be, let's say, not an important character in it but a peripheral character," he says. "Someone will go into Elaine's, and there I'll be, played by some schlemiel, because I'm conceived of as a schlemiel, and he'll have glasses on, and he'll be a gloom-ridden recluse who shivers at the thought of going out into the country—some execrable exaggeration of what people think I am. And that will be my hell. If I'm ever in a work of fiction as part of the atmosphere, they'll be doing to me the same unjust things as when I show Ernest Hemingway sitting at a bar talking the way he talks."

In the nearer term—this fall, to be precise—Allen will find himself the subject of a two-part, three-hour *American Masters* documentary directed by Oscar nominee Robert Weide (*Lenny Bruce: Swear to Tell the Truth*), to whom Allen granted unprecedented access to his personal and professional life during the making of last year's *You Will Meet a Tall Dark Stranger*. "Now, I say this with no false modesty: I cannot imagine why anyone would want to see it," Allen deadpans.

"It's funny, I'm always interested in those things about people that I like, so I guess there will be people who will be interested. But to me, I feel there's not enough. With the exception of my one encounter with scandal with Mia [Farrow], my life's been very, very dull. I mean, I work, I've always worked, and even that thing with Mia was really blown way out of proportion by the press; the actual facts are not very fascinating. But there's been nothing to even approach that in terms of excitement in my life."

Allen pauses for a moment, as if contemplating some bigger picture. "It's not the kind of life, let's say, that Hemingway led, where he'd be deep-sea fishing off Cuba and then hunting lions or kudu in Africa, and then his plane crashes but he survives after going missing for two weeks in the jungle. Mine's been very middle-class."

Woody Allen on *Blue Jasmine*

Catherine Shoard / 2013

Published in the *Guardian*, September 26, 2013. Copyright Guardian News & Media Ltd 2013. Reprinted by permission.

Woody Allen does not look like a samurai. He looks, at seventy-seven, like a Woody Allen action doll, so tiny and iconic you have to sit on your hands so as not to pick him up and put him on the mantelpiece. His green shirt balloons round his body, baggy slacks winched up high. I'm lucky I have a morning slot, he says, extending dinky fingers—these days, he's snoring by four. He smiles mildly, left eye creased, hearing aid in one ear. The world knows Woody as a lover not a fighter. As he approaches eighty, that hasn't changed.

And yet it is to a Japanese assassin, a stone-cold swordsman, that his two most recent collaborators compare him. John Turturro, who directed Allen as an unlikely pimp in the forthcoming *Fading Gigolo*, says it first. "Sure, a samurai," he shrugs. "He's one of the toughest people I've met." Then Cate Blanchett, whom Allen directed in *Blue Jasmine*. She seizes on the word with something approaching relief. "Yeah! A very little samurai with glasses. I think he'd like that description."

He doesn't. Or, at least, he doesn't recognize it. It takes three takes before he twigs what I'm saying. "A *samurai*?" he says, finally. "I'd hardly say a samurai." He laughs, aghast. But they're right. Woody is a warrior. He just doesn't know it yet.

The first shock of his new film is its quality. Our critic Peter Bradshaw gave *Blue Jasmine* five stars and hailed it as his best in twenty years. For the Allen aficionado, accustomed to diminishing returns, it feels less like the oft-hailed "return to form" than a minor miracle.

Its ferocity is the second. *Midnight in Paris*, his biggest box-office earner to date, might have lulled you into assuming late-stage Allen was pipe-and-slippers stuff. But *Blue Jasmine* is a bruiser of a movie, a Greek tragedy that dispatches a Park Avenue princess with a massive slap.

The idea came from Soon-Yi, his wife of sixteen years, who told him about the friend of a friend—the wife of a financier who imploded after learning her husband was unfaithful and involved in Ponzi-ish fraud. Critics have feasted on the age-of-Madoff topicality. Allen is unconvinced.

"No. I had none of that in mind," he says. "I don't engage with public events any more than I ever did. In real life of course I vote, I campaign for people I like, I'm interested in public events. But in writing I'm not, and I wasn't here in any way. It's strictly accidental."

Jasmine, broke and shaky, goes to stay with adopted sister Ginger (Sally Hawkins) in her boxy San Francisco flat. Doom isn't definite. She scrapes a job as a dental receptionist, attracts a glossy suitor in Peter Sarsgaard. But, in the background, we're drip-fed details of what went wrong before. And, almost as ominous, we see the attempts of shelf-stacker Ginger, under Jasmine's influence, to swap her car-mechanic fiancé, Chilli, for a more middle-class model.

Okay: it's not topical. And Allen is skeptical about theories that say it's a modern spin on *A Streetcar Named Desire*. So maybe it's a public service broadcast? A warning for siblings who might egg each other over the precipice? (Allen and Soon-Yi have two adoptive daughters of their own, now teenagers.)

Allen shuts the lid politely. "A cautionary fable? No. I just thought it was an interesting psychological situation for a woman to be in. This is not a character I'd have written forty years ago. I wouldn't have had the skill to do it, and I didn't come in contact with this type of woman until I got older, because I live in an upscale neighborhood in New York."

Allen's career can be charted through his gender adventures. In his "early, funny" films, women were sexy accessories. Then came the Diane Keaton years and the Mia Farrow era, and a stream of female characters that rank as some of the most richly and compassionately realized ever. Following the Farrow split in 1992, a slide back towards stereotype. The love letters regressed into caricatures. And now, out of nowhere, a masterpiece.

Allen has spoken before about his fondness for "kamikaze women," who destroy you in the fallout; Jasmine is cut from the same cloth, yet untroubled by charm. As the film unfolds, you expect revelations that will heighten your sympathy. What you get is further incriminating evidence. It's a character study. It's also character assassination.

I was surprised, I say, he wasn't more on side with someone who seeks solace in a fantasy world. "Well, you're just asking for trouble, if you do that," he says, concern in his voice. "It's very seductive and I've done it a certain amount, but it does take a terrific toll. If you try and live your life with other people in offices and in the street and in your social intercourse I think it can be brutal."

Jasmine forever protests it is feelings which maketh the man, not hard facts. Again, not total anathema to Allen, you'd think. But he's adamantly anti. "Ninety-nine per cent of decisions are predicated on feelings—instinctive, emotional, fears, conflicts, unresolved childhood problems. They're our dominant motivating factor, not reason or rationality or common sense. And that's why the world is in a terrible, terrible state. Human relations are hard and brutal and painful, and the world is in a dreadful state politically. And that's because feelings govern almost everything in every sphere."

It is in giving in to them that Jasmine seals her fate. At a pivotal moment, she succumbs to what Allen calls, in both script and conversation, a "tantrum." That's what snaps his tolerance. "She could have gotten a divorce, forgiven him, had a talk with him, moved out of the house. But she just hit the ceiling blindly and went on a rampage that brought destruction upon her whole household. She never stopped to think out the consequences of her raging moment. You see tantrums in adults all the time. You're driving on the highway and a car bumps you and the driver gets out and he's ready to tear your head off."

But do some people have a greater propensity for self-destruction? "Yes, absolutely." Why? "Well, I think that's genetic. Or at least somewhat genetic and somewhat nurture. The genetic component works in terms of a proclivity towards tantrums, and depending on the kind of childhood they've had, how much rage they assimilate, injustices and terrible things or perceived failure work together on you as you grow up."

Allen may have witnessed such combustions. But he seems forever unflappable. Sure, he plays neurotics, but beneath that twitchy exterior there's a clear head, sturdy heart and—according to Diane Keaton—"balls of steel." He prizes poise, particularly in himself.

"I think he's incredibly disciplined," says Blanchett, backing up that samurai theory. "People talk about how hands-off he is and how he likes to give actors free rein but he knows exactly what he doesn't want. He eats the same thing for breakfast, wears the same clothes every day. I mean, he washes them—but he has twenty of that same Ralph Lauren silhouette."

And such intensity of focus doesn't sit ill with Allen's self-deprecation. The more you really *do* think that "80 percent of success is showing up," the more you organize your life around arriving on time. The virtues of graft were drummed in by his parents, Nettie, a bookkeeper, and Martin, an engraver—so successfully that at seventeen Woody was earning more than them both combined, rattling out gags for comedians and columnists. By nineteen, he was on $1,500 a week and working for Sid Caesar. He still makes a film a year, on time, on budget, like clockwork. (When we first meet in Paris, he's just finished shooting a Riviera romance with Colin Firth and Emma Stone. A fortnight later, we speak on the phone, and he's fresh from finishing the rough cut.)

This traditionalism can take you aback. It's easy to forget, watching him talk, viewing old films, even seeing him goof about with a gaggle of kids in *Fading

Gigolo, that Allen is the product of pre-war New York. At one point, I'm disparaging about Jasmine's attempts to coat-tail up the social ladder. But, says Allen, women are entitled to feel entitled.

"I think it's a reasonable feeling, the hope to meet somebody who can give them a life of some security and enjoyment. Someone who'll give them something better than they have—or, in upper-class families, at least as good as what they have. They don't wanna marry down. I imagine that would be not too thrilling a proposition."

He chuckles dryly. Men have long had it more straightforward, he thinks. "They feel they have more control. They'll get a job or they'll steal the money or they'll do something to better their circumstances. They're not dependent on their spouse for improvement.

"Now, of course, feminists changed all of that, which is great. But they didn't change it for every class or for every woman. There are still deep roots women are influenced by. They feel they'll grow up, they'll go to school, they'll meet some guy and he will take over the reins. They may do some work but they're not going to head up a law firm or something—they won't have time, raising the kids. Guys are more used to the business of making their own lives and women have traditionally married men who they feel have an obligation to take care of them in some way."

So how does that make men feel? "I don't think that men have been comfortable with feminist progress," he says, unblinking. "They're used to growing up in a society where women have a role to play and so do the men. Some enlightened men have welcomed and encouraged and supported it. But I'm not so sure if you look deeply even into them that it hasn't been a little bit of an effort to accept women in roles that they're completely entitled to. If you asked most men in the privacy of their own home they might say: I liked it better when a woman got married and took care of the kids and I went out to work and the equation was clearly defined. Women should be free to have anything and everything they want in terms of all of those rights. It should be a given, not be a privilege. But it is undoing a more primitive situation."

So societal structures are struggling to keep up? "That's true. It's happened very rapidly. I think if you look one hundred years from now, the situation will be much more graceful. You won't have the old history to fall back on. You'll have a feminist dynamic to refer to."

He frowns. It's not just genes, not just habit. It's class, too. He lives, he says, in the kind of "sophisticated environment" that makes liberal-mindedness easy. "I've never had to go off to a factory and need somebody home to take care of the children."

The compassion is keen. The friendliness sincere. As he gets older, he says, his fellow-feeling only grows. "Over the years you get to see what a struggle life is for most people, how tough it is, how easy it is to be judgmental and criticize and stand outside of situations and impart your wisdom and judgment. But over the decades I've got more tolerant of people's flaws and mistakes. Everybody makes a lot of them. When you're younger you feel: 'Hey, this person is evil' or 'This person is a jerk' or stupid or 'What's wrong with them?' Then you go through life and you think: 'Well, it's not so easy.' There's a lot of mystery and suffering and complication. Everybody's out there trying to do the best they can. And it's not such an easy business."

He grins again, glasses glinting, soft and sweet. He means it. It's just that it's impossible to reconcile such benevolence with the mercilessness of his new movie. But perhaps that's for the good. The day Allen has it all worked out is the day he might stop making movies. Let's just hope he sticks to his guns. Embraces the way of the sword, even.

Index

Academy aperture, 15
Academy Awards, ix, xiii, xvii, xix, xx, 60, 65, 75–76, 140, 168, 178, 183. *See also* Chronology, xxiv–xxx
acting: and directing in same film, 13, 104, 126; theater acting, 23, 51
acting skills, Allen's, 16, 58, 215, 228
Adair, Virginia Hamilton, 160
Adam's Rib, 15
admission prices, 23
aging, thoughts on, 164, 201–2, 220–21
Aiello, Danny, 81
Airplane!, 65, 207
Albee, Edward, 125
"Albert (The Logical Positivist) Corillo," 121
Alda, Alan, 134, 143–44
Alexander, Jane, 50
Alice, x, xvii, 103, 105, 124; magical/supernatural elements in, xviii, 158–59, 232
Allen, Bechet, 164
Allen, Manzie, 164
Allen, Woody
    abstinence from drugs, 35, 170
    Academy Awards and nominations, xiii, xix, 75–76, 168, 178, 183
    aging, 164, 201–2, 220–21
    appearance/manner, 21, 24, 132, 164, 181, 235
    athletic ability, 132, 216
    character
        anxiety, 39, 56, 59, 132, 144–45, 147, 149
        compartmentalization, 147, 167–68, 171
        confidence, 196
        cynic and idealist, 32
        discipline, sense of, 200, 237
        "imperfectionist," 144
        pessimism, 41, 175
        reserve, 132
        self-deprecation, 214–15, 237
        self-loathing, 41
        seriousness, xi, 22, 41, 132
        workaholic, 56, 60
        work ethic, 132
    childhood, xxii, 38–39, 85, 109, 132, 200–201, 217–20
    children, xvii, 115–18, 119, 133, 147–48, 164, 166, 197, 222, 236
    comedic influences, 33–34
    disguises, xi, 23, 37, 74
    draft status, 4-F, 32
    dress, 21, 22, 23, 57, 172, 181, 235, 237
    education
        City College of New York, 40
        Hebrew school, 38
        Midwood High School, 109, 190
        New York University, 40, 137, 216–17
        P.S. 99, 140
    fantasies, 42
    favorite comedians, 28, 208
    favorite films/directors, xii, xx, 28, 110, 207, 222–23
    friends, 55, 74, 140–41

glasses, 24, 84, 109, 167, 181, 216, 235, 239
goals, xiii, 41–42, 66
grandparents, 197
heroes, xii, 32–33
as Jew, xii, xxii, 38, 66, 80, 158, 175, 181, 183, 200, 208–9
lifestyle, 60, 74–76, 171, 198, 205
marriages, 57
　Previn, Soon-Yi, 174, 197, 215, 221, 235–36
obsessions, 23, 56
offices
　Brill Building sound studio, 84
　Park Avenue editing suite, 91, 131, 173, 176, 204, 231
　West 57th Street, 60
painting as hobby, 198
parents, xxii, 38, 134–35, 175, 199–200, 218–20, 222
　in films, 20
persona, 20, 137, 208–9, 233
　on-screen, ix, xxi, 19–20, 84, 132, 171, 181, 208–9, 214–15
phobias, 171, 173, 209
political views, 28–32
productivity, xvi, 60, 127, 140, 181, 183
regrets, xxii, 200–201
relationships
　Farrow, Mia, 67–68, 73, 91, 147, 154–55, 166–67
　Keaton, Diane, 58, 140
　Previn, Soon-Yi, xvii, 114–18, 133, 134, 146–49, 166–67, 209
religion, views on, 38–39, 49, 157, 181
residences
　Fifth Avenue penthouse, NYC, xiv, 55, 60, 67, 91, 109, 131, 149, 173, 205
　one-room apartment, NYC, 206
　townhouse, Carnegie Hill, NYC, 173
　townhouse, East Seventies, NYC, 205
　Southampton, 205
scandal/legal battle with Farrow, xvii, 110, 114–18, 133, 147, 166–68, 234
sports
　childhood interest in, 38, 86
　Giants fan, 38, 86
　Knicks fan, 23, 84, 86, 189
staff, cook and driver, 57
tragic view of life, 39–40
and women, 140–42, 236
work habits, xxi, 51–54, 60–63, 82
Almodóvar, Pedro, 186
Altman, Robert, 110, 126, 163
American Masters (TV series), 163, 233–34
Anderson, Maxwell, 123
anhedonia, 56, 213
Animal House, 65
Anna Karenina (Tolstoy), 92
Annie Hall, ix, xiii, xvi–xvii, 28, 43–46, 69, 84, 100, 127, 135, 163, 212; Academy Awards, ix, xiii, xix, 60, 75–76, 183; Allen's character in, 63, 154, 171, 174, 217; box office, 65, 90, 111; budget, 96; camera movement in, 52; characters, 169; cinematography, 45, 124; dinner scene, 218; discarded titles, 43, 56, 213; dissatisfaction with, 64; as dramatic comedy, 60, 64, 180; improvisation in, 62; jokes in, 62; Diane Keaton's character in, 43, 58, 70, 141; length of shoot, 53; locations, 87, 179; and *Manhattan* compared, 48, 56; Marshall McLuhan in, 70; middle-class values in, xiv, 51; origin of story, 64; possible sequel, 174; structure, 76; style, 43–44
Another Woman, ix–x, xv, xvii, 124, 155, 158, 180, 228

INDEX

antiwar movement, 32
Antonioni, Michelangelo, xii, 17, 28, 202
anxiety, existential, 39, 209
Anything Else, xix, 169, 203; Allen's character in, 171
Arden, Eve, 86
Armstrong, Louis, xii, 32, 70, 133, 201
Arnold, Gary, xiii, xv, 43–46, 71–78
Aronson, Letty, 135, 173–74
art: cinema as, 164; views on, xiii, 48–49, 153–54, 233
artist, problem of the, xviii, 124–25
aspect ratio, 15
audience: Allen's, 37, 64, 67, 133–34, 162, 172; for comedy, 22; for plays, 62; relationship with, xiv, 68–69, 221–22; testing films with, 61, 63
auteur status, 163, 164
autobiographical content, in Allen's films, xiv, xix, 63, 67–68, 77, 84, 87, 154, 170, 188–89, 215–17
awards: Academy Awards, ix, xiii, xvii, xix, xx, 60, 65, 75–76, 140, 168, 178, 183; foreign, 76; Golden Globes, 180. *See also* Chronology, xxiv–xxx

Bach, Johann Sebastian, 129
Baker, Russell, 26, 61
Balcony, The, 40
ballet and dance, 42
Balzac, Honoré de, 166
Bananas, ix, xi, 3–5, 11–12, 20, 21, 60, 69, 79, 138, 183, 189; Allen's character in, 19; box office, 27; budget, 43; camera movement in, 9; improvisation in, 14–15; jokes in, 8, 10, 16, 44; locations, 14, 18; political satire in, 9; slapstick in, 16, 180; structure, 76; style, 11, 18
Barcelona, 183–84, 193–94; filming in, xxi, 205

Barcelona (film), 184
Bardem, Javier, 183–86, 190, 193
Barrault, Marie-Christine, 70
Barrymore, Drew, 134, 136
Basinger, Kim, 156
Bates, Kathy, 232
BBC, 173
Beatty, Warren, 6
Bechet, Sidney, 131, 225–26, 231
Beckett, Samuel, 40, 125
Beekman, The, 91, 131
Beethoven, Ludwig van, xix, 129
Belgravia, London, 164, 176
Benayoun, Robert, xvi, 79–82, 92; *Beyond Words*, 91
Benchley, Robert, 33, 61, 138
Bergman, Ingmar, xii, xx, 28, 32, 34, 44, 58, 62, 69–70, 96, 100, 107, 133, 152, 158, 159, 163, 165, 181, 207, 227–28; influence on *Interiors*, 65–66; *Magic Lantern, The*, 227
Berle, Milton, 20, 81
Berman, Shelley, 208
best films, Allen's, xv, 135, 163, 169, 180, 183
Beyond Words (Benayoun), 91
Bicycle Thief, The, xx, 99–100, 139, 222
bisexuality, views on, 35
Biskind, Peter, xxi, 161–75
Björkman, Stig, 101–8; *Woody Allen on Woody Allen*, xvii
black and white, xv, 51, 52, 159, 227
blacklisting, 28–29
Blanchett, Cate, 235, 237
Blazing Saddles, 27
Blue Angel, 136, 137
Blue Jasmine, x, xx, xxiii, 235–39
Bogart, Humphrey, 78, 121
Bogdanovich, Peter, 163
Boone, Pat, xv
Born Yesterday (film, 1950), xx, 16, 110, 130

Born Yesterday (film, 1993), 109, 130
Born Yesterday (play), 125
Botticelli, Sandro, 159
Bourne, Mel, 81
box office/grosses, 43, 65, 111, 139, 172, 178; *Annie Hall*, 65, 90, 111; *Bananas*, 27; *Bullets over Broadway*, 139; *Deconstructing Harry*, 172; foreign, 172; *Hannah and Her Sisters*, 90, 111, 139, 172; *Love and Death*, 27; *Manhattan*, 111; *Melinda and Melinda*, 172; *Midnight in Paris*, 235; *Mighty Aphrodite*, 139; *Sleeper*, 27
Bradshaw, Peter, 235
Branagh, Kenneth, 176
Brando, Marlon, 19, 95, 143
Brick, Richard, 170
Brickman, Marshall, 74, 88, 140, 166, 169–70; collaboration with Allen, xvii, 55, 64, 215, 221
Brill Building, 84
Broadway Danny Rose, xv, xvi, xvii, 79, 80–82, 86, 112, 121, 125, 135, 163; Mia Farrow's character in, xvi, 81–82, 141; improvisation in, 81, 123
Broadway theater, 20, 23, 125
Bronx, 86, 204. See also New York City
Bronx Tale, A, 122
Brooklyn, 38, 85, 190, 205, 206. See also New York City
Brooklyn Dodgers, 38, 86
Brooks, Mel, 27, 65, 136, 180
Brown, David, 13
Bruce, Lenny, 33, 208
budgets/costs, 18, 43, 69, 73–74, 96, 111, 127–28, 139, 173, 178, 196–97; *Annie Hall*, 96; *Bananas*, 43; *Bullets over Broadway*, 139; *Hannah and Her Sisters*, 139; *Husbands and Wives*, 102; *Match Point*, 178; *Mighty Aphrodite*, 139; *Scoop*, 173
Bullets over Broadway, xvii–xviii, 112, 118, 120–26, 133, 144, 155, 163, 190, 202; Academy Awards and nominations, xvii, 168; box office, 139; budget, 127, 139; camera movement in, 124; improvisation in, 113, 122; locations, 111, 120; style, 113–14; Dianne Wiest's character in, 128–29, 141
Bullets over Broadway (musical version), xxix
Buñuel, Luis, xii, xx, 28, 165; character in *Midnight in Paris*, 226
Burrows, Abe, 118
Buxton, Frank, 5

Caesar, Sid, xv, 27–28, 60, 110, 190, 191, 237
Caesars Palace, 118
Cagney, James, 122, 190
Caine, Michael, xviii, 94, 95, 113, 228–29
camera movement, xiv, 9–10, 52, 124
Camus, Albert, 40
Canby, Vincent, x, 165, 168, 169
Cannes Film Festival, 177
Cannon, Jimmy, 86
Cape Fear (1991), 106
Carroll, Kathleen, xi, 21–23
Carter, Helena Bonham, 118
Casino Royale, 6
Cassandra's Dream, 188–89, 193
Cassavetes, John, 19, 123
casting, 53, 81, 95–96, 104, 122, 128, 142, 167–68, 178, 184, 186
Catskills, 80, 208
Cavett, Dick, 57, 88
Celebrity, 176
Champlin, Charles, x, xiv, xv, 67–70
Chaplin, Charlie, xi, xiii, 3, 7, 8, 9, 15, 16, 19, 22, 42, 44, 64, 85, 110, 136, 137, 138, 146, 163, 214
Che! (film), 14
Chekhov, Anton, 66, 70, 92, 228

Ciment, Michel, xviii–xix, 120–30, 152–60
cinematography, xiii, 10, 42, 45, 52–53, 112, 123–24, 225; dark cinematography, 45, 124
Circle Magic Shop, 85
Citizen Kane, xx, 99–100, 139
City College of New York, 40
City Lights, 8, 11
Claremont College, 208
clarinet playing, xix, 36, 62, 139, 150–51, 230; at Michael's Pub, 26, 68, 75, 82, 84, 118, 133, 150, 167
Clark, Norma Lee, 50
Clarkson, Patricia, 185, 188, 196
Clockwork Orange, A, 20
Cloquet, Ghislain, 45
close-ups, xviii, 113, 191
Coates, Susan, 117
Coen brothers, 186
Cohn, Sam, 111, 139, 165
Coleman, Ornette, 36
collaboration: with cinematographers, xiii, 10, 45, 52–53, 112, 123–24, 225; with editors, 76, 108, 224–25; with writers, 4–5, 64, 109–10, 121, 215
Coltrane, John, 36
Come Blow Your Horn, 64
comedian, career as, xi, 25, 37, 208, 216. *See also* nightclub act; stand-up comedy
comedians, 28, 33–34, 208
comedy: and aspect ratio, 15; children in, 197; and drama compared, 180; dramatic comedies, 60, 64, 76, 180; film genre, xiii, 22, 44; filmmaking style for, xiv, 52; Jewish comedies, 80; narrative in, 7–8; philosophy/views on, xi, 22, 26, 179–80, 224–25; physical, xiii, 16, 44; and tragedy compared, 58; visual humor in, 7

commercial success, 26, 27, 43, 65, 76; in foreign markets, 66, 69
Coney Island, 63, 217
Connecticut, 83, 115, 148
Connery, Sean, 200
Coppola, Francis Ford, 110
Cosby, Bill, 208
costs of films. *See* budgets/costs
Cotillard, Marion, 232
creating, delight in, 198
Cries and Whispers, 151
Crimes and Misdemeanors, x, xv, xvii, 105, 124, 163, 170, 175, 177, 183, 188; reshooting/changes, 179
critics, 25–26, 65, 99, 105, 163; French, 40; Israeli, 157; New York, 162, 165, 168–69
Cruz, Penélope, 183–86, 190–91, 193
Cukor, George, 130
Curse of the Jade Scorpion, The, xix, 169, 177, 179, 192
Cusack, John, 126

Dalí, Salvador, 29; character in *Midnight in Paris*, 226
Daniels, Jeff, 81, 100
Dante Alighieri: *The Divine Comedy*, 159
David, Larry, 188, 196, 211, 214–15
Davis, Judy, 103–4, 106, 143, 156; Academy Award nomination, 140
Davis, Miles, 36
Davis, Sammy, Jr., 81
Day at the Races, 15
day for night, 52
Dayton, Ohio, 83
death, views on, 39, 56, 202
Death Wish, 205
Deconstructing Harry, ix, xviii–xix, 133, 147, 152–60, 163, 170, 188; Allen's character in, xix, 154; box office, 172; editing, 156;

Jewish heritage in, 158; magical/supernatural elements in, 159
defocusing (special effect), 155
De Niro, Robert, 122, 207
De Sica, Vittorio, xx, 100
Dickens, Charles, 166
Didion, Joan, 65
Dillinger, John, 4
Dinner at Eight, 125
Di Palma, Carlo, 102, 112, 123–24, 225
directing, 112, 187; and acting in same film, 13, 104, 126; directing actors, 143–44, 155–56, 195–96; directing women, 70; technique, 113
directors as creators, 125
Discreet Charm of the Bourgeoisie, The, 165
dissolves, 191
Divine Comedy, The (Dante), 159
dolly shots. *See* camera movement
Don't Drink the Water, 14, 64, 118, 133
Donner, Clive, 6
Dostoyevsky, Fyodor, 104–5, 131, 158, 166
Doumanian, Jean, 55, 74, 139, 168; lawsuit against, 162, 169
Doyle, Arthur Conan, 131
drama: chamber drama, 180; and comedy compared, 180; dramatic comedies, 60, 64, 76, 180
dramatic films, xiii, 44, 58, 77, 124, 179–80; filmmaking style for, xiv, 52
DreamWorks, 172, 181
drugs, views on, 35, 57, 170
Duck Soup, 3, 8

Ebbets Field, 86
editing, xiv, 53, 61, 76, 98, 108, 156, 187, 224–25; elliptical editing, 156; rhythm in, 52
Eiffel Tower performance, 30
8 ½, 164

Elaine's, 55, 74, 84, 171, 233
Ellington, Duke, 85, 109
El Morocco, 190
Elvira Madigan, 11
England, filming in, 173, 178
escape, search for, 134, 146, 226
Europe: filming in, xxi, 183, 190, 197, 205; popularity in, x, 66, 69, 138–39
European style in Allen's films, 69
Everyone Says I Love You, xvii, xviii, 132–33, 134–36, 142, 145–46, 152, 154, 206; improvisation in, 144; magical/supernatural elements in, xix, 146, 159; songs, 135–36
Everything You Always Wanted to Know about Sex* (*but Were Afraid to Ask), ix, xi, 4, 21, 22, 51; Allen's character in, 19; budget, 18; cinematography, 45; length of shoot, 53; style, 9–11, 18, 69
Ewing, Patrick, 86
Exorcist, The, 163

Fading Gigolo, 235, 237–38
fame, perils of, 37, 68
fantasy in films. *See* magic and the supernatural in films
Farrow, Dylan, xvii, 115–17, 133, 147–48, 166
Farrow, Mia, xv, 74, 79, 81, 93, 100, 184, 229, 236; apartment on Central Park West, 87, 91; in *Broadway Danny Rose*, xvi, 81–82, 141; children, xvii, 115–18, 133, 147–48, 166; country house in Connecticut, 83, 193; relationship with Allen, 67–68, 73, 91, 147, 154–55, 166–67; scandal/legal battle with Allen, xvii, 110, 114–18, 133, 147–48, 166–68, 234
Farrow, Moses, xvii, 133, 166
Farrow, Satchel (Ronan), xvii, 115–17, 133, 148, 166

fascism, 31
Fatal Attraction, 174
Faulk, John Henry, 30
Faulkner, William, 68
Feldman, Charles K., 6
Fellini, Federico, 62, 158, 165, 166, 202, 207
female characters, 34–35, 140–42, 236; in *Hannah and Her Sisters*, 93–94
Ferber, Edna, 130
Ferrell, Will, 176
Fields, W. C., 15, 85, 214
Film Comment, ix
film genres, 125–26
filmmaking and Allen: artistic freedom/control, ix, xii, 11–12, 27, 82, 127, 138–39, 165, 172–73, 178; attention to detail, 17–18, 44–45, 63; best/favorites among own films, xiii–xiv, 51, 111, 126, 202–3; dark films, 69, 105, 188–89; failure, feelings of, 25, 44, 64, 65, 99–100, 110–11; financial arrangements, 139, 173, 178, 197; length of shoots, 53, 63, 81; personal style, 11, 18–19, 113; replacing cast members, 112–13, 143, 186; secrecy, 18, 28, 178; self-assessment, xvi, 76–77, 111, 164–65, 179, 202; themes, 171–72; visual aspect, 10, 80; working methods, xiv, xxi, 10–11, 51–54, 61–63, 76, 81, 101–2, 186–88; writing/directing/acting, xi, 27, 60, 90, 104, 128, 132, 139
Film Quarterly, ix
final cut, xii, 12, 27
Firth, Colin, 237
Fitzgerald, F. Scott: character in *Midnight in Paris*, 232
Five Easy Pieces, 163
Flatbush, Brooklyn, 21, 60, 63, 85, 134, 204, 217. *See also* New York City
Floating Light Bulb, The, 69, 81
Fonda, Jane, 29

Ford, Gerald, 31–32
Forte, Nick Apollo, 112
Foster, Phil, 208
Foundas, Scott, xxi, 176–82, 231–34
400 Blows, The, xx, 163, 164
Fox Searchlight, 172
France: filming in, xxi; popularity in, x, 69, 139
Frankie and Johnnie's, 86
French Connection, The, 163
Freud, Sigmund, 167, 175, 182
Friedkin, William, 163
From the Life of the Marionettes, 107
Front, The, 28–29

gags in films. *See* jokes in films
gag writing. *See* joke writing
gangster films, 121–22
Garbarz, Franck, xviii–xix, 152–60
Garner, Errol, xix
Gelbart, Larry, 136, 180
Genet, Jean, 40
Germany, popularity in, 139
Gershwin, George, 129
Getting Even, 137
Gianni Schicchi (Puccini), xxix
Gleason, Jackie, 28, 85, 220
God, views on, 39, 175
Godard, Jean-Luc, 96–97, 106–7, 181
Godfather, The, 13, 121
Golden Age fallacy, 227
Golden Globes, 180. *See also* Chronology, xxiv–xxx
Goldwater, Barry, 30
Gomez, Lefty, 182
GoodFellas, 110
Good Mother, The, 104
Göring, Hermann, 168
Gould, Elliot, 5
Gould, Glenn, 201

Graduate, The, 27
Grand Bouffe, The, 23
Grand Illusion, xx, 139, 168
Grant, Cary, 78
Greenhut, Robert (Bobby), 52, 54, 111, 112
Griffith, Kristin, 49, 50
Griffith, Melanie, 130
Grosbard, Ulu, 69
Gross, Terry, xxiii, 211–23
Grossberg, Jack, 18
grosses. *See* box office/grosses

Hackett, Buddy, 208
Halberstadt, Ira, xiii–xiv, 47–54
Hall, Rebecca, 183–86
Hamlisch, Martin, 129
Hamptons, Long Island, 176, 205
handheld shots, xvii, 18, 101, 124, 180
Hanks, Tom, 126
Hannah and Her Sisters, ix, xv, xvii, xviii, 85, 90–100, 105, 107, 113, 135, 140, 143, 163, 170; Academy Awards, 168, 183; Allen's character in, 87, 94, 228–29; box office, 90, 111, 139, 172; budget, 139; cast, 90, 95–96; characters, 93–94, 169; ending, 95, 228–29; locations, 87, 88, 89, 91; reshooting/changes, xvi, 97
Harper, Jessica, 229
Hawkins, Sally, 236
Hawn, Goldie, 134, 142
Hayes, Peter Lind, 39
Heckert, Jim, 224
Hell, depiction of, 158–59
Hellman, Lillian: *Julia*, 48
Hemingway, Ernest, 68, 234; character in *Midnight in Paris*, 232, 233
Hemingway, Margaux, 81
Hemingway, Mariel, 57, 58, 221
Hepburn, Katharine, 15
Hershey, Barbara, 93, 140, 143

High Noon, xx
Hinckley, John, 78
Hitchcock, Alfred, x
Hitler, Adolf, 40
Hoboken, N.J., 206
Hoffman, Dustin, 13, 19, 126, 127
Holliday, Judy, 15, 16, 130
Hollywood Ending, xix, 162, 169, 177, 179
Home Box Office, 45
homosexuality, views on, 35
Honeymooners, The, 110, 220
Hope, Bob, xv, 58–59, 180
Horowitz, Vladimir, 201
Houdini, Harry, 131
Hubert's Flea Circus and Museum, 85
humor. *See* comedy; jokes in films; joke writing; stand-up comedy
Hurt, Mary Beth, 47, 49–50
Husbands and Wives, ix–x, xvii, 101–8, 111, 118, 133, 155, 163, 165, 180, 183, 188, 202; budget, 127; characters, 169; editing, 108; handheld shots in, 101, 124; improvisation in, 103; style, xvii, 101–2, 113
Huston, Anjelica, 175
Huston, John, 177

illusion, importance of, xviii–xix, 135, 145
imaginary, depiction of the, 159
immortality, views on, 48–49, 56, 153
improvisation in films, 14–15, 113, 122–23; *Annie Hall*, 62; *Broadway Danny Rose*, 81, 123; *Bullets over Broadway*, 113, 122; *Everyone Says I Love You*, 144; *Husbands and Wives*, 103; *September*, 145
Industrial Light and Magic, 155
Inge, William, 125
insanity defense, 78
Interiors, ix, xiii, xviii, 47–54, 57–58, 60, 63, 65–66, 69, 70, 77, 100, 124, 127, 180;

camera movement in, 52; cast, 50–51, 70; characters, 47–50; cinematography, 52; critical reception, 65; Mary Beth Hurt's character in, 49–50; Diane Keaton's character in, xiii, 47–49, 50, 58; length of shoot, 53; locations, 52; visual aspect, 80
Ionesco, Eugène, 40
Israel, 157
Italy, popularity in, 138
It's a Mad, Mad, Mad, Mad World, 15

Jackman, Hugh, 161, 180
jazz, 36, 129–30; New Orleans–style, xix, 36, 150
jazz playing, xix, 60, 75, 82, 118, 133, 150, 182, 183, 198, 213
Jewishness, xii, xxii, 38, 66, 158, 175, 176, 181, 200, 208–9; Jewish comedies, 79–80; Jewish humor, 66, 183
Joffe, Charles H., 11, 54, 57, 136, 168
Johansson, Scarlett, 161–62, 177, 178, 179, 180, 183–86, 190, 194–95
Johnson, Bunk, 150
Johnson, Lyndon, 30
Johnson, Van, 81
jokes in films, 7–11, 16, 22, 26, 44, 51, 52; *Annie Hall*, 62; *Bananas*, 8, 10, 16, 44; Jewish, 66; *Love and Death*, 44; *Manhattan*, 59; *Sleeper*, 44; *Take the Money and Run*, 16
joke writing, 39, 60, 136–37, 190, 219, 237
Jolie, Angelina, 179
Jones, Kent, 224–30
Jordan, Michael, 165
Jordan, Richard, 49, 50–51
Jules and Jim, 163
Julia (Hellman), 48
jump cuts, xvii, 15, 101, 105–6, 108, 113, 156, 180

Kael, Pauline, 165, 177
Kafka, Franz, 40
Kakutani, Michiko, xv–xvi
Kanin, Garson, 125
Kaplan, Fred, xix
Kaufman, George S., 33, 130
Kazan, Elia, 11, 58
Keaton, Buster, xi, xiii, 3, 9, 15, 19, 22, 44, 136, 165
Keaton, Diane, 33, 57–58, 81, 88, 106, 143, 144, 147, 151, 184, 186, 236, 237; Academy Award, 140; in *Annie Hall*, 43, 58, 70, 141; friendship with Allen, 63, 74; in *Interiors*, xiii, 50, 58; in *Manhattan*, 58; relationship with Allen, 58, 140; singing role, 100
Kelley, Ken, xii–xiii, 24–42
Kelly, Gene, 146
Khondji, Darius, 225
Kierkegaard, Søren, xxi, 25, 40, 182
Kissinger, Henry, 4
Klein, Joe, xvi–xvii, 83–89
Knicks, 23, 42, 84, 86, 133, 189, 198
Konigsberg, Allan Stewart. *See* Allen, Woody
Konigsberg, Martin, 134–35, 218–20, 237
Konigsberg, Nettie, 134–35, 174, 218–20, 237
Krim, Arthur, 71, 138–39, 165, 178
Kroft, Steve, 117
Kubrick, Stanley, 45
Kurosawa, Akira, 163, 165, 175

LA Opera, xxix
Lahr, John, ix, xviii–xix, 131–51
Landau, Martin, 175
Lang, Fritz, 158
language, Allen's use of, 80
Lasser, Louise, 5, 14–15, 57, 131
Last Picture Show, The, 163

Laugh-In, 34
Laurel and Hardy, 85, 110
L'Avventura, 164
Lax, Eric, 135
Leave It to Beaver, 197
Le Cirque, 144, 206
Lee, Gypsy Rose, 85
Lennon, John, 69
Lenny Bruce, 233
Leonard, Jack E., 208
Lewis, Jerry, 7, 112
Lewis, Juliette, 105–6
Lindsay, John, 30
Lipstick, 58
Lloyd, Harold, xi, 22
Lloyd Webber, Andrew, 177
locations: *Annie Hall*, 87, 179; *Bananas*, 14, 18; *Bullets over Broadway*, 111, 120; *Hannah and Her Sisters*, 87, 88, 89, 91; *Interiors*, 52; *Manhattan*, 55, 89, 91, 165; *Match Point*, 176; *Midnight in Paris*, 225, 231–32; *The Purple Rose of Cairo*, 83; *Take the Money and Run*, 18; *Vicky Cristina Barcelona*, 183–84, 193–94. See also Manhattan (New York City); New York City
location scouting, 83, 112, 120, 123, 179
London, 161–62, 166, 176, 184; filming in, xxi, 193–94, 205
Long Day's Journey Into Night, 197
Los Angeles, 23
Los Olvidados, xx
love, views on, 36–37, 228
Love and Death, ix, 26, 28, 32, 35, 36, 45–46, 138, 176; box office, 27; cinematography, 42, 45; jokes in, 44; length of shoot, 53; structure, 76; style, xiii–xiv, 43, 51
Lubitsch, Ernst, 229
luck, force of, xii, xxi, 27, 36–37, 57, 167, 175, 177–78

Lyman, Rick, xx

MacMurray, Fred, 207
Madison Square Garden, 86
Madoff, Bernard, 236
Madonna, 155
magic, early interest in, 39, 56, 131, 159, 232
magic and the supernatural in films, xviii–xix, 146, 158–59, 227–28, 232
Magic in the Moonlight, 237
Magic Lantern, The (Bergman), 227
Mamber, Stephen, xi, 3–20
Mandocki, Luis, 130
Manhattan, ix, xiv, xvi–xvii, 51–52, 55–59, 69, 84, 105, 129, 163, 183, 229; Allen's character in, 63, 154; and *Annie Hall* compared, 48, 56; awards, 76; box office, 111; dissatisfaction with, 64, 110–11; as dramatic comedy, 60, 64, 76, 180; ending, 221; jokes in, 59; Diane Keaton's character in, 58; locations, 55, 89, 91, 165; opening scene, 204–6, 225; R rating, 55; structure, 76
Manhattan (New York City): Broadway, 80–82, 85; Central Park, 89, 111, 205; early memories of, xix, 80–82, 85–86, 109; filming in/location for films, xx, 66, 86–89, 90, 120; Greenwich Village, 87, 88, 216; image in movies, 205; love of, 205; SoHo, 87; Times Square/42nd Street, 85–86, 87, 88; Upper East Side, 87–88; Upper West Side, 87, 88. See also New York City
Manhattan Film Center, 131
Manhattan Filmmakers' Cooperative, 91
Manhattan Murder Mystery, xvii, 118, 121, 124, 133, 144; budget, 127
Marbury, Stephon, 189
marijuana, 35
Marshall, E. G., 49, 53

Marx, Groucho, xii, 23, 28, 32, 151, 180, 214
Marx, Harpo, 23, 146
Marx Brothers, xi, xii, 3, 7, 15, 22, 28, 32–33, 42, 85, 95, 110, 229
M*A*S*H, 163
Maslin, Janet, x, 168, 169
master shot technique, 113, 123, 144
Match Point, x, xx–xxi, xxi, 161, 163, 172–73, 174–75, 176–81, 183, 189, 193, 202, 225; budget, 178; locations, 176
Matisse, Henri, 201
Mays, Willie, xii, 32, 150
Mazursky, Paul, 53
McAdams, Rachel, 232
McCabe & Mrs. Miller, 163
McCann, Graham, x
McCarthy, Eugene, 30
McCarthy, Joseph, 29
McGovern, George, 30
McGrath, Douglas, xvii–xviii, xxi–xxii, 109–19, 140, 190–203; collaboration with Allen, xvii, 109–10, 121, 190, 215
McKellen, Sir Ian, 142
McLuhan, Marshall, 70, 182
McShane, Ian, 161
meaning of life, xiii, 39, 48, 56
Medavoy, Mike, 168
Melinda and Melinda, xix, 169, 176, 177; box office, 172
Mendelssohn, Felix, 73, 193
Men of Crisis: The Harvey Wallinger Story, 3–4
Merrick, David, 23
Michael's Pub, 26, 68, 75, 82, 84, 118, 133, 150, 167
Midnight in Paris, x, xx, xxiii, 225–27, 229; box office, 235; locations, 225, 231–32; magical/supernatural elements in, 232; music, 225–26
Midsummer Night's Sex Comedy, A, xv, 71–74, 192–93, 226; camera movement in, 124; as dramatic comedy, 76; magical/supernatural elements in, 159, 232; structure, 76
Mighty Aphrodite, 118, 133, 142, 154, 155, 158, 167–68; box office, 139; budget, 139
Miller, Arthur, 125
Miramax, 139
Mitchell, Elvis, 168–69
Mitchum, Robert, 29
Modern Times, 8
Modigliani, Amadeo: character in *Midnight in Paris*, 232
Monk, Thelonious, xix, 36
Moore, Demi, 156
Morse, Susan, 108
mortality, sense of, 56, 68, 149, 153
Mortimer, Emily, 161, 176
Moss, Adam, 204–10
Moss, Robert F., xiv, 60–66
Mostel, Zero, 30, 211, 213–14
Motorcycle Diaries, The, 177
moviegoing, early memories of, 45, 81, 85, 109, 134
movies about the movies, 126
Mozart, Wolfgang Amadeus, 70
Mundy, Robert, xi, 3–20
Murphy, Michael, 55, 74
music: in Allen's films, xix, 100, 129, 138, 146, 194, 225–26; love of, xix, 130, 201, 213. *See also* clarinet playing; jazz; opera

narration in films, 7–8, 157
Nashville, 163
Neeson, Liam, 104
NET pseudo-documentary (withdrawn before telecast), 3–4
Neville, Sir John, 142
Newhart, Bob, 208
Newsweek, 165

New York, New York, 126
New York City: filming in/location for films, xvii, 84, 86–89, 111–12, 196–97; image in movies, 205; love of, xii, xvi–xvii, xxii, 23, 82, 83–89, 119, 129, 165–66, 197, 204–6. *See also* Brooklyn; Bronx; Flatbush, Brooklyn; Manhattan (New York City)
New York *Daily Mirror*, 204
New Yorker, 25, 33, 34, 82, 91, 121, 125, 132, 137–38, 183, 198
New York Giants (baseball team), 38, 86
New York Stories, x, xv, 159, 163, 196, 232
New York Times, ix, x, xvi, xx, 26, 55, 161, 162, 165, 168–69, 174
New York University, 40, 137, 216–17
New York Yankees, 182
Nichols, Mike, 11, 136
Nichols and May, 33, 208
Nicholson, Jack, 29, 127, 192
nightclub act, 20, 118–19, 136–37, 190
Night in Casablanca, A, 23
Nixon, Richard, 31–32
No Country for Old Men, 186
Nolan, Lloyd, 96
nostalgia, 45, 105, 232–33
novelistic approach to filmmaking, 105
Nykvist, Sven, 123, 159

Obama, Barack, 226
"Oedipus Wrecks," x, xv, 163; magical/supernatural elements in, 159, 232
O. Henry Award, 137
O'Neill, Eugene, 123
Opening Night, 123
opera, xxix
Orion, 71, 73, 82, 139, 165, 168, 178
Orton, Joe, 146
Ory, Kid, 36
Oscars. *See* Academy Awards

O'Shea, Milo, 81
O'Sullivan, Maureen, 96
O'Toole, Peter, 6, 231
Ozymandias syndrome, 153

Pacino, Al, 207
Page, Geraldine, 49, 50–51, 70
Palminteri, Chazz, 122, 130
Paper Moon, 163
Paramount, 12–13
Paramount Theater, 85, 109
Paris, 59, 83, 119, 166, 197, 225, 231–32
Parker, Charlie, 36
Parker Meridien, 150
Passion of Anna, The, 227
Penn, Sean, 170
Perelman, S. J., 33, 138, 151
persona, 20, 137, 208–9, 233; on-screen, ix, xxi, 19–20, 84, 132, 171, 181, 208–9, 214–15
Persona, 70
Picasso, Pablo, 180, 201; character in *Midnight in Paris*, 226, 232
Piermont, N.Y., 83
Player, The, 126, 163
Play It Again, Sam, 4, 8, 12, 13, 14, 16, 21, 22, 140; Allen's character in, 19
playwriting, 132; and screenwriting compared, 13–14
Pleskow, Eric, 71, 138–39
political correctness, 157
political views, 28–32
Pollack, Sydney, 103, 104, 133, 140
Pollock, Jackson, 180
Polo Grounds, 86
Porter, Cole, 86, 88, 129, 131, 173
Powell, Bud, 201
Powell, William, 207
Prentiss, Paula, 6
Previn, André, 114, 117, 166

Previn, Soon-Yi, xvii, 114–18, 133, 134, 140, 146–49, 164, 166–67, 174, 209, 215, 221, 235–36
Prizzi's Honor, 177
producers, 54, 128
Prokofiev, Sergei, 106
promotion, xiii, 43, 181, 199
prostitutes as characters, 158
Pryor, Richard, 33–34
psychiatrist characters, 155
psychoanalysis, 41, 56, 78, 166–67, 170–71, 209; in films, 155
psychological conflicts, xiii, 44
Puccini, Giacomo, xxix
Puerto Rico, 14
Purple Rose of Cairo, The, ix, xv, xvii, 79, 80, 89, 93, 111, 120, 135, 163, 165, 183, 202–3, 226; ending, 94–95; location, 83; magical/supernatural elements in, xviii, 158–59; reshooting/changes, xvi

Radio Days, xv, xvii, 100, 120, 165, 196; budget, 127–28
Rafelson, Bob, 163
Rampling, Charlotte, 70
Rao's restaurant, 141
Rashomon, xx, 139, 165
record albums, Allen's, 37, 118, 183
reincarnation, views on, 39
Reinhardt, Django, 170
religion, views on, 38–39, 49, 157, 181
Renoir, Jean, xx, 28
reputation, changes in, 164
reshooting, xiv, xvi, 10–11, 53, 62, 63, 91–92, 97–99, 102, 113, 179, 187
Return of the Pink Panther, The, 46
Reuben, David, 5
reviews, 99, 163, 199
Rhys-Meyers, Jonathan, 161, 176
Rich, Frank, xiv, 55–59

Rilke, Rainer Maria, 228
Ripley's Believe It or Not, 85
Ritt, Martin, 30
Roberts, Julia, 134, 145, 156
Roberts, Tony, 74, 100, 140
Robinson, Edward G., 207
Robinson, Sugar Ray, xii, 32
rock 'n' roll, 36
Rolling Stone, ix
Rollins, Jack, 11, 54, 136
Rome, 166, 183–84, 197; filming in, xxi
Rose, Mickey, 4–5, 79, 215
Rosen, Harlene, 57
Rosenblum, Ralph, 53, 61; *When the Shooting Stops*, 76
Ross, Herbert, 4, 12–13
Roth, Philip, 38
Roth, Tim, 134
Rowlands, Gena, xviii, 113
Runyon, Damon, 81, 86, 121
Russell, Bertrand, 40
Russian literature, 104–5; predeliction for, 92
Russian Tea Room, 83

Sahl, Mort, xv–xvi, 20, 31, 33, 137, 208
Saraband, 228
Sarris, Andrew, 165
Sarsgaard, Peter, 236
Sartre, Jean-Paul, 40
satire, political, 9
Schickel, Richard, 133–34; *Woody Allen: A Life in Film*, x
Schultz, Nancy, 115, 117
Scoop, 161–62, 172, 180, 193; budget, 173
Scorsese, Martin, 110, 126, 127, 173
Scott, A. O., 168–69, 174–75
Scott, George C., 30
screenwriting, 13, 105, 186–87; collaboration, 4–5, 64, 109–10, 121, 215; comedy,

7–8; dialogue, 7, 14, 62; female roles, 140–42; and playwriting compared, 13–14; writing during filming, 61–62
script changes/cutting, 14, 53, 113, 122, 179, 187–88, 228–29
self-indulgence, 70
Sellers, Peter, 6, 231
sentimentality in comedy, 44
September, xv, xvii, 124, 145; reshooting/changes, 179
September 11 terrorist attacks, 210
serious films. *See* dramatic films
Seventh Seal, The, xx, 100, 164, 222, 227
70mm, 15
Shadows and Fog, x, xvii, 103, 133, 180; budget, 127–28; cinematography, 124
Shane, xx, 122, 222
Shelley, Percy Bysshe, 153
Shepard, Sam, 145
Sherlock Junior, 165
Shoard, Catherine, 235–39
Shoot the Piano Player, 163
Shop around the Corner, The, xx
Shulman, Max, 33
Side Effects, 137
silent films, 44, 136
Simon, Danny, 136
Simon, John, 65
Simon, Neil, 64, 180
Simon, Paul, 62
single shot technique. *See* master shot technique
60 Minutes, 117, 148
slapstick, 16, 180
Sleeper, ix, xi, xii, 21, 22, 28, 51, 59, 60, 138, 183; box office, 27; cinematography, 45; jokes in, 44; length of shoot, 53; slapstick in, 180; style, 43
Sleepy Hollow, N.Y., 72

Small Time Crooks, xix, 169, 172
Smith, Liz, 73
Sorrow and the Pity, The, 174, 177
Sorvino, Mira, 118; Academy Award, 140
South America, popularity in, 69
Southampton, N.Y., 52, 205
special effects, xiii, 45, 81, 146, 155
Stallone, Sylvester, 99
stand-up comedy, xv–xvi, 60, 118–19, 132, 137–38, 190, 208, 224
Stapleton, Maureen, 49, 50–51, 70
Stardust Memories, xiv, 63, 67–70, 80, 111, 126, 133–34, 153, 229; Allen's character in, 68–69, 77; audience reaction, xiv, 67, 77; as dramatic comedy, 60
stars, casting/treatment of, 155–56
Stein, Gertrude: character in *Midnight in Paris*, 232, 233
Stevens, George, 110
Stillman, Whit, 184
Stir Crazy, 69
Stone, Emma, 237
Stork Club, 205
St. Petersburg, 166
Stravinsky, Igor, 106
Streetcar Named Desire, A, 236
Streisand, Barbra, 173
Stritch, Elaine, 179
Sturges, Preston, 229–30
Sullivan's Travels, 229–30
Sunset Boulevard, 121
supernatural elements in films. *See* magic and the supernatural in films
Swanson, Gloria, 121
Swear to Tell the Truth, 233
Sweet and Lowdown, xviii–xix, 170, 183
Sweetland Films, 139
Sydow, Max von, 95–96

Take the Money and Run, ix, xi, 3–4, 7–8, 11–12, 20, 21, 60, 71, 76, 79, 112, 165, 183, 188, 189, 204; Allen's character in, 19; camera movement in, 9; documentary style in, 9; editing, 224; jokes in, 16; locations, 18; style, 18–19, 52
Taylor, Cecil, 36
Taylor, Juliet, 104, 112, 142, 167–68, 214, 226
Teahouse of the August Moon, 19
Thalia, 84
Thomas, Isiah, 86, 189
Thoreau, Henry David: *Walden*, 57
Throne of Blood, xx
Thurber, James, 33
Tilly, Jennifer, 122; Academy Award nomination, 140
Time, 26, 165, 166
Tobias, Scott, xxi, 183–89
Tobin, Yann, xviii, 120–30
Tolstoy, Leo, 104; *Anna Karenina*, 92
Tomlin, Lily, 34
Toulouse-Lautrec, Henri de, 158
tragedy: and comedy compared, 58
Tri-Star, 168
Truffaut, François, xx, 163, 165, 202
Turgenev, Ivan, 104
Turturro, John, 235
Twain, Mark, 175
'21' Club, 86
2001, 45, 128

Ullman, Tracey, 122
Unfaithfully Yours, 229
United Artists (UA), 11–12, 21, 27, 43, 45–46, 71, 82, 111, 138, 139, 165, 178

Vaughan, Arky, 86
Vicky Cristina Barcelona, xx–xxi, 183–86, 188, 193–95, 199, 212; locations, 183–84, 193–94; music, 194; style, 190–91
Vidor, King, 110

Walden (Thoreau), 57
Walker, Alexander, xvi, 90–100
Walsh, David, 10, 45
Waterston, Sam, 49
Wayne, David, 19
Wayne, John, 78
Weide, Robert, 233–34
Welles, Orson, 100, 110
Westerns, 122
Whatever Works, xx–xxi, xxiii, 188, 196, 211, 213–15
What's New Pussycat?, 5, 6–7, 231
What's Up, Tiger Lily?, 5–6, 21, 183
When the Shooting Stops (Rosenblum), 76
White Heat, 122
"Whore of Mensa, The," 137–38
Wiest, Dianne, 93, 98, 100, 106, 121, 140–41, 144, 229; Academy Awards, 140, 168; in *Bullets over Broadway*, 128–29, 141
Wilde, Oscar, 146
Wilder, Billy, 121
Wild Strawberries, xx, 152, 227
Wilk, Judge Elliott, 114, 115–16
Williams, Robin, 155, 160
Williams, Tennessee, 61, 66
Willis, Gordon, xiii, 45, 52–53, 69, 81, 91, 100, 123, 124, 179, 225
Wilson, Earl, 190
Wilson, Owen, 226, 231–32
Winchell, Walter, 190
Winters, Jonathan, 34, 208
Without Feathers, 25, 137
Wizard of Oz, The, 110
women, affinity for, 140–42
women characters, 34–35, 140–42, 236; in *Hannah and Her Sisters*, 93–94

women's movement, 35, 238
Wood, Evan Rachel, 188, 196, 215
Woody Allen: A Life in Film (Schickel), x
Woody Allen on Woody Allen (Björkman), xvii
World Trade Center, 210
writing: comedy, 44; essays and short stories, 60, 61; feedback, 62; habits/method, 34, 60–63, 191; jokes, 39, 60, 136–37, 190, 219, 237; for the *New Yorker*, 25, 33, 34, 82, 125, 132, 137–38, 183, 198; playwriting, 132; playwriting and screenwriting compared, 13–14; rewriting, 61; for Sid Caesar, 60, 110, 190. *See also* screenwriting
Wyler, William, 110

Yale–New Haven Hospital, 115, 148, 166
Young Frankenstein, 27
Youngman, Henny, 208
You Will Meet a Tall Dark Stranger, 234

Zelig, ix, xv–xvi, 80, 81, 111, 163, 172, 177, 192, 202; length of shoot, 81; magical/supernatural elements in, xviii, 159

www.ingramcontent.com/pod-product-compliance
Lightning Source LLC
Chambersburg PA
CBHW021954220426
43663CB00007B/815